FROMM

EasyGuide

TO

BOSTON, CAPE COD
& THE ISLANDS

By
Marie Morris & Laura Reckford

Easy Guides are   ✦ Quick To Read   ✦ Light To Carry
✦ For Expert Advice   ✦ In All Price Ranges

FrommerMedia LLC

Published by
FROMMER MEDIA LLC

ISBN 978-1-62887-110-4 (paper), 978-1-62887-111-1 (e-book)

Editorial Director: Pauline Frommer
Editor: John Rambow
Production Editor: Heather Wilcox
Cartographer: Roberta Stockwell
Cover Design: Howard Grossman

For information on our other products or services, see www.frommers.com.

Frommer Media LLC also publishes its books in a variety of electronic formats. Some content that appears in print may not be available in electronic formats.

Manufactured in the United States of America

5 4 3 2 1

AN IMPORTANT NOTE

The world is a dynamic place. Hotels change ownership, restaurants hike their prices, museums alter their opening hours, and buses and trains change their routings. And all this can occur in the several months after our authors have visited, inspected, and written about these hotels, restaurants, museums and transportation services. Though we have made valiant efforts to keep all our information fresh and up-to-date, some few changes can inevitably occur in the periods before a revised edition of this guidebook is published. So please bear with us if a tiny number of the details in this book have changed. Please also note that we have no responsibility or liability for any inaccuracy or errors or omissions, or for inconvenience, loss, damage, or expenses suffered by anyone as a result of assertions in this guide.

CONTENTS

ABOUT THE AUTHORS

Freelance writer and editor **Marie Morris** is the author of this guide's Boston coverage. She is based in the North End, where she has lived long enough to pass for a native but not long enough to acquire a Boston accent. She grew up in New York and graduated from Harvard University, where she studied American history. Marie has worked for Newser.com, "02138" magazine, "The Boston Herald," "Boston" magazine, and "The New York Times." She's the author and coauthor of numerous Frommer's guides to Boston, including "Frommer's Boston Day by Day."

Laura Reckford, who covered Cape Cod and the Islands, is the owner of "Cape Cod Wave" (CapeCodWave.com), an online magazine celebrating the culture and character of Cape Cod. She is also the news director at Cape Cod Broadcasting, which consists of WQRC 99.9, Ocean 104.7 FM, FCC Classical 107.5, Cape Country 104, and CapeCod.com.

ABOUT THE FROMMER'S TRAVEL GUIDES

For most of the past 50 years, Frommer's has been the leading series of travel guides in North America, accounting for as many as 24 percent of all guidebooks sold. I think I know why.

Although we hope our books are entertaining, we nevertheless deal with travel in a serious fashion. Our guidebooks have never looked on such journeys as a mere recreation, but as a far more important human function, a time of learning and introspection, an essential part of a civilized life. We stress the culture, lifestyle, history, and beliefs of the destinations we cover and urge our readers to seek out people and new ideas as the chief rewards of travel.

We have never shied from controversy. We have, from the beginning, encouraged our authors to be intensely judgmental, critical—both pro and con—in their comments, and wholly independent. Our only clients are our readers, and we have triggered the ire of countless prominent sorts, from a tourist newspaper we called "practically worthless" (it unsuccessfully sued us) to the many rip-offs we've condemned.

And because we believe that travel should be available to everyone regardless of their incomes, we have always been cost-conscious at every level of expenditure. Although we have broadened our recommendations beyond the budget category, we insist that every lodging we include be sensibly priced. We use every form of media to assist our readers and are particularly proud of our feisty daily website, the award-winning Frommers.com.

I have high hopes for the future of Frommer's. May these guidebooks, in all the years ahead, continue to reflect the joy of travel and the freedom that travel represents. May they always pursue a cost-conscious path, so that people of all incomes can enjoy the rewards of travel. And may they create, for both the traveler and the persons among whom we travel, a community of friends, where all human beings live in harmony and peace.

Arthur Frommer

THE BEST OF BOSTON, CAPE COD & THE ISLANDS

N early 400 years of history, some of the most beautiful beaches in the world, and a wealth of diversions and attractions combine to make Boston, Cape Cod, and the islands of Martha's Vineyard and Nantucket irresistible destinations for travelers from around the world.

One of the oldest American cities, Boston packs a lot into a small footprint, with abundant culture, historic sites, shopping for every budget, terrific dining, lovely scenery, and plenty of sports (both watching and doing). It's a crowded, welcoming destination—even areas choked with sightseers are in or near residential neighborhoods, and countless locals are former students at the area's many excellent colleges. With so much to offer, Boston is perfect for a quick visit or a longer stay.

Summertime is really what first draws the crowds to Cape Cod and the Islands, but the colorful history, arts, and culture of the region keep them coming back throughout the year. When it comes to this 70-mile-long peninsula, it's a matter of choosing which of the 15 towns to use as your base, and then heading out to explore, from the bridges in Bourne to the tip in Provincetown.

Martha's Vineyard, an island that's a 45-minute ferry ride from the Cape, has six towns, all with very distinct personalities, from the slightly honky-tonk Oak Bluffs to the bucolic community of Chilmark to the refined allure of Edgartown.

Nantucket is 30 miles out to sea, and parts of it can seem frozen in the 19th century, its Main Street looking not that different from the version found by Herman Melville when researching "Moby-Dick." Still, the elegant shops and restaurants on the island have the quality—and price—of urban centers like New York and Boston.

BOSTON'S best AUTHENTIC EXPERIENCES

o **A Walk Around the North End:** Boston's Little Italy (but don't call it that!) has an old-world flavor you won't want to miss. Explore the shops on Salem Street, and be sure to stop for coffee and a pastry at a Hanover Street *caffè*. See p. 71.

- **A Ride on a Duck:** Board an amphibious vehicle and let **Boston Duck Tours** (p. 92) show you the city from an irresistible angle. The sightseeing ride includes a dip in the Charles River—for the "duck," not for you.

- **A Stroll (or Jog) Along the River:** The paved path that hugs both shores of the Charles accommodates pedestrians, runners, skaters, and cyclists. The Esplanade (adjacent to the Back Bay) offers both people-watching and gorgeous greenery; the Cambridge side has fabulous views of the Boston skyline.

- **A Visit to the Top of the Prudential Tower:** At the **Skywalk Observatory** here (p. 86), you'll see Boston like a local—a middle-school student on a field trip. Kids of all ages from around the world love the 50th-floor views and interactive displays.

- **A Day at the MFA:** The **Museum of Fine Arts** (p. 86) is world-class. The whole place overflows with breathtaking works, including a surprising number of master-pieces so familiar that seeing them is like running into an old friend.

- **A Newbury Street Safari:** From the genteel Arlington Street end to the cutting-edge Massachusetts Avenue end, Boston's legendary shopping street is a solid mile of pure temptation: art galleries, boutiques, jewelry and gift shops. See p. 97.

- **Quality Time with the Red Sox:** Baseball fans revere **Fenway Park** (p. 125), the creaky, cramped home of the Boston Red Sox. If you can't go to a game, plan on a tour—it's the oldest park in the major leagues (1912). Kids love it, and parents saving a bundle by not paying for game tickets tend to agree.

BOSTON'S best RESTAURANTS

- **Best for a Special Occasion:** Established but innovative, adventurous but comfort-able, **Hamersley's Bistro** (p. 61) is a can't-miss destination for that big birthday or anniversary. Julia Child encouraged chef-owner Gordon Hamersley to open the restaurant and then became a loyal customer—need I say more?

- **Best for Seafood:** Like the culinary equivalent of a medical specialist, **Legal Sea Foods** (p. 55) does one thing and does it exceptionally well. It's a chain for a great reason: People can't get enough of the freshest seafood around.

- **Best Burgers:** A Harvard Square standby, **Mr. Bartley's Burger Cottage** (p. 66) is famous for its juicy burgers, the world's best onion rings, and a down-to-earth atmo-sphere that's increasingly rare in a chain-choked neighborhood.

- **Best for a Business Lunch:** Skip the expense-account splurge and impress your colleagues by knowing about the top-notch food and no-frills atmosphere at the **Sultan's Kitchen** (p. 60).

- **Best Pizza:** With its jam-packed dining room and fiery oven, the original **Pizzeria Regina** (p. 60) looks like Hollywood's idea of a pizza joint. After one bite of the slightly smoky crust, you'll be sending Martin Scorsese to the back of the line.

- **Best Classic Boston Experience:** Know-it-alls sneer about the touristy clientele, but the **Union Oyster House** (p. 58) is popular with both locals and visitors. Dating to 1826, it's the place to go for traditional New England food, including oysters shucked while you watch.

BOSTON'S best HOTELS

- **Best Value:** The **Newbury Guest House** (p. 51) is ideal for travelers who want to take advantage of the Back Bay's excellent shopping. You can't beat the Newbury Street location, and room rates include breakfast. Motorists will want to check out the **MidTown Hotel** (p. 50), which offers comfortable, no-frills rooms and the cheapest guest parking in the Back Bay.

○ **Best Splurge:** The **Boston Harbor Hotel** (p. 44) has it all: Huge rooms, magnificent views, impeccable service, luxurious health club and spa, terrific pool, and a great location adjacent to a marina where you can moor your yacht. Across the river, Cambridge's **Charles Hotel** (p. 52) offers a similar combination of amenities, location, and pampering service (no place for a yacht, though).

○ **Best for Romance:** The intimate atmosphere and elegant furnishings make a suite at the **Eliot Hotel** (p. 49) a great spot for a rendezvous. If you and your beloved need some time apart, close the French doors and maintain eye contact while in separate rooms

○ **Best for Business Travelers:** The **Seaport Hotel** (p. 45) was a pioneer in the so-called Innovation District before that name even existed. It offers great access to the airport and convention center, plus all the features a tycoon (or would-be tycoon) could want. In tech-happy East Cambridge, the **Kendall Hotel** (p. 54) is a welcome retreat. It's in a 19th-century firehouse.

BOSTON'S best FOR FAMILIES

○ **A Visit to Faneuil Hall Marketplace:** Street performers, crowds from all over the world, the food court, restaurants, bars, and shops make **Faneuil Hall Marketplace** (p. 67) Boston's most popular destination. It's across the street from the harbor, where a stroll along the water can help your crew decompress.

○ **An Exploration of the Museum of Science:** Kids can't get enough of the **Museum of Science** (p. 73). Fascinating displays and tons of interactive exhibits cover every branch of science and inquiry without ever feeling like homework.

○ **An Excursion to the Public Garden:** A perfect retreat during or after a busy day of sightseeing, the **Public Garden** (p. 84) is home to the beloved **Swan Boats** and to the **"Make Way for Ducklings"** statues. The Mallard family from the beloved children's book relaxed here, and so will you.

○ **A Trip to the Boston Children's Museum:** The hands-on exhibits, noisy galleries, and overall air of discovery and excitement make the **Boston Children's Museum** (p. 91) catnip for the elementary-school set.

○ **A Thrill "Ride":** The **Mugar Omni Theater** at the Museum of Science (p. 74) and the 3-D **Simons IMAX Theatre** at the New England Aquarium (p. 74) offer intrepid visitors hair-raising experiences in the safety of a comfortable auditorium. Most of the large-format films concentrate on the natural world.

BOSTON'S best FREE (OR CHEAP) THINGS TO DO

○ **Picnic by the Water:** Head for the harbor or river, relax on a park bench or patch of grass, turn off your phone, and enjoy the spectacular scene. Whether it's sailboats or ocean liners, seagulls or scullers, there's always something worth watching.

○ **Visit a Museum:** Schedule your visit to take advantage of free or discounted admission. The **USS *Constitution* Museum** (p. 83) is free all the time; the **Institute of Contemporary Art** (p. 72) is free after 5pm Thursday; and the **Museum of Fine Arts** (p. 86) asks for a voluntary contribution after 4pm Wednesday. After 5pm on Friday, the **Boston Children's Museum** (p. 91) costs just $1.

o **Take a Ranger-Led Tour:** The National Park Service offers tours of historic attractions all over eastern Massachusetts. The ranger's knowledge can elevate a visit to a park, a house, a neighborhood, or even a government installation (like the Charlestown Navy Yard; p. 83) from good to great.

o **Check Out a College Concert or Show:** Countless student groups just want an attentive audience. And imagine the credit card commercial: "Ability to say you recognized the talent of [insert name of big star] in a student production? Priceless."

o **Ride on a Skunk:** In place of horses, the **Rose Kennedy Greenway Carousel** (p. 90) has animals native to Massachusetts, including lobsters, owls, and even an adorable skunk. A ticket costs $3.

BOSTON'S best OF OUTDOORS

o **A Ride across the Harbor:** The 10-minute commuter **ferry** (p. 38) that connects Long Wharf and the Charlestown Navy Yard is a treasure hidden in plain sight. You might notice the boat traffic on the Inner Harbor as you make your way around downtown; for just $3, you can be part of it.

o **An Island Excursion:** The **Boston Harbor Islands National Recreation Area** (p. 95) is something of a hidden secret, just offshore but a world away. Start at the visitor center, on the Rose Kennedy Greenway, before venturing to a destination so accessible and interesting that you won't believe how uncrowded most of it is.

o **An Interlude at a Cafe:** Outdoor seating in a place with great people-watching is a great way to recharge. A passing parade of shoppers and students (on Newbury St. and in Harvard Square) may be more interesting than suits and ties (downtown and the rest of the Back Bay), but if the breeze and the iced cappuccino are cool, what's not to like? See "Where to Eat" (p. 55).

o **A Free Concert:** The Boston area's cultural scene has no real off-season. During the summer, many musicians and musical groups take their acts outside—to parks, plazas, and even a barge (behind the Boston Harbor Hotel). Plan well and you can enjoy music alfresco almost every night.

CAPE COD'S & THE ISLANDS' best AUTHENTIC EXPERIENCES

o **A Drive along the Old King's Highway:** Cape Cod's Route 6A stretches 34 miles through seven towns. A former stagecoach route, this super-scenic road is the place to go for a taste of what makes Cape Cod so special, with some antiquing on the side. See p. 133.

o **Surf-casting in Osterville:** Do what the locals do and cast a fishing line from the shore and see if you can catch dinner. You can fish from any beach on Cape Cod, but **Dowses Beach** is a particularly scenic one, with Nantucket Sound on one side and a calm inlet on the other.

o **A Day at a Cape Cod National Seashore Beach:** Try **Cahoon's Hollow** in Wellfleet, with its magnificently high dunes, or **Race Point** in Provincetown, where you can sometimes see whales and seals. But whichever National Seashore beach you choose, you'll enjoy a pristine stretch of sand that goes for miles. See p. 205.

o **Admire the Captains' Houses in Martha's Vineyard:** A stroll on **North Water Street** in Edgartown from Main Street to Edgartown Light is a walk through time to the mid–19th century, when most of these magnificent homes were built. See p. 11.

o **Use Two Wheels, Not Four:** No need to bring your car to Martha's Vineyard. A **bike** works just fine to explore the down island towns. The scenic ride from Vineyard Haven to Oak Bluffs, with harbor views, is a good place to start.

o **Fun in the Sun:** Bring the family to **Jetties Beach** (p. 250) and settle in for the day. There are boat rentals, volleyball, playground, skate park, restaurants and more at Nantucket's most full-service beach.

CAPE COD'S & THE ISLANDS' best RESTAURANTS

o **Best Super-Authentic Italian:** It didn't take long for locals to realize that what's cooking at Falmouth's little **Osteria La Civetta** (p. 145) is something very special and authentic. This is the kind of place where the owners send the chefs to Italy in the off-season to learn new techniques.

o **Best for Special Occasions:** Cape Cod's **28 Atlantic** (p. 182) offers the most elegant dining in the region. Floor-to-ceiling plate-glass windows give you a panoramic view of Pleasant Bay, and the menu is loaded with delicacies from around the world.

o **Best Food in a Historic Inn:** An elegant entry in the Lower Cape dining scene, the **Bramble Inn and Restaurant** (p. 177) attracts those who don't mind a rather steeply priced, four-course, fixed-price dinner. The five intimate dining rooms are decorated with antique china and fresh flowers, and the chef, Ruth Manchester, is a local favorite.

o **Best Place to See and Be Seen on Nantucket:** The exquisite beachfront restaurant at the Cliffside Beach Club, **Galley Beach** (p. 246), is the place to go if you want to feel like you are in a spread of "Travel + Leisure" magazine. Delicious food, too.

o **Best for Seafood:** Talented chef-owners have made **Straight Wharf** (p. 247) *the* place for upscale dining on Nantucket. Make your reservation for 8pm so that you can sit on the outside deck and watch the sun set over the harbor.

o **Best for a Fancy Meal on Martha's Vineyard:** Edgartown's **Atria** (p. 221) gets rave reviews for its locavore cuisine, with influences from all over, and high-caliber service.

CAPE COD'S & THE ISLANDS' best HOTELS

o **Best Value:** Maybe it's no surprise that the **Old Sea Pines Inn** (p. 178), in Brewster, is a charmer with a lot of personality—it was once the Sea Pines School of Charm and Personality for Young Women. For decades, it has offered an old-fashioned, reasonably priced Cape Cod vacation.

o **Best Splurge: Wequassett Resort and Golf Club** (p. 181), near Chatham, occupies its own little peninsula on Pleasant Bay and offers excellent sailing and tennis clinics; it's also next to the Cape's premier golf course. You'll be tempted to just relax, though—especially if you score one of the clapboard cottages that are right on the water.

- **Best for Romance:** Chatham's **Captain's House Inn** (p. 183) exudes good taste. Most rooms have fireplaces, elegant paneling, and antiques throughout; the rooms are sumptuous yet cozy.
- **Best Amenities:** Provincetown's **Brass Key Guesthouse** (p. 199), a compound of five historic buildings, is run by the kind of innkeepers who think of everything: The pillows are goose-down, the showers have wall jets, and complimentary ice tea is delivered poolside.
- **Best Hotel on the Beach:** Nantucket's **Cliffside Beach Club** (p. 240) may not be as fancy as some, but there's a sublime "beachiness" to it all: simply decorated rooms; cheerful, youthful staff; a sea of antique wicker in the clubhouse; and, of course, all the blue, yellow, and green umbrellas lined up on the beach.
- **Best Historic Ambiance:** Made up of a cluster of 18th- and 19th-century houses that are linked by formal gardens, the **Charlotte Inn** (p. 216), on Martha's Vineyard, has old-world charm and rooms that bring to mind an English gentlemen's club.

CAPE COD'S & THE ISLANDS' best FOR FAMILIES

- **A Visit to Heritage Museums and Gardens:** The three buildings here house a unique group of collections, including classic cars, Native American artifacts, and tin soldiers—and there's also a 1912 carousel that gives unlimited rides. See p. 138.
- **Mini-Golf on the Cape:** The whole area is mini-golf heaven, and among the most appealing destinations for it is **Pirate's Cove,** which has two 18-hole courses outfitted with caves, footbridges, waterfalls, and a bit of macabre humor too.
- **A Day of Trampolines, Go-Carts, and Bumper Boats:** Want your kids to sleep well? Take them to Rte. 28 in Harwich. The **Trampoline Center** is loads of fun, **Bud's Go-Karts** welcomes hot-rodders as young as 8, and **Bumper Boats** is just down the road.
- **An Excursion to Cape Cod Museum of Natural History:** This interactive museum in Brewster, with displays covering whale noises, a beehive, live tanks of fish, and 85 acres of trails, is anything but dull.

CAPE & ISLANDS' best FREE (OR CHEAP) THINGS TO DO

- **Picnic in the Park:** While everyone else is experiencing beach rage trying to find parking at one of Falmouth's popular saltwater beaches, you can park for free at **Grews Pond,** in Chatham's own forest. The area stays relatively uncrowded, even in the middle of summer. Goodwill Park and wander shady paths around the pond.
- **Stroll Down Main Street:** The most entertaining of the Cape's "Main Streets" is Provincetown's **Commercial Street,** where buskers, hawkers, musicians, and drag queens all vie for your attention. The other three contenders for window shopping

and people-watching would have to be the Main Streets of Falmouth, Hyannis, and Chatham.

o **Arts and Music by the Harbor:** All summer the Bismore and Aselton parks on Hyannis's Inner Harbor are the places for free concerts, plays, and art exhibits, including the seven Harbor Your Arts artist shanties—booths where local painters, potters, and other crafters work daily in the summer.

o **Take Yourself Out to a Ball Game:** Many people plan their Cape Cod vacations around the schedule of their favorite team in the **Cape Cod Baseball League.** This is a training ground for the Major League, and one of the top summer leagues in the country.

o **Listen to a Town Band Concert:** Whether it's at the **Oak Bluffs Bandshell** on Martha's Vineyard, at the **Chatham Bandshell** on the Cape, or another town, you can bring a blanket and a picnic and gather with other families for a free old-fashioned band concert. Check with local chambers of commerce to find out what night the trombones might be coming out.

o **Get a Bird's-Eye View:** For a small donation you can climb up the 94 steps of the 1795 bell tower of the **Old North Church** in Nantucket —it's a glorious view.

BOSTON, CAPE COD & THE ISLANDS IN CONTEXT

W hat draws visitors to Boston, Cape Cod, Martha's Vineyard, and Nantucket? Some come for the historic attractions and abundant cultural offerings, others for the beaches and outdoor activities. Seafood lovers and avid shoppers find a lot to enjoy throughout eastern Massachusetts. Convention-goers, vacationing families, and fall foliage "leaf peepers" flock to Boston, the main gateway to New England and its magnificent scenery. And every summer, travelers from around the world find their way to the seaside paradise an hour south of the city. Cape Cod encompasses 15 towns and numerous villages, each with its own personality. The nearby islands—quaint Martha's Vineyard and elegant Nantucket—are uniquely enjoyable destinations. Read on to learn more about this fascinating region, including information about the best times to visit and the weather you can expect.

BOSTON TODAY

Boston embodies nearly 4 centuries of contrasts and contradictions—blue blood and blue collar, Yankee and Irish, Brahmin banker and budget-conscious student. In the 21st century, it's evolved into a magnet for students and intellectuals from all over the world. The Boston area is a hotbed of innovation. Cambridge and the South Boston waterfront are home to high-tech leaders in every field, from gaming to genetic engineering. Downtown Boston continues to evolve, with the parks of the mile-long Rose Kennedy Greenway (which replaced an ugly elevated highway) increasingly popular among locals and visitors alike.

Today you'll find a metropolis of some 637,000 at the heart of the Greater Boston area, which encompasses 83 cities and towns that are home to 4.5 million people. Health care and tourism are pillars of the local economy, as is higher education. In fact, eastern Massachusetts sometimes feels like one big campus. You've probably heard that Boston is a college town, but you may not realize just how true that is until you're here. The real-estate market is booming, and the city is one of the most expensive places in the country to live—and to visit, if you don't budget carefully.

And as they have for more than a century, immigrants flock to the Boston area. In the last quarter-century, the Asian and Latino populations have soared.

Whatever their origins, most Bostonians share at least a passing interest in sports. ("How about those Red Sox?" is an all-purpose icebreaker.) The Boston Bruins, Boston Celtics, and New England Patriots have enjoyed great success in the 21st century, but they play in the shadow of one of the most beloved teams in baseball. The Boston Red Sox won the World Series in 2004 (for the first time since 1918), 2007, and 2013, cementing their status as New England's favorite franchise.

The biggest sports story of century, however, was the heartbreaking bombings at the finish line of the 2013 Boston Marathon. In the international spotlight that accompanied the incomprehensible tragedy, Bostonians showed the resilience, resolve, and sense of community that have characterized the spirit of New England since its earliest days.

CAPE COD & THE ISLANDS TODAY

The Cape Cod of today is many things at once: a popular vacationland, a mecca for wealthy second-home owners, a historic fishing village, a hip urban scene, a sleepy retirement community, a suburban subdivision, and even a bedroom community for Boston. The Cape still resembles the classic Patti Page song "Old Cape Cod," with plenty of "sand dunes and salty air," and even "quaint little villages here and there," but it is also a modern destination. Towns wrestle with how to maintain vibrant year-round communities as wealthy second-home owners buy up properties and drive up the cost of living for the average Joe. Towns also struggle to preserve each community's authentic character. As for Martha's Vineyard and Nantucket: The rich are richer, and the struggle is greater. The islands' character is even more at risk from the dreaded sameness of corporate America, because they are both still so unique.

A BRIEF HISTORY

In November 1620, a gaunt and exhausted band of Pilgrims traveling on a rickety boat called the *Mayflower* landed on the tip of the Cape in what is now Provincetown and established the Plymouth Colony. (Nearby Plymouth was their second stop.) At the far east end of Commercial Street in Provincetown, a rock marks the spot where the Pilgrims are believed to have landed.

The Cape's cultural history really begins with the Wampanoag tribe, a name that translates as "The People of the First Light." This Native American tribe inhabited the northeast coast and used the area that is now the town of Mashpee on the Upper Cape as one of their bases. The Pilgrims were greeted by Wampanoag tribe members, among them Squanto, who is said to have stayed with the newcomers for the 1½ years that they lived in Plymouth, teaching them the ways of the New World. The Wampanoags were friendly to the Europeans, offering them food during the cold winter and showing them how to farm crops in the sandy soil. The Pilgrims seem to have repaid them with smallpox and some beaver pelts.

The Puritans who permanently settled Boston in 1630—like the Pilgrims, they fled Europe to escape religious persecution—also enjoyed peaceful relations with natives, members of the small, Algonquian-speaking Massachuset tribe that grew corn on some harbor islands but lived farther inland. Thanks to its excellent location on a deep, sheltered harbor, Boston, which became the capital of the Massachusetts Bay colony in 1632, quickly grew into a center of shipbuilding, trading, and fishing. All these years later, fresh-caught seafood remains an important element of the local cuisine.

The 18th Century

The Plymouth and Massachusetts Bay colonies were united in 1692, and appointed governors ruled the province of Massachusetts Bay for most of the 18th century. As dissatisfaction with the government in England escalated, Boston emerged as a center of revolutionary activity. In the Boston Massacre of 1770, five colonists were killed in a scuffle with British troops. The first to die was a former slave named Crispus Attucks. The site, represented by a circle of cobblestones, sits on what is now State Street, and the colonists' graves are nearby, in the Granary Burying Ground on Tremont Street.

In December 1773, three British ships laden with tea sat at anchor in Boston Harbor (roughly where present-day Atlantic Ave. meets the Evelyn Moakley Bridge), waiting for to be unloaded. Before that could happen, the rabble-rousing Sons of Liberty, stirred up after a spirited public meeting at what's now the Old South Meeting House, boarded the ships and dumped 342 chests of tea into the harbor. The anti-tax protest, soon known as the "Boston Tea Party," endures today as the inspiration for one of the most divisive movements in modern American politics. You can visit replicas of the vessels at the Boston Tea Party Ships & Museum, on the Fort Point Channel; the meet-inghouse stages a re-creation of the inflammatory rally every December.

In 1775, royal troops dispatched to destroy the colonists' stockpiles of weapons left Boston by boat from what's now Charles Street, between Boston Common and the Public Garden. A lantern signal soon illuminated the steeple of the Old North Church, alerting Paul Revere to their route—the "two if by sea" made famous nearly a century later by Cambridge resident Henry Wadsworth Longfellow in his 1861 poem "Paul Revere's Ride" ("Listen my children and you shall hear / Of the midnight ride of Paul Revere"). The romantic but inaccurate account of the events of April 18 and 19, 1775, is a must if you plan to walk the Freedom Trail.

The British won the Battle of Bunker Hill in Charlestown on June 17, 1775, but at the cost of half their forces. The redcoats abandoned Boston the following March 17. On July 4, 1776, the Continental Congress adopted the Declaration of Independence. Although many Bostonians fought in the 6-year war that followed, Boston itself saw no more battles.

Isolated from the action on the mainland yet connected to the rest of the world by the sea, Cape Cod and the islands were growing in importance. Before the Cape Cod Canal was dug and the bridges were constructed (in the 1930s), the shipping route around the arm of the Cape carried the reputation as "the graveyard of the Atlantic," for all the shipwrecks among the treacherous shoals and currents off the Cape.

Whaling was a prominent and lucrative industry from about 1750 to about 1850, when it began to wane. Whalers proved to be some of the most successful seafarers in the Cape's history. To make bountiful catches, whalers traveled around the world; when they returned, they inevitably brought souvenirs home. The homes of successful sea captains on the Cape and islands became virtual museums containing treasures from across the globe. Nantucket was an important whaling port, and its wealth was renowned. The Nantucket Whaling Museum houses exhibits that show the history of whaling and the bounty it enabled seafarers to bring home.

Whaling was also important to the economy of Boston, which again became a center of business after the Revolution, when fishing and trade with the Far East dominated. The influential merchant families who became known as Boston Brahmins spearheaded a cultural renaissance that flourished even after the War of 1812 ravaged international shipping, ending Boston's commercial heyday. As banking and manufacturing rose in importance, Boston took a back seat to New York and Philadelphia in size and influence. But the city became known for its intellectual community and its fine art and architecture, including the luxurious homes you see today on Beacon Hill.

The 19th Century

In 1822, Boston became a city. From 1824 to 1826, Mayor Josiah Quincy oversaw the landfill project that moved the waterfront away from Faneuil Hall. The market building constructed at that time, which still stands, was named in his honor. It's at Dock Square, one of many locations, all over the city, named for long-gone geographical features. In the 19th century, landfill work tripled the city's area, creating badly needed space. The largest of the projects, started in 1835 and completed in 1882, was the transformation of the Back Bay from mud flats and marshes into the elegant neighborhood you see today.

By the mid-1800s, Ralph Waldo Emerson, Oliver Wendell Holmes, Henry Wadsworth Longfellow, Nathaniel Hawthorne, Louisa May Alcott, John Greenleaf Whittier, Walt Whitman, and Henry David Thoreau had appeared on the literary scene in the city sometimes known as the "Athens of America." William Lloyd Garrison published the weekly "Liberator" newspaper, a powerful voice in the antislavery movement. Boston became an important stop on the Underground Railroad, the secret network the abolitionists developed to smuggle runaway slaves into Canada. The Black Heritage Trail passes by a number of sites related to the Railroad.

Meanwhile, on Nantucket, the Great Fire of 1846 destroyed the town center, which was rebuilt with the riches from whaling journeys. An economic bust in the late 19th century meant that nothing was changed for decades, and the town has been virtually preserved from that mid-19th-century period, cobblestone streets and all. Edgartown on Martha's Vineyard also thrived during this period, and there are numerous examples of the majestic sea captains' houses—mostly still private homes—along North Water Street. A large concentration of sea captains' houses lines Route 6A in Brewster, nicknamed "The Sea Captains' Town." This is a good place to admire widow's walks, those rooftop porches that were said to allow the wives of sea captains to scan the horizon in anticipation of the return of their men.

During the Civil War (1861–65), abolitionist sentiment dominated Boston—to such a degree that only names of members of the Union Army appear on the rolls listing the war dead in Harvard's Memorial Hall, which is open to the public. Massachusetts's contributions to the war effort included enormous quantities of firearms, shoes, blankets, tents, and men.

The black abolitionist Frederick Douglass, a former member of the Massachusetts Anti-Slavery Society, helped recruit the 54th and 55th Massachusetts Colored Regiments. The 1989 movie "Glory" tells the story of the 54th, the first army unit made up of free black soldiers, and its white commander, Col. Robert Gould Shaw. The regiment's memorial, a gorgeous bas-relief by Augustus Saint-Gaudens, stands on Boston Common opposite the State House.

The railroad boom of the 1820s and 1830s and the flood of immigration that began soon after had made New England an industrial center. Then as now, Boston was the region's unofficial capital. Before and after the Civil War, immigrants from Ireland poured into the city, the first ethnic group to do so in great numbers since the French Huguenots in the early 18th century. Early resistance to the newcomers began to fade away as the new arrivals gained political power, and the first Irish mayor was elected in 1885.

By that time, Boston's class split was a chasm, with the influx of immigrants adding to the social tension. The Irish led the way and were followed by Italian, Portuguese, and Eastern-European Jewish immigrants. Each group had its own neighborhoods, houses of worship, schools, newspapers, and livelihoods that intersected only occasionally with "proper" society.

Even as the upper crust was sowing cultural seeds that would wind up enriching everyone—the Boston Symphony, the Boston Public Library, and the Museum of Fine Arts were established in the second half of the 19th century—its prudish behavior gained Boston a reputation for making snobbery an art form. In 1878 the censorious Watch and Ward Society was founded (as the New England Society for the Suppression of Vice), and the phrase "banned in Boston" soon became well known.

The late 19th century also brought the beginnings of the tourism industry to the Cape and islands. The first tourists were looking toward the heavens, but they were not seeking the sun. They came—by the hundreds—for religious retreats. In Oak Bluffs, on Martha's Vineyard, Methodists gathered in a grove near the harbor for revivalist camp meetings. The canvas tents they erected for the extended religious revivals were eventually expanded into tiny cottages. Today visitors can stroll around and see the "gingerbread cottages," with their elaborate Victorian-era scrollwork and brightly colored details. The Cottage Museum tells the history of the camp meetings.

Across Vineyard Sound, in the village of Woods Hole in Falmouth, a different kind of summer tourist was discovering the area. Scientists—especially oceanographers—interested in spending their summer vacations surrounded by other scientists were beginning to gather for seminars. Founded as a summer lab in 1888, the Marine Biological Laboratory is now an international center for biological research, education, and training. Woods Hole is also home to the Woods Hole Oceanographic Institution, founded in 1930 and dedicated to ocean research, education, and exploration.

The 20th Century

Around 1900 a group of artists from New York, led by Charles Hawthorne, discovered Provincetown, a tiny fishing village at the tip of the Cape, where the native population of fishermen, many of them Portuguese, had developed a colorful community. The artists, who set up their easels on the piers and the tiny lanes, made it even more colorful. As writers and intellectuals followed, the area became a hotbed of bohemia, a kind of Greenwich Village of the north. The liberal, artsy, open-mindedness of the populace made the area a popular spot for gays, and Provincetown is now one of the country's top gay resorts. Elsewhere on the Cape and islands, from around the 1890s to the 1930s, summer cottage communities began to spring up all over. Two particularly picturesque summer cottage communities are Falmouth Heights, a village along the south shore of Falmouth, where Victorian-era cottages were built on and around a central hill, and Siasconset—known as 'Sconset—on Nantucket, where the tiny cottages are all near the ocean, and festooned with climbing roses and ringed by white picket fences.

In Boston, the new century saw the rise of the Irish-American politician. The forebears of the Kennedy clan had appeared on the scene—John F. "Honey Fitz" Fitzgerald, Rose's father, was elected mayor in 1910—and the city slowly transformed yet again as WASPs and Catholics struck an uneasy truce. By the time Honey Fitz's grandson John Fitzgerald Kennedy was elected to the U.S. Senate, in 1952, Boston was in the midst of another transformation. World War II had bolstered the Depression-ravaged industrial economy, and the war's end touched off an unprecedented economic shift. Shipping declined, along with New England's textile, shoe, and glass industries, at the same time that students on the GI Bill poured into area colleges and universities. MIT grads in particular helped spark the rise of the local high-tech economy. It remains a worthy competitor for Silicon Valley, with diverse elements that include defense contractors, software leaders, and biotech and venture capital firms.

The Kennedy mystique, meanwhile, endures. The family had vacationed on the Cape for decades, and the glamour of seeing JFK sailing his yacht, the *Honey Fitz,* off Hyannis Port gave Cape Cod worldwide panache in the 1960s. Some say the place has never recovered. Hyannis, which is actually a village in the town of Barnstable, is by far the most built-up part of the Cape. The Kennedy compound is still in Hyannis Port, and many family members still consider it home. The Kennedy family's favorite pastimes, such as sailing in Nantucket Sound, continue through the generations. JFK also did his part to preserve the Cape. In August 1961, he signed a bill designating 27,000 acres from Chatham to Provincetown as a new national park, the Cape Cod National Seashore.

The postwar baby boom and the international social upheaval of the 1960s hit the Boston area hard. In the mid-1970s, Boston proper was the center of a school-busing crisis. Sparked by a court-ordered school desegregation plan enacted in 1974, it touched off riots, violence, and a white boycott.

In pop culture, Boston's gift to classic TV comedy is a show that performed so poorly in its first season that NBC nearly canceled it. "Cheers" (1982–93), based on a local pub then called the Bull & Finch, became so popular that the original bar changed its name and opened a spin-off in Faneuil Hall Marketplace.

The 21st Century

Boston has gone through many upgrades in in the past couple decades. The $15 billion highway-construction project known as the Big Dig wrapped up, and by 2007, the new Rose Fitzgerald Kennedy Greenway had transformed a mile-long swath of downtown into gorgeous parkland at the edge of the cleaned-up harbor. And the nearby part of the South Boston waterfront now known as the Seaport District is booming (though the city won't stop trying to make "Innovation District" happen). Alongside long-established businesses relocating from downtown and the Back Bay, the neighborhood is home to dozens of tech companies.

An economic shift has also come to the Cape and islands. Although the industry has suffered in recent years because of overfishing, the area is still home to many who make their living by harvesting from the sea. In some families, the profession goes back for generations. Stop by the Fish Pier in the Lower Cape town of Chatham after noon to see fishermen unloading their catches. This too is an important part of the history of the region.

It's not all scenery and seafood, of course—for instance, the Catholic Church's sex-abuse scandal first came to light in the Boston Archdiocese, a major presence in this predominantly Catholic area. And the crime spree mounted by James "Whitey" Bulger—whose capture in 2011 after 16 years on the run made international headlines—was a black eye for local and federal law enforcement. Meanwhile, social divisions were fading. In 2003, the Massachusetts Supreme Judicial Court ruled that not allowing same-sex couples to marry violated the state constitution, institutionalizing a live-and-let-live attitude that had already taken hold outside the courtroom. The election of Deval Patrick, who in 2006 became the second African American since Reconstruction (after Virginia's Douglas Wilder) elected governor, was a similar big deal that the locals treated as no big deal.

Thanks in no small part to the college students who clog rapid transit and drive property values out of sight—and who stick around after graduation, keeping the cutting edge nice and sharp—the Boston area continues to grow and change. By contrast, even with development taking its toll, the Cape and islands retain a certain timelessness. Standing on a pristine seashore looking out at the churning Atlantic Ocean, and putting all of America behind you, to paraphrase Henry David Thoreau, continues to be one of the most cherished experiences for those visiting Cape Cod.

WHEN TO GO

Boston attracts throngs of visitors year-round. Between April and November, the city sees hardly any slow times. Make reservations as early as possible if you plan to visit during busy periods, especially college graduation season (May and early June) and foliage season, from mid-September to early November. Spring and fall are popular times for conventions. Families pour into the area in July and August, but summer actually isn't the most expensive time to visit: That's foliage season, when many leaf-peepers stay in the Boston area or pass through on the way to other New England destinations. December is less busy but still a convention time—look for weekend bargains.

Cape Cod and the islands, once strictly warm-weather destinations, traditionally open the season with a splash on Memorial Day weekend—traffic is horrendous, and ferries are booked solid—and shutter up come Labor Day. Things slow down between late May and late June, then explode. The weekend closest to July 4th is another major mob scene, July is the second-busiest month of the year, and August is by far the most popular month for visiting the region. Summer ends with Labor Day, a heavily trafficked weekend you'll probably want to avoid.

Cape Cod now welcomes more and more tourists in the spring and fall. During these shoulder seasons, lodging tends to cost less, and a fair number of restaurants and attractions are open. Most important, traffic is manageable. November and December don't quite qualify as "off season" on the Cape and islands. Some say the most crowded time on Nantucket is during the Christmas Stroll in early December. Martha's Vineyard also rolls out the red carpet in December.

During the coldest months, January through March, tourist-oriented establishments on the Cape and islands traditionally close, but some tough it out. To avoid disappointment, check schedules ahead of time. This is also Boston's (relatively) slow time, when many hotels offer great deals, especially on weekends. However, winter is when unpredictable weather plagues the Northeast, often affecting travel schedules.

Climate

You've probably heard the saying about New England weather: "If you don't like it, wait 10 minutes." Variations from day to day or morning to afternoon (if not minute to minute) can be enormous. You can roast in March and freeze in June, shiver in July and sweat in November. Dressing in layers is always a good idea.

BOSTON

Spring and fall are the best bets for moderate temperatures, but **spring** ("mud season") is brief—it can settle in as late as early May, and snow sometimes falls in April. Pack an umbrella as well as shoes that keep your feet dry. **Summers** are hot, especially in July and August, and can be uncomfortably humid. This is also when the wind can shift in a matter of minutes, cooling the city with a burst of wind off the ocean—an extra layer (even just a long-sleeved T-shirt) can really come in handy. **Fall** is when you're most likely to catch a comfortable run of dry, sunny days and cool nights. **Winters** are cold and usually snowy—bring a warm coat, a hat and gloves, and sturdy boots.

THE CAPE & ISLANDS

The Gulf Stream renders the Cape and islands generally about 10° warmer in winter than the mainland, and offshore winds keep them about 10° cooler in summer (you'll probably need a sweater most evenings). The only downside of being surrounded by water is the other wet stuff: no, not rain, fog! Typically it's sunny about 2 days out of 3—not bad odds. And the foggy days can be rather romantic. Pack some good books for when it pours. Check out www.ackweather.com for up-to-date wind, surf, and tide conditions for the Cape and islands.

Boston's Average Temperatures & Rainfall

	JAN	FEB	MAR	APR	MAY	JUNE	JULY	AUG	SEPT	OCT	NOV	DEC
TEMP. (°F)	30	31	38	49	59	68	74	72	65	55	45	34
TEMP. (°C)	–1	–1	3	9	15	20	23	22	18	13	7	1
PRECIPITATION (in.)	3.8	3.5	4.0	3.7	3.4	3.0	2.8	3.6	3.3	3.3	4.4	4.2

Hyannis's Average High & Low Temperatures

	JAN	FEB	MAR	APR	MAY	JUNE	JULY	AUG	SEPT	OCT	NOV	DEC
TEMP (°F)	37/20	37/20	44/28	53/37	63/46	72/56	78/62	70/62	71/53	62/43	52/35	42/25
TEMP (°C)	3/–7	3/–7	7/–2	12/3	17/8	22/13	26/17	21/17	22/12	17/6	11/2	6/–4

Holidays

Banks, government offices, post offices, schools, and many stores, restaurants, and museums close on the following legal national holidays: January 1 (New Year's Day), the third Monday in January (Martin Luther King, Jr., Day), the third Monday in February (Presidents Day), the last Monday in May (Memorial Day), July 4 (Independence Day), the first Monday in September (Labor Day), the second Monday in October (Columbus Day), November 11 (Veterans' Day/Armistice Day), the fourth Thursday in November (Thanksgiving Day), and December 25 (Christmas). The Tuesday after the first Monday in November is Election Day, a federal government holiday in presidential-election years (every 4 years, next in 2016). Massachusetts state offices and some businesses close for **Patriots' Day** on the third Monday in April.

Calendar of Events

The **Massachusetts Office of Travel & Tourism** (© **800/227-MASS** [227-6277] or 617/973-8500; www.massvacation.com) provides visitor information, including details of countless events, for the whole state. See "Visitor Information" in chapters 4, 5, and 6 for destination-specific sources.

JANUARY

Martin Luther King, Jr., Birthday Celebration, various Boston-area locations. Events include musical tributes, gospel concerts, museum displays and programs, readings, speeches, and panel discussions. Third Monday in January.

FEBRUARY

African-American History Month, various Boston-area locations. Programs include special museum exhibits, children's activities, concerts, films, lectures, discussions, readings, and tours of the Black Heritage Trail led by National Park Service rangers (© **617/742-5415;** www.nps.gov/boaf). All month.

Chinese New Year, Chinatown. The dragon parade (which draws a big crowd no matter the weather), fireworks, and raucous festivals are part of the celebration. Special programs take place at the **Children's Museum** (© **617-426-8855;** www.bostonchildrens museum.org). For more details, visit **www. chinatownmainstreet.org**. The holiday falls between January 21 and February 19. February 19, 2015, and February 8, 2016.

MARCH

St. Patrick's Day Celebrations, various Boston-area locations. Concerts, talks, special restaurant menus, and other offerings celebrate the heritage of this very Irish-American city. Note that organization that runs the parade, held along Broadway in South Boston, is private and therefore free to bar any group it wants to from marching. That includes gays and, at least once in recent years, antiwar veterans. March 17; parade is on the closest Sunday.

APRIL

Big Apple Circus (© **800/922-3772;** www. bigapplecircus.org), City Hall Plaza, Government Center. The New York–based "one-ring wonder" performs in a heated tent with all seating less than 50 feet from the ring. Proceeds support the Boston Children's Museum. Early April to mid-May.

Red Sox Opening Day, Fenway Park, Boston. Even if your concierge is a magician, this is an extremely tough ticket. Check ahead (© **877/RED-SOX-9** [733-7699]; www.redsox.com) when tickets go on sale in December. If you can't get tickets to Opening Day, try to see the morning game on **Patriots' Day,** the third Monday in April. The early start allows spectators to watch the Boston Marathon afterward. Early and mid-April.

Swan Boats Return to the Public Garden. Since their introduction in 1877, the Swan Boats (© **617/522-1966;** www.swanboats. com) have been a symbol of Boston. Like real swans, they go away for the winter. Mid-April.

Patriots' Day, North End, Lexington, and Concord. Festivities commemorate and reenact the events of April 18 and 19, 1775.

Lanterns glow in the steeple of the **Old North Church** (© **617/523-6676;** www. oldnorth.com). Participants dressed as Paul Revere and William Dawes ride from the North End to Lexington and Concord to warn the minutemen that "the regulars are out" (not that "the British are coming"— most colonists considered themselves British). For information on reenactments and other events, check the websites of the **Paul Revere House** (© **617/523-2338;** www. paulreverehouse.org) and the **Battle Road Committee** (www.battleroad.org). Third Monday of April (Apr 20, 2015; Apr 18, 2016).

Boston Marathon, Hopkinton, Massachusetts, to Boston. International stars and local amateurs join in the world's oldest and most famous marathon (www.bostonmarathon. org). The event begins on April 15. On race day, competitors start in stages, with the first setting out around 9am. Fans are welcome— subject to stringent security measures instituted after 2013—until the last weekend warriors stagger across the Boylston Street finish line in the late afternoon. Third Monday of the month.

Freedom Trail Week, various Boston-area locations. This is a school vacation week, with plenty of crowds and diversions. Family-friendly events include tours, concerts, talks, and other programs related to Patriots' Day, the Freedom Trail, and the American Revolution. Third week of April.

Daffodil Festival, Nantucket. Spring's arrival is heralded with masses of yellow blooms adorning everything in sight, including a cavalcade of antique cars. Call © **508/228-1700.** April 27 to 29.

Brewster in Bloom, Brewster. You'll find open houses, a crafts fair and flea market, and hot-air balloons. The Old King's Highway (Rte. 6A) is lined with thousands of daffodils. Call © **508/896-3500,** or visit www. brewsterinbloom.org. Late April to early May.

Independent Film Festival of Boston, various locations. Features, shorts, and documentaries by international filmmakers make up the schedule for this increasingly buzz-worthy event. Check ahead (www.

iffboston.org) for the schedule. Late April to early May.

MAY

Lilac Sunday, Arnold Arboretum, Jamaica Plain. The arboretum (© **617/524-1717; www.arboretum.harvard.edu**) allows picnicking only once a year, on Lilac Sunday. From sunrise to sunset, wander the grounds and enjoy the sensational spring flowers, including more than 400 varieties of lilacs in bloom. Mid-May.

Street Performer Spring Showcase, Faneuil Hall Marketplace. Everyone but the pigeons gets into the act as musicians, magicians, jugglers, sword swallowers, and artists strut their stuff. Late May

Dexter Rhododendron Festival, Sandwich. Heritage Museums and Gardens—at the peak of bloom—sells offshoots of its incomparable botanical collection. Call © **508/ 888-3300.** Late May.

Nantucket Wine Festival, Nantucket. Vintners from all over converge on Nantucket for wine tastings and cuisine provided by some of the island's top chefs. The Grand Cru is the main event. Call © **508/228-1128,** or visit www.nantucketwinefestival.com. Late May.

Figawi Sailboat Race, Hyannis to Nantucket. This is the largest—and wildest—race on the East Coast. Intense partying in Hyannis and on Nantucket surrounds this popular event. Call © **508/221-6891,** or visit www.figawi. com. Memorial Day weekend.

JUNE

Boston Pride Parade, South End to Government Center (© **617/262-9405; www.bostonpride.org**). The largest gay pride march in New England is the highlight of a weeklong celebration. The parade, on the second weekend of the month, starts in the South End and ends at City Hall Plaza, where the Boston Pride Festival takes place. Early June.

Hong Kong Dragon Boat Festival, Charles River near Harvard Square, Cambridge (www. bostondragonboat.org). Teams of paddlers synchronized by a drummer propel boats with dragon heads and tails as they race 1,640 feet. The winners go to the national

championships; the spectators go to a celebration of Chinese culture and food on the shore. Second or third Sunday of June.

Cambridge River Festival (© **617/349-4380;** www.cambridgeartscouncil.org), Memorial Drive from John F. Kennedy Street to Western Avenue. A salute to the arts, the festival incorporates live music, dancing, children's activities, crafts and art exhibits, and international food on the banks of the Charles River. *Note:* In 2014, the festival temporarily relocated to Central Square; check ahead before setting out. Mid-June.

Arts Alive Festival, Falmouth. Dozens of artists and performers sell artwork, and put on performances at this weekend-long event that opens with a town dance on the library lawn. Call © **508-548-8500,** or visit www. artsfalmouth.org/artsalive. Mid-June.

Nantucket Film Festival, Nantucket. This annual event focuses on storytelling through film and includes showings of films, documentaries, staged readings, panel discussions, and screenplay competitions. Sponsors include "Vanity Fair" magazine, so you may see a celebrity or two. Call © **508/325-6274,** or visit www.nantucketfilmfestival.org. Mid-June.

Provincetown International Film Festival, Provincetown. Focusing on alternative film, this fete has brought out such celebrities as John Waters and Lily Tomlin. Call © **508/ 487-FILM** [3456], or visit www.ptownfilm fest.org. Mid-June.

St. Barnabas Strawberry Festival, Falmouth. Indulge in strawberry shortcake, barbecue, and lots of children's games on the grounds of St. Barnabas Church, by the Village Green. Call © **508/548-8500.** Mid-June.

Aptucxet Strawberry Festival, Bourne. The Aptucxet Trading Post Museum, a replica of the country's first store, features crafts demonstrations and fresh strawberry shortcake. Call © **508/759-9487.** Late June.

Provincetown Portuguese Festival, Provincetown. This cultural event celebrates Provincetown's Portuguese heritage with music, dancing, exhibits, food, a parade, fireworks, and the traditional Blessing of the Fleet. Call ✆ **508/246-9080,** or visit www.provincetownportuguesefestival.com. Late June.

JULY

Independence Day celebrations, various locations. The entire region gets into the spirit. Weeklong **Boston Harborfest** (www.bostonharborfest.com) focuses on maritime history, with concerts, cruises, fireworks, and much more. July 4.

Boston Pops Concert & Fireworks Display, Hatch Shell, on the Esplanade, Boston. Spectators start showing up at dawn (overnight camping is not permitted) to stake out a good spot on the lawn. Others show up at the last minute—the Cambridge side of the river, near Kendall Square, and the Longfellow Bridge are good spots to watch the spectacular aerial show. The program includes the "1812 Overture," with real cannon fire and church bells. Visit www.july4th.org. July 4.

Wampanoag Pow Wow, Mashpee. Native American tribes from around the country converge for traditional dances and games. Call ✆ **508/477-0208,** or visit www.mashpeewampanoagtribe.com. July 4th weekend.

Edgartown Regatta, Martha's Vineyard. A highly social sailing event. Call ✆ **508/627-4361,** or visit www.edgartownyc.org/regatta.php. July 19 to 21.

Barnstable County Fair, East Falmouth. This old-fashioned, 9-day agricultural extravaganza is complete with prize produce and livestock and, of course, rides and a midway. There are concerts nightly. Call ✆ **508/563-3200,** or visit www.barnstablecountyfair.org. July 21 to 28.

Woods Hole Film Festival, Falmouth. A 2-week festival that features small independent films in various venues. Call ✆ **508/495-FILM** [3456], or visit www.woodsholefilmfestival.org. Late July.

Puerto Rican Festival & Parade, Franklin Park, Boston. This 3-day event, instituted in 1967, is part street fair, part cultural celebration, with plenty of live music and traditional food. Visit www.puertoricanfestivalofma.com. Late July or early August.

AUGUST

Italian-American Feasts, North End, Boston. These weekend street fairs begin in July and end in late August with the two biggest: the Fisherman's Feast and the Feast of St. Anthony. The sublime (fresh seafood prepared while you wait, live music, dancing in the street) mingles with the ridiculous (carnival games, tacky T-shirts, fried-dough stands). Visit www.fishermansfeast.com or www.saintanthonysfeast.com for a preview. Weekends throughout August.

In the Spirit Arts Festival, Martha's Vineyard. Oak Bluffs celebrates its cultural diversity with food, music, and children's fun. Call ✆ **508/693-0085.** Early August.

Pops by the Sea, Hyannis. Celebrity "conductors"—such as Olympia Dukakis—enliven this outdoor concert with the Boston Pops Esplanade Orchestra. Call ✆ **508/775-2201.** Early August.

Carnival Week, Provincetown. The gay community's annual blowout features performers, parties, and an outrageous costume parade. Call ✆ **508/487-2313.** August 12 to 17.

Falmouth Road Race, Falmouth. Joggers and world-class runners turn out in droves—10,000 strong—for this annual race that covers just over 7 miles. Entry registration is by lottery and ends in May. **Note:** Unregistered runners are not allowed to participate. Call ✆ **508/540-7000,** or visit www.falmouthroadrace.com. August 12.

Agricultural Society Livestock Show and Fair, Martha's Vineyard. In West Tisbury, you'll find a classic country carnival and a celebration of the Vineyard's agricultural tradition. Call ✆ **508/693-9549,** or visit www.mvas.vineyard.net/fair.php. Mid-August.

August Moon Festival, Chinatown, Boston. A celebration of the harvest and the coming of autumn, the festival includes dragon and lion dances during the parade through the crowded streets, and demonstrations of crafts and martial arts. It's also an excuse to stuff yourself with tasty mooncakes. For details, visit www.chinatownmainstreet.org. Mid-August.

Illumination Night, Martha's Vineyard. The Oak Bluffs campground is lit with hundreds of Japanese lanterns. Campground officials keep this event a secret until the last minute, so it's hard to plan ahead. Call ✆ **508/693-0085.** Late August.

Oak Bluffs Fireworks and Band Concert, Martha's Vineyard. The summer's last blast. Call ✆ **508/693-0085.** Late August.

SEPTEMBER

Scallop Festival, Falmouth. This annual weekend event features food, crafts, rides, musical entertainment, and more. Call ✆ **508/759-6000,** or visit www.bourne scallopfest.com. Early September.

Windmill Weekend, Eastham. This jolly community festival includes a sand-art competition, road races, band concerts, an arts and crafts show, and professional entertainment. The highlight of this weekend is the square dance held under the historic windmill. Call ✆ **508/255-3444,** or visit www.eastham windmillweekend.com. Early September.

Cambridge Carnival International, Kendall Square, Cambridge (✆ **617/863-0476;** www.cambridgecarnival.org). This Afro-Caribbean-style celebration of diversity and unity features live music, food, kids' activities, and a parade of costumed revelers. Sunday after Labor Day.

Boston Film Festival (✆ **617/523-8388;** www.bostonfilmfestival.org), various locations. Independent films continue on the festival circuit or make their premieres, sometimes following a lecture by an actor or filmmaker. Most screenings are open to the public without advance tickets. Mid-September.

Martha's Vineyard Striped Bass and Bluefish Derby, Martha's Vineyard. In its 56th year, the region's premier fishing derby and one of the country's oldest is a month-long classic contest. Call ✆ **508/693-0085,** or visit www.mvderby.com. Mid-September to mid-October.

OCTOBER

Oktoberfest, Harvard Square, Cambridge. This immense street fair is a magnet for college students, families, street performers, musicians, and crafts vendors. Visit www.

harvardsquare.com. Second Sunday of October.

Wellfleet OysterFest, Wellfleet. Spend a weekend learning about and tasting Wellfleet's world-famous oysters at this weekend-long street festival, including arts, crafts, and live music. Call ✆ **508/349-2510,** or visit www.wellfleetoysterfest.org. Weekend (beginning on Fri) after Columbus Day.

An Evening with Champions, Bright Athletic Center, Allston. World-class ice skaters and promising local students stage two or three performances to benefit the Jimmy Fund, the children's fundraising arm of the Dana-Farber Cancer Institute. Sponsored by Harvard's **Eliot House** (✆ **617/942-1392;** www.aneveningwithchampions.org). Mid-October.

Yarmouth Seaside Festival, Yarmouth. Enjoy a parade, fireworks, arts and crafts, contests, and sporting events. Call ✆ **800/732-1008** or 508/778-1008, or visit www.yarmouthseasidefestival.com. Mid-October.

Boston Book Festival, Copley Square. The area in front of the Boston Public Library fills with bookworms and vendors, while speeches and panel discussions take place in Trinity Church and other nearby venues. Check ahead (✆ **617/945-9552;** www.bostonbookfest.org) for specifics and tickets, or just show up. Mid- to late October.

Head of the Charles Regatta, Boston and Cambridge. High school, college, and post-collegiate rowing teams and individuals—some 4,000 in all—race in front of tens of thousands of fans along the banks of the Charles River and on the bridges spanning it. The Head of the Charles (✆ **617/868-6200;** www.hocr.org) has an uncanny tendency to coincide with a crisp, picturesque weekend. Late October.

NOVEMBER

Thanksgiving Celebrations, Plymouth. Festivities start the weekend before, with **America's Hometown Thanksgiving** (✆ **508/746-1818;** www.usathanksgiving.com), which includes a craft and food festival, tours and other educational activities, and a huge parade. Thanksgiving Day menus at **Plimoth**

Plantation, which re-creates the colony's first years, include a buffet and a Victorian Thanksgiving feast. Reservations (℡ **800/ 262-9356** or 508/746-1622; www.plimoth. org) are accepted beginning in June. Contact **Destination Plymouth** (℡ **508/ 747-7533;** www.seeplymouth.com). Thanksgiving Day.

Lighting of the Pilgrim Monument, Provincetown. The Italianate tower turns into a monumental Christmas ornament as carolers convene below. Call ℡ **508/487-1310.** Thanksgiving Eve (late Nov).

Chatham's Christmas by the Sea, Chatham. A month of townwide events includes historic-inn tours, carolers, hayrides, open houses, a dinner dance, and an appearance by Santa. Call ℡ **508/945-5199.** Late November through December.

DECEMBER

"The Nutcracker," Opera House, Boston. Boston Ballet's annual holiday extravaganza is one of the country's biggest and best. This is *the* traditional way to expose Buy tickets (℡ **617/695-6955;** www.bostonballet.org) as soon as you plan your trip, ask whether your hotel offers a "Nutcracker" package, or cross your fingers and check when you arrive. Thanksgiving weekend through late December.

Christmas Stroll, Nantucket. The island briefly stirs from its winter slumber for one last shopping/feasting spree, attended by costumed carolers, Santa in a horse-drawn carriage, and a "talking" Christmas tree. This event is the pinnacle of **Nantucket Noel,** a month of festivities starting in late November. Ferries and lodging establishments book up months before this event, so you'll need to plan ahead. Call ℡ **508/228-1700.** Early December.

Falmouth Christmas by the Sea, Falmouth. Weekend-long seasonal entertainment features carolers, holiday lights, Santa, and a parade along the historic and lavishly decorated Falmouth Village Green. Call ℡ **508/ 548-8500.** Early December.

Holly Folly, Provincetown. The annual gay and lesbian holiday festival guesthouse tours, holiday parties, the Reindeer Run, concerts, and more. Call ℡ **508/487-2313,** or visit www.ptown.org/HollyFolly.asp. Early December.

Yarmouth Port Christmas Stroll, Yarmouth Port. Stroll along the Old King's Highway for open houses, visits with Santa, and caroling. Call ℡ **508/778-1008.** Early December.

Boston Tea Party Reenactment, Old South Meeting House (℡ **617/482-6439;** www. oldsouthmeetinghouse.org) and Tea Party Ships and Museum, Congress Street Bridge (℡ **855/TEA-1773** [832-1773] or 617/338-1773; www.bostonteapartyship.com), Boston. Chafing under British rule, American colonists rose up on December 16, 1773, to strike a blow where it would cause real pain—in the pocketbook. A re-creation of the pre-party rally at the meetinghouse is a lively all-ages audience-participation event; the continuation at the ships and museum involves tea-tossing. Mid-December.

Black Nativity (℡ **617/585-6366;** www. blacknativity.org), Blackman Auditorium, Northeastern University, 342 Huntington Ave., Boston. Poet Langston Hughes wrote the "gospel opera," and a cast of more than 100 brings it to life. Produced by the National Center of Afro-American Artists. Mid-December.

Christmas Revels, Sanders Theatre, Cambridge. This multicultural celebration of the winter solstice features the holiday customs of a different culture each year. Themes have included 17th-century Europe, American folk traditions, and Victorian England. Be ready to sing along. For information and tickets, contact the **Revels** (℡ **617/972-8300;** www. revels.org). Last 2 weeks of December.

First Night, various locations statewide. **Boston** pioneered the arts-oriented, no-alcohol, citywide New Year's Eve celebration. It begins in the early afternoon and includes a parade, ice sculptures, art exhibitions, theatrical performances, and indoor and outdoor entertainment. Some attractions require tickets, but for most you just need a First Night button, available for less than $20 at visitor centers and stores around the city. Fireworks light up the sky above Boston Common just before 7pm and over Boston Harbor at midnight. For details, contact **First Night** (© **857/600-1590;** www.firstnight.org) or check local websites.

Following Boston's lead, **Chatham** puts on a festive evening featuring local performers. Call © **508/945-5199,** or visit www.firstnightchatham.com. In **Sandwich,** First Night ends at 9pm but features an illuminated parade and lots of music and food all over town. Visit www.firstnightsandwich.com. December 31.

SUGGESTED ITINERARIES

3

Picture this: You're on vacation, going from place to place at a reasonable pace, exploring areas and subjects that interest you, taking breaks when and where you need them, and not fretting over a rigid checklist. Or you're obsessively following a minute-by-minute schedule, saying "ought" and "should" a lot, and generally acting as though breaking out of your usual routine is a chore, not an opportunity. The first approach sounds better, right? Read on for strategies that can help you organize your schedule and still have a great time.

ICONIC BOSTON

Every trolley-tour company in town (p. 92) claims that it can show visitors the city in a single day, which is technically true. If you just want to *see* as much as possible as quickly as possible, climb aboard. A more fulfilling way to explore Boston is to schedule fewer activities—using a trolley tour, if you like, for an overview and point-to-point transportation—and spend some quality time on each one. Even a single day can give you a taste of what makes Boston such a popular destination; here I'll offer 1-, 2-, and 3-day plans that focus on experiences unique to Boston. You won't have time for full immersion, of course, but you can touch on some singular destinations and experiences. Begin with the downtown area, home to the city's oldest and most historic neighborhoods. *Start: Boston Common (Red or Green Line to Park St.) or Faneuil Hall (Orange or Green Line to Haymarket).*

---

1 The Freedom Trail ★★★

Following the whole 2.5-mile (4km) Freedom Trail (p. 76) can consume the better part of a day, but several options that concentrate on the downtown part of the walk take 2 hours or so. Your goal is to cover—at whatever pace suits you, as carefully or as casually as you like—the first two-thirds of the trail, from **Boston Common** through **Faneuil Hall.** Start at the Boston Common Visitor Information Center with a pamphlet describing the self-guided tour or with the audio tour available from the Freedom Trail Foundation, or opt for a guided tour (p. 76).

2 Faneuil Hall Marketplace ★★

The combination of retail, dining, street performers, and history makes indoor-outdoor Faneuil Hall Marketplace an insanely popular tourist destination. Budget for shopping, or just grab a seat on a bench and enjoy some great people-watching.

3 Quincy Market 💭 ★★

The main level of Faneuil Hall Marketplace's central building, **Quincy Market**, is a gigantic food court. You can eat at the marketplace, but for a more relaxed experience, head toward the harbor. Cross Surface Road and enjoy your snack or lunch in the seating area around the Rose Kennedy Greenway carousel, or continue across Atlantic Avenue to Christopher Columbus Waterfront Park (next to the Marriott), overlooking the marina. If you'd rather eat indoors, head across the street to the **Union Oyster House** ★, 41 Union St. (𝄴 **617/227-2750;** p. 58).

4 Paul Revere House ★★★

My favorite Freedom Trail stop is this little 17th-century home overlooking a picturesque cobblestone square. See p. 81.

5 The North End ★★★

The Freedom Trail continues here with another famous Paul Revere hangout, the fascinating **Old North Church** ★. But there's more to this historic neighborhood than just history. The city's "Little Italy" (locals never call it that) is a great place for wandering around. See p. 71.

6 Hanover Street 💭

Coffee outlets throughout the city serve good espresso and cappuccino; the North End adds an authentic Italian accent. Pair your caffeine with a fresh pastry at a bakery or **caffè**, and take in the scene on the North End's main drag. Top choices: **The Thinking Cup,** 236 Hanover St. (𝄴 **857/233-5277);** **Caffè Vittoria,** 296 Hanover St. (𝄴 **617/227-7606);** and **Caffè dello Sport,** 308 Hanover St. (𝄴 **617/523-5063**). See p. 71.

7 The Waterfront

On this part of the tour, downtown Boston's small size pays off: In almost any direction, the gorgeous harbor is a short stroll from the North End. As the day winds down, you can take a **sightseeing cruise** ★★ (p. 93) from Long Wharf or Rowes Wharf—though a **ferry** ride from Long Wharf to Charlestown and back may be better for your schedule and budget. If cruises aren't for you or are out of season, explore the **New England Aquarium** ★ (p. 74) or the **Boston Children's Museum** ★★ (p. 91). If those don't appeal to you, head for the nearby

---

One Singular Sensation

On a 1-day visit, consider concentrating on just **one or two things** you're most excited about, plus a good meal or two. If what really gets you going is the Museum of Fine Arts, the Museum of Science, Newbury Street's art galleries and boutiques, the Boston Harbor Islands, or the Harvard campus, you have a good excuse for not doing more—and for a return trip to Boston!

Iconic Boston

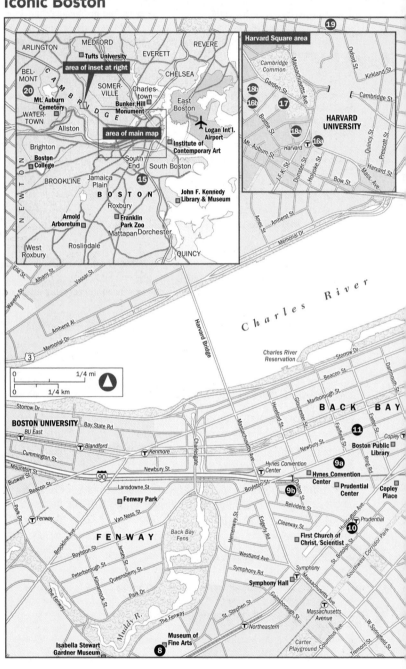

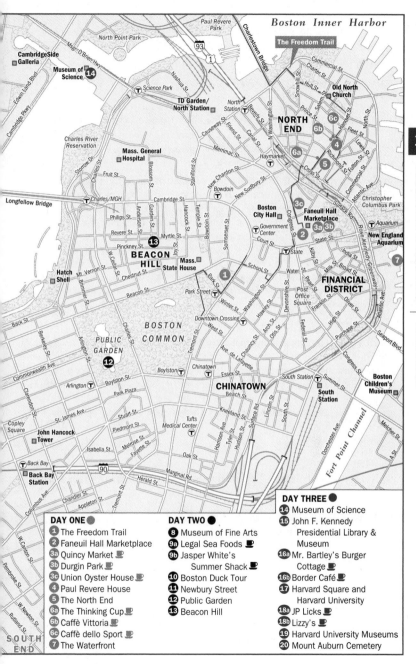

DAY ONE ●
1. The Freedom Trail
2. Faneuil Hall Marketplace
3a. Quincy Market 🍽
3b. Durgin Park 🍽
3c. Union Oyster House 🍽
4. Paul Revere House
5. The North End
6a. The Thinking Cup 🍽
6b. Caffè Vittoria 🍽
6c. Caffè dello Sport 🍽
7. The Waterfront

DAY TWO ●
8. Museum of Fine Arts
9a. Legal Sea Foods 🍽
9b. Jasper White's
   Summer Shack 🍽
10. Boston Duck Tour
11. Newbury Street
12. Public Garden
13. Beacon Hill

DAY THREE ●
14. Museum of Science
15. John F. Kennedy
   Presidential Library &
   Museum
16a. Mr. Bartley's Burger
   Cottage 🍽
16b. Border Café 🍽
17. Harvard Square and
   Harvard University
18a. JP Licks 🍽
18b. Lizzy's 🍽
19. Harvard University Museums
20. Mount Auburn Cemetery

Seaport District (also known as the South Boston Waterfront) and visit the inspiring **Institute of Contemporary Art** ★★ (p. 72). It's a 20- to 30-minute walk or 10-minute cab ride.

Or—it's not the Waterfront, but bear with me—abandon the sightseeing after the Paul Revere House and go **shopping** in the Back Bay, starting with a stroll along Newbury Street.

Iconic Boston in 2 Days

Today you'll explore beyond downtown and investigate subjects other than history. The Back Bay, Beacon Hill, and other destinations contrast invitingly with the colonial extravaganza of the Freedom Trail. If you can, book an afternoon Duck Tour, but don't worry if you can't—this is a flexible itinerary. Start at the:

8 Museum of Fine Arts ★★★

Be at the museum (T: Green Line E to Museum of Fine Arts or Orange Line to Ruggles) when it opens, 10am daily. Check the website beforehand to help structure your visit, and consider taking the first guided tour of the day, which begins at 10:30am. The museum has a cafeteria, cafe, and restaurant, but I'd suggest saving your appetite for the next stop. See p. 86.

9 Shops at Prudential Center 🍴

One of my favorite branches of **Legal Sea Foods** ★★★ (p. 55) is here, on the main level off Boylston Street. If you prefer something lighter, the food court is nearby. Or walk 5 minutes to the Back Bay branch of **Jasper White's Summer Shack** ★★. See p. 64.

10 Boston Duck Tour ★★★

This is the most entertaining motorized way to see the city. On a reconditioned World War II amphibious landing vehicle, you see the top attractions, pick up some historical background, and take a ride on the Charles River. See p. 92.

Duck Tours don't operate from January through March (unless they're needed for a Patriots Super Bowl victory parade) or on weekdays in December. An excellent alternative is a **Boston Symphony Orchestra** ★★★ or **Boston Pops** ★★ concert at Symphony Hall (p. 113), a short walk from either the MFA or the Prudential Center.

11 Newbury Street

Newbury Street has the best shopping in New England. One block away, Boylston Street also offers excellent retail therapy.

12 The Public Garden ★★★

Newbury Street begins across Arlington Street from the most beautiful park in Boston. The Public Garden (p. 84) is lovely year-round—a visit will brighten up even the grayest off-season day—and the **"Make Way for Ducklings"** sculptures (p. 84) are always delightful. In warm weather, leave time for a **Swan Boat ride** (p. 84).

13 Beacon Hill ★★★

The most picturesque neighborhood in town is a festival of red brick, cobblestones, and gorgeous architectural details. **Charles Street,** the main thoroughfare, is shopping destination with a refreshing lack of chain stores. Wander on your own or seek out a guide—on summer weekdays, a **Boston By Foot** tour starts at 5:30pm.

Iconic Boston in 3 Days

Now you'll probably want to venture beyond Boston proper. (If not, you can easily extend the suggestions for the first 2 days to fill a third—for instance, complete the Freedom Trail or return to the Museum of Fine Arts, where admission is good for two visits within 10 days.) This itinerary may look skimpy, but it's packed with interesting activities. Begin by picking a morning destination.

14 Museum of Science ★★★

If you prefer science to history or want to stay close to downtown, head to the Museum of Science (T: Green Line to Science Park). Otherwise, you're off to Dorchester (T: Red Line to JFK/UMass, then free shuttle bus) to see the:

15 John F. Kennedy Presidential Library and Museum ★★

Although these two museums are very different from each other, they are both well worth a trip and a full morning. The Museum of Science (p. 73), with its wealth of hands-on exhibits, is a great destination for families; adults and older kids who have studied American history can't get enough of the Kennedy Library (p. 72). Both museums open at 9am. Both have cafeterias, but I recommend that you wait to have lunch in Harvard Square.

16 Eat Like a College Kid 🍴

My favorite Harvard Square lunch destinations are casual places where sightseers fit right in. **Mr. Bartley's Burger Cottage** ★★, 1246 Massachusetts Ave. (☎ **617/354-6559;** p. 66), is my top choice anywhere for onion rings, not to mention great burgers. It's closed Sunday. **The Border Café,** 32 Church St. (☎ **617/864-6100**), serves terrific Tex-Mex specialties.

17 Harvard Square & Harvard University

I consider these one big stop because the school couldn't exist without the neighborhood, and vice versa. Allow some time to wander around and enjoy the gentrified-boho atmosphere. Take a tour, which begins at the university's Information Center, or head out on your own. "The Square" is also fun for **shopping.**

18 Ice Cream 🍴

Harvard Square has some of the best ice cream shops in this ice-cream-obsessed part of the world. **JP Licks,** 1312 Massachusetts Ave. (☎ **617/492-1001**), and **Lizzy's,** 29 Church St. (☎ **617/354-2911**), are equally delicious, so check the daily specials if you can't decide. Take your treat to Harvard Yard.

19 Harvard University Museums ★★

The Harvard Museum of Natural History and the adjacent Peabody Museum (p. 87) are equally welcoming to kids and adults. The Harvard Art Museums (p. 88), which will reopen in late 2014 after more than 5 years of renovation, are just the right size for exploring in a couple of hours. All of the university museums close at 5pm.

If the weather's fine, you may prefer to point yourself toward:

20 Mount Auburn Cemetery ★★

A short distance from Harvard Square, Mount Auburn Cemetery is a gorgeous, fascinating destination. See p. 89.

BOSTON FOR FAMILIES

My best advice for seeing Boston with the family is unconventional: Skip the Freedom Trail. Ignore me if your offspring are old enough and interested enough to suggest the trail on their own. The other 99 percent of you can plan on two big activities and some well-earned downtime.

1 Museum of Science ★★★

Be there when the museum (T: Green Line to Science Park) opens, at 9am, and know where you're going. Use the website to find can't-miss exhibits and the schedule for the Omni theater and planetarium. The dining options here are good, but if you can hold out, wait to eat lunch elsewhere.

2 Faneuil Hall Marketplace ☕

Even the pickiest kids can find something they like at **Quincy Market,** which offers plenty of more sophisticated options for the adults. In fine weather, **Christopher Columbus Waterfront Park** (see "Iconic Boston" stop 3, above) is a great picnic spot with both a playground and a fountain.

3 New England Aquarium ★

Check the schedule for feeding the seals in the New Balance Foundation Marine Mammal Center (at the back of the main level), and plan around them. *Tip:* Don't try to visit the aquarium and the Children's Museum (see below) in 1 afternoon. Split up if your kids vary widely in age, or plan a trip on another day to the attraction you skip.

4 Boston Children's Museum ★★

Kids under 10 love this museum, where crowds fluctuate depending on school vacation and day-camp schedules. Let larger groups pass you, and you'll have better access to the exhibits.

5 Greenway food trucks and carts ☕

In spring, summer, and fall, the Rose Kennedy Greenway boasts an enticing variety of snack options, from barbecue to cupcakes. In a pinch, there's a **7-Eleven** at 70 East India Row (enter from Atlantic Ave. at Milk St.; ☏ **617/227-9534**).

6 Rose Kennedy Greenway ★★

The most child-friendly parts of the mile-long Greenway are near places you've already visited. Ride the seasonal carousel (across from Faneuil Hall Marketplace), check out the displays at the adjacent Boston Harbor Islands Pavilion, frolic in the Rings Fountain (at Milk St.), or just explore the art and sculpture as you unwind and plan your evening.

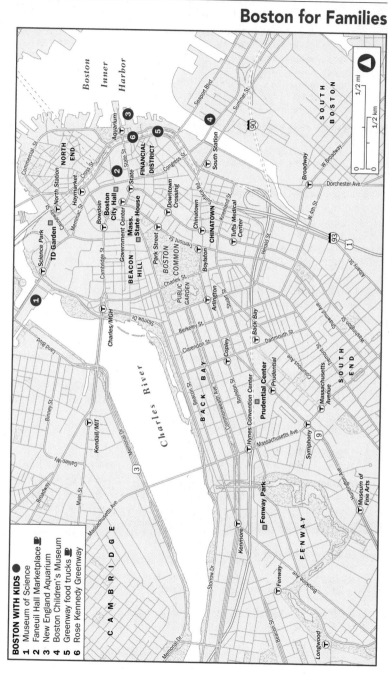

BOSTON WITH KIDS ●
1 Museum of Science
2 Faneuil Hall Marketplace 🍴
3 New England Aquarium
4 Boston Children's Museum
5 Greenway food trucks 🍴
6 Rose Kennedy Greenway

Mix and match the itineraries in this chapter to accommodate your schedule and interests, allowing plenty of time for travel from Boston to the Cape, Martha's Vineyard, or Nantucket—or vice versa. An excellent way to break up the car or bus trip in either direction is with a stop in **Plymouth.** See p. 126 for details.

ICONIC CAPE COD IN 3 DAYS

If you're lucky, you'll have a week to spend finding out what Cape Cod has to offer. Cape Cod stretches 75 miles (120km), and its 15 towns are all worth visiting. But if you have only 3 days, it's best to stick with the high points, with visits to the towns of Falmouth, Barnstable, and Provincetown. You'll bike down the Shining Sea Bikeway in Falmouth and explore the science community of Woods Hole. You'll motor down the Old King's Highway and visit the Cape's unofficial "capital" of Hyannis, where you can pay homage to JFK's Camelot legacy. Finally you'll take in art, culture, and the liveliest street scene this side of Manhattan at the Cape's tip in Provincetown.

1 Falmouth's Village Green

On your first day, head over the Bourne Bridge south on Rte. 28 to Falmouth. After the traffic light, take the six left to reach Falmouth's charming Village Green, which is flanked by two historic churches and surrounded by a dozen historic buildings, including the Falmouth Museums on the Green (p. 151). The museum tells the story of the town through exhibits in three buildings, the 1790 Julia Wood House, the mid-18th-century Conant House, and the Dudley Hallett Barn. Founded in 1660 by Quakers from Sandwich, Falmouth proved to be remarkably arable territory. Today, with over 33,000 year-round residents, it's the second-largest town on the Cape, after Barnstable. Continue east a few steps from the Village Green to reach

2 Main Street ★★

Here you can find stores selling books, clothes, art, and gifts—and a dozen restaurants and ice cream shops. Wander several blocks down to Peg Noonan Park on the left, where in the summer you'll find free live music on Friday evenings and a farmers' market on Thursdays. Don't miss the nearby shops in the Queens Buyway. Here you can rent a bike, buy a cup of coffee, and find more souvenirs.

3 Coffee Obsession ☕

Some of the best coffee in town can be found at this cafe ★★ (p. 147), which is a favorite of locals. It has a real "college town" vibe, especially on Open Mic Nights, which take place on occasional evenings year-round.

4 Shining Sea Bikeway ★★★

Rent a bike at Corner cycle in the Queens Buyway and explore all or part of the 12-mile (19.3km) Bikeway. The Falmouth Chamber of Commerce has maps for the entire path, complete with historical notes and points of interest. From the

Village Green, it's a quick ride down Locust Street to the bike path for a 3-mile (4.8km) ride that skirts the coastline (on a warm day, you can stop to take a dip in Vineyard Sound) down to Woods Hole.

On day 2, starting from Falmouth, take Rte. 28 back to the traffic rotary at the Bourne Bridge. Instead of going over the bridge, take the first right off the rotary and drive alongside the canal, under the Sagamore Bridge, to the town of Sandwich. The road turns into Rte. 6A, also known as the Old King's Highway.

5 Old King's Highway ★★★

The beauty of exploring the Old King's Highway is you can make as many or as few stops as you like. There's a lot to see—glassblower's workshops, pottery studios, antiquarian bookstalls, antiques stores, and marvelous gift shops. People love to drive this long winding road, a former stagecoach route, just to look at the house, which represent a veritable history of Early American home construction, from classic Capes to colonial, federal and Victorian styles of architecture.

6 Barnstable Restaurant and Tavern ★★ 🍺

Have a beverage and a snack on the front patio former stagecoach stop, at 3176 Main St./ Rte. 6A, and you'll have a view of the Superior Courthouse across the street, a magnificent slate-gray building with stately columns. This is old New England at its most charming. See p. 160.

To get to Hyannis, you can take Rte. 6 to exit 6 (Rte. 132) or follow the Old King's Highway (Rte. 6A) for about 15 miles (24km) from the Sagamore Bridge to Rte. 132. Take Rte. 132 through the airport rotary and down Barnstable Rd. to the town's Main Street.

7 Hyannis ★★

To bask in the Kennedys' Cape Cod experience, visit the John F. Kennedy Hyannis Museum. There is a documentary on Kennedy narrated by Walter Cronkite and several rooms' worth of memorabilia. The Kennedy Memorial, just above Veterans Beach on Ocean Street, is a moving tribute. Main Street itself has vibrant arts district. Other interesting attractions within walking distance of Main Street are the Cape Maritime Museum on South Street, and the Union Museum on North Street.

8 Provincetown ★★★

Save Provincetown for day 3. This boisterous, fascinating place is a year-round destination, but it really comes alive in summer. The dozens of shops along Commercial Street are all open well into the evening, and some people come here just for the fabulous shopping. Others come for the art galleries and still others for the dining. From Macmillan Pier (in the center of town), you can take a sail on the *Bay Lady II* or a whale-watching tour to Stellwagen Bank. Some of the best beaches on the Cape are just down the road at Herring Cove and Race Point.

9 Patio ★ 🍺

P'town has a number of sidewalk cafes perfect for people-watching, including this one, at 328 Commercial Street. Plop yourself down at a sidewalk table, and watch the parade of colorful locals and visitors. See p. 209.

BOSTON

4

Ask 10 visitors why they decided to travel to Boston, and you might get a dozen answers. Whether it's for a museum show, a music festival, a convention, a Red Sox game, a college visit, a weekend getaway, or a longer stay, Boston makes a great destination. You probably already have some connection to Boston—a relative studying here, a neighbor who dreams of qualifying for the Marathon, a child who won't rest until she goes on a whale watch, a co-worker who always wears a Red Sox cap, a friend who's getting into genealogical research. Even if you don't, you'll find Boston a uniquely enjoyable destination, compact in size but with a virtually inexhaustible supply of activities and diversions. Pick out a suitcase that has room for your walking shoes, and get ready for your own adventure. The interests that draw you here can monopolize your schedule, but you'll have a better experience if you make some room for serendipity—on your schedule and in your attitude.

ESSENTIALS

Visitor Information

Before you leave home, contact the **Greater Boston Convention & Visitors Bureau** (© **888/SEE-BOSTON** [733-2678] or 617/536-4100; www.bostonusa.com); the **Cambridge Office for Tourism** (© **800/862-5678** or 617/441-2884; www.cambridgeusa.org); and the **Massachusetts Office of Travel & Tourism** (© **800/227-MASS** [227-6277] or 617/973-8500; www.massvacation.com). All three are active on Facebook, Twitter, and other social-media platforms.

After you arrive, you'll find maps, pamphlets, discount coupons, and other useful materials in many hotel lobbies. National Park Service rangers staff the **Boston National Historical Park Visitor Center,** on the first floor of Faneuil Hall (© **617/242-5642;** www.nps.gov/bost; T: Blue or Orange Line to State St.), and lead seasonal free tours of the Freedom Trail. The center is open daily from 9am to 6pm. The ranger-staffed center at the **Charlestown Navy Yard** (© **617/242-5601**) is open 9am to 5pm daily (closed Mon in winter).

The Convention & Visitors Bureau operates the **Boston Common Information Center,** 148 Tremont St., on Boston Common, which is open Monday through Friday from 8:30am to 5pm, Saturday and Sunday from 9am to 5pm; and an information desk on the main level of the **Prudential Center,** 800 Boylston St. It's open Monday through Friday from 9am to 5:30pm, Saturday and Sunday from 10am to 6pm.

The Cambridge Office for Tourism runs the **Cambridge Visitor's Information Center,** a kiosk in the heart of Harvard Square, near the T entrance at the intersection of Massachusetts Avenue, John F. Kennedy Street, and Brattle Street. It's open Monday through Friday from 9am to 5pm, Saturday and Sunday from 9am to 1pm.

There's a small outdoor information booth at **Faneuil Hall Marketplace,** between Quincy Market and the South Market Building. It's staffed in the spring, summer, and fall Monday through Saturday from 10am to 6pm, Sunday from noon to 6pm.

APPS   Search your preferred app store for "Boston," and be picky about what you download—you're here to see the sights, not your mobile device. Start with the excellent, free **National Park Service** Boston National Historical Park app. And before relying on any app that claims to deliver information about events, make sure it's been updated recently.

City Layout

When Puritan settlers established Boston in 1630, it was one-third the size it is now. Much of the city reflects the original layout, a confusing arrangement that can disorient even longtime residents. Legend has it that the street pattern originated as a network of cow paths, but it owes more to 17th-century London and long-gone property lines. Old Boston abounds with alleys, dead ends, one-way streets, streets that change names, and the names of long-gone geographical features. On the plus side, every "wrong" turn **downtown,** in the **North End,** or on **Beacon Hill** is a chance to see something interesting that you might otherwise miss.

The most prominent feature of downtown Boston is the five-sided park known since the 1630s as **Boston Common.** Its borders are the 1-block-long Park Street (an important subway interchange) and Beacon, Charles, Boylston, and Tremont streets. **Washington Street,** which runs southwest from Boston City Hall all the way to the Rhode Island border, is the most "main" street downtown. Another important street is **Massachusetts Avenue,** usually called "Mass. Ave." It stretches 9 miles, from Boston's Roxbury neighborhood through the South End, the Back Bay, Cambridge, and Arlington, to Lexington.

Nineteenth-century landfill projects transformed much of the city, altering the shoreline and creating the **Back Bay,** where the streets form a grid (and even go in alphabetical order, starting at the Public Garden: Arlington, Berkeley, Clarendon, Dartmouth, Exeter, Fairfield, Gloucester, and Hereford, then Mass. Ave.). The adjacent **South End** is the only other central neighborhood laid out in anything close to a logical pattern.

In general, there's no rhyme or reason to the street pattern, compass directions are virtually useless, and there aren't enough street signs. Often the best way to find an address is to call ahead and ask for directions, including to landmarks—this is true even if you have GPS on your phone or in your car—or leave extra time for wandering around. If the directions involve a T stop, be sure to ask which exit to use; most stations have more than one.

The Neighborhoods in Brief

These are the areas most popular with visitors. When Bostonians say **"downtown,"** they usually mean the first seven or eight neighborhoods defined here; there's no "midtown" or "uptown." Boston's neighborhoods, especially those downtown, are so small and close together that the borders are somewhat arbitrary. Whether you're picking a hotel or just planning a lunch date, the important distinction is **downtown vs. the Back Bay vs. Cambridge**—not, for example, Faneuil Hall Marketplace vs. the adjacent Financial District.

Neighborhoods outside central Boston include South Boston, East Boston, Dorchester, Roxbury, West Roxbury, Hyde Park, Roslindale, and Jamaica Plain. With a couple of exceptions (noted here), Boston is generally safe, but you should always take the precautions you would in any large city, especially at night. **Note:** I include some compass points here to help you read your map, but that's not how the locals will give you directions: They typically just point.

The Waterfront This narrow area runs along the Inner Harbor, on **Atlantic Avenue** and **Commercial Street** from the Charlestown Bridge (on N. Washington St.) to South Station. Once filled with wharves and warehouses, today it's the place for luxury condos, marinas, restaurants, and offices. Also here are the New England Aquarium and embarkation points for harbor cruises and whale-watching expeditions. The **Rose Kennedy Greenway** roughly parallels the coast for a mile from South Station to North Station.

The North End Crossing the Rose Kennedy Greenway as you head east toward the Inner Harbor brings you to one of the city's oldest neighborhoods. Long an immigrant stronghold, it was predominantly Italian for most of the 20th century. It's now less than half Italian American; many newcomers are young professionals who walk to work in the Financial District. Nevertheless, you'll hear Italian spoken in the streets and find a wealth of Italian restaurants, *caffès*, and shops. The main streets are **Hanover Street** and **Salem Street.**

North Station Technically part of the North End but just as close to Beacon Hill, this area around **Causeway Street** is home to the **TD Garden** (sports and performance arena), **North Station,** and many nightspots and restaurants. The neighborhood—sometimes called the West End or the Bulfinch Triangle—is improving, but wandering the side streets alone late at night is not a good idea.

Faneuil Hall Marketplace Employees aside, locals tend to be scarce at Faneuil Hall Marketplace (also called Quincy Market, after its central building). An irresistible draw for out-of-towners and suburbanites, this cluster of restored market buildings—bounded by the Waterfront, the North End, Government Center, and **State Street**—is the city's most popular attraction. You'll find restaurants, bars, a food court, retail stores and pushcarts, and Faneuil Hall itself. **Haymarket,** a stone's throw away on **Blackstone Street,** is home to an open-air produce market on Fridays and Saturdays.

Government Center Here, stark modern design breaks up Boston's traditional architecture. Flanked by Beacon Hill, Downtown Crossing, and Faneuil Hall Marketplace, Government Center is home to state and federal offices, City Hall, and a major T stop (which is closed through 2016 for construction). Its most prominent feature, the red-brick wasteland of City Hall Plaza, lies between **Congress** and **Cambridge streets.**

The Financial District Bounded loosely by Downtown Crossing, **Summer Street, Atlantic Avenue,** and **State Street,** the Financial District has long been the city's banking, insurance, and legal center; in recent years, the Seaport District has emerged as a serious rival. Bars and restaurants near the Greenway are popular with after-work crowds and sightseers, but most of the area is quiet at night and on weekends.

Seaport District/South Boston Waterfront Across the Fort Point Channel from the Waterfront neighborhood, this booming area (sometimes called the Innovation District) grows busier by the day. The main convention center is here, and numerous startups, tech companies, and law firms have originated or moved here since the turn of the century. New restaurants, many of them branches of chains, are proliferating. Still, convention-goers dominate. **Seaport Boulevard, Northern Avenue,** and **Summer Street** are the main drags. The renovated warehouses in the area closest to the channel, known simply as **Fort Point,** were once home to many artists, but rampant development is forcing them out.

Downtown Crossing The intersection that gives Downtown Crossing its name is at

Washington Street where Winter Street becomes Summer Street. The Freedom Trail runs along one edge of this shopping and business district between Boston Common, Chinatown, the Financial District, and Government Center. The neighborhood, already busy during the day, gets increasingly lively in the evening, thanks to new condos and businesses, thriving theaters, and students from Emerson College and Suffolk University.

Charlestown One of the oldest areas of Boston—across the Inner Harbor from downtown—Charlestown is home to the Bunker Hill Monument and USS *Constitution* ("Old Ironsides"), the final stops on the Freedom Trail. Gentrification has diversified a once predominantly white neighborhood, but pockets remain that have earned their reputation for insularity.

Beacon Hill Narrow tree-lined streets, brick and cobblestone alleyways, and Federal-style architectural showpieces dominate this largely residential area in the shadow of the State House. Two of the loveliest and most exclusive spots in Boston are here: Mount Vernon Street and Louisburg (pronounced "Lewis-burg") Square. Bounded by Government Center, Boston Common, the Back Bay, and the river, Beacon Hill is where you'll find Massachusetts General Hospital. Charles Street, which divides the Common from the Public Garden, is the main street of Beacon Hill. Other important thoroughfares are Beacon Street, on the north side of the Common, and Cambridge Street.

Chinatown/Theater District One of the largest Chinese communities in the country is a small area jammed with Asian restaurants, bakeries, groceries, and shops. Chinatown takes up the area between Downtown Crossing and the Massachusetts Turnpike extension. The main street is Beach Street. Three theaters are on Washington Street, closer to Downtown Crossing, but the heart of the Theater District is at Tremont and Stuart streets; be careful there at night, after the crowds thin out.

The South End Cross Stuart Street or Huntington Avenue heading south from the

Back Bay, and you enter a landmark district packed with Victorian row houses and little parks. The South End has a large gay community and some of the city's best restaurants. Tremont Street (particularly the end closest to downtown), Washington Street, and, increasingly, Harrison Avenue all draw diners and shoppers. Long known for its ethnic, economic, and cultural diversity, the neighborhood is now thoroughly gentrified nearly all the way to Mass. Ave. *Note:* Don't confuse the South End with South Boston, on the other side of I-93.

The Back Bay Fashionable since its creation out of landfill more than a century ago, the Back Bay overflows with gorgeous architecture and chic shops. It lies between the Public Garden, the river, Kenmore Square, and either Huntington Avenue or St. Botolph Street, depending on who's describing it. Students dominate the area near Mass. Ave. but grow scarce as property values soar near the Public Garden. Major thoroughfares include Boylston Street, which starts at Boston Common and runs into the Fenway; largely residential Beacon Street and Commonwealth Avenue (say "Comm. Ave."); and boutique central, Newbury Street. Access to Cambridge isn't the greatest, but there's so much to do here that you may not care.

Kenmore Square The landmark white-and-red CITGO sign that dominates the skyline above the intersection of Commonwealth Avenue, Beacon Street, and Brookline Avenue tells you that you're approaching Kenmore Square. Its shops, bars, restaurants, and clubs attract students from adjacent Boston University. The Hotel Commonwealth, the most prominent place to stay in the neighborhood, lends a touch of class to a generally rowdy neighborhood, which gets even busier when the Red Sox are in town and baseball fans pour into the area on the way to Fenway Park, 3 blocks away.

The Fenway Between Kenmore Square and the Longwood Medical Area, the Fenway neighborhood encompasses Fenway Park, the Museum of Fine Arts, the Isabella Stewart Gardner Museum, and innumerable students. Boston University, Northeastern

"Charlie," hero of the Kingston Trio song "Charlie on the MTA," is the face of the T's automated fare-collection system, which uses two different reloadable passes that store prepaid fares as well as daily, weekly, and monthly passes. The **CharlieCard** is a plastic smart card with an embedded chip. Fares are cheaper with a CharlieCard, but to get one, you have to find a T employee or a retail location (check **www.mbta.com** for a list). Visit a self-service kiosk—at the entrance to each subway station and in each terminal at the airport—to load value onto a CharlieCard using cash or a credit or debit card, or to buy a **CharlieTicket,** a heavy paper pass with a magnetic strip. CharlieCards can also be reloaded online. Note that the CharlieTicket goes into the front of the subway turnstile and pops out of the top (or in and out of the bus fare box), while the CharlieCard registers when you hold it in front of the rectangular reader on the turnstile or fare box.

University, and Harvard Medical School are the largest educational institutions in and near the Fenway. The area's southern border is **Huntington Avenue,** the honorary "Avenue of the Arts" (or, with a Boston accent, "Otts"), where you'll find the Christian Science Center, Symphony Hall (at the corner of Mass. Ave.), and the MFA. Parts of Huntington can be a little risky, so if you're leaving the museum at night, stick to the Green Line or hail a cab, and try to travel in a group.

Cambridge Boston's neighbor across the Charles River is a separate city. The areas you're likely to visit lie along the MBTA Red Line. **Harvard Square** is a magnet for students, sightseers, and well-heeled shoppers. It's an easy walk along Mass. ave. southeast to **Central Square,** a gentrifying area dotted with ethnic restaurants and music clubs; a short stroll away is boho **Inman Square,** a stronghold of independent businesses. North along shop-lined Mass. Ave. from Harvard Square is **Porter Square,** a mostly residential neighborhood with quirky shops. Around **Kendall Square** you'll find MIT and many technology-oriented businesses.

GETTING AROUND

On Foot

If you can manage a fair amount of walking, this is the way to go. You can best appreciate Boston at street level, and walking the narrow, picturesque streets takes you past many gridlocked cars.

It pays to be alert, even more than in a typical large city. Look both ways before crossing, even on one-way streets, where many bicyclists and some drivers ignore signs and the law. The "walk" cycle of many downtown traffic signals is dangerously brief, and a small but significant part of the driving population considers red lights optional anyway. Keep a close eye on the kids, especially in crosswalks. And you're all wearing comfortable shoes, right?

By Public Transportation

The **Massachusetts Bay Transportation Authority,** or MBTA (© **800/392-6100** or 617/222-3200; www.mbta.com), is known as "the T," and its logo is a black letter T in a white circle. It runs subways, trolleys, buses, and ferries in and around Boston and many suburbs, as well as the commuter rail, which extends as far as Providence, Rhode Island. The automated fare-collection system is a bit involved, but getting the hang of it is easy, and T employees who staff stations during busy times can answer questions. (Download the mTicket app if you're planning to use the commuter rail.)

BY SUBWAY & TROLLEY

The T dates to 1897, making it the oldest system in the country. Although it's generally reliable, you should still leave extra time and carry cab fare if you're on the way to a vital appointment, because you may need to ascend to the street and hail a taxi. (The ancient Green Line is the least dependable.) The system is generally safe, but always watch out for pickpockets, especially during the holiday shopping season. And keep in mind that downtown stops are so close together that walking is often faster than riding.

The Red, Green, Blue, and Orange lines make up the subway system (beyond downtown, some stops are aboveground). The commuter rail to the suburbs is purple on system maps and is sometimes called the Purple Line. The Silver Line is a fancy name for a bus line; route **SL1** runs from South Station to the airport via the South Boston waterfront, including the convention center and the Seaport Boston World Trade Center (the **SL2** stays on the downtown side of the harbor and serves the cruise ship terminal area). At press time the fare on the subway and Silver Line routes SL1 and SL2 is **$2.10** if you use a CharlieCard (transfers to local buses are free), **$2.65** with a CharlieTicket. Children 11 and under ride free with a paying adult. Route and fare information and timetables are available through the website (www.mbta.com) and at centrally located stations. If you're planning to use the T regularly during your visit, you'll probably want to download a schedule app.

Service begins at around 5:15am and ends around 12:30am on weeknights. Under a 1-year pilot program started in 2014, service on Friday and Saturday nights extends until about 2:30am. A sign in every station gives the time of the last train in either direction; if you're planning to be out late and don't see a sign, ask the attendant in the booth near the entrance.

BY BUS

The MBTA runs buses and "trackless trolleys" (buses with electric antennae) that provide service around town and to and around the suburbs. The local routes you're most likely to use are **no. 1,** along Massachusetts Avenue from Dudley Square in

---

Discount Transit Passes

The MBTA's 1-day and 7-day **LinkPasses** (© **888/844-0355;** www.mbta.com) can be a great deal—if you plan to use public transit enough. Passes cover unlimited travel on the subway and local buses, in commuter rail zone 1A, and on the Inner Harbor ferry. The cost for 24 hours is $12, which translates to a lot of riding before you start to save money. The 7-day pass, which costs $19, is more likely to be a good deal. Passes can be loaded onto CharlieCards or Charlie-Tickets. You can order them in advance over the phone or on the Web (minimum 10; at press time, shipping is free), or buy them when you arrive at any kiosk or retail location. Long-term visitors may find one of the numerous monthly commuter passes a better deal than a visitor-oriented LinkPass.

Roxbury through the Back Bay and Cambridge to Harvard Square; **no. 92** and **no. 93,** which connect Haymarket and Charlestown; and **no. 77,** along Mass. Ave. north of Harvard Square to Porter Square, North Cambridge, and Arlington. Two branches of the **Silver Line** run through the South End on Washington Street to Dudley Station in Roxbury and are part of the bus fare structure (the higher subway fare applies to routes SL1 and SL2). Route **SL4** serves South Station (Essex St. at Atlantic Ave.), and Route **SL5** starts and ends on Temple Place, near Downtown Crossing between Washington and Tremont streets.

The fare on the local bus and Silver Line routes SL4 and SL5 at press time is **$1.60** with a CharlieCard (transferring to the subway costs 55¢), **$2.10** with a CharlieTicket or cash. Children 11 and under ride free with a paying adult. If you're paying cash, exact change is required. Service hours are shorter than the subway's, and some routes don't operate on weekends. The weekend late-night pilot program (see above) also applies to some busy bus routes; check the website for details.

BY FERRY

The MBTA Inner Harbor ferry connects **Long Wharf** (near the New England Aquarium) with the **Charlestown Navy Yard**—it's a good way to get back downtown from "Old Ironsides" and the Bunker Hill Monument. The one-way fare is $3.25, or show your LinkPass. Visit www.mbta.com or call ℂ **617/227-4321** for more information, including schedules.

By Taxi

Taxis are expensive and not always easy to find. Hailing a cab on the street is legal but can be tough at busy times—seek out a cabstand or call a dispatcher.

Cabs usually queue up near hotels. There are also waiting areas at Faneuil Hall Marketplace (on North St. and in front of 60 State St.), South Station, and Back Bay Station, and on either side of Massachusetts Avenue in Harvard Square, near the Harvard Coop bookstore and Au Bon Pain.

To call ahead for a cab in Boston, try the **Independent Taxi Operators Association** (ℂ 617/426-8700; www.itoataxi.com), **Boston Cab** (ℂ 617/536-5010; www.boston cab.us), **Top Cab/City Cab** (ℂ 617/266-4800 or 617/536-5100; www.topcab.us), or **Metro Cab** (ℂ 617/782-5500; www.boston-cab.com). In Cambridge, call **Ambassador Brattle/Yellow Cab** (ℂ 617/492-1100 or 617/547-3000; www.ambassadorbrattle. com) or **Checker Cab** (ℂ 617/497-1500). Boston Cab will dispatch a wheelchair-accessible vehicle upon request; advance notice is recommended.

The Boston fare structure: The first ⅐ mile (when the flag drops) costs $2.60, and each additional ⅐ mile is 40¢. Wait time is extra, and the passenger pays all tolls. On trips leaving Logan Airport, you're on the hook for $10.10 in fare and fees, including the tunnel toll, before the cab even moves. Charging a flat rate is not allowed within the city; the police department (see below) publishes a list of flat rates for trips to the suburbs.

The city requires that Boston cabdrivers accept credit cards, and every vehicle has a card reader fastened to the divider. Drivers resisted the rule at first, and anecdotal evidence suggests that some "broken" card readers will suddenly come online if you say you don't have enough cash to pay.

Always ask for a receipt in case you have a complaint or lose something and need to call the company. If you want to report a problem or have lost something in a Boston cab, contact the police department's **Hackney Unit** (ℂ **617/343-4475;** www.cityof boston.gov/police/hackney); its website has the list of suburban flat fares. The

Cambridge License Commission (✆ **617/349-6140;** www.cambridgema.gov/license/Hackney.aspx) also regulates cabs; visit the website to see the flat fees for trips from hotels to Logan Airport.

By Water Taxi

Water taxis serve stops around the waterfront, including the airport, in covered boats. They operate daily year-round, from 7am until at least 7pm (later in the summer). One-way fares start at $10. Reservations are recommended but not required; you can call from the dock for pick-up. The operators are **Boston Harbor Cruises** (✆ **617/422-0392** or 617/227-4320; www.bostonharborcruises.com/water-taxi) and **Rowes Wharf Water Transport** (✆ **617/406-8584** or 617/261-6620; www.roweswharfwatertransport.com).

By Car

If you plan to visit only Boston and Cambridge, **you do not need a car** to get around. With its pricey parking and narrow, one-way streets, not to mention abundant construction, Boston in particular is an out-of-town driver's nightmare. Cambridge is slightly less confusing to navigate, but you'll probably pay to park there, too. If you arrive by car, **park at the hotel** and use the car for day trips. If you decide to rent a vehicle for a day trip or a visit to Cape Cod, here's the scoop.

RENTALS

Wait to pick up the car until you need it, to save yourself the hassle of driving and parking. Most major firms have offices in the consolidated car-rental facility at Logan Airport and in central Boston, and many have other area branches. Rentals that originate in Boston carry a **$10 convention center surcharge;** you can get around it by picking up your car in a nearby suburb, but the savings may not be worth the hassle.

In general, Boston doesn't conform to the pattern of a big city that empties on weekends, when business travelers leave town and rental-car rates plummet. At busy times—especially on summer weekends and during foliage season—reserve a car well in advance.

To rent from the major national chains, you must be at least 25 years old and have a valid driver's license and credit card. Some companies allow drivers aged 21 to 24 to rent, subject to a steep daily fee. And some chains enforce a maximum age; if you're over 70, check ahead to avoid an unpleasant surprise.

If you plan to smoke in your rental car, make sure the company allows it—most don't—or be prepared to pay a substantial cleaning charge for lighting up in a non-smoking vehicle.

If you're visiting from abroad and plan to rent a car in the United States, keep in mind that foreign driver's licenses are usually recognized in the U.S., but you may want to consider obtaining an international driver's license. International visitors should also note that quoted rates in the U.S. almost never include insurance and taxes. Be sure to ask your rental agency about those additional fees, which can significantly increase your total cost.

Money-saving tips: Rent the smallest car you're comfortable driving and you'll save on gas (petrol). The price per gallon at press time is around $4; the posted price includes taxes. One U.S. gallon equals 3.8 liters or .85 imperial gallons.

If you belong to Boston-based **Zipcar** or another car-sharing service, check ahead to see whether your membership is good in the Boston area. And if you don't mind taking a short T ride to (potentially) save a bundle, check rates at Enterprise and Hertz neighborhood locations. Most branches will pick you up at the nearest train station or bus stop if the office isn't close to public transit.

See the "By Car" section under "Getting There" in chapter 7 for information about driving (or not) to eastern Massachusetts.

PARKING

It's difficult to find your way around Boston and practically impossible to find parking in some areas. Most spaces on the street are metered (and patrolled until as late as 8pm Mon–Sat) or are open to nonresidents for 2 hours or less between 8am and 6pm. The penalty is a $45 ticket—the same as a full day at the most expensive garage. Read the sign or meter carefully. Some areas allow parking only at certain hours. Rates vary in different sections of the city ($1.25/hr. downtown). At press time, three different payment systems, including traditional meters, are in use. All accept cash—some require quarters—and some also take debit and credit (MC, V) cards. Time limits range from 15 minutes to 2 hours.

If you blunder into a tow-away zone, retrieving the car will cost well over $100 and a lot of running around. The **city tow lot** (© 617/635-3900) is at 200 Frontage Rd., South Boston. Take a taxi, or ride the Red Line to Andrew and flag a cab.

It's best to **leave the car in a garage or lot and walk,** but be aware that Boston's parking is the second most expensive in the country (after Manhattan's). A full day at most garages costs no more than $30, but some downtown facilities charge as much as $45, and hourly rates typically are exorbitant. Many lots charge a lower flat rate if you enter and exit before certain times or if you park in the evening. Some restaurants offer reduced rates at nearby garages; ask when you make reservations. Regardless of where you park, visit the attendant's booth as you exit on foot to ask whether any local businesses offer discounted parking with a purchase and validation; you may get lucky.

DRIVING RULES

When traffic permits, drivers may turn right at a red light after stopping, unless a sign is posted saying otherwise (as it often is downtown). The speed limit on most city streets is 30mph.

Seat belts are mandatory for adults and children; children 11 and under may not ride in the front seat; and infants and children 7 and under must be strapped into car seats in the back seat. You can be stopped just for having an unbelted child in the car, though not for traveling with an unsecured adult. Texting while behind the wheel is against the law for drivers of all ages, and cellphone use of any kind by motorists 17 and under is illegal except in an emergency.

By Bicycle

The streets of downtown Boston are less dangerous than they once were, but still not as safe as they could be. Don't consider bicycling if you're not fairly experienced or not completely comfortable sharing the road with aggressive motorists. Even Cambridge, which has a longstanding network of bike lanes, can be difficult to negotiate if you're not familiar with the area. Nevertheless, **Hubway** bike sharing (© **855/9HUB-WAY** [948-2929]; www.thehubway.com) is very popular, with stations throughout Boston and Cambridge as well as parts of Somerville and Brookline. At press time, passes cost $6 for 24 hours, $12 for 72 hours. Check the website a list of retailers—including numerous centrally located drugstores—that sell helmets at a discount, or bring one with you. Then *wear one.*

[FastFACTS] BOSTON

Doctors & Hospitals

The front-desk staff at your hotel can often recommend a doctor, or you can use one of the referral services available through local hospitals. They include Massachusetts General Hospital (📞 800/711-4644) and Brigham and Women's Hospital (📞 855/278-8010).

Local hospitals include **Massachusetts General Hospital,** 55 Fruit St. (📞 617/726-2000; www.massgeneral.org), and **Tufts Medical Center,** 800 Washington St. (📞 617/636-5000; www.tuftsmedicalcenter.org). Both are downtown. At the Harvard Medical Area on the Boston-Brookline border are **Beth Israel Deaconess Medical Center,** 330 Brookline Ave. (📞 617/667-7000; www.bidmc.org); **Brigham and Women's Hospital,** 75 Francis St. (📞 617/732-5500; www.brighamandwomens.org); and **Boston Children's Hospital,** 300 Longwood Ave. (📞 617/355-6000; www.childrenshospital.org). In Cambridge are **Mount Auburn Hospital,** 330 Mount Auburn St. (📞 617/492-3500; www.mountauburnhospital.org), and **Cambridge Hospital,** 1493 Cambridge St. (📞 617/665-1000; www.cha.harvard.edu/cambridge).

CVS MinuteClinics (📞 866/389-2727; www.minuteclinic.com) are walk-in facilities that deal with ear infections, strep throat, and such, but not with serious emergencies. At press time, the closest one to downtown Boston is in the CVS at the Porter Square Shopping Center, 36 White St., off Mass. Ave., Cambridge.

Emergencies

Call 📞 **911** for fire, ambulance, or the police. Dialing 911 on a cellphone connects you to a state police dispatcher, who transfers the call to the local authorities. The Boston police direct emergency number is 📞 617/343-4911.

Internet Access

Internet access is widely available in the Boston area, and Wi-Fi is often (but not always) free. Many coffee shops, restaurants, and other businesses have free Wi-Fi, as does Logan Airport, all Boston Public Library locations, the Rose Kennedy Greenway, the Quincy Market rotunda at Faneuil Hall Marketplace, and Christopher Columbus Waterfront Park and Norman B. Leventhal Park at Post Office Square.

If you're traveling without a computer or other device, ask the front-desk staff at your hotel for suggestions or visit a branch of **FedEx Office** (www.fedexoffice.com). Locations include 2 Center Plaza, Government Center (📞 617/973-9000); 10 Post Office Sq., Financial District (📞 617/482-4400); and 187 Dartmouth St. (📞 617/262-6188), Back Bay; and in Cambridge, 1 Mifflin Place (Mount Auburn St. and University Rd.), Harvard Square (📞 617/497-0125), and 600 Technology Sq. (Main and Portland sts.), Kendall Square (📞 617/494-5905). You'll pay about 35¢ a minute to use a computer.

Pharmacies

Hospital emergency departments can usually help you fill a prescription. At press time, the only 24-hour pharmacy in central Boston is the Copley Square **CVS,** 587 Boylston St. (Dartmouth St.), Back Bay (📞 617/437-8414). In Cambridge, head for the **CVS** at the Porter Square Shopping Center, 36 White St., off Mass. Ave. (📞 617/876-5519). In Harvard Square, the **CVS** at 1426 Mass. Ave. (📞 617/354-4420) is open 24/7, but the pharmacy keeps shorter hours.

Safety

The Boston area is generally safe, especially in the neighborhoods you're likely to visit. Nevertheless, you should take the same precautions you would in any other large North American city. Stash wallets and billfolds in your least accessible pocket, don't wave around maps or expensive electronics, and take off your headphones (or at least turn the volume way down) when you're walking alone. In general, trust your instincts—a dark, deserted street is probably deserted for a reason.

It's a good idea to stay out of parks (including Boston Common, the Public Garden, the Esplanade, the Rose Kennedy Greenway, and Cambridge Common) at night unless you're in a crowd. Specific areas to avoid at night include Boylston Street between Tremont and Washington streets, and Tremont Street from Stuart to Boylston streets. Try not to walk alone late at night in the Theater District or on the side streets around North Station. Public transportation in the areas you're likely to visit is busy and safe, but service stops between 12:30 and 1am (around 2:30am on weekends). If you're going to be out late, carry cab fare and a charged phone programmed with the number of at least one cab company.

WHERE TO STAY

Boston hotels are convenient—the central city is so small that nearly every location is a good one—but generally expensive. Many lodgings reflect the city's historic character: Renovations have transformed decades- and even century-old buildings into worthy competitors for brand-new hotels. Thanks to the mix of new construction and repurposed structures, strict zoning laws and building codes, and varying market conditions at the time of construction, Boston hotels offer wildly varying room sizes and amenities. Don't assume that every hotel has every option you expect in a certain price range—a pool, hypoallergenic rooms, 24-hour room service, pet accommodations—but do keep checking until you find one that does.

These listings omit the national and international chains, most of which have a presence in the booming Greater Boston market. If you know the brand, you probably know what to expect. They include the business-traveler magnets Hilton (and its DoubleTree and Embassy Suites brands), Hyatt, Loews, Marriott (in all its incarnations, including Courtyard, Renaissance, and Residence Inn), and Starwood (parent company of Le Méridien, Sheraton, W, and Westin); the leisure-oriented Best Western, Holiday Inn, Radisson, Ramada, and Wyndham; the boutique-hotel trendsetter Kimpton; and the luxury operators Fairmont, Four Seasons, InterContinental, Langham, Mandarin Oriental, Millennium, Ritz-Carlton, and Sonesta.

The scarcest lodging option in the immediate Boston area is the moderately priced chain motel, a category almost completely driven out by soaring real estate prices. And especially at busy times, brands that are bargains elsewhere may be pricey here—twice what you're used to paying, if not more. If an establishment with "Boston" in its name seems unusually cheap, double-check the location—it may be farther from downtown than you think.

Rates in this chapter are for a double room (except where noted); if you're traveling alone, single rates may be lower. The rates given here do not include the 5.7 percent state hotel tax. Boston and Cambridge add a 2.75 percent convention center tax on top of the 6 percent city tax, making the total a whopping 14.45 percent. Not all suburbs impose a local tax, so some towns charge only the state tax. These listings cover Boston, Cambridge, and Brookline.

Getting the Best Deal

The **rack rate** is the maximum rate that a hotel charges for a room. Hardly anybody pays it, however, except sometimes in high season. To cut costs:

o **Ask for a rate, then ask about special rates or other discounts.** You may qualify for corporate, student, military, senior/AARP, AAA, or other discounts. Nail down the standard rate before you ask for your discount.

- **Book online.** Many hotels offer Internet-only discounts or supply discounted rooms to **Priceline.com, Hotwire.com,** or **Expedia.com.** Some chains guarantee that the price on their websites is the lowest available; check anyway.
- **Bid online.** Priceline and Hotwire use different methods to get to the same goal: a deal on a room in a hotel whose name you don't learn until after you pay. If "opaque" booking makes you nervous, explore **BiddingForTravel.com** or **Better Bidding.com** to get a sense of the properties available.
- **Dial direct.** When booking a room in a chain hotel, you'll often get a better deal from the hotel's reservation desk than from the chain's main number.
- **Remember the law of supply and demand.** Business-oriented hotels are busiest during the week, so you can expect weekend discounts. Leisure hotels are most crowded and expensive on weekends, so discounts may be available midweek.
- **Visit in the winter.** Boston-bound bargain hunters who don't mind cold and snow (sometimes *lots* of snow) aim for January through March, when hotels offer great deals, especially on weekends.
- **Avoid excess charges and hidden costs.** Ask how much the hotel charges for parking and whether there's a charge for staying in the garage past room checkout time on the last day of your stay. Use your cellphone instead of making expensive calls from hotel phones. Seek out a hotel that includes Internet access in the room rate (many older properties and hotels that do a lot of expense-account business don't). And don't be tempted by the minibar: Prices tend to be outrageous. Finally, ask about local taxes, service charges, and energy surcharges, which can increase the cost of a room by 15 percent or more.
- **Book an efficiency.** A room with a kitchenette allows you to shop for groceries and even cook. This is a big money saver, especially for families on long stays.
- **Enroll in frequent traveler programs,** which court repeat customers. Members of some programs enjoy free Wi-Fi access, which can save as much as $15 a day.

Alternative Accommodations

Turn to the Internet for information about short-term rentals at every price point, from dirt-cheap (a tiny room in a suburban apartment some distance from public transit) to over-the-top (a fancy private home in a highly desirable location). Many property owners require a minimum stay and a security deposit or cleaning fee.

Popular options include **Airbnb** (www.airbnb.com), **FlipKey** (www.flipkey.com), **HomeAway** (www.homeaway.com), and **Vacation Rentals by Owner** (www.vrbo.com). If you're on a budget and enjoy meeting strangers, look into **Couchsurfing International** (www.couchsurfing.org).

For a longer visit, consider a home swap through **Home Exchange** (www.homeexchange.com) or **HomeLink International** (usa.homelink.org).

If you prefer to have someone else do the work, a B&B agency can save you a lot of calling around and find a lodging that accommodates your likes and dislikes, allergies, dietary restrictions, tolerance for noise and morning chitchat, and anything else you consider important. Rates are generally competitive with hotel prices. Many B&Bs require a minimum stay of at least 2 nights, and most offer winter specials (discounts or 1-night-free deals).

The following organizations can help you find a B&B in Boston, Cambridge, or the greater Boston area:

- **B&B Agency of Boston** (© **800/248-9262** or 617/720-3540, 0800/89-5128 from the U.K.; www.boston-bnbagency.com)

- **Bed and Breakfast Associates Bay Colony** (✆ **888/486-6018** or 617/720-0522; www.bnbboston.com)
- **Host Homes of Boston** (✆ **800/600-1308** outside MA or 617/244-1308; www.hosthomesofboston.com)
- **Inn Boston Reservations** (✆ **617/236-2227;** www.innbostonreservations.com)

Downtown & Vicinity

Businesspeople and sightseers dominate the hotels in this area, which includes the neighborhoods defined earlier in this chapter as the Waterfront, the North End, North Station, Faneuil Hall Marketplace, Government Center, the Financial District, the Seaport District/South Boston Waterfront, Downtown Crossing, Beacon Hill, and Chinatown/Theater District.

BEST FOR   Travelers who want easy access to the downtown and waterfront attractions, the Seaport District (home of the convention center and the Seaport World Trade Center), and the airport.

DRAWBACKS   Touristy atmosphere, distance from the Back Bay and Cambridge, mostly expensive.

EXPENSIVE

Ames Boston Hotel ★   The city's first skyscraper, the Ames Building opened in 1893 and became a hotel in 2007. It's an unusual place, with an uber-traditional Richardsonian Romanesque exterior and a stripped-down interior that contrasts invitingly with the comfy-cozy beds. Wood floors—again, unusual—sleek furnishings, and the predominantly white-and-gray color scheme add to the minimalist feel of the guest rooms, which are laid out in 11 different configurations. Vistas from the higher floors are sensational; rooms facing State Street have oblique water views.

1 Court St. (at Washington and State sts.). ✆ **888/293-4112** or 617/979-8100. www.ameshotel.com. 114 units. Apr–Nov from $499 double, from $850 suite; Dec–Mar from $249 double, from $500 suite. Children 17 and under stay free in parent's room. Packages available. Valet parking $42. T: Green or Blue Line to Government Center or Orange Line to State. **Amenities:** Restaurant and bar; concierge; exercise room; Wi-Fi (free).

Boston Harbor Hotel ★★★   One of the best hotels in Boston faces the harbor and the Rose Kennedy Greenway, but the fantastic location is just one reason to stay here: Others include the superb service, a great pool and spa, excellent restaurants, and plush, luxurious rooms. The hotel even has an outdoor skating rink, under the landmark arch at the heart of the Rowes Wharf complex. In the guest rooms, mahogany furniture creates a residential feel; blue decor predominates, echoing the harbor, which is visible from most guest rooms. If you plan to be away from the hotel a lot, save a few bucks and book a city-view unit. There's no such thing as a small room: All are at least 500 square feet. Accommodations start on the eighth floor of the 16-story structure, part of a red-brick hotel-residential-office complex that opened in 1987.

70 Rowes Wharf (at Atlantic Ave. near High St.). ✆ **800/752-7077** or 617/439-7000. www.bhh.com. 230 units. $345–$795 double; from $685 suite. Extra person $50. Children 17 and under stay free in parent's room. Weekend, family, spa, and other packages available. Valet parking $47; self-parking $43 weekdays; $40 weekends. T: Red Line to South Station or Blue Line to Aquarium. Pets accepted. **Amenities:** 2 restaurants; 3 bars, including seasonal outdoor bar; babysitting; concierge; well-appointed health club & spa; 60-ft. lap pool; room service; seasonal outdoor skating rink; Wi-Fi (free).

The Liberty Hotel ★★   The hook here is a good one: The entrance and public areas (as well as 18 guest rooms) are in the former Charles Street Jail, built in 1851.

price CATEGORIES

Expensive	$300 and up
Moderate	$200–$300
Inexpensive	Under $200

The granite edifice has enormous windows that illuminate an octagonal atrium. An adjoining 16-story tower is home to the rest of the guest rooms and the fitness center, which was completely renovated in 2014. Accommodations and bathrooms are large and luxurious, all cool neutrals with stainless-steel accents. Units on the river side of the building also face busy Storrow Drive, but the view in the other direction is of a hospital; given a choice, I'd opt for the river and ask to be on the highest possible floor.

215 Charles St. (at Cambridge St.). ✆ **617/224-4000.** www.libertyhotel.com. 298 units. $295–$550 double; $600–$1,000 suite. Children 17 and under stay free in parent's room. Weekend and other packages available. Valet parking $47. T: Red Line to Charles/MGH. Small pets accepted. **Amenities:** 2 restaurants; bar; concierge; 24-hr. exercise room; room service; Wi-Fi (free).

Seaport Hotel ★★   This is the only independent lodging in the rapidly evolving Seaport neighborhood; it completed extensive renovations of its guest rooms in 2014. Already comfortable, they're now downright luxurious, with upscale linens, pillow-top mattresses, and custom Stickley furniture that has neat details like wheels on the desks. Rooms on higher floor of the 18-story building enjoy magnificent views. Tech-oriented and eco-conscious (it has its own rooftop beehives), the hotel is a great choice if you have business in the Seaport—the World Trade Center is across the street—or the Financial District. Also nearby is the Boston Children's Museum; families can look into weekend packages and plan on spending some time in the pool. The hotel operates a shuttle to downtown destinations and an electric water taxi.

1 Seaport Lane (btw. Seaport Blvd. and Congress St.). ✆ **877/732-7678** or 617/385-4000. www.seaportboston.com. 426 units. $189–$479 double; from $589 suite. Children 16 and under stay free in parent's room. Weekend and family packages available. Valet parking $44; self-parking $34. T: Red Line to South Station, then Silver Line SL1/SL2 to World Trade Center or 20-min. walk. Or water taxi to World Trade Center. Pets under 50 lb. accepted. **Amenities:** Restaurant; cafe; lounge; concierge; bikes; well-equipped health club; 50-ft. indoor pool; room service; spa; Wi-Fi (free).

XV Beacon ★★   The best boutique hotel in Boston will rent you an iPad to use in front of the gas fireplace while you wait for the towel heater to work: It mixes traditional style and 21st-century tech better than any other option. The 10-story hotel has just seven units per floor, decorated in subdued shades of brown and tan. Each has Frette linens, a TV in the bathroom, and lots of other amenities. If you must have a pool or a huge fitness facility, look elsewhere; if you'd prefer plush accommodations and great service, this might be the place for you.

15 Beacon St. (at Somerset St., 1 block from the State House). ✆ **877/982-3226** or 617/670-1500. www.xvbeacon.com. 63 units, some with shower only. From $355 double; from $1,200 suite. Valet parking $46. T: Red or Green Line to Park St., or Blue Line to Bowdoin. Dogs accepted ($25 MSPCA donation). **Amenities:** Restaurant; bar; babysitting; concierge; exercise room; access to nearby health club ($15); room service; Wi-Fi (free).

MODERATE

The Boxer Boston ★   On a nondescript street near North Station, the 1904 flat-iron-shape building stands out; the odd exterior means that every guest room has a

Boston Hotels

Ames **17**

Anthony's Town House **23**

Boston Common Hotel & Conference Center **11**

Boston Harbor Hotel **19**

The Boxer Boston **14**

Chandler Inn Hotel **9**

Charlesmark Hotel **4**

Eliot Hotel **2**

Fifteen Beacon **16**

40 Berkeley **8**

Friend Street Hostel **15**

Harborside Inn **18**

Hostelling International—Boston **22**

Hotel Commonwealth **1**

Hotel 140 **10**

Inn @ St. Botolph **6**

InterContinental Boston **21**

John Jeffries House **12**

The Lenox Hotel **5**

The Liberty Hotel **13**

Longwood Inn **24**

The MidTown Hotel **7**

Newbury Guest House **3**

Seaport Hotel **20**

XV Beacon **16**

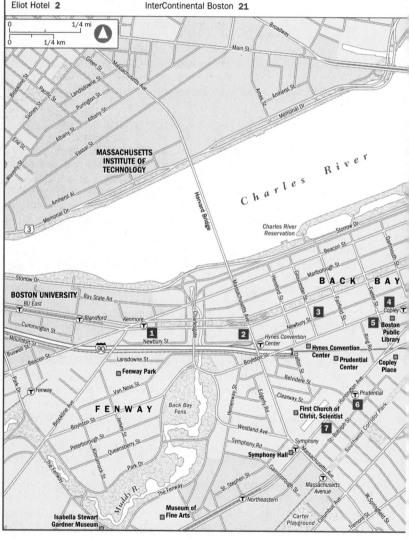

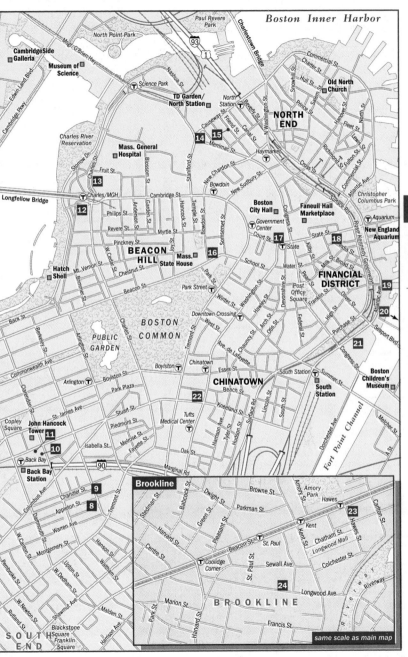

unique layout, including triangular units in the pointy end (and a handful of rooms with twin-and-full-size bunk beds). All have blue-gray walls and custom furnishings that make the small rooms feel more spacious than they are, as well as marble-clad bathrooms. Rooms on higher floors of the nine-story building (there's just one elevator) are farther from street noise, but the views are uninspiring no matter how high you go.

107 Merrimac St. (at Lancaster St., 1 block from Causeway St.). *Ⓒ* **617/624-0202.** www.theboxer boston.com. 79 units, most with shower only. $169–$399 double; $199–$489 executive king. Children 17 and under stay free in parent's room. Packages and AAA, AARP, military, and long-term discounts available. Valet parking $44; self-parking $30 in nearby garage. T: Green or Orange Line to North Station. Pets under 50 lb. accepted ($50 nonrefundable fee). **Amenities:** Restaurant and lounge; concierge; exercise room; room service; Wi-Fi (free).

INEXPENSIVE

Friend Street Hostel If Hostelling International (see below) is sold out, this might be an acceptable fallback. The location, a half-block from North Station, is the main selling point. The clientele tends toward young international backpackers who don't mind the noisy location and lack of elevator in the three-story building. Bunk beds are in 6- and 10-person rooms (all male, all female, and mixed). The hostel has a kitchenette, laundry facilities, TV, and air-conditioning; rates include bed linens but not towels, which are available for rent.

234 Friend St. (btw. Causeway St. and Valenti Way). *Ⓒ* **617/248-8971.** www.friendstreethostel. com. 42 beds. From $45 per bed. Rates include continental breakfast. T: Green or Orange Line to North Station. **Amenities:** Wi-Fi (free).

Harborside Inn ★★ On the edge of the Financial District, the Harborside Inn, a former warehouse built in 1858, is a great deal, and the Greenway and Faneuil Hall Marketplace are right across the street. Every unit has a unique layout and a pillow-top bed, with sleek custom teak furnishings and nautical-themed art. The only tough decision here is whether to ask for a room that faces the street (noisier) or the eight-story atrium; if you're a really light sleeper, a handful of "cabin" rooms have no windows at all.

185 State St. (btw. Atlantic Ave. and the Custom House Tower). *Ⓒ* **617/723-7500.** www.harbor sideinnboston.com. 116 units. $129–$299 double. Extra person $15. Packages and long-term rates available. Rates may be higher during special events. Off-site parking $29; reservation required. T: Blue Line to Aquarium, or Blue or Orange Line to State. **Amenities:** Lounge; concierge; access to nearby health club ($10); Wi-Fi (free).

Hostelling International–Boston ★ This sprawling hostel was an immediate success when it opened in 2012. The public areas in the six-story LEED-certified building look like part of a contemporary boutique hotel. The dorm-style accommodations aren't as pretty—it's a hostel, after all—but the bright walls and efficient floor plans make them more pleasant experience than you might expect. Most units (all men, all women, and mixed) hold three bunk beds, with shared bathrooms. For a private bathroom, book one of the 22 private units. You can use the provided linens or bring your own, but a local law forbids sleeping bags. The clientele is the customary mix of backpackers, students, youth groups, and thrifty travelers of all ages.

19 Stuart St. (off Washington St.). *Ⓒ* **888/464-4872** or 617/536-9455. www.bostonhostel.org. 481 beds. Members of Hostelling International–American Youth Hostels $50–$65 per bed, nonmembers $53–$68 per bed; members $190–$200 per private unit, nonmembers $193–$203 per private unit. Children 3–12 half-price, children under 3 free. Rates include continental breakfast. T: Orange Line to Tufts Medical Center or Green Line to Boylston. **Amenities:** Coffee shop; Wi-Fi (free).

John Jeffries House ★★ This red-brick inn looks like a dorm because it used to be one (for nurses working nearby), and its genteel reproduction-Victorian decor fits right in on Beacon Hill. Guest rooms and bathrooms are snug but not cramped; most units have kitchenettes. With cars, trains, and ambulances whizzing past, this isn't a perfect place if you need dead silence—definitely ask for a room that faces the garden—but it's quieter than you might expect, and a great deal for the location.

14 David G. Mugar Way (off Charles St. at Charles Circle). ℂ **617/367-1866.** www.johnjeffries house.com. 46 units. $154–$199 double. Rates include continental breakfast. Validated valet parking $25 in nearby garage. T: Red Line to Charles/MGH. **Amenities:** Room service; Wi-Fi (free).

Back Bay & Vicinity

Boston's widest variety of lodgings is in this area, which for our purposes includes the South End, Kenmore Square, and a slice of suburban Brookline.

BEST FOR Anyone who wants to be where the action is. The Back Bay is the best place in the Boston area for shopping and people-watching. Budget-conscious travelers have more options here than in any other centrally located part of town.

DRAWBACKS Room rates can be extremely high, especially during citywide events such as the Marathon. Tour groups overrun the neighborhood year-round, especially during foliage season. The most convenient T access is on the unreliable Green Line. Reaching Cambridge isn't easy or consistently fast (the subway can be as slow as the pokey No. 1 bus).

EXPENSIVE

Eliot Hotel ★★ The 79 suites (other units are standard doubles) are by far the most residential-feeling hotel accommodations in Boston. And on this part of tony Commonwealth Avenue—close to Newbury Street, Kenmore Square, and (across the river) MIT—the residences feel really comfortable. From the subtly patterned carpets, bed linens, and upholstery to the marble-clad bathrooms and French doors between rooms in the suites, it's all exquisite. Courtly, personalized service only adds to the charm of the place.

370 Commonwealth Ave. (at Mass. Ave.). ℂ **800/443-5468** or 617/267-1607. www.eliothotel.com. 95 units, most with shower only. $235–$395 double; $355–$545 1-bedroom suite; $580–$890 2-bedroom suite. Extra person $30. Children 17 and under stay free in parent's room. Valet parking $36. T: Green Line B, C, or D to Hynes Convention Center. Pets accepted. **Amenities:** Restaurant; sashimi bar; babysitting; concierge; free access to nearby health club; room service; Wi-Fi (free).

Hotel Commonwealth ★ Fresh off a room renovation that was completed in 2014, the Hotel Commonwealth is in great shape. The spacious accommodations look and feel plush, and are decorated in rich neutrals with splashes of dark red—a nod to the Red Sox (Fenway Park's a few blocks away). Fenway rooms overlook the ballpark, but with the Massachusetts Turnpike in the foreground; Commonwealth rooms are larger, with views of the traffic in busy Kenmore Square. All units have large bathrooms, Frette robes, and oversize desks.

500 Commonwealth Ave. (at Kenmore St.). ℂ **866/784-4000** or 617/933-5000. www.hotel commonwealth.com. 149 units. $239–$499 double; $269–$569 jr. suite; $459–$899 suite. Extra person $20. Children 17 and under stay free in parent's room. Packages and AAA discount available. Valet parking $46. T: Green Line B, C, or D to Kenmore. Pets accepted ($125 fee). **Amenities:** 2 restaurants; bar; concierge; exercise room; room service; Wi-Fi (free).

The Lenox Hotel ★★ The Lenox wrapped up a complete overhaul of its guest rooms in 2014, transforming a style you might call "pleasant high-end hotel" to "dramatic yet relaxing," in shades of brown and gray with tufted-leather headboards and garnet accents. At the heart of the Back Bay, the Lenox is well positioned to compete with the huge chain hotels nearby, and it delivers business features along with personalized service that its competitors can't match. This isn't the place if you need extensive fitness facilities, but in every other regard it's a great choice.

61 Exeter St. (at Boylston St.). ✆ **800/225-7676** or 617/536-5300. www.lenoxhotel.com. 214 units, some with shower only. $215–$425 double; $289–$545 junior suite; from $770 1-bedroom fireplace suite. Children 16 and under stay free in parent's room. Corporate, weekend, and family packages available. Valet parking $45. T: Green Line to Copley. **Amenities:** Restaurant; bar; pub; babysitting; concierge; small exercise room; room service; Wi-Fi (free).

MODERATE

The 16 units at the **Inn @ St. Botolph,** 99 St. Botolph St. (at W. Newton St.; ✆ **617/236-8099;** www.innatstbotolph.com; T: Green Line E to Prudential), are so popular that they're almost always booked, but check anyway; they are in a residential neighborhood a block from Huntington Avenue and the Prudential Center. Guests pretty much fend for themselves, which is perfect if you like the atmosphere of an upscale B&B but not mingling with the staff and other guests. The lavishly decorated suites have self-catering kitchens (management supplies the breakfast fixings) and Wi-Fi but no other services besides a small exercise room. Rates for a double in high season start at $209.

Chandler Inn Hotel ★ Just 2 blocks from the Back Bay, the Chandler Inn feels like a pricier boutique hotel. The eight-story building holds small but well-designed rooms, which are decorated in cool neutrals with splashes of orange and equipped with plasma TVs and marble bathrooms; all have individual climate control. The staff is welcoming and helpful. Off-season rates are excellent.

26 Chandler St. (at Berkeley St.). ✆ **800/842-3450** or 617/482-3450. www.chandlerinn.com. 56 units. $109–$279 double. Children 11 and under stay free in parent's room. Parking $27 in nearby garage. T: Orange Line to Back Bay. Pets under 25 lb. accepted ($50 fee). **Amenities:** Restaurant and bar; access to nearby health club ($10); Wi-Fi (free).

Charlesmark Hotel ★★ The Charlesmark occupies a convenient location that's now tinged with tragedy: overlooking the Boston Marathon finish line. The six-story building, erected in 1892, predates the race, and its conversion into a budget-boutique hotel created a worthy competitor for this neighborhood's many large chains. Guest rooms are small but have pillow-top mattresses and mini-fridges. They feel like ship cabins, with built-ins that help alleviate the space crunch. The included breakfast makes this place a bargain, but note that there's only one elevator.

655 Boylston St. (btw. Dartmouth and Exeter sts.). ✆ **617/247-1212.** www.thecharlesmark.com. 40 units, most with shower only. $129–$249 double. Rates include continental breakfast. Children stay free in parent's room. Self-parking $28 in nearby garage. T: Green Line to Copley. **Amenities:** Lounge; access to nearby health club ($15); Wi-Fi (free).

The MidTown Hotel ★ In a neighborhood packed with chain business hotels, the MidTown feels almost like a suburban motel: It's just two stories, with a seasonal outdoor pool. Many of guests are part of tour groups or here for conventions; others are families who can book adjoining rooms and enjoy easy access to the Prudential Center, across the street. The well-maintained guest rooms are large and utilitarian, decorated in standard contemporary hotel style; bathrooms are small. Huntington Avenue can be busy, especially if there's an event at Symphony Hall; request a room at the back of the building if traffic noise bothers you. And if you're driving, note that the parking here is among the cheapest in central Boston.

220 Huntington Ave. (at Cumberland St., 1 long block from Mass. Ave.). $\textcircled{C}$ **800/343-1177** or 617/262-1000. www.midtownhotel.com. 159 units. $119–$309 double; from $139 suite. Extra person $15. Children 17 and under stay free in parent's room. Parking $25. T: Green Line E to Prudential or Orange Line to Massachusetts Ave. Dogs accepted ($30 fee). **Amenities:** Concierge; access to nearby health club ($5–$10); outdoor pool; Wi-Fi ($10/day).

Newbury Guest House ★★   Newbury Street is Boston's most elegant shopping area, and this inn is a perfect fit—without the designer prices. The Newbury Guest House consistently sells out, especially in the summer and fall, so try to book as soon as you lock up your travel plans. The accommodations, in a trio of brick 19th-century townhouses, are comfortable and cozy but not cramped. The well-kept guest rooms have pale walls and white linens with dark furniture and accents. In the largest units, bay windows face busy Newbury Street; this isn't an issue in cold weather, but in the summer, light sleepers may be happier with a room overlooking the alley.

261 Newbury St. (btw. Fairfield and Gloucester sts.). $\textcircled{C}$ **800/437-7668** or 617/670-6000. www. newburyguesthouse.com. 32 units, some with shower only. $139–$279 double. Extra person $20. Rates include continental breakfast. Packages and off-season discounts available. Rates may be higher during special events. Parking $20 (reservation required). T: Green Line B, C, or D to Hynes Convention Center. **Amenities:** Restaurant; access to nearby health club ($25); Wi-Fi (free).

INEXPENSIVE

Check ahead for information about **40 Berkeley,** 40 Berkeley St. (at Appleton St.; $\textcircled{C}$ **617/375-2524;** www.40berkeley.com), which was sold in April 2014 and appears poised for redevelopment. At press time, the former YWCA was operating as a hostel-style "entry-level hotel," with more private rooms than a typical hostel but with bathrooms (and a handful of suites with private bathrooms). The seven-story building is in a great South End location on the edge of the Back Bay. Rates for a single room in high season start at around $100, which includes breakfast and Wi-Fi.

Anthony's Town House   What you see is what you get: This family-owned guesthouse is a well-maintained old four-story brownstone where guests share bathrooms, use the stairs (there's no elevator), and enjoy a homey, no-frills experience. Many international travelers and budget-minded Americans love the place, over the Brookline border about a mile from Kenmore Square. Rooms have high ceilings and Queen Anne– or Victorian-style furnishings (but no phones), and bathrooms have enclosed showers. Ask about family units, which accommodate up to five. Although the Beacon Street trolley isn't especially noisy by city standards, light sleepers should ask for a room at the back. *Note:* No credit cards are accepted, but ATMs are nearby; make sure you know your daily withdrawal limit.

1085 Beacon St. (at Hawes St.). $\textcircled{C}$ **617/566-3972.** www.anthonystownhouse.com. 10 units, none with private bathroom. $78–$108 double; from $125 family room. Extra person $10. Weekly rates and winter discounts available. Limited free parking; off-premises parking $10. T: Green Line C to Hawes St. **Amenities:** Wi-Fi (free).

Boston Common Hotel & Conference Center ★   While developers plan its imminent replacement, this eight-story hotel remains a great find in an even better location. It's nowhere near the Common, but Copley Square is less than 2 blocks away, and Back Bay Station is even closer. This is not the lap of luxury: Decorated in generic-hotel style, rooms are small and bathrooms tiny. Solo travelers might not appreciate the fact that many guests are traveling with the groups who flock here, but the great rates and friendly staff help make up for that. Hotel 140, which is nearby, sometimes has lower rates, but the winter deals here are great.

40 Trinity Place (off Stuart St.). © 617/933-7700. www.bostoncommonhotel.com. 64 units. $109–$229 double. Rates include continental breakfast. Extra person $10. Children 17 and under stay free in parent's room. Validated self-parking $28 in nearby garage. T: Orange Line to Back Bay or Green Line to Copley. **Amenities:** A/C, TV, hair dryer, Wi-Fi (free) in public areas.

Hotel 140 ★   If your hotel room is your castle, this is not the place for you—but if you're looking for a comfortable, reasonably priced place to sleep and shower, this former YMCA hits the mark—it's on floors five through eight of a 14-story building a block from Copley Square. In size, the rooms are about what you'd expect, but the unfrilly style—neutrals with pops of pattern and color—helps camouflage how small they are. The Boston Common Hotel, around the corner, is the main competition; it's more traditional in style and sometimes beats this hotel on price.

140 Clarendon St. (at Stuart St.). © **800/714-0140** or 617/585-5600. www.hotel140.com. 59 units (all with shower only). $119–$339 double. Packages and AAA, AARP, and long-term rates available. Self-parking $27 in adjacent garage. T: Orange Line to Back Bay. **Amenities:** Exercise room; access to nearby health club; Wi-Fi (free).

Longwood Inn   This renovated Victorian-style guesthouse sits in a residential part of Brookline, about equidistant from Coolidge Corner and the Harvard Medical Area. A stay here feels like visiting a relative—not fancy, but comfortable and welcoming. All but one of the well-kept, pleasantly decorated guest rooms have their own bathroom; the other unit's facilities are across the hall. Guests have the use of a kitchen, dining room, and coin-op washer and dryer, and there's seating on a pleasant porch and patio. The playground, tennis courts, and running track at the public school next door are open to the public.

123 Longwood Ave. (at Marshall St., 1 block from Kent St.). © **617/566-8615.** www.longwood-inn.com. 22 units, 4 with shower only. Apr–Nov $144–$174 double; Dec–Mar $104–$134 double. Extra person $10. 1-bedroom apt (sleeps 4-plus) $124–$164. Weekly rates available. Free parking. T: Green Line D to Longwood or C to Coolidge Corner. **Amenities:** Wi-Fi (free).

Cambridge

Across the Charles River from Boston, Cambridge has its own attractions and excellent hotels. Graduation season (May and early June) is especially busy, but campus events can cause high demand at unexpected times, so plan ahead.

BEST FOR   Anyone with business in Cambridge, as well as visitors who need access to downtown Boston and the South Boston waterfront, which are relatively easy to reach on the T from both the Harvard Square area and East Cambridge.

DRAWBACKS   Access to the Back Bay and South End can be slow, expensive, or both. Budget options are limited, and parking at most hotels is almost as expensive as parking in Boston.

EXPENSIVE

The Charles Hotel ★★★   The Charles, which turned 30 in 2014, is among the best hotels in the Boston area, and certainly the best in Cambridge—with rates to match. Unlike a lot of high-end hotels, it's maintained a consistent guest room style: simple yet luxurious, with custom Shaker-style furnishings and abundant amenities. Floor-to-ceiling windows make the decent-sized rooms feel bigger than they are. With Harvard Square on one side and the Charles River on the other, the nine-story brick

Cambridge Hotels

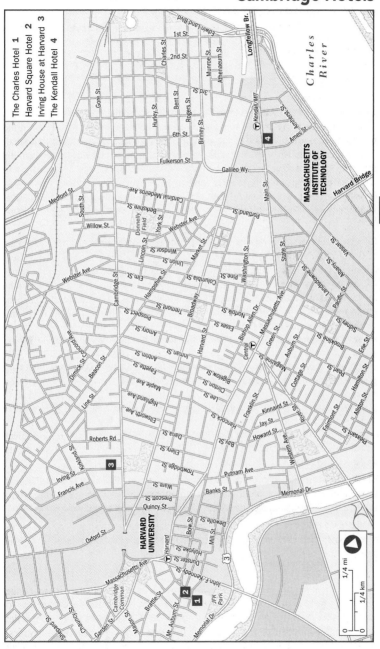

The Charles Hotel **1**
Harvard Square Hotel **2**
Irving House at Harvard **3**
The Kendall Hotel **4**

hotel draws Harvard parents and other visitors, demanding business travelers, and vacationing families. They all get the same type of personalized service the hotel lavishes on the occasional passing celebrity.

1 Bennett St. (at Eliot St., 1 block from Mount Auburn St.). 📞 **800/882-1818** or 617/864-1200. www.charleshotel.com. 295 units. $299–$599 double; from $409 suite. Off-season discounts and weekend packages available. Valet or self-parking $34. T: Red Line to Harvard. Pets accepted ($50 fee). **Amenities:** 2 restaurants; 2 bars; Regattabar jazz club; concierge; bikes; free access to adjacent health club w/pool, Jacuzzi, and sauna; room service; adjacent spa; Wi-Fi (free).

MODERATE

Harvard Square Hotel A friend accustomed to traveling first class laughed as he described the basic style of his room here—then acknowledged that it had everything he needed. The great location of the six-story brick building is its main selling point. As my friend admitted, the accommodations are comfortable and—except at the busiest times—reasonably priced. Rooms aren't large, but the lack of frills and lots of shiny white surfaces help make the most of limited space. True, you can't have a masseuse or a lobster sent to your room (at least not easily), but how much time are you really planning to spend in your room?

110 Mount Auburn St. (at Eliot St.). 📞 **800/458-5886** or 617/864-5200. www.harvardsquarehotel. com. 73 units, some with shower only. $139–$259 double. Extra person $20. Children 16 and under stay free in parent's room. Packages, corporate rates, AAA and AARP discounts available. Parking $35. T: Red Line to Harvard. **Amenities:** Coffee shop; dining privileges at Harvard Faculty Club; Wi-Fi (free).

The Kendall Hotel ★ A 19th-century firehouse and a seven-story 20th-century annex make up this hotel in the heart of Kendall Square. It feels like a giant B&B, and not just because of the generous breakfast: Patchwork quilts, bright paint on the walls, country-style furniture, and personalized service add to the artsy, quirky atmosphere. Units in the low-rise firehouse are closer to street noise and subway vibrations than rooms in the seven-story annex. *Tip:* On weekends, free street parking usually isn't too hard to find (if you don't mind walking a couple of blocks).

350 Main St. (at Dock St.). 📞 **866/566-1300** or 617/577-1300. www.kendallhotel.com. 77 units. $129–$349 double. $13/night service fee (includes buffet breakfast, Internet and fitness center access, weeknight reception with wine). Children 17 and under stay free in parent's room. Weekend and other packages and long-term discounts available. Limited self-parking $25. T: Red Line to Kendall/MIT. **Amenities:** Restaurant, access to nearby health club, Wi-Fi.

INEXPENSIVE

Irving House at Harvard ★ In a great location just off the Harvard campus, this sprawling 1893 building—four stories, with no elevator—sits on a quiet residential street. In true down-to-earth Cambridge fashion, it's convenient and welcoming but not luxurious or stylish: Think one crucial step up from a dorm, with smallish, comfortably appointed rooms. The price is right, the breakfast is tasty, the staff is friendly, and the parking is free. Note that single rooms are cheaper than doubles but share hallway bathrooms and don't have TVs.

24 Irving St. (off Cambridge St.). 📞 **877/547-4600** or 617/547-4600. www.irvinghouse.com. 44 units, some with shower only. $150–$300 double. Rates include buffet breakfast. Children 6 and under stay free in parent's room. Off-season and long-term discounts available. Free parking (except during Harvard commencement). T: Red Line to Harvard, 15-min. walk. **Amenities:** Access to nearby health club ($8); Wi-Fi (free).

WHERE TO EAT

In Boston, top-notch creations emerge from kitchens all over town, from the fanciest special-occasion destinations to the humblest food trucks. The **North End** is known for Italian food, and the city's hottest restaurant scenes are in the **South End,** the **Fenway,** and the **Seaport District,** which includes **Fort Point.** Across the river, **Cambridge** offers a tasty mix of upscale places, neighborhood stalwarts, cheap student hangouts, and ethnic restaurants. Vegetarians and vegans (as well as those who eat gluten-free) have more options than ever before. And many visitors just want to know where they can get a big lobster. This section aims to help every diner find something that hits the spot.

Downtown & Vicinity

Restaurants in these neighborhoods draw much of their business from hungry tourists, expense-account travelers (including convention-goers avoiding the Seaport District's chains), and local office workers in search of a quick lunch that won't ruin their budgets. In the **North End,** the weekend is rush hour—if you plan to have dinner there, aim for Sunday through Thursday.

EXPENSIVE

Daily Catch ★ SOUTHERN ITALIAN/SEAFOOD   The Daily Catch in the North End seats just 20, but that's only part of the reason there's often a line outside. The food really is worth waiting for. This is the place if you love garlic, calamari, or both—but unlike some restaurants that mess up anything trickier than deep-frying, this is a great choice for more complicated dishes: Try the monkfish Marsala. All food is prepared to order, and some dishes arrive still in the frying pan. Note that this location, the original one, is cash only. The **Seaport** branch is fancier (and takes credit cards) but still has the homey vibe that's made the Daily Catch popular since 1973.

323 Hanover St. (btw. Richmond and Prince sts.). *©* **617/523-8567.** www.dailycatch.com. Main courses $17–$27. Daily 11:30am–10pm. Validated parking available. T: Green or Orange Line to Haymarket. Also at the Moakley Federal Courthouse, 2 Northern Ave. (*©* **617/772-4400;** Mon–Thurs 11am–9:30pm, Fri 11am–10:30pm, Sat noon–10:30pm, Sun 1–9pm; T: Silver Line SL1/SL2 to Court House).

Legal Sea Foods ★★★ SEAFOOD   I chose to list this branch of the family-owned chain because I enjoy the idea of eating fish while looking at an aquarium, but you can't go wrong at any Legal Sea Foods location in the Boston area. From the simplest broiled filet to the celebrated clam chowder to the fanciest shellfish concoction, everything here is ultra-fresh, made from top-quality ingredients, and prepared with care. Ask your well-versed server for advice if you can't decide, or just order a big lobster. The wine list and dessert menu are also terrific. The flagship location, **Legal Harborside,** is a three-level space at 270 Northern Ave. in the Seaport District (*©* **617/477-2900**)—it's a hassle to get to, but it's the only branch with a water view.

---

price CATEGORIES

Categories refer to the average cost of an individual main course at dinner, not the cost of a meal.		
	Expensive	$20 and up
	Moderate	$10–$19
	Inexpensive	Under $10

Boston Restaurants

Bangkok City **5**
The Barking Crab **23**
Ben & Jerry's **9, 13, 34**
Bertucci's **4**
Blue Dragon **25**
Chacarero **21**
Daily Catch **15, 22**
Davio's Northern Italian
   Steakhouse **33**
The Elephant Walk **1**
Emack & Bolio's **7**

Flour Bakery & Cafe **24, 26, 31**
Galleria Umberto Rosticceria **15**
Great Taste Bakery
   & Restaurant **38**
Hamersley's Bistro **28**
Jasper White's Summer Shack **6**
Legal Sea Foods **8, 12, 22, 35**
Myers + Chang **29**
Neptune Oyster **16**
P. F. Chang's China Bistro **11, 36**
Pizzeria Regina **14**

The Salty Pig **27**
South End Buttery **30**
Sultan's Kitchen **20**
Sweet Cheeks Q **2**
Taranta Cucina
   Meridonale **17**
Tasty Burger **3**
Toro **32**
Union Oyster House **18**
Wagamama **10, 19**
Xinh Xinh **37**

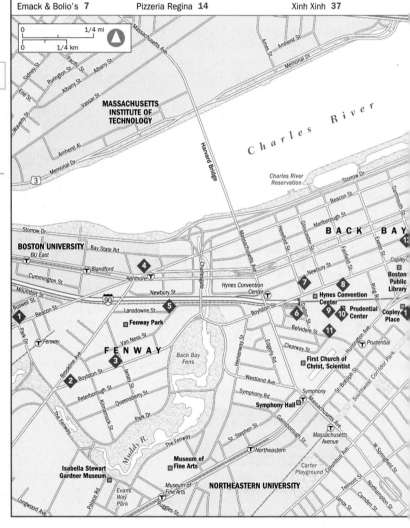

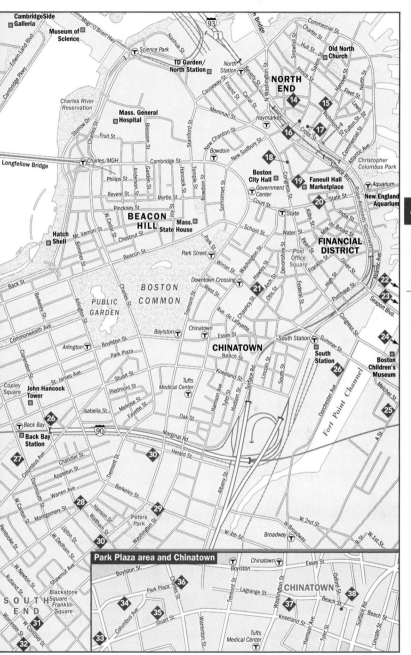

255 State St. (1 block from Atlantic Ave.). ☎ **617/742-5300.** www.legalseafoods.com. Main courses $11–$19 at lunch, $14–$35 at dinner; lobster market price. Mon–Thurs 11am–10pm; Fri–Sun 11am–11pm. T: Blue Line to Aquarium. Other locations at the Prudential Center, in Park Sq., at Copley Place, in Harvard Sq., in Kendall Sq., and in the 3 domestic terminals at Logan Airport.

Taranta Cucina Meridionale ★★ SOUTHERN ITALIAN/PERUVIAN   The unusual combination of Peruvian and Italian is enough to draw curious diners here once; the excellent food and service keep fans coming back. They want cassava-root gnocchi with spicy lamb ragù, macadamia-crusted salmon with a pisco-and-blood-orange sauce, and the signature pork chop with a sweet-hot glaze of sugar cane and *rocoto* pepper. The brick-walled dining room and open kitchen are visible from the street, through open French windows when the weather's fine; for more privacy and less noise, ask for a table upstairs.

210 Hanover St. (btw. Cross and Parmenter sts.). ☎ **617/720-0052.** www.tarantarist.com. Main courses $19–$36. Daily 5:30–10pm. T: Green or Orange Line to Haymarket.

Union Oyster House ★ SEAFOOD/NEW ENGLAND   Opened in 1826, the Union Oyster House brags that it's "America's oldest restaurant in continuous service." Right on the Freedom Trail, it attracts legions of tourists (and when he was a senator, John F. Kennedy was a regular). But I've stopped being surprised when locals want to meet me here—it's a classic for a reason. Simple food, well prepared, is the not-so-secret formula: super-fresh oysters shucked while you watch, clam chowder, broiled or fried seafood, gingerbread or Boston cream pie, done! Now get back on the Freedom Trail.

41 Union St. (btw. North and Hanover sts.). ☎ **617/227-2750.** www.unionoysterhouse.com. Main courses $10–$25 (most under $18) at lunch, $22–$34 at dinner; lobster market price; children's menu $6–$12. Sun–Thurs 11am–9:30pm (lunch menu until 5pm); Fri–Sat 11am–10pm (lunch until 6pm). Union Bar daily 11am–midnight (lunch until 3pm, late supper until 11pm). Validated and valet parking available. T: Green or Orange Line to Haymarket.

MODERATE

The Barking Crab ★ SEAFOOD   With indoor-outdoor seating and a busy after-work bar scene, the Barking Crab has something for everyone. Overlooking the Fort Point Channel in the increasingly corporate Seaport District, this is a casual place that's close enough to the Boston Children's Museum to attract families. Come here for simple fried, steamed, and broiled fish and shellfish, deftly prepared and served without any pretensions. Then look around and enjoy the contrasts of the waterfront: clam shack picnic tables and skyscrapers.

Boston's Food Trucks

Like a lot of other dining trends, food trucks conquered New York before sweeping Boston—but Boston has embraced them warmly. You'll find trucks that serve everything from barbecue to Uyghur specialties to cupcakes to Vietnamese sandwiches along the **Rose Kennedy Greenway,** outside the **Boston Public Library** in Copley Square, and next to **Boston City Hall** every day in warm weather and at the **SoWa Open Market** (p. 98) on summer Sundays. **Clover Food Truck** (p. 66) originated and has three brick-and-mortar locations in Cambridge. Visit **www.cityofboston. gov/foodtrucks/schedule-tabs.asp** for locations, schedules, and links to vendors.

Try to be near Downtown Crossing at lunchtime at least once during your visit and seek out **Chacarero,** 101 Arch St., off Summer Street (© **617/542-0392;** www.chacarero.com). It serves other things, but the lines are for the scrumptious Chilean sandwiches, served on house-made bread. Order chicken, beef, or vegetarian, ask for it "with everything"—tomatoes, cheese, avocado, hot sauce, and (unexpected but delicious) green beans—and dig in. The lines are long but move fairly quickly, and for less than $10, you can feel like a savvy Bostonian.

88 Sleeper St. (btw. Northern Ave. and Seaport Blvd.). © **617/426-2722.** www.barkingcrab.com. Reservations accepted only for parties of 6 or more. Main courses $10–$25; sandwiches $7–$21 (most less than $15); fresh seafood market price. Sun–Wed 11:30am–10pm; Thurs–Sat 11:30am–11pm; bar closes 1 hr. after kitchen. Closed 3 weeks in Jan. T: Red Line to South Station and 10-min. walk or Silver Line to Court House; or Blue Line to Aquarium and 10-min. walk.

Blue Dragon ★★ ASIAN/GASTROPUB Celebrity chef Ming Tsai got it just right when he opened this casual, slight rowdy spot in the Fort Point neighborhood: It was an instant hit. It's perfect for groups of friends sharing dishes, and surprisingly popular for business lunches. Asian with trendy gastropub isn't an obvious combo, but bar food and strong flavors are a delicious match. Friendly servers, who have to shout to be heard, can offer guidance on the dishes, which might include.fish and chips with flaky panko rather than beer batter and black-vinegar aioli rather than malt vinegar, or shepherd's pie with Indonesian curried lamb. The only dish that doesn't work for me is the curiously bland pad Thai.

324 A St. (at Melcher St.). © **617/338-8585.** www.bluedragonboston.com. Reservations not accepted. Plates and platters $9–$30. Mon–Sat 11:30am–midnight; bar closes 1 hr. after kitchen. T: Red Line to South Station and 10-min. walk.

Neptune Oyster ★ SEAFOOD Eating at Neptune can be annoying: There's usually a wait, the tiny dining room (only 42 seats) is crowded and noisy, and the staff seems constantly harried. Just remind yourself that it wouldn't be so crowded if it weren't so good. This is the best seafood place in the North End—some say in all of Boston—and the quality doesn't flag even on the busiest weekend night. Start with oysters, enticingly displayed in the window on beds of ice. Move on to anything that sounds good; even the burger is terrific, but I prefer to concentrate on the seafood specials. The signature dish is the lobster roll, served either cold with mayonnaise or hot with butter.

63 Salem St. (off Cross St.). © **617/742-3474.** www.neptuneoyster.com. Reservations not accepted. Main courses $16–$35; lobster market price. Sun–Thurs 11:30am–9:30pm; Fri–Sat 11:30am–10:30pm. Raw bar closes 1 hr. after kitchen. T: Green or Orange Line to Haymarket.

INEXPENSIVE

Galleria Umberto Rosticceria ★ ITALIAN Lunch here is a true Boston experience, especially if you like Sicilian-style (thick crust) pizza—one friend of mine says it's the best in the city. Join the line that forms moments after the doors open; your fellow patrons will be office workers and North End locals as well as sightseers. Check out what's on their paper plates: *arancini* (rice balls stuffed with ground beef, peas, and cheese, then deep-fried); meat, vegetable, and cheese calzones; and maybe best of all, *panzarotti* (potato croquettes molded around mozzarella and fried). And that amazing pizza, served by the slice. Have your cash out (no credit cards here), ask for a soft drink or beer, and grab a table.

289 Hanover St. (btw. Richmond and Prince sts.). © **617/227-5709.** All items less than $5. No credit cards. Mon–Sat 10:45am–2:30pm. Closed July. T: Green or Orange Line to Haymarket.

Great Taste Bakery & Restaurant ★ CANTONESE/DIM SUM   The excellent Hong Kong–style and Chinese-American classics are only half the story at this lively storefront restaurant. Great Taste is also one of the only restaurants in Boston that serves dim sum a la carte—in other words, made to order, not wilting on a steam cart. Shrimp and chive dumplings (separately or together) are delectable. Of the larger dishes, I especially like salt-and-pepper seafood of all kinds, hot pots ("casserole specials" on the menu), and anything with Chinese broccoli. One door down, the excellent bakery half of the business sells not-too-sweet Chinese sweets (walnut cookies, egg tarts) and Western-style layer cakes.

61–63 Beach St. (off Hudson St.). © **617/426-6688.** www.bostongreattastebakery.com. Reservations not accepted. Main courses $5–$16 (most items less than $12); dim sum $2.50–$5. Sun–Thurs 6:30am–10pm, Fri–Sat 6:30am–11pm. T: Orange Line to Chinatown.

Pizzeria Regina ★★ PIZZA   Regina's opened in 1926, when the North End was solidly Italian and homesick Neapolitans wanted a taste of the old country. Today's patrons might also be homesick—they tend to be out-of-towners drawn here by the restaurant's well-deserved reputation and not averse to waiting for a table. Although pizza with the same name is available at other locations, and they all use the same ingredients—specially aged cheese, tomatoes canned just for Regina's, house-made sausage—the decades-old brick oven here makes all the difference. And the atmosphere in the jam-packed dining room doesn't hurt. Ask the waitress, who might call you "honey," for a well-done pie, let it cool a little, and dig in.

11½ Thacher St. (at N. Margin St.). © **617/227-0765.** www.pizzeriaregina.com. Pizza $13–$22. Sun–Thurs 11:30am–11:30pm; Fri–Sat 11:30am–12:30am. T: Green or Orange Line to Haymarket.

Sultan's Kitchen ★★ TURKISH/MIDDLE EASTERN   You've probably had kebabs, Middle Eastern salads, and perhaps even Turkish food before, but they probably weren't this good. The line is out the door of this spot around the corner from Faneuil Hall marketplace because the local office workers know quality and value when they find it. That line snakes past display cases filled with eye-catching salads, braised and roasted vegetables, and meat dishes. Study the boards above the cash register, then ask for a combination of salads and *meze* (appetizers). Order your food to go, and head outside for a picnic. "Eat Well Like the Sultans," indeed.

116 State St. (at Broad St.). © **617/570-9009.** www.sultans-kitchen.com. Sandwiches $6–$9; main courses $9–$12. Mon–Fri 11am–8:30pm; Sat 11am–4pm. T: Orange or Blue Line to State.

Xinh Xinh ★★ VIETNAMESE   Pronounced "sin sin," this restaurant is just a nondescript storefront, but the food makes it a standout all the same. The menu is voluminous, and the cheery staff can help you narrow down your options. If you've been curious about a particular obscure dish or just want an introduction to the cuisine, you'll find something that suits. This is a great place to try *pho,* the classic Vietnamese noodle soup, and *bun,* another classic that combines rice vermicelli, meat or tofu, and cool garnishes into a saladlike taste sensation. You can't go wrong with lemongrass chicken, available in multiple dishes, and you should always check out the specials board—when the every-day food is this good, "special" really means something.

7 Beach St. (at Knapp St., 1 block from Washington St.). © **617/422-0501.** Main courses $6–$14 (most less than $11). Daily 10am–10pm. T: Orange Line to Chinatown.

Back Bay & Vicinity

Like many fashionable neighborhoods, the **Back Bay** is home to lots of mediocre, pricey restaurants. There's good food in this area if you know where to look—mostly in the **South End** and the **Fenway.** Both neighborhoods abound with good options at all price points.

EXPENSIVE

Davio's Northern Italian Steakhouse ★★ STEAKS/NORTHERN ITALIAN

You want steak, and your date wants pasta. Your spice-phobic uncle is in town, but you're craving garlic. Your biggest client needs attention, and everything has to be perfect. Problem solved. Davio's executes its quadruple-jump-level difficult combination with panache and even a sense of humor—this is the place that invented Philly cheese steak spring rolls. The rest of the menu is more straightforward: top-notch steaks and sides, inventive seafood, wonderful pasta, sublime risotto. The dining room hums, but the noise level is surprisingly reasonable considering that the bar is in the middle of the space. It's not cheap, but considering the quality of the food and service, lunch here is one of Boston's best deals.

75 Arlington St. (at Stuart St., 2 blocks from the Public Garden). ⓒ **617/357-4810.** www.davios. com. Reservations recommended. Main courses $9–$43 at lunch (most less than $25), $17–$51 at dinner; 4-course tasting menu $75. Mon–Fri 11:30am–3pm; Sun–Tues 5–10pm (lounge menu until 11pm), Wed–Sat 5–11pm (lounge menu until midnight). Validated and valet parking available. T: Green Line to Arlington.

Hamersley's Bistro ★★★ FRENCH/AMERICAN

The best restaurant in the South End opened in 1987 and has outlasted all challengers thanks to a combination of culinary genius and first-class service. The dish that's never off the menu is perfect roast chicken with garlic, lemon, and parsley, but I fall for the seafood dishes, like prosciutto-wrapped roasted trout with Gulf shrimp. Owner Gordon Hamersley presides (literally—he's the tall line chef in the Red Sox cap) over a kitchen that embraced the seasonal-local-organic philosophy long before it was trendy. Classic French technique transforms top-notch ingredients, many from New England, into the unforgettable cuisine that made Julia Child a fan back in the day. Desserts are among the best in town, and there's seasonal outdoor seating.

553 Tremont St. (at Clarendon St.). ⓒ **617/423-2700.** www.hamersleysbistro.com. Reservations recommended. Main courses $26–$44. Sun–Thurs 5:30–9:30pm; Fri–Sat 5:30–10pm; Sun brunch 11am–2pm. Closed 1st week. of Jan. Valet parking available. T: Orange Line to Back Bay.

MODERATE

Bangkok City ★ THAI

Across the street from the Berklee College of Music, Bangkok City draws a substantial number of students with excellent food at a good price. It's a fine choice for the usual suspects, like satays, fried rice, and pad Thai, but I prefer the option of picking a protein and a curry sauce, served with plenty of veggies and rice. Servers are unobtrusive, but helpful if you ask for advice. Shades separate the large dining room from the busy street, and gold accents and elephant statues add to the hideaway feel. You can't have the umbrella drink that would complete the illusion, but beer goes perfectly with this food.

167 Massachusetts Ave. (btw. Belvidere and St. Germain sts.). ⓒ **617/266-8884.** www.bangkok cityrestaurantboston.com. Main courses $7–$10 at lunch, $10–$19 at dinner; whole fish market price. Mon–Sat 11:30am–3pm; Mon–Thurs 5–10pm; Fri 5–10:30pm; Sat 3–10:30pm; Sun 5–10pm. T: Green Line B, C, or D to Hynes Convention Center.

The Elephant Walk ★★ FRENCH/CAMBODIAN   Venture beyond Kenmore Square to cross two international borders at the Elephant Walk. The well-prepared French dishes are classics, such as roast chicken and *boeuf bourguignon,* but it's with the Cambodian side of the menu that the kitchen shines. The stir-fries and noodle dishes are wonderful, but my favorite dishes are the less familiar *amor royal* (spicy steamed coconut-milk custard, served with rice) and *loc lac* (beef tenderloin chunks flavored with pepper, garlic, and mushroom soy). Vegetarians, vegans, and diners with gluten issues eat very well here, and the welcoming staff can offer helpful suggestions.

900 Beacon St. (at Park Dr.). ✆ **617/247-1500.** www.elephantwalk.com. Reservations recommended. Main courses $8–$20 at lunch (most items less than $13), $15–$23 at dinner; dinner tasting menu $30 for 3 courses, $34 for 4 courses. Mon–Fri 11:30am–2:30pm; Sun–Thurs 5–10pm; Fri–Sat 5–11pm; Sun brunch 11:30am–2:30pm. Valet parking available at dinner. T: Green Line C to St. Mary's St. Also at 2067 Massachusetts Ave., Porter Sq., Cambridge (✆ **617/492-6900,** Mon–Fri 11:30am–10pm, Sat–Sun 5–10pm, Sun brunch 11:30am–2:30pm; T: Red Line to Porter).

Myers + Chang ★★ PAN-ASIAN   Try to come here with a group and explore the menu, which incorporates flavors and dishes from all over Asia. The familiar and unusual dishes are just right for sharing. Mix and match noodles, dumplings, salad, and full main courses; your server can tell you if you're ordering enough (or too much) food. Many dishes carry a fair amount of heat; quench the fire with sake or a cocktail. The glass-walled room, on a busy South End corner, grows loud at night; eat during the day—the weekend dim sum brunch is a winner—if you don't want to shout to be heard.

1145 Washington St. (at E. Berkeley St.). ✆ **617/542-5200.** www.myersandchang.com. Main courses $9–$16 at lunch, $13–$19 at dinner. Sun–Thurs 11:30am–10pm, Fri–Sat 11:30am–11pm (lunch Mon–Fri until 5pm, dim sum brunch Sat–Sun until 5pm). T: Silver Line SL4/SL5 to E. Berkeley St.

The Salty Pig ★ CHARCUTERIE   In a touristy location next to the Copley Place mall, the Salty Pig is a welcome surprise. The specialty is house-cured pork, aka "salty pig parts." You order from a selection of meats, pâtés, and sausages, choose one or more of the excellent cheeses and condiments, and wait while the kitchen assembles your charcuterie "board." If that doesn't appeal, the salads, sandwiches, and pizzas are terrific. This is a good place for foodies eating with less adventurous diners, parents with kids, and even carnivores with vegetarians. The dining room is noisy in the evening; in fine weather, you can sit on the patio.

130 Dartmouth St. (btw. Huntington and Columbus aves.). ✆ **617/536-6200.** www.thesaltypig. com. Pizzas, pastas, and main courses $11–$18; board items $2–$8. Daily 11am–1am. T: Orange Line to Back Bay.

South End Buttery AMERICAN   Originally an excellent bakery, the Buttery became a cafe and eventually a restaurant. South Enders eat here all day, starting with luscious baked goods for breakfast on the go. The ovens crank out terrific bread for sandwiches at lunch, which also features salads and hearty soups made in-house. Consider a midafternoon cupcake, but don't spoil your dinner. The back and downstairs dining rooms turn into a sit-down comfort-food restaurant (meatloaf, roasted salmon, chicken pot pie) in the evening, and for weekend brunch. At all three meals, takeout is a popular option.

314 Shawmut Ave. (at Union Park St.). ✆ **617/482-1015.** www.southendbuttery.com. Cafe items $2.25–$9 (most under $7); soups, sandwiches and salads $6–$10; brunch items $4–14; dinner main courses $13–$29 (most under $21). Cafe daily 6:30am–8pm. Dinner Sun–Wed 5:30–10pm, Thurs–Sat 5:30–11pm; Sat–Sun brunch 10am–3pm. T: Orange Line to Back Bay or Silver Line SL4/SL5 to Union Park.

Sweet Cheeks Q ★ BARBECUE   A highlight of the Fenway's booming restaurant scene, Sweet Cheeks opened in 2011, eclipsing every other Boston-area barbecue joint. The brainchild of chef-owner Tiffani Faison (of "Top Chef" fame), it serves all-natural pork, beef, and poultry, sourced locally when possible, prepared Texas-style in a 2-ton smoker. "Trays" of meats hold a single generous serving alongside two side dishes, with plenty of napkins. Although the main courses—ribs, pulled pork, brisket, fried chicken—are scrumptious, the best item on the menu is the buttermilk biscuits. Wash it all down with a craft cocktail, served in a Mason jar, or a domestic microbrew. Sit on the patio if you can; this might be the noisiest restaurant in Boston, which is saying something.

1381 Boylston St. (btw. Brookline Ave. and Kilmarnock St.). ✆ 617/266-1300. www.sweetcheeksq. com. Main courses $9–$14 at lunch, $11–$26 at dinner. Sun–Tues 11:30am–10pm, Wed–Sat 11:30am–11pm (lunch Mon–Fri until 5pm). T: Green Line D to Fenway.

Toro ★★ SPANISH/TAPAS   For my money, this is the best lunch restaurant in Boston. It's better known for its dinner scene, but noise and an interminable wait don't make a great experience. Delectable Barcelona-style tapas at your own pace, preferably at a table on the surprisingly pleasant sidewalk? That's more like it. Start with the house special grilled corn, making sure everyone gets a piece. Mix up hot and cold, meat and seafood, vegetables and more vegetables. The friendly waitstaff can help you decide whether to order more. Just make sure to try the lunch-only *milanesa bocadillo*—a chicken cutlet sandwich that's worth the trip all by itself.

1704 Washington St. (near E. Springfield St.). ✆ 617/536-4300. www.toro-restaurant.com. Tapas $5–$15 at lunch, $8–$16 at dinner; salads and sandwiches $8–$10 at lunch, main courses $15–$38 at dinner. Mon–Fri noon–3pm; Mon–Thurs 5:30–10:15pm, Fri 5:30–11:45pm, Sat 5–11:45pm, Sun 5–10:15pm; Sun brunch 10:30am–2:30pm. Valet parking available at dinner Thurs–Sat. T: Silver Line SL4/SL5 bus to Mass. Ave.

INEXPENSIVE

Flour Bakery & Cafe AMERICAN/BAKERY   From a single location in the South End, Flour grew into a little local chain that serves irresistible baked goods all day and wildly popular lunches. Lines are long at all four locations from shortly before noon until nearly 2pm. The hearty sandwiches (on bread made in house), salads, and soups are so good that you might not mind having to wait for dessert. But the desserts are amazing—cookies like house-made "Oreos," macaroons, tarts, out-of-this-world sticky buns, and more.

131 Clarendon St. (at Stuart St.). ✆ 617/437-7700. www.flourbakery.com. Bakery items $2–$6; sandwiches and salads $5–$9. Mon–Fri 7am–8pm, Sat 8am–6pm, Sun 9am–5pm. T: Green Line to Copley or Orange Line to Back Bay. Check website for locations in the South End, in Fort Point, and outside Central Sq.

Tasty Burger AMERICAN   A block from Fenway Park, Tasty Burger serves exactly what it says. The excellent ⅓-pound burgers would be a deal anyway, and the fact that they're made of grass-fed beef means they're a steal. You'll pay extra if you want more than lettuce and tomato on your patty. You can also get a terrific hot dog, crispy chicken sandwich, or turkey or veggie burger. The best side dish is onion rings, available straight up or mixed half-and-half with French fries. The Harvard Square location stays open till 4am and has a pool table, but the renovated-service-station design of the Fenway original gets me every time. At both, you'll see students and families all day, bar- and club-hoppers in the evening.

1301 Boylston St. (at Yawkey Way). ✆ 617/425-4444. www.tastyburger.com. Main courses $4–$7. Daily 11am–2am. T: Green Line B, C, or D to Kenmore, then 10-min. walk. Also at 40 John F. Kennedy St. (at Mt. Auburn St.), Cambridge. Same phone. T: Red Line to Harvard.

Cambridge & Vicinity

The Cambridge side of the river, as in Boston, has places for penny-pinching students as well as the tycoons many of them aspire to become.

EXPENSIVE

East Coast Grill & Raw Bar ★★★ SEAFOOD/BARBECUE Founder Chris Schlesinger sold the East Coast Grill in 2012 after 27 years at the helm, and luckily the new regime inherited a commitment to ultra-fresh seafood, quality meats, deftly deployed heat (both fire and spice), strong drinks, and friendly service. If you don't have a reservation, be ready to wait at the noisy, neon-bright bar, anticipating food that mixes New England ingredients, equatorial flavors, and classic barbecue. Seafood tacos are my favorite starter, but the raw bar always appeals. Main courses range from shrimp and grits to Latin-spiced mahimahi to bounteous portions of Texas-style brisket, Kansas City–style ribs, and eastern North Carolina pulled pork (or all three).

1271 Cambridge St. (off Prospect St.). ℂ **617/491-6568.** www.eastcoastgrill.net. Main courses $16–$30; fresh seafood market price. Sat 11am–2:30pm; Sun–Thurs 5:30–10pm; Fri–Sat 5:30–10:30pm; Sun brunch 11am–2:30pm. Validated parking available. T: Red Line to Central, then a 10-min. walk on Prospect St., or Red Line to Harvard, then no. 69 (Harvard-Lechmere) bus to Inman Sq.

Giulia ★★ ITALIAN Between Harvard and Porter squares stands this little slice of Rome. In a long, narrow former bar, it serves inventive starters and delectable main courses that rely on meat, poultry, and fish. But the headliner is the handmade pasta, whipped up every afternoon at the long table in front of the open kitchen. I'm still thinking about pappardelle with wild-boar sauce, which I ate with one eye on my friend's farro noodles with rabbit sauce. Everything about this place, which opened in December 2012, is just so: excellent cocktails, well-edited wine list, classic yet imaginative cuisine, and warm, thoughtful service. Make a reservation.

1682 Massachusetts Ave. (at Sacramento St.). ℂ **617/441-2800.** www.giuliarestaurant.com. Main courses $17–$36. Mon–Thu 5:30–10pm, Fri–Sat 5:30–11pm. T: Red Line to Harvard or Porter.

Jasper White's Summer Shack ★★ SEAFOOD Ride the Red Line to the Cambridge-Arlington border and the Summer Shack, a perfect example of what happens when an acclaimed chef (that'd be Jasper White) embraces casual, family-friendly dining: magic. The clam shack is a New England beach institution, and this cavernous space feels like an extra-extra-large one. The menu matches the seashore ambience—raw and cooked shellfish, lobster rolls, hot dogs, all sorts of fried seafood—with the added zing of gourmet lobster preparations and amazing specials. The Summer Shack in Boston's **Back Bay** is less atmospheric but still delicious; it's especially popular before and after Red Sox games and Symphony performances.

149 Alewife Brook Pkwy. (at Cambridgepark Dr., opposite Alewife Station). ℂ **617/520-9500.** www.summershackrestaurant.com. Main courses $8–$36 (most $25 or less); sandwiches $5–$15; lobster and specials market price. Mon–Thurs 11:30am–9:30pm (lunch menu until 5pm); Fri 11:30am–10:30pm (lunch menu until 5pm); Sat noon–10:30pm; Sun noon–9pm. Free parking. T: Red Line to Alewife. Also at 50 Dalton St. (at Scotia St., 1 block from Boylston St.), Boston (ℂ **617/867-9955**), Apr–Oct Sun–Wed 11:30am–10pm, Thurs–Sat 11:30am–11pm; Nov–Mar Mon–Wed 5–10pm, Thurs–Fri 5–11pm, Sat 11:30am–11pm, Sun 11:30am–10pm. T: Green Line B, C, or D to Hynes Convention Center.

MODERATE

The Friendly Toast AMERICAN The Friendly Toast serves upscale diner food in a kitsch-encrusted space plopped incongruously in the midst of Kendall Square's tech paradise. Surrounded by vintage ads and memorabilia, you can dig into large

Cambridge Restaurants

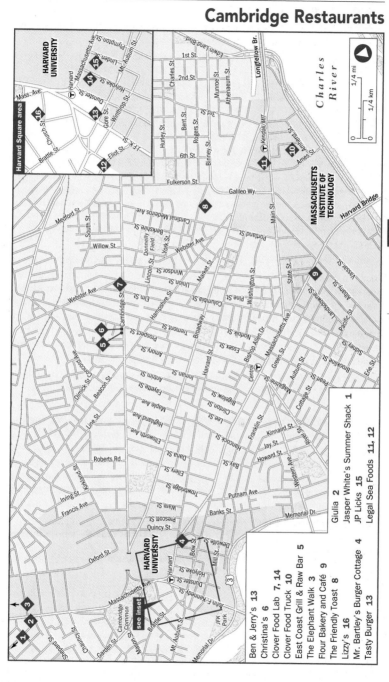

Ben & Jerry's **13**
Christina's **6**
Clover Food Lab **7, 14**
Clover Food Truck **10**
East Coast Grill & Raw Bar **5**
The Elephant Walk **3**
Flour Bakery and Café **9**
The Friendly Toast **8**
Lizzy's **16**
Mr. Bartley's Burger Cottage **4**
Tasty Burger **13**

Giulia **2**
Jasper White's Summer Shack **1**
JP Licks **15**
Legal Sea Foods **11, 12**

No less an expert than Ben Cohen of Ben & Jerry's has called Boston "a great place for ice cream." That goes for Cambridge, too—residents of both cities famously defy even the most frigid weather to get their fix. I like Cambridge's options better: Try **JP Licks,** 1312 Massachusetts Ave. (© **617/492-1001;** www.jplicks.com); **Ben & Jerry's,** in the Garage mall, 36 John F. Kennedy St. (© **617/864-2828;** www.benjerry.com); or **Lizzy's,** 29 Church St. (© **617/354-2911;** www.lizzysicecream.com)—all in Harvard Square—or **Christina's,** 1255 Cambridge St., Inman Square (© **617/492-7021;** www.christinasicecream.

com). Favorite Boston destinations include **Emack & Bolio's,** 290 Newbury St., Back Bay (© **617/536-7127;** www.emackandbolios.com), and 255 State St., across from the New England Aquarium (© **617/367-0220**); and **JP Licks,** 659 Centre St., Jamaica Plain (© **617/524-6740**). **Ben & Jerry's** also has stores in Boston at the Prudential Center, 800 Boylston St. (© **617/266-0767**); 174 Newbury St., Back Bay (© **617/536-5456**); and 20 Park Plaza, a block from the Public Garden (© **617/426-0890**). JP Licks and Emack & Bolio's also have locations in Cambridge, Somerville, and Brookline.

portions of breakfast food (served all day) and comfort food like mac and cheese, burgers, and overstuffed burritos. The crazy lines for weekend brunch make sense after you've seen the menu, which is clearly the work of someone with experience battling hangovers. Among the omelets and pancakes, you'll find dishes like spicy mashed potatoes with chorizo, fried eggs, and chipotle sauce, and "drunkard's French toast," with Grand Marnier–raspberry sauce.

1 Kendall Sq. (Broadway and Hampshire St.). © **617/621-1200.** www.thefriendlytoast.com. Breakfast items $5–$13; main courses $10–$13. Sun–Tue 8am–10pm, Wed–Thu 8am–11pm, Fri–Sat 8am–1am. T: Red Line to Kendall/MIT, 10-min. walk.

Mr. Bartley's Burger Cottage ★★ AMERICAN

Since 1960, Mr. Bartley's has pulled in Harvard students and Cambridge locals with its big, juicy burgers. The menu names them after celebrities, politicians, and pop-culture trends, with corny explanations (the iPhone burger, "'Siri'ously delicious"), but only the names change. Also holding steady are the wacky vintage signs, posters, ads, and other throwback amusements that plaster the walls of the jam-packed dining room. You can decide for yourself what you want on your burger, so I'll offer just one piece of advice: Order the onion rings. Bartley's accepts cash only and closes on Sunday.

1246 Massachusetts Ave. (btw. Plympton and Bow sts.). © **617/354-6559.** Burgers $11–$15; main courses, salads, and sandwiches $6–$10; children's menu $5–$6. Mon–Sat 11am–9pm. Closed Memorial Day, July 4, Labor Day, Dec 25–Jan 1. T: Red Line to Harvard.

INEXPENSIVE

Clover Food Lab ★ VEGETARIAN/VEGAN

In a purpose-built space in Harvard Square, Clover is basically an experiment. Will people eat food that's marketed as good for them if it's also priced right, readily available, and delicious? Signs point to yes. It's a good bet that many of the people lining up for chickpea-fritter sandwiches, rosemary French fries, and the ever-changing selection of sandwiches, salads, and soups don't even know or care that the food is vegetarian. They just know that they like it. An MIT and Harvard alumnus founded Clover in 2008 with one food truck; today, the policy of using local organic produce whenever possible looks visionary. Visit the website for the scoop on Clover's aggressively green, socially conscious business model.

7 Holyoke St. (off Mass. Ave.). (C) **617/640-1884.** www.cloverfoodtruck.com. All items $6 or less. Daily 7am–10pm. T: Red Line to Harvard. Check website for other brick-and-mortar and truck locations.

EXPLORING BOSTON

Central Boston is relatively compact, but that doesn't mean you can cram an infinite number of activities and destinations into a single day. It's possible—but not advisable—to take in most of the major attractions in 2 or 3 days if you don't linger anywhere too long. For a more enjoyable, less rushed visit, plan fewer activities and spend more time on them. For descriptions of suggested itineraries, see chapter 2.

Downtown & Vicinity

Faneuil Hall Marketplace ★★ MARKET   Since Boston's most popular attraction opened in 1976, cities all over the country have imitated the "festival market" concept. Each complex of shops, food counters, restaurants, bars, and public spaces reflects its city, and Faneuil Hall Marketplace is no exception. Its popularity with visitors and suburbanites is so great that you might think that the only Bostonians here are employees.

The marketplace includes five buildings—the central three-building complex is on the National Register of Historic Places—on brick and stone plazas that teem with crowds shopping, eating, performing, cheering for the performers, and people-watching. In warm weather, it's busy from early morning until well past dark. **Quincy Market** (you'll also hear the whole complex called by that name) is the Greek revival–style building at the center of the marketplace.

The central corridor of Quincy Market is the food court, where you can find anything from a fresh-shucked oyster to a full Greek dinner to sweets of all sorts. On either

Eyes in the Skies

For a smashing view of the airport, the harbor, and the South Boston waterfront, stroll along the harbor or Atlantic Avenue to Northern Avenue. On either side of this intersection are buildings with free observation areas. Be ready to show an ID to gain entrance. The space on the 14th floor of **Independence Wharf,** 470 Atlantic Ave., is open daily from 11am to 5pm. Across the way is **Foster's Rotunda,** on the ninth floor of 30 Rowes Wharf, in the Boston Harbor Hotel complex. It's open Monday to Friday from 11am to 4pm.

Boston Attractions

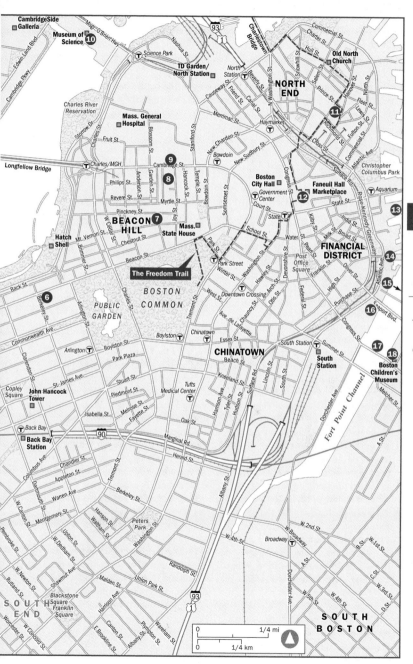

side of this building, under glass canopies, are full-service restaurants and bars—including one made to look like the one on the TV show **"Cheers"**—as well as push-carts that sell everything crafts created by New England artisans as well as lots of hokey souvenirs. In the plaza between the **South Canopy** and the South Market building is an **information kiosk,** and throughout the complex you'll find numerous outlets of retail chains. On warm evenings, the tables that spill outdoors from the restaurants and bars fill with people.

The original **Faneuil Hall ★** gets lost in the shuffle, but it's worth a visit. The first floor holds a National Park Service Visitor Center. See p. 80 for a full description.

Btw. North, Congress, and State sts. and John F. Fitzgerald Surface Rd. ℂ **617/523-1300.** www. faneuilhallmarketplace.com. Marketplace Mon–Sat 10am–9pm; Sun noon–6pm. Mon–Thu closing time may be earlier in winter. Food court opens earlier; bars and some restaurants close later. T: Orange Line to Haymarket or State, or Blue Line to Aquarium or State.

Boston Tea Party Ships & Museum TOUR   The Boston Tea Party—a December 1773 uprising that helped lead to the American Revolution—lasted just a few hours, but its legacy endures. On visit here, you'll see a show that tells the story through exhibits, a film, and live performances. Talented actors interpret scripts that draw on

Boston Sightseeing Deals

As you plan your visit, consider these money-saving options. Check their respective websites for info about buying each pass.

If you concentrate on the included attractions, a **Boston CityPass** (ℂ 888/330-5008; www.citypass.com/boston) offers great savings. It's a booklet of tickets (so you can go straight to the entrance) to the Museum of Fine Arts, Museum of Science, New England Aquarium, Skywalk Observatory, and either the Harvard Museum of Natural History or the Old State House. The price represents a 47 percent savings for adults—*but only if you visit all five attractions.* It feels like an even better deal on a steamy day when the line at the aquarium is long. At press time, the cost was $54 for adults, $39 for children 3 to 11, subject to change as admission prices rise. The passes, good for 9 days from first use, also include discounts at other local businesses.

The **Go Boston Card** (ℂ 800/887-9103; www.gobostoncard.com) includes admission to 51 New England attractions, plus dining and shopping discounts, a guidebook, and a 2-day trolley pass.

Getting the most for your money requires some serious planning. The card, which can be loaded onto a smartphone, costs $53 for 1 day, $75 for 2 days, $122 for 3 days, $168 for 5 days, and $197 for 7 days, with discounts for children and winter travelers (some of the included businesses close in the winter). The **Go Select Boston** pass covers a single admission to two or more of the 39 included attractions and is good for 30 days. The price varies with the options you choose.

If you're a Bank of America or Merrill Lynch credit or debit card holder, the **Museums on Us** program gets you into cultural institutions around the country free on the first full weekend of each month. Participating establishments in eastern Massachusetts are the Museum of Fine Arts and the MIT Museum. Visit http://museums.bankofamerica.com for details. On **"Free Fun Fridays"** in the summer, the Massachusetts-based Highland Street Foundation (www.highlandstreet.org) foots the bill for admission to cultural institutions around the state. Check the website for specifics.

WELCOME TO THE north end

The Paul Revere House and the Old North Church are the best-known buildings in the **North End ★★★**, which is Boston's "Little Italy" (although locals *never* call it that). Home to Italian immigrants and their assimilated children, numerous Italian restaurants and private social clubs, and many historic sites, this is one of the oldest neighborhoods in the city. It was home in the 17th century to the **Mather family** of Puritan ministers, who might be shocked to see the merry goings-on at the festivals and street fairs that take over different areas of the North End on weekends in July and August.

The Italians and their descendants (and the yuppie neighbors who have crowded many of them out since the 1980s) are only the latest immigrant group to dominate the North End. In the 19th century, this was an Eastern-European Jewish enclave and later an Irish stronghold. In 1890, President Kennedy's mother, Rose Fitzgerald, was born on Garden Court Street and baptized at St. Stephen's Church on Hanover Street.

Modern visitors might be more interested in a Hanover Street *caffè*, the perfect place to have coffee or a soft drink and feast on sweets. **Mike's Pastry ★★**, 300 Hanover St. (*©* **617/742-3050;** www.mikespastry.com), is a bakery that does a frantic takeout business and has tables where you can sit down and order one of the confections on display in the cases. The signature item is cannoli (tubes of crisp-fried pastry filled with sweetened ricotta cheese); the cookies, cakes, and other pastries are excellent, too. You can also sit and relax at **Caffè Vittoria** or **Caffè dello Sport,** on either side of Mike's.

Before you leave the North End, stroll down toward the water and see whether there's a **bocce** game going on at the courts on Commercial Street near Hull Street. The European pastime is both a game of skill and an excuse to hang around and shoot the breeze—in Italian and English—with the locals, mostly older men. It's so popular that the neighborhood has courts both outdoors, in the Langone Playground at Puopolo Park, and indoors, at the back of the adjacent Steriti Rink, 561 Commercial St.

historic documents and the latest technology (including holograms) to give visitors a sense of why 18th-century Bostonians were in a revolutionary mood. The largest artifacts are faithful full-size replicas of two of the three merchant ships raided during the original Tea Party (another is under construction). It's worth noting that this for-profit institution is a museum in name only: The 1-hour guided tour of the exhibits doesn't allow visitors to wander on their own. But one of the displays is a wooden chest that was cast overboard during the Tea Party—a passing teenager recovered it the next morning—and the performances are well-researched, with plenty of audience participation. Families enjoy it, especially if middle-school kids who have studied the American Revolution are along. To save on admission, order tickets online, and look into discounts that may be available if you take a tour with Old Town Trolley (like this establishment, owned by Historic Tours of America). Check ahead for information about the annual **Boston Tea Party reenactment,** on December 16; it begins at the Old South Meeting House (see listing below) and continues with a march to the ships, where spectators cheer for the "colonists" as they festoon the water with tea.

Congress St. Bridge (btw. Dorchester Ave. and Sleeper St.). *©* **855/TEA-1773** (832-1773) or 617/338-1773. www.bostonteapartyship.com. Admission $25 adults, $22 seniors and students, $15 children 4–12, free for children 3 and under. Summer and fall daily 10am–5pm; tours every 15 min. Check ahead for winter and spring hours. T: Red Line to South Station; walk north on Atlantic Ave. 1 block (past Federal Reserve Bank), turn right onto Congress St., then walk 1 long block to bridge.

Institute of Contemporary Art ★★ MUSEUM   The ICA is a dynamic presence in the constantly changing Seaport District neighborhood. In 2014, the museum expanded its summer programming, which already included free admission and concerts on Thursday evenings, with Friday evening events focusing on music, art, and even cooking. Year-round, the ICA is Boston's go-to destination for contemporary art in every imaginable medium, thoughtfully presented and invariably inspiring. The brilliant curators zero in on emerging artists whose work complements a small but superb permanent collection of 20th- and 21st-century art. The ICA also schedules numerous events, including lectures, discussions, and musical performances, that help even the most casual or reluctant visitor appreciate the importance of art in everyday life. As you approach the entrance, detour and walk around the building, taking in the innovative architecture (by the New York firm Diller Scofidio + Renfro) that effectively makes the building the largest artifact in the ICA's collections. The waterfront cafe has seasonal patio seating, and the excellent gift shop is well worth a visit.

100 Northern Ave. (off Seaport Blvd. at E. Service Rd.). © **617/478-3100.** www.icaboston.org. Admission $15 adults, $13 seniors, $10 students, free for children 17 and under and those visiting only the cafe. Free to all Thurs after 5pm and to families (up to 2 adults with children 12 and under) last Sat of month Jan–Nov. Sat–Sun, Tues–Wed, and some Mon holidays 10am–5pm; Thurs–Fri 10am–9pm. T: Silver Line SL1/SL2 bus to Courthouse.

John F. Kennedy Presidential Library and Museum ★★   In the half-century since the assassination of the 35th president, John Kennedy has taken on an almost mythic aura. His presidential library helps put him and his legacy in context—with the expected dash of hero worship, but in evenhanded fashion overall. The museum, in the Dorchester neighborhood of Boston, is easy to reach from downtown by T or car. Touring the galleries is usually a self-guided experience, but check ahead to see whether docent-led tours are available during your visit.

The Black Heritage Trail

The 1.5-mile **Black Heritage Trail ★★** covers sites on Beacon Hill that preserve the history of 19th-century Boston. The neighborhood was the center of the free black community, and the trail links stations of the Underground Railroad, homes of famous citizens, and the first integrated public school in the city. You can take a free 2-hour guided tour with a ranger from the National Park Service's **Boston African American National Historic Site** (© **617/742-5415;** www.nps.gov/boaf). Tours start at the **Shaw Memorial** (Memorial to Robert Gould Shaw and the Massachusetts 54th Regiment), on Beacon Street across from the State House. They're available Monday through Saturday from Memorial Day to Labor Day, and by request at other times; call ahead for a reservation. Or go on your own, using a brochure (available at the Museum of African American History and the Boston Common and Faneuil Hall visitor centers) that includes a map and descriptions of the buildings. The only buildings on the trail that are open to the public are the **African Meeting House** and the **Abiel Smith School,** which make up the **Museum of African American History** (p. 73). Check ahead for special programs year-round.

The JFK Library, designed by I. M. Pei and opened in 1979, offers visitors an immersive experience that incorporates video, audio, photos, souvenirs, artifacts, memorabilia, documents, and more. It could be overwhelming, but the curators work to help visitors put the exhibits in perspective. Temporary displays that focus on particular people and topics—the inaugural address, folk art, the president's mother—make good use of the library's collections. Subjects of the permanent exhibits include the Oval Office (with a replica of the room), First Lady Jacqueline Bouvier Kennedy, Attorney General Robert F. Kennedy, and the Cuban Missile Crisis. Before entering the galleries, visitors view a 17-minute film edited to create the illusion that Kennedy himself is narrating an account of his early life. In the next-to-last gallery, news reports of the assassination and its aftermath playing in a loop—Walter Cronkite chokes me up every time. The exhibits end in a huge glass-walled chamber overlooking Dorchester Bay and the Boston skyline.

Columbia Point. ✆ **866/JFK-1960** or 617/514-1600. www.jfklibrary.org. Admission $14 adults, $12 seniors and students with ID, $10 youths 13–17, free for children 12 and under. Surcharges may apply for special exhibitions. Daily 9am–5pm. Closed Jan 1, Thanksgiving, and Dec 25. T: Red Line to JFK/UMass, then take free shuttle bus (every 20 min.). By car, take Southeast Expressway (I-93/ Rte. 3) south to exit 15 (Morrissey Blvd./JFK Library), turn left onto Columbia Rd., and follow signs to free parking lot.

Museum of African American History ★★ MUSEUM   On the North Slope of Beacon Hill, the 1806 **African Meeting House** is the country's oldest extant black church, but it's better known as the "Black Faneuil Hall," in honor of the fact that it once rang with speeches by Frederick Douglass and other prominent abolitionists. The meeting house and the **Abiel Smith School** (1834) make up this fascinating museum, which is the last stop on the **Black Heritage Trail** (p. 72). Along with its campus on Nantucket, the museum tells the story of the free and enslaved blacks who helped shape American history beginning in the colonial era. The Smith School, the first public school built expressly for African-American children, now holds three floors of exhibits. The story they tell makes an important and inspiring complement to the Revolutionary War–era history that dominates downtown Boston. With thoughts of the Underground Railroad in your head, you'll look at Beacon Hill in a new light.

If you are heading here in 2014 or 2015, check ahead for details of the museum's variety of Freedom Rising programs, which commemorate the 150th anniversary of the Civil War.

46 Joy St. ✆ **617/725-0022.** www.maah.org. Admission $5 adults, $3 seniors and youths 13–17, free for children 12 and under. Mon–Sat 10am–4pm. Closed Jan 1, Thanksgiving, and Dec 25. T: Red or Green Line to Park St., Red Line to Charles/MGH, or Blue Line to Bowdoin (weekdays only).

Museum of Science ★★★ MUSEUM   The internet will be your best friend as you plan a visit to this fascinating institution. In addition to buying tickets online, you can check out the hundreds of exhibits and plot a path through the sprawling galleries that lets you explore topics of particular interest to you. To make the most of your time on a single visit, do a little homework.

Refreshingly, that will probably be the only part of this experience that does feel like homework. The point of the museum is to introduce children, the target audience, to important scientific concepts as painlessly as possible. From nanotechnology to dinosaurs, the moon (as a destination) to the sun (as an energy source), everything is fair game. Adults love this place, too—I especially like the **Hall of Human Life,** which explores biology and genetics; **Mapping the World Around Us,** where visitors learn how to create their own maps; and **Catching the Wind,** which uses the museum's own turbines to illuminate wind energy's role in green technology. What do all of these have in common? They use a full range of multimedia displays, participatory exhibits, and hands-on activities to teach without lecturing. Check ahead for details of regularly changing temporary exhibits. high-profile science-oriented touring shows usually make a stop here, so check ahead when you hear about one that interests you.

The IMAX **Mugar Omni Theater ★★★** shows films that focus on the natural world, and the domed **Charles Hayden Planetarium ★★** is also a high-def theater equipped with "immersive video" that schedules laser music shows.

1 Science Park, off O'Brien Hwy. on bridge to Cambridge. ✆ **617/723-2500.** www.mos.org. Admission to exhibit halls $23 adults, $21 seniors, $20 children 3–11, free for children 2 and under; to Butterfly Garden or 3-D Digital Cinema (available only with exhibit hall admission) $6 adults, $5.50 seniors, $5 children 3–11. Admission to Omni Mugar Theater or planetarium $10 adults, $9 seniors, $8 children 3–11, free for children 2 and under. Discounted combination tickets available. July 5–Labor Day Sat–Thurs 9am–7pm, Fri 9am–9pm; day after Labor Day–July 4 Sat–Thurs 9am–5pm, Fri 9am–9pm. Check ahead for extended hours during school vacations. Closed Thanksgiving and Dec 25. T: Green Line to Science Park.

4

New England Aquarium ★ AQUARIUM   In 2013, the aquarium completely overhauled its centerpiece, the aptly named **Giant Ocean Tank.** The 200,000-gallon tank, encircled by a four-story spiral ramp, is now home to an enlarged Caribbean coral reef and more than 1,000 fishes. The best news for visitors is the most apparent: During the overhaul, dozens of viewing windows were replaced with larger, clearer panels. Together, tanks throughout the building house more than 30,000 fish and aquatic mammals, starting just before the entrance with a colony of **Atlantic harbor seals,** identified on panels above their enclosure.

Once inside, the first large exhibit is home to rockhopper, little blue, and African **penguins.** Turn left to visit the 25,000-gallon **Shark and Ray Touch Tank,** where the expansive water surface makes some of the resident animals accessible to visitors who want to "pet" them. Also on this level is a new exhibit, the **Blue Planet Action Center.** It highlights the numerous threats modern human society poses to the oceans, but it's not all bad news—visitors learn about possible remedies and view shark eggs and babies as well as (in a separate enclosure) baby lobsters. Climb the ramp to the third level to reach another touch tank, the **Edge of the Sea** exhibit, with horseshoe crabs, sea stars, and sea urchins. Or head for the back of the ground level and the open-air **New Balance Foundation Marine Mammal Center.** The resident colony of fur seals and sea lions—again, look for their names on the identifying panels around the exhibit—is especially interesting when trainers are working with the animals. Look for the schedule (usually three sessions a day) when you arrive.

In an adjacent building is the separate-admission **Simons IMAX Theatre ★★★,** which screens 3-D films. Check ahead for the schedule, and consider buying a discounted combination ticket.

The aquarium is worth at least a half-day visit; try to get there early. On weekends year-round and every day in the summer, lines can be long and crowds uncomfortably large, leading to frustration and, often, tears. Consider investing in a Boston CityPass or Go Boston Card (see the "Boston Sightseeing Deals" box on p. 70).

Central Wharf (Milk St. and Old Atlantic Ave.). ✆ **617/973-5200.** www.neaq.org. Admission $25 adults, $23 seniors, $18 children 3–11, free for children 2 and under and for those visiting only the outdoor exhibits, cafe, and gift shop. July–Labor Day Sun–Thurs 9am–6pm, Fri–Sat and holidays 9am–7pm; day after Labor Day–June Mon–Fri 9am–5pm, Sat–Sun and holidays 9am–6pm. Simons IMAX Theatre: ✆ **866/815-4629.** Tickets $10–$13 adults, $8–$11 seniors and children 3–11. Daily from 9:30am. Discounted combination tickets available. Closed Thanksgiving and Dec 25 and until noon Jan 1. T: Blue Line to Aquarium.

The Harborwalk & Walk to the Sea

The **Harborwalk** ★★ traces 47 miles of Boston's shoreline, allowing public access to multimillion-dollar views of the water. In theory, it extends from East Boston to Dorchester; in practice, it isn't continuous. Distinctive royal blue signs with a white logo and text point the way along the Harborwalk, which is an ideal route to take from downtown to the Institute of Contemporary Art, in the Seaport District. The ambitious project has been in the works since 1984 and is more than three-quarters complete. Learn more by visiting the website, **www.boston harborwalk.com**, which features a map and a free downloadable audio tour.

Intersecting the Harborwalk is the 1-mile **Norman B. Leventhal Walk to the Sea** ★ (www.walktothesea.com), which begins on Beacon Street in front of the State House and ends at the tip of Long Wharf. It tracks 4 centuries of Boston history with compelling narration on freestanding trail markers; visit the website to download a map and get more information. The Walk to the Sea makes an excellent compromise if you don't have the time or energy to tackle the whole Freedom Trail or Black Heritage Trail, both of which it intersects.

Nichols House Museum ★ HISTORIC HOME   A stroll around Beacon Hill leaves many visitors pining to know what the stately homes look like inside. This grand residence is one of the only places to satisfy that curiosity. The 1804 home, designed by the celebrated architect Charles Bulfinch, holds beautiful antique furnishings, art, carpets, and tapestries collected by several generations of the Nichols family. Its most prominent occupant, Rose Standish Nichols (1872–1960), was a suffragist and a pioneering landscape designer. Her legacy includes not just family heirlooms but objects she brought back from her many travels to the thoroughfare that author Henry James (who lived at no. 131) called "the only respectable street in America."

55 Mount Vernon St. ℂ **617/227-6993.** www.nicholshousemuseum.org. Admission $8, free for children 12 and under. Apr–Oct Tues–Sat 11am–4pm; Nov–Mar Thurs–Sat 11am–4pm; tours every 30 min. T: Red or Green Line to Park St.

Otis House ★★ HISTORIC HOME   Charles Bulfinch designed this gorgeous 1796 mansion for his friends Harrison Gray Otis, an up-and-coming young lawyer who later became mayor of Boston, and his wife, Sally. The 1960s restoration was one of the first in the country to use computer analysis of paint, and the result was revolutionary: It revealed that the walls were drab because the paint had faded, not because the colors started out dingy. Furnished in the style to which a wealthy family in the young United States would have been accustomed, the Federal-style building is a colorful, elegant treasure. Guided tours (the only way to see the property) discuss the architecture of the house and post-Revolutionary social, business, and family life, and touch on the history of the neighborhood.

Tip: **Historic New England** owns and operates the Otis House and dozens of other properties throughout the region. Contact the organization (ℂ 617/227-3956; www.historicnewengland.org) for information on its properties, visiting hours, and admission fees.

141 Cambridge St. (entrance on Lynde St.). ℂ **617/994-5920.** www.historicnewengland.org. Guided tour $10 adults, $9 seniors, $5 students. Wed–Sun 11am–4:30pm; tours every 30 min. T: Blue Line to Bowdoin or Red Line to Charles/MGH.

THE FREEDOM TRAIL

A line of red paint or red brick on the sidewalk, the 2.5-mile **Freedom Trail ★★★** links 16 historic sites, many of them associated with the Revolution and the early days of the United States. The route cuts across downtown and the North End on the way to Charlestown. Markers identify the stops, and plaques point the way from one to the next. For a map of the Freedom Trail, see the inside front cover of this book.

This section lists the stops on the trail in the customary order, from Boston Common to the Bunker Hill Monument. It's important to remember that this is the *suggested* route, laid out after a local journalist cooked up the idea in 1958. Nobody's checking on you. You don't have to visit every stop or even go in order—you can skip around, start in Charlestown and work backward, visit different sights on different days, or even omit some sights. Be flexible, and that goes double if you're traveling with children.

A hard-core history fiend who peers at every artifact and reads every plaque can easily spend 4 hours along the trail. A family with restless kids will probably appreciate the enforced efficiency of a free 90-minute ranger-led tour. Tours leave from the **Boston National Historical Park Visitor Center,** inside Faneuil Hall, Congress Street at North Street (© 617/242-5642; www.nps.gov/bost). Visit the website for schedules and descriptions of the available tours, which run daily from mid-April through November. The first-come, first-served tours are limited to 30 people (rangers distribute stickers starting 30 min. before tour time) and not available in bad weather.

The nonprofit **Freedom Trail Foundation** (© 617/357-8300; www.thefreedom trail.org) and its interactive website are excellent resources as you plan your visit. The foundation's costumed **Freedom Trail Players** lead 90-minute tours (online prices $12 adults, $10 seniors and students, $7 children 6–12) of the trail. You can also buy an MP3 download ($15) of a 2-hour tour narrative, "Walk into History," which was commissioned by the foundation and which includes interviews, sound effects, and music that help bring the sites to life.

The best time to start on the trail is in the morning. During the summer and fall, aim for a weekday if possible. Try not to set out later than midafternoon, because attractions will be closing and you'll run into the evening rush hour.

Boston Common PARK/GARDEN   In 1634, when their settlement was just 4 years old, the town fathers paid the Rev. William Blackstone £30 for this property. In 1640 it was set aside as common land. The 45 or so acres of the country's oldest public park have served as a cow pasture, a military camp, and the site of hangings, protest marches, and visits by dignitaries. The **Frog Pond** makes a pleasant spot to splash around in the summer and skate in the winter. At the Boylston Street side of the Common is the **Central Burying Ground,** where you can see the grave of the famed portraitist Gilbert Stuart. There's also a bandstand where you might take in a free concert or play, and many beautiful shade trees.

Although the city refurbished it recently, the Common still seems run-down (especially compared to the gorgeous Public Garden), but it buzzes with activity all day. You might see a demonstration, a musical performance, a picnic lunch—almost anything other than a cow. Cattle have been banned since 1830, which seems to be one of the few events related to the Common that isn't commemorated with a plaque.

One of the loveliest markers is on this route; head up the hill inside the fence, walking parallel to Park Street. At Beacon Street is the **Shaw Memorial ★★★**, designed by Augustus Saint-Gaudens to celebrate the deeds (indeed, the very existence) of Col. Robert Gould Shaw and the Union Army's **54th Massachusetts Colored Regiment,** who fought in the Civil War. You might remember the story of this American army unit, the first one to be made up of free black soldiers, from the 1989 movie "Glory."

To continue on the Freedom Trail: Cross Beacon Street.

Btw. Beacon, Park, Tremont, Boylston, and Charles sts. Visitor information center: 148 Tremont St. *C* **888/733-2678** or 617/536-4100. www.bostonusa.com. Mon–Fri 8:30am–5pm; Sat–Sun 9am–5pm. T: Green or Red Line to Park St.

Massachusetts State House GOVERNMENT BUILDING   Boston is one of the only American cities where a building whose cornerstone was laid in 1795 (by Gov. Samuel Adams) can be the "new" anything. Nevertheless, this is the new State House, as opposed to the Old State House (see below). The great Federal-era architect Charles Bulfinch designed the central building of the state capitol, and in 1802 copper sheathing manufactured by Paul Revere replaced the shingles on the landmark dome. Gold leaf now covers the dome; during World War II blackouts, it was painted black. The state legislature, or Massachusetts General Court, meets here. The House of Representatives congregates under a wooden fish, the **Sacred Cod,** as a reminder of the importance of fishing to the local economy. Take a self-guided tour, or call ahead to schedule a conducted tour.

Whether or not you go inside, be sure to study some of the many statues outside. The subjects include **Mary Dyer,** a Quaker hanged on the Common in 1660 for refusing to abandon her religious beliefs, and **Pres. John F. Kennedy.** The 60-foot monument at the rear (off Bowdoin St.) illustrates Beacon Hill's original height, before the top was hacked off to use in 19th-century landfill projects.

To continue on the Freedom Trail: Walk down Park Street (which Bulfinch laid out in 1804) to Tremont Street.

Beacon St. at Park St. *C* **617/727-3676.** www.sec.state.ma.us/trs/trsgen/genidx.htm. Mon–Fri 8:45am–5pm. Free tours Mon–Fri 10am–3:30pm. T: Green or Red Line to Park St., or Blue Line to Bowdoin.

Park Street Church CHURCH   Author Henry James called this 1809 structure with a 217-foot steeple "the most interesting mass of bricks and mortar in America." The church has accumulated an impressive number of firsts: The first Protestant missionaries to Hawaii left from here in 1819; the prominent abolitionist William Lloyd Garrison gave his first antislavery speech here on July 4, 1829; and "America" ("My Country 'Tis of Thee") was first sung here on July 4, 1831. You're standing on **"Brimstone Corner,"** named either for the passion of the Congregational ministers who declaimed from the pulpit or for the fact that gunpowder (made from brimstone) was stored in the basement during the War of 1812. This was part of the site of a huge granary (grain storehouse) that became a public building after the Revolutionary War. In the 1790s, the sails for USS *Constitution* ("Old Ironsides") were manufactured in that building.

To continue on the Freedom Trail: Walk away from the Common on Tremont Street.

1 Park St. *C* **617/523-3383.** www.parkstreet.org. Tours late June to Aug Tues–Fri 9am–4pm, Sat 9am–3pm, and by appointment. Sun services year-round 8:30 and 11am, 4pm. T: Green or Red Line to Park St.

Granary Burying Ground ★ CEMETERY   This graveyard, established in 1660, was once part of Boston Common. You'll see the graves of patriots **Samuel Adams, Paul Revere, John Hancock,** and **James Otis;** merchant **Peter Faneuil;** and Benjamin Franklin's parents. Also buried here are the victims of the **Boston Massacre** (see below) and the wife of Isaac Vergoose, who is believed to be **"Mother Goose"** of nursery rhyme fame. Note that gravestone rubbing, however tempting, is illegal in Boston's historic cemeteries.

To continue on the Freedom Trail: Turn left as you leave the cemetery and continue 1½ blocks on Tremont Street.

Tremont St. at Bromfield St. Daily 9am–5pm (until 3pm in winter). T: Green or Red Line to Park St.

King's Chapel and Burying Ground CHURCH/CEMETERY

Architect Peter Harrison sent the plans for this Georgian-style building from Newport, Rhode Island, in 1749. Rather than replacing the existing wooden chapel, the granite edifice was constructed around it. Completed in 1754, it was the first Anglican church in Boston. George III sent gifts, as did Queen Anne and William and Mary, who presented the communion table and chancel tablets (still in use today) before the church was even built. The Puritan colonists had little use for the royal religion; after the Revolution, this became the first Unitarian church in the new nation. Today, the church conducts Unitarian Universalist services using the Anglican Book of Common Prayer. It schedules public concerts (p. 112) every Tuesday at 12:15pm and some Sundays at 5pm.

The **burying ground ★★**, on Tremont Street, is the oldest in the city; it dates to 1630, 56 years before the congregation was organized. Among the colonial headstones (winged skulls are a popular decoration) are the graves of **John Winthrop,** the first governor of the Massachusetts Bay Colony; **William Dawes,** who rode with Paul Revere; **Elizabeth Pain,** the reputed model for Hester Prynne in Nathaniel Hawthorne's novel "The Scarlet Letter"; and **Mary Chilton,** the first female colonist to step ashore on Plymouth Rock.

To continue on the Freedom Trail: Follow the trail back along Tremont Street and turn left onto School Street.

58 Tremont St. ℭ **617/523-1749.** www.kings-chapel.org. Chapel: Summer Sun 1:30–4pm; Mon and Thurs–Sat 10am–4pm; Tues–Wed 10–11:15am and 1:30–4pm. Year-round Sat 10am–4pm. Check website for spring and fall hours. Closed to casual tourists during religious services. $2 donation suggested. Services Sun 11am, Wed 12:15pm. Burying ground: Daily 8am–5:30pm (until 3pm in winter). T: Orange or Blue Line to State.

First Public School/Benjamin Franklin Statue MONUMENT/MEMORIAL

A colorful folk-art **mosaic** embedded in the sidewalk marks the site of the first public school in the country. Founded in 1634, 2 years before Harvard College, the school educated Samuel Adams, Benjamin Franklin, John Hancock, and Cotton Mather. The original building (1645) was demolished to make way for the expansion of King's Chapel, and the school moved across the street. Other alumni include Charles Bulfinch, Ralph Waldo Emerson, George Santayana, Arthur Fiedler, and Leonard Bernstein. Now called Boston Latin School, the prestigious institution later moved to the Fenway neighborhood and started admitting girls.

Behind the fence in the courtyard to your left is the **Benjamin Franklin statue,** the first portrait statue erected in Boston (1856). Franklin was born in Boston in 1706 and was apprenticed to his half-brother James, a printer, but they fought constantly. In 1723, Benjamin ran away to Philadelphia. Plaques on the base of the statue describe Franklin's numerous accomplishments. The lovely granite Second Empire–style building behind the statue is **Old City Hall** (1865), designed by Arthur Gilman (who laid out the Back Bay) and Gridley J. F. Bryant. The administration moved to Government Center in 1969, and the building now houses commercial tenants.

To continue on the Freedom Trail: Follow School Street to Washington Street.

School St. at City Hall Ave. (btw. Tremont and Washington sts.). T: Blue or Orange Line to State.

Old Corner Bookstore Building ARCHITECTURE   Built in 1718, this building stands on a plot of land that was once home to the religious reformer Anne Hutchinson, who was excommunicated and expelled from Boston in 1638 for heresy. In the 19th century, the brick building held the publishing house of Ticknor & Fields, which effectively made this the literary center of America. Publisher James "Jamie" Fields counted among his friends Henry Wadsworth Longfellow, James Russell Lowell, Henry David Thoreau, Ralph Waldo Emerson, Nathaniel Hawthorne, and Harriet Beecher Stowe.

To continue on the Freedom Trail: Turn right and walk 1 block.

3 School St. T: Blue or Orange Line to State.

Old South Meeting House ★ HISTORIC SITE   Look for the beautifully restored clock tower that tops this religious and political gathering place, best known as the site of an important event that led to the Revolution. On December 16, 1773, a restive crowd of several thousand, too big to fit into Faneuil Hall, gathered here. They were waiting for word from the governor about whether three ships full of tea—priced to undercut the cost of smuggled tea and force the colonists to trade with merchants approved by the Crown—would be sent back to England from Boston. The ships were not, and revolutionaries haphazardly disguised as Mohawks cast the tea into the harbor. The meetinghouse commemorates that uprising, the **Boston Tea Party.** You can even see a vial of the tea.

Originally built in 1669 and replaced by the current structure in 1729, the building underwent extensive renovations in the 1990s. In 1872, a devastating fire that destroyed most of downtown stopped at Old South, a phenomenon considered evidence of the building's power. The exhibit **"Voices of Protest"** tells the story of the events that unfolded here.

The meetinghouse frequently schedules speeches, readings, panel discussions, and children's activities, often with a colonial theme. Every December 16, it stages a reenactment of the debate that led to the Tea Party—it's especially fun for kids, who can participate in the heated debate. Check ahead for schedules.

To continue on the Freedom Trail: Exit through the gift shop and look across Milk Street to see **Benjamin Franklin's birthplace.** In a little house at 17 Milk St., Franklin was born in 1706, the 15th child of Josiah Franklin. The house is long gone, but look at the second floor of what's now 1 Milk St. When the building went up after the Great Fire of 1872, the architect guaranteed that the Founding Father wouldn't be forgotten: A bust and the words BIRTHPLACE OF FRANKLIN adorn the facade.

Now backtrack on Washington Street (passing Spring Lane, one of the first streets in Boston and originally the site of a real spring) and follow it to State Street.

310 Washington St. ⓒ **617/482-6439.** www.osmh.org. Admission $6 adults, $5 seniors and students with ID, $1 children 6–17, free for children 5 and under. Freedom Trail ticket (with Old State House and Paul Revere House; available Apr–Nov) $13 adults, $3 children. Daily Apr–Oct 9:30am–5pm; Nov–Mar 10am–4pm. Closed Jan 1, Thanksgiving, Dec 24–25. T: Blue or Orange Line to State St.

Old State House Museum ★ MUSEUM   Did you know that Paul Revere didn't say "The British are coming"? Even rebellious colonists generally considered themselves British, as the newest Old State House Museum exhibit will remind you. **"A British Town: The Council Chamber in Boston before the American Revolution,"** which opened in 2014, re-creates the appearance of the royal governor's meeting room in this building during the 1760s. Other exhibits in the museum, which the Bostonian Society runs, include a fun interactive experience that focuses on the building's history, and a multimedia presentation exploring the Boston Massacre. A Paul Revere print depicting the Massacre is on view, as is tea from the Boston Tea Party. Changing exhibits focus on other topics that help explain the evolution of Boston, using the society's historic photographs and artifacts. Explore on your own or take a 20-minute guided tour, available every hour on the hour.

The 1713 Old State House, a little brick building, is itself an artifact. After the Revolution, it was the state capitol until 1798. The lion and unicorn—symbols of British rule—on the facade are replicas of the originals, which the new Americans burned the day the Declaration of Independence was first read in Boston.

To continue on the Freedom Trail: Leave the building, turn left, and walk half a block.

206 Washington St. (C) **617/720-1713.** www.bostonhistory.org. Admission $10 adults, $8.50 seniors and students, free for children 18 and under. Freedom Trail ticket (with Old South Meeting House and Paul Revere House; available Apr–Nov) $13 adults, $3 children. June–Aug daily 9am–6pm; Sept–Mar daily 9am–5pm. Closed Jan 1, first week of Feb, Thanksgiving, Dec 25. T: Blue or Orange Line to State.

Boston Massacre Site MONUMENT/MEMORIAL A ring of cobblestones marks the location of the skirmish that helped consolidate the spirit of rebellion in the colonies. On March 5, 1770, angered at the presence of royal troops in Boston, colonists threw snowballs, garbage, rocks, and other debris at a group of redcoats. The soldiers panicked and fired into the crowd, killing five men. Their graves, including that of Crispus Attucks, the first black man to die in the Revolution, are in the Granary Burying Ground.

To continue on the Freedom Trail: Turn left onto Congress Street and walk down the hill, covering 1 long block. Faneuil Hall will be on your right.

State St. at Devonshire St. T: Blue or Orange Line to State.

Faneuil Hall ★ HISTORIC SITE   Built in 1742 (and enlarged using a Charles Bulfinch design in 1805), this building was a gift to Boston from prosperous merchant Peter Faneuil. This "Cradle of Liberty" rang with speeches by orators such as Samuel Adams—whose statue stands outside the Congress Street entrance—in the years leading to the Revolution. Abolitionists, temperance advocates, and suffragists also used the hall as a pulpit. The upstairs is still a public meeting and concert hall. Downstairs is the visitor center for the downtown part of the **Boston National Historical Park.** It has exhibits focusing on Boston history and—in keeping with the nearly 3-century history of retail in this space—a bookstore.

National Park Service rangers give **free historical talks** every half-hour from 9am to 5pm in the second-floor auditorium.

To continue on the Freedom Trail: Leave Faneuil Hall, cross North Street, and follow the trail through the "Blackstone Block." These buildings, among the oldest in the city, give a sense of the scale of 18th- and 19th-century Boston. In the park at the corner of North and Union streets are two sculptures of legendary Boston mayor (and congressman and federal prisoner) **James Michael Curley,** the inspiration for the protagonist of Edwin O'Connor's 1956 novel "The Last Hurrah." Beyond the sculptures, you'll see six tall glass columns arranged parallel to Union Street. Pause here.

Dock Sq. (Congress St. and North St.). (C) **617/242-5642.** www.nps.gov/bost. Free admission. Daily 9am–5pm; no public access during special events. T: Green or Orange Line to Haymarket.

The New England Holocaust Memorial ★★ MONUMENT/MEMORIAL   Erected in 1995, these six glass towers designed by Stanley Saitowitz spring up in the midst of attractions that celebrate freedom, reminding us of the consequences of its absence. The pattern on the glass, which at first appears merely decorative, is actually 6 million random numbers, one for each Jew who died during the Holocaust. As you pass through, pause to read the inscriptions.

To continue on the Freedom Trail: Follow Hanover Street across the Rose Kennedy Greenway to reach the North End, which begins at Cross Street. Take Hanover Street 1 block to Richmond Street, passing the post office on your right. Turn right, go 1 block, and turn left.

Union St. btw. North and Hanover sts. ℗ **617/457-8698.** www.nehm.org. T: Orange or Green Line to Haymarket.

Paul Revere House ★★★ HISTORIC HOME   One of the most pleasant stops on the Freedom Trail, this 2½-story wood structure presents history on a human scale. Revere (1734–1818) was living here when he set out for Lexington on April 18, 1775, a feat immortalized in Henry Wadsworth Longfellow's poem "Paul Revere's Ride" ("Listen my children and you shall hear / Of the midnight ride of Paul Revere"). Inside are neatly arranged and identified 17th- and 18th-century furnishings and artifacts, including the famous Revere silver, considered some of the finest anywhere. The oldest house in downtown Boston, it was built around 1680, bought by Revere in 1770, and put to a number of uses before being turned into a museum in 1908.

The thought-provoking tour is self-guided, with staff members around in case you have questions. The format allows you to linger on the artifacts that hold your interest. Revere and his two wives had a total of 16 children—he called them "my lambs"—and he supported the family with a thriving silversmith's trade. At his home, you'll get a good sense of the risks he took in the run-up to the Revolutionary War. Across the courtyard is the home of Revere's Hichborn cousins, the **Pierce/Hichborn House ★**. The 1711 Georgian-style home is a rare example of 18th-century middle-class architecture. It's suitably furnished and shown only by guided tour (usually twice a day at busy times). Contact the Paul Revere House for schedules and reservations.

A new **Education and Visitor Center,** in an 1835 building adjoining the house, is slated to open in late 2014. The center will give visitors with disabilities access to the second floor of the Revere House.

Before you leave North Square, look across the cobblestone plaza at **Sacred Heart Church.** It was established in 1833 as the Seamen's Bethel, a church that ministered to the mariners who frequented the area. Wharves ran up almost this far in colonial days; in the 19th century, this was a notorious red-light district.

To continue on the Freedom Trail: The trail leaves the square on Prince Street and runs along Hanover Street past Clark Street. (The first church you see, on Hanover St., is St. Stephen's.) Before turning onto Prince Street, take a few steps down Garden Court Street and look for no. 4, on the right. The private residence was the birthplace of Rose Fitzgerald, later Rose Kennedy, Pres. John F. Kennedy's mother.

19 North Sq. ℗ **617/523-2338.** www.paulreverehouse.org. Admission $3.50 adults, $3 seniors and students, $1 children 5–17, free for children 4 and under. Freedom Trail ticket (with Old South Meeting House and Old State House; available Apr–Nov) $13 adults, $3 children. Apr 15–Oct daily 9:30am–5:15pm; Apr 1–14 and Nov–Dec daily 9:30am–4:15pm; Jan–Mar Tues–Sun 9:30am–4:15pm. Closed Jan 1, Thanksgiving, and Dec 25. T: Green or Orange Line to Haymarket, or Blue Line to Aquarium.

James Rego Square (Paul Revere Mall) PARK/GARDEN   A pleasant brick-paved park also known as "the Prado," the mall holds a famous equestrian statue of Paul Revere—a great photo op. Take time to read some of the **tablets ★** on the left-hand wall that describe famous people and places in the history of the North End.

To continue on the Freedom Trail: Walk around the fountain and continue to Salem Street, heading toward the steeple of the Old North Church.

Hanover St. at Clark St. T: Green or Orange Line to Haymarket.

Old North Church ★ CHURCH   Look up! In this building's original steeple, sexton Robert Newman hung two lanterns on the night of April 18, 1775, to signal Paul Revere that British troops were setting out for Lexington and Concord in boats across the Charles River, not on foot. We know that part of the story in Longfellow's words: "One if by land, and two if by sea."

Officially named Christ Church, this is the oldest church building in Boston (1723). The design is in the style of Sir Christopher Wren. The 190-foot spire, long a reference point for sailors, appears on navigational charts to this day.

Members of the Revere family attended this church; their plaque is on pew 54. Famous visitors have included presidents James Monroe, Theodore Roosevelt, Calvin Coolidge, Franklin D. Roosevelt, and Gerald R. Ford; and Queen Elizabeth II. Markers and plaques appear throughout; note the bust of George Washington, reputedly the first memorial to the first president. The **gardens** ★ on the north side of the church (dotted with more plaques) are open to the public. On the south side of the church, volunteers maintain an 18th-century garden.

Free presentations that introduce the self-guided tour begin periodically during open hours year-round. For a more complete look at the church, take a **Behind the Scenes tour** ($8 adults, $6 seniors and students, $5 children 11 and under). The tour includes visits to the steeple and the crypt. It's offered on weekends in March, daily from April through December, and the rest of the year by appointment. Tickets are available in the gift shop.

To continue on the Freedom Trail: Cross Salem Street onto Hull Street and walk uphill toward Copp's Hill Burying Ground. On the left you'll pass 44 Hull St., a fine example of the phenomenon known as the "spite house," which is built to annoy neighbors by cutting off a view, for instance. The 10-foot-wide house is the narrowest in Boston.

193 Salem St. ✆ **617/523-6676.** www.oldnorth.com. $3 donation requested. Jan–Feb Tues–Sun 10am–4pm; Mar–May daily 9am–5pm; June–Oct daily 9am–6pm; Nov–Dec daily 9:30am–4:30pm. Closed to visitors Thanksgiving, Dec 25. Services (Episcopal) Sun 9 and 11am, Thurs 6pm. T: Orange or Green Line to Haymarket.

Copp's Hill Burying Ground ★ CEMETERY   Boston's second-oldest cemetery (1659) is the burial place of Cotton Mather and his family, the sexton Robert Newman, and Prince Hall. Hall, a prominent member of the free black community that occupied the north slope of the hill in colonial times, fought at Bunker Hill and established the first black Masonic lodge. The highest point in the North End, Copp's Hill was the site of a windmill and of the British batteries that destroyed the village of Charlestown during the Battle of Bunker Hill on June 17, 1775. Charlestown is clearly visible (look for the masts of the USS *Constitution*) across the Inner Harbor. No gravestone rubbing is allowed.

To continue on the Freedom Trail: Follow Hull Street down the hill to Commercial Street (be careful crossing Commercial at the dangerous intersection with Hull) and follow the trail to North Washington Street, then across the bridge to Charlestown. Signs and the trail lead to the Charlestown Navy Yard.

Off Hull St. near Snowhill St. Daily 9am–5pm (until 3pm in winter). T: Green or Orange Line to North Station.

USS Constitution ★★ HISTORIC SITE In 2015, 200 years after retiring from combat with an undefeated record, **"Old Ironsides"** will enter dry dock for 3 years of restoration. You'll still be able to view the lovely black-hulled vessel, one of the U.S. Navy's six original frigates; check ahead to see whether guided 30-minute tours, led by active-duty sailors in 1812 dress uniforms, are available during your visit. Before boarding, all visitors aged 18 and up must show a government photo ID and pass through security. *Tip:* If you're traveling with kids, be sure to check out the interactive site **www.asailorslifeforme.org** before you visit.

The ship was constructed in the North End from 1794 to 1797 at a cost of $302,718 (about $4 million in current dollars, adjusted for inflation), using bolts, spikes, and other fittings from Paul Revere's foundry. As the United States built its naval and military reputation, the *Constitution* battled French privateers and Barbary pirates, repelling the British fleet during the War of 1812, participating in 33 engagements, and capturing 20 vessels. The frigate earned its nickname during a battle on August 19, 1812, when shots from HMS *Guerriere* bounced off its thick oak hull as if it were iron.

In 1830, Oliver Wendell Holmes's poem "Old Ironsides" helped launch a preservation movement that rescued the frigate from destruction. When the *Constitution* is afloat, tugs tow it into the harbor every **Fourth of July** for its celebratory "turnaround cruise," which includes a naturalization ceremony for new U.S. citizens.

Adjacent to the ship in Building 5, National Park Service rangers staff the **Navy Yard Visitor Center** (☎ 617/242-5601; www.nps.gov/bost), where a 10-minute video about the history of the installation runs in a loop.

To continue on the Freedom Trail: Walk straight ahead to the museum entrance.

Charlestown Navy Yard. ☎ **617/242-7511.** www.history.navy.mil/ussconstitution. Free tours. Apr–Sept Tues–Sun 10am–6pm; Oct Tues–Sun 10am–4pm; Nov–Mar Thurs–Sun 10am–4pm. Year-round tours every 30 min. until 30 min. before closing, subject to dry-dock-related closings. Closed Jan 1, Presidents Day, Thanksgiving, and Dec 25. T: Ferry from Long Wharf (Blue Line to Aquarium); or Green or Orange Line to North Station, then a 10-min. walk.

USS Constitution Museum ★ MUSEUM With the *Constitution* in dry dock from 2015 through 2018, the museum is even more important in helping visitors experience the early days of the U.S. Navy. In the first-floor galleries, visitors can watch a 19-minute video and learn more about the *Constitution*'s history, perhaps with help from an interactive computer display or one of the staff members and volunteers who answer questions and give brief, informative talks. The second floor is where the action is: The exhibit **"All Hands on Deck: A Sailor's Life in 1812"** is an interactive delight, especially for kids. Visitors learn about working the lines that control a frigate's sails, firing a cannon, and even relaxing in a hammock (that one's pretty self-explanatory). Allow at least an hour to explore the timelines, try the hands-on activities, and check out the fascinating artifacts, including gorgeous model ships.

To continue on the Freedom Trail: Follow the trail up Constitution Road, crossing Chelsea Street, and continue to the Bunker Hill Monument. A more interesting, slightly longer route runs from Chelsea Street and Rutherford Avenue (back where you entered Charlestown) across City Square Park and up Main Street to Monument Street.

Off First Ave., Charlestown Navy Yard. ☎ **617/426-1812.** www.ussconstitutionmuseum.org. Free admission; suggested donation $5–$10 adults, $3–$5 children, $15–$20 families. Apr–Oct daily 9am–6pm; Nov–Mar daily 10am–5pm. Closed Jan 1, Thanksgiving, and Dec 25. T: Ferry from Long Wharf (Blue Line to Aquarium), or Green or Orange Line to North Station, then a 10-min. walk.

Bunker Hill Monument MONUMENT/MEMORIAL   The 221-foot granite obelisk, a landmark that's visible from miles away, honors the memory of the colonists who died in the Battle of Bunker Hill on June 17, 1775. The rebels lost the battle, but nearly half the British troops were killed or wounded, a loss that contributed to their leaders' decision to abandon Boston 9 months later. The Marquis de Lafayette, the celebrated hero of the American and French revolutions, helped lay the monument's cornerstone in 1825. He is buried in Paris under soil taken from the hill. A punishing flight of 294 steps leads to the top of the monument. It's not a can't-miss experience unless you're traveling with children you'd like to tire out. There's no elevator, and although the views of the harbor and the Zakim–Bunker Hill Bridge are good, the windows are quite small. *Note:* Depending on visitor traffic, you may need to present a climbing pass before entering the monument; check ahead.

Across the street is the excellent ranger-staffed **Battle of Bunker Hill Museum ★**, 43 Monument Sq. (at Monument Ave.). The centerpiece is a panoramic mural that depicts the battle in not-too-gory detail, accompanied by displays and dioramas that help set the scene.

To return to downtown Boston: From the Charlestown Navy Yard, a **ferry** to Long Wharf leaves every half-hour from 6:45am to 8:15pm on weekdays (every 15 min. 6:45–9:15am and 3:45–6:45pm), and every half-hour on the quarter-hour from 10:15am to 6:15pm on weekends. The 10-minute trip costs $3 (or show your Link-Pass), and the dock is an easy walk from "Old Ironsides." Alternatively, walk to Main Street, at the foot of Bunker Hill, and take **bus no. 92** toward Haymarket (Green or Orange Line).

Monument Sq., Charlestown. ℂ **617/242-5641.** www.nps.gov/bost. Free admission. Monument daily 9am–4:30pm (until 5:30pm July–Aug). Museum daily 9am–5pm (until 6pm July–Aug). T: Orange Line to Community College, 10-min. walk.

Back Bay & Vicinity

Boston's best-known park is the spectacular **Public Garden ★★★**, bordered by Arlington, Boylston, Charles, and Beacon streets. Something lovely is in bloom at the country's first botanical garden at least half the year. The spring flowers are particularly impressive, especially if your visit happens to coincide with the first really warm days of the year. It's hard not to enjoy yourself when everyone around you seems ecstatic just to be seeing the sun.

For many Bostonians, the official beginning of spring coincides with the return of the **Swan Boats ★★** (ℂ **617/522-1966;** www.swanboats.com). Although the Swan Boats don't move fast, they'll transport you. The pedal-powered vessels—the attendants pedal, not the passengers—plunge into the lagoon on the Saturday before Patriots' Day, the third Monday of April. The surrounding greenery and placid water help lend a 19th-century aura to the attraction, which the Paget family has operated since 1877. They operate daily from 10am to 5pm in the summer, daily from 10am to 4pm in the spring, and weekdays noon to 4pm and weekends 10am to 4pm from the day after Labor Day to mid-September. The cost for the 15-minute ride is $3 for adults, $2.50 for seniors, $1.50 for children 2 to 15, free for kids under 2.

Boston Public Library LIBRARY   The central branch of the city's library system is an architectural and intellectual monument. The original 1895 building, a National Historic Landmark designed by Charles F. McKim, is an Italian Renaissance–style masterpiece that fairly drips with art. The **lobby doors** are the work of Daniel Chester French (who also designed the Abraham Lincoln statue in the memorial in

Washington, the "Minute Man" statue in Concord, and the John Harvard statue in Cambridge). The **murals** are by John Singer Sargent and Pierre Puvis de Chavannes, among others. Visit the lovely **courtyard ★** or peek at it from a window on the stairs. The adjoining addition, of the same height and material (pink granite), was designed by Philip Johnson and opened in 1972. Ask the staff at the information desk about changing exhibits. The **Courtyard** restaurant serves lunch Monday through Friday and afternoon tea Wednesday through Friday, and the **Map Room Café** is open Monday through Saturday 9am to 5pm.

Free **Art & Architecture Tours** (www.bpl.org/central/tours.htm) run daily; check the schedule on the website.

700 Boylston St., Copley Sq. 🕐 **617/536-5400.** www.bpl.org. Free admission. Mon–Thurs 9am–9pm; Fri–Sat 9am–5pm; Sun 1–5pm. Closed Sun June–Sept and legal holidays. T: Green Line to Copley.

Gibson House Museum ★ HISTORIC HOME   Virtually unchanged since 1954, when the last member of the family that owned it died, the 1859 Gibson House is never the same twice—you always notice something new. That's because the lovely brownstone holds so much *stuff*, from paintings and sculpture to an ornate high chair to a straw boater hat. The tour covers both the family chambers and the rooms where the servants toiled—think "Downton Abbey" with different accents. Check ahead for the schedule of lectures and other special events.

137 Beacon St. 🕐 **617/267-6338.** www.thegibsonhouse.org. Admission $9 adults, $6 seniors and students, $3 children under 12. Tours on the hour Wed–Sun 1–3pm. Closed Jan 1, July 4, Thanksgiving, and Dec 25. T: Green Line to Arlington.

Isabella Stewart Gardner Museum ★★   The transformation of the Gardner Museum since 2012, when the then-109-year-old museum opened its first addition, has been nothing short of astounding. In 2014, the Gardner mounted its first fashion exhibition, and in 2015 it's planning shows that focus on the contemporary French artist Jean-Michel Othoniel and on Renaissance painter Carlo Crivelli. How can this be, if the terms of founder Isabella Stewart Gardner's will famously forbid changes to the 1903 museum? A dramatic addition designed by Renzo Piano takes the pressure off the main building, originally called Fenway Court and built in the style of a Venetian *palazzo* around a greenery-filled courtyard. The new building holds the everyday functions—the entrance, administrative offices, cafe, and gift shop, plus gallery space and a concert hall. Problem solved.

Gardner (1840–1924) was a prominent patron of the arts—and the Red Sox—who moved to Boston as a bride and shook up the stuffy establishment. Her legacy is a beloved symbol of her adopted city, overflowing with art from Europe, America, and Asia as well as furniture and architectural details from European churches and palaces, all painstakingly arranged just as you see it today. The art historian Bernard Berenson consulted on the acquisitions of work by artists such as Botticelli, Raphael, Rembrandt, Matisse, Whistler, Sargent, and, notably, Titian—many scholars acknowledge Gardner's **"Europa"** as his finest work.

At the heart of Fenway Court, which opened as a museum after Mrs. Gardner's death, is the magnificent skylit **courtyard,** filled year-round with fresh flowers from the museum's own greenhouses.

280 the Fenway (btw. Evans Way and Palace Rd.; enter from Evans Way). 🕐 **617/566-1401.** www.gardnermuseum.org. Admission $15 adults, $12 seniors, $5 college students with ID. Free for children 17 and under, and adults named Isabella with ID. Wed and Fri–Mon 11am–5pm, Thu 11am–9pm. Closed July 4, Thanksgiving, and Dec 25. T: Green Line E to Museum of Fine Arts.

Museum of Fine Arts ★★★ MUSEUM   One fact says volumes about the MFA's philosophy: In 2014, the museum staged its first crowdsourced exhibit. Far from being stuffy or exclusive, the institution strives to make itself as user-friendly as possible—even if it that means running an online popularity contest that ends with the winners featured on both a museum wall and Pinterest. (In something of an upset, van Gogh beat out Monet for the top spot.)

Renovated galleries housing French Impressionist and post-Impressionist works and the arts of the Pacific also opened in 2014, but they were somewhat overshadowed by the debut of the **Kunstkammer Gallery.** Translated as "collector's cabinet," a *Kunstkammer* is more like a treasure chest. Trendy 17th-century aristocrats showed off their collections of natural and manufactured objects in these rooms; this gallery's displays include intricate clocks, automata (think Hugo Cabret), and even some 21st-century artifacts: iPads.

The museum is still refining its sprawling **Art of the Americas Wing ★★★**, which transformed the institution when it opened in 2010. Considering the scope of the collections, it's no surprise that some visitors park themselves here, among some of the MFA's best-known and best-loved works (by Gilbert Stuart, John Singleton Copley, and Childe Hassam, among many, many others). Others prefer to concentrate on the **Impressionist ★★★** holdings (including works by Gaugin, Degas, and Renoir, and dozens of Monets), Asian and Old Kingdom Egyptian collections, classical art, American furniture and silver, prints, photographs, and decorative arts. Still others, traveling with their kids, concentrate on the numerous family-friendly displays and programs.

If you can't decide, do yourself a favor and don't try to see everything on your own. Take a free **guided tour** (daily except Mon holidays) that concentrates on a particular topic or focuses on the highlights of the collections (daily 10:30am and 1:30pm, Wed 6:15pm). The expensive-but-worth-it admission fee (which covers two visits within 10 days) is an investment, and you'll want to make the most of it. A Boston CityPass or Go Boston Card (see the "Boston Sightseeing Deals" box on p. 70) can give you a break on the ticket price.

Visitors enter the museum from Huntington Avenue or the Fenway; leave the Green Line and backtrack about a half-block, pausing to admire the sculpture on the lawns. The Sharf Information Center distributes floor plans and is the meeting place for guided tours (see above). The museum has a cafeteria, two cafes, and a fine-dining restaurant, two excellent gift shops (plus satellites when large traveling exhibitions are in town), and two auditoriums.

The interactive website is invaluable as you organize your visit. Check the website ahead to locate pieces and galleries that interest you, and note the schedules of tours and special exhibitions. During the lifespan of this book, they will include **"Gold and the Gods: Jewels of Ancient Nubia"** (through 2017) and **"Gordon Parks: Back to Fort Scott"** (Jan 17–Sept 13, 2015).

465 Huntington Ave. ℂ **617/267-9300** or 617/369-3395 (tour info). www.mfa.org. Admission $25 adults, $23 students and seniors, $10 children 7–17 on school days after 3pm (otherwise free), free for children 6 and under. Admission good for 2 visits within 10 days. Voluntary contribution ($25 suggested) Wed after 4pm. Free admission to Museum Shop, library, and restaurants. Sat–Tues 10am–4:45pm; Wed–Fri 10am–9:45pm. Closed Jan 1, Patriots' Day, July 4, Thanksgiving, and Dec 25. T: Green Line E to Museum of Fine Arts or Orange Line to Ruggles.

Skywalk Observatory at the Prudential Center ★★ OBSERVATORY   The enclosed observation deck on the 50th floor of the Prudential Tower offers a 360-degree view of Boston and far beyond. You can see for miles, even (when it's clear) as far as the mountains of New Hampshire to the north and the beaches of Cape Cod to the southeast. Away from the windows, interactive audiovisual exhibits chronicle the city's history, and two short films screen in the on-site theater. Also here are fascinating exhibits, including video presentations about refugees, on the history of immigration to Boston. The admission price includes a narrated audio tour, available in versions targeted to adults and children. Call before visiting, because the space sometimes closes for private events.

800 Boylston St. (at Fairfield St.). © **617/859-0648.** www.topofthehub.net/skywalk.php. Admission $16 adults, $13 seniors and college students with ID, $11 children 6th grade and under. Mar–Oct daily 10am–10pm; Nov–Feb daily 10am–8pm. T: Green Line E to Prudential.

Cambridge

Boston and Cambridge are so closely associated that many people believe they're the same place—a notion that both cities' residents and politicians are happy to dispel. Cambridge is a separate city, with a number of appealing attractions and a fun, youthful vibe that sets it apart from its (relatively) more serious neighbor. Cantabrigians are often considered more liberal and educated than Bostonians, which is another idea that's sure to get you involved in a lively discussion.

HARVARD SQUARE & VICINITY

"The Square" is a busy crossroads where college and high school students, professors and instructors, commuters, street performers, and sightseers mingle. Visit the **Cambridge Visitor's Information Center** kiosk, near the T entrance in the middle of Harvard Square at the intersection of Massachusetts Avenue, John F. Kennedy Street, and Brattle Street, where trained volunteers dispense maps and brochures and answer questions Monday through Friday from 9am to 5pm, Saturday and Sunday from 1 to 5pm. The website of the Cambridge Office for Tourism (www.cambridgeusa.org), which operates the booth, lists organized tours.

Stores and restaurants line all three streets that spread out from the center of Harvard Square and the streets that intersect them. If you follow **Brattle Street** to the residential area just outside the square, you'll arrive at a part of town known as **"Tory Row"** because many residents were loyal to King George during the Revolution.

Harvard University

Free student-led tours of the Harvard campus leave from the **Information Center** in the Smith Campus Center, 1350 Massachusetts Ave. (© **617/495-1573;** www.harvard. edu/visitors). Call or surf ahead for times; reservations aren't necessary, but there are no tours during exams or between semesters. The Information Center is open Monday through Saturday 9am to 5pm and has maps, illustrated booklets, and self-guided walking-tour directions in nine languages, as well as a bulletin board where flyers publicize campus activities. The website includes links to audio tours and an app with a mobile tour.

Harvard Museum of Natural History and Peabody Museum of Archaeology & Ethnology ★ MUSEUM The best-known exhibit at the Harvard Museum of Natural History is, by far, the **Glass Flowers ★★★**. From 1887 to 1936, German father and son Leopold and Rudolf Blaschka created the 3,000 astonishingly accurate models of 847 plant species, and they have entranced museum visitors for decades. In 2014, the HMNH introduced the Blaschkas to a new audience with the opening of **Sea Creatures in Glass,** an exhibition devoted to marine invertebrates. These models predate the Glass Flowers, but they show the same artistry in every waving tentacle.

To reach the Blaschka collections, visitors must climb (or ride) to the third floor of the museum. Take it slow and explore the galleries, especially if you're traveling with kids; they may not care about glass models, but they're sure to find a friend in the **zoological collections ★★**, which preserve creatures of all sizes, from insects to dinosaurs. Thoughtfully curated and dotted with engaging interactive, hands-on, and multimedia displays, the museum is just the right size for a visit of a half-day or longer.

From the third floor, you'll have direct access to the galleries of the **Peabody Museum of Archaeology & Ethnology ★**. Rather than trying to define "ethnology," I've described this museum to young visitors by saying that it's like a natural history museum with people instead of animals. You might see dazzling contemporary and historical photographs, items recovered during an archeological dig, or an artifact of an indigenous culture, such as a magnificent totem pole. In the engrossing **Hall of the North American Indian,** 500 artifacts from 10 cultures tell hundreds of stories.

Both museums schedule numerous special events and programs; check ahead. The websites provide copious information to help all visitors, especially families, make the most of their time.

Harvard Museum of Natural History: 26 Oxford St. ⓒ **617/495-3045.** www.hmnh.harvard.edu. Peabody Museum: 11 Divinity Ave. ⓒ **617/496-1027.** www.peabody.harvard.edu. Admission to both $12 adults, $10 seniors and students, $8 children 3–18, free for children 2 and under. Check website for free hours for MA residents. Daily 9am–5pm. Closed Jan 1, Thanksgiving, Dec 24–25. T: Red Line to Harvard. Cross Harvard Yard, keeping John Harvard statue on right. Exit Harvard Yard; facing the Science Center, bear right as you cross the plaza. First left is Oxford St. Check website for parking info.

Harvard Art Museums ★★ MUSEUM   After more than 6 years under renovation, the **Fogg Museum,** the **Busch-Reisinger Museum,** and the **Arthur M. Sackler Museum** are on schedule to reopen in late 2014. The institutions' new configuration has been clear for a while—there's glass everywhere. The Renzo Piano Building Workshop designed the renovation and expansion, building on the original 1925 design by Coolidge, Shepley, Bulfinch & Abbott. The Fogg is at the center of the complex, and at the center of the Fogg is the **Calderwood Courtyard,** which is open to the public free of charge. The dramatic space, with graceful travertine arches and columns below and soaring glass panels above, is breathtaking. You can also check out the new cafe and shop without paying for admission, but think twice: The collections of American, European, and especially Asian art make this one of the best small museums in the country.

32 Quincy St. and 485 Broadway. ⓒ **617/495-9400.** www.harvardartmuseums.org. Check ahead for open days and hours, admission fees, and parking information. T: Red Line to Harvard, cross Harvard Yard diagonally from the T station and exit onto Quincy St., turn left, and walk to the next corner. Or turn your back on the Coop and follow Massachusetts Ave. to Quincy St., then turn left and walk 1 long block to Broadway.

Longfellow House–Washington's Headquarters National Historic Site ★ HISTORIC HOME   This lovely yellow mansion was the longtime home of Henry Wadsworth Longfellow (1807–82). The poet first lived here as a boarder in 1837. When he and Fanny Appleton married, in 1843, her father made the stately 1759 house a wedding present. The furnishings and books inside are original to Longfellow, who lived here until his death, and his descendants. During the siege of Boston in 1775–76, the house served as the headquarters of Gen. George Washington, with whom Longfellow was fascinated. On a tour—the only way to see the house—you'll learn about the history of the building and its famous occupants. The gardens and grounds are a good refuge after some time in busy Harvard Square.

105 Brattle St. (at Longfellow Park). $©$ **617/876-4491.** www.nps.gov/long. Free admission and tours. House late May to Oct Wed–Sun 9:30am–4:30pm; tours on the hour, 10am–4pm. Closed Nov to late May. Gardens and grounds daily dawn–dusk. T: Red Line to Harvard, then 10-min. walk on Brattle St.

Mount Auburn Cemetery ★★ CEMETERY   Three important colonial burying grounds—Granary, King's Chapel, and Copp's Hill—are in Boston (see "The Freedom Trail," earlier in this chapter), but the most famous cemetery in the area is in Cambridge.

Mount Auburn Cemetery, the final resting place of many well-known Americans, is also famous simply for existing. Dedicated in 1831, it was the first of the country's rural, or garden, cemeteries. The establishment of burying places removed from city centers reflected practical and philosophical concerns: Development was encroaching on urban graveyards, and the ideas associated with Transcendentalism and the Greek revival gave communing with nature precedence over organized religion. Since the day it opened, Mount Auburn has been a popular place to retreat and reflect.

Visitors to this National Historic Landmark find history and horticulture coexisting with celebrity. The graves of Henry Wadsworth Longfellow, Oliver Wendell Holmes, Julia Ward Howe, and Mary Baker Eddy are here, as are those of Charles Bulfinch, James Russell Lowell, Winslow Homer, the Transcendentalist leader Margaret Fuller, and the abolitionist Charles Sumner. In season, you'll see gorgeous flowering trees and shrubs (the Massachusetts Horticultural Society had a hand in the design).

Stop at the **visitor center** in Story Chapel (daily 9am–4pm Apr–Oct; closed Sun Nov–Mar and year-round during burials) for an overview and a look at the changing exhibits, or ask at the office or front gate for brochures and a map. Visit **http://mountauburn.toursphere.com/en/** to select a free self-guided tour. Note that animals and recreational activities such as jogging, biking, and picnicking are not allowed.

The **Friends of Mount Auburn Cemetery** conducts workshops and lectures and coordinates walking tours; call the main number for topics, schedules, and fees.

580 Mount Auburn St. (at Brattle St.). $©$ **617/547-7105.** www.mountauburn.org. Free admission. May–Sept daily 8am–7pm; Oct–Apr 8am–5pm (call ahead in spring and fall to check closing time). T: Red Line to Harvard, then 25-min. walk on Brattle St. or bus no. 71 or 73. By car (5 min.) or on foot, take Mount Auburn St. or Brattle St. west from Harvard Square; just after they intersect, gate is on the left.

KENDALL SQUARE

East Cambridge is a high-tech wonderland, which makes perfect sense when you see it on a map—MIT is everywhere.

Massachusetts Institute of Technology (MIT)

The public is welcome at the MIT campus, 2 miles or so from Harvard Square, across the Charles River from Beacon Hill and the Back Bay. Visit the **Events & Information Center,** 77 Massachusetts Ave. ($©$ **617/253-4795;** web.mit.edu/institute-events/events), to take a free guided tour (weekdays at 11am and 3pm, or download the app) or to pick up a copy of a self-guided walking tour.

MIT's campus is known for its art and architecture. The excellent **outdoor sculpture** collection includes works by Picasso and Alexander Calder, and notable modern buildings include designs by Frank Gehry, Eero Saarinen, and I. M. Pei. Gehry designed the **Stata Center**, a curvilinear landmark on Vassar Street off Main Street.

Fumihiko Maki, a Pritzker Prize winner, designed the **Media Lab** complex, 20 Ames St. (at Amherst St.).

To get to MIT, take the MBTA Red Line to Kendall/MIT. The scenic walk from the Back Bay takes you along Massachusetts Avenue over the river straight to the campus. By car from Boston, cross the river at the Museum of Science, Cambridge Street, or Massachusetts Avenue and follow signs to Memorial Drive, where you can usually find parking during the day.

MIT Museum ★ MUSEUM Science and technology collide with art at this museum. Best known for its exhibits of holography and robots, it packs a lot into a relatively small space. The collections contain artifacts you don't see at general-interest institutions, like thermometers, slide rules, historic architectural plans, and even medical devices. Normally I'd suggest that you check ahead for topics of interest—the website is enlightening and helpful—but this is one place where I also recommend just showing up and exploring. Smaller children aren't the museum's target audience, but anyone above age 10 or so with even a passing interest in science and technology will enjoy it. Be sure to check out the entertaining gift shop.

Tip: The **List Visual Arts Center** (℃ **617/253-4680**; http://web.mit.edu/lvac), home to MIT's contemporary art collections, is about 5 minutes away—and it's free. Head to the Wiesner Building, 20 Ames St. (btw. Main and Amherst sts.), Tuesday through Sunday from noon to 6pm, until 8pm on Thursday.

265 Massachusetts Ave. (Building N51, at Front St.). ℃ **617/253-5927.** web.mit.edu/museum. Admission $10 adults; $5 seniors, students, and children 5–17; free for children under 5. Free last Sun of month, Sept–June. Daily 10am–5pm year-round; until 7pm Thu July–Aug. Closed major holidays. T: Red Line to Central, then 10-min. walk.

Especially for Kids

What can the children do in Boston? A better question might be "What *can't* they do?" Just about every major attraction either is designed to appeal to kids or easily adapts to do so.

The already beloved Greenway Carousel (www.rosekennedygreenway.org), which opened in 2013, is across the street from Faneuil Hall Marketplace, near the intersection of Atlantic Avenue and Cross Street. The custom-sculpted animals—including lobsters, owls, butterflies, and a skunk—are delightful, as are the music selection and the good-size seating area that surrounds the ride. It's open daily in the summer (Sun–Thurs 11am–7pm, Fri–Sat 11am–9pm), fewer days and shorter hours in the spring and fall, and closed in the winter except for special events, such as First Night. A ride costs $3.

The following attractions are covered extensively elsewhere in this chapter; here's the boiled-down version for busy parents.

Destinations that offer something for every member of the family include the **Boston Tea Party Ships & Museum** (℃ **855/TEA-1775** [832-1775]; p. 70); **Faneuil Hall Marketplace** (℃ **617/338-2323;** p. 34); the **Museum of Fine Arts** (℃ **617/267-9300;** p. 86), which offers special weekend and after-school programs; and the USS *Constitution* **Museum** (℃ **617/426-1812;** p. 83).

Hands-on exhibits and large-format films are the headliners at the **New England Aquarium** (℃ **617/973-5200;** p. 74), where you'll find the Simons IMAX Theatre, and at the **Museum of Science** (℃ **617/723-2500;** p. 74), home to the Mugar Omni Theater as well as the Hayden Planetarium.

The allure of seeing people the size of ants draws young visitors to the **Skywalk Observatory at the Prudential Center** (☏ 617/859-0648; p. 86). And they can see actual ants—although they might prefer the dinosaurs—at the **Harvard Museum of Natural History** (☏ 617/495-3045; p. 87).

Older children who have studied modern American history will enjoy a visit to the **John F. Kennedy Presidential Library and Museum** (☏ 617/929-4523; p. 72). Middle-schoolers who enjoyed Esther Forbes's "Johnny Tremain" will probably get a kick out of the **Paul Revere House** (☏ 617/523-2338; p. 81). Young visitors who have read Robert McCloskey's classic "Make Way for Ducklings" will relish a visit to the **Public Garden** (p. 84), and fans of E. B. White's "The Trumpet of the Swan" certainly will want to ride on the **Swan Boats** (☏ 617/522-1966; p. 84). Considerably less tame, and much longer, are **whale watches** (p. 94).

Boston Harbor Cruises, 1 Long Wharf (☏ 877/733-9425 or 617/227-4321; www. bostonharborcruises.com), offers a 40-minute experience called **Codzilla,** which it bills as a "high-speed thrill boat ride." The boat, which has a scary face painted on the hull, leaves Long Wharf daily from mid-May through early October; from the shore, you may be able to hear delighted screaming. Tickets cost $29 for adults, $27 for seniors, and $25 for children 3 to 11; reservations are recommended.

The walking-tour company **Boston By Foot ★★** (☏ 617/367-2345; www.boston byfoot.org) offers **"Boston By Little Feet"** for children 6 to 12 years old. The 1-hour walk gives a child's-eye view of the architecture along the Freedom Trail and of Boston's role in the American Revolution. Children must be accompanied by an adult, and a map is provided. Tours run from May through October and begin at the statue of Samuel Adams on the Congress Street side of Faneuil Hall. They begin Saturday at 10am and Sunday at 1pm, plus Friday at 10am in July and August, rain or shine. The cost is $10 per person, free for children 5 and under.

Boston Children's Museum ★★ Like its target audience of kids under 11, this museum constantly changes. In a renovated warehouse (see? change!) overlooking the Fort Point Channel, it's packed with opportunities to explore literally everything that children can get their hands on. Visitors in 2015 will have the chance to learn about the **"Children of Hangzhou,"** Chinese sister city to Boston (through May) and explore nutrition and fitness in **"Healthyville"** (May–Sept).

Permanent exhibits start right in the glass-walled lobby, where you'll find the entrance to the three-level **New Balance Climb.** As kids find their way through the "full-body puzzle," negotiating ramps and nets, adults watch from the stairs. In the galleries, it's all about experiential learning, an approach the museum has promoted since its founding, in 1913 (the only older American children's museum is in Brooklyn). Let the kids set the itinerary and timetable here.

Also constantly changing is the museum's Fort Point neighborhood, with one exception: the 40-foot-high red-and-white milk bottle out front, a useful landmark as you're heading (or running) toward the entrance.

308 Congress St. (Museum Wharf), at Sleeper St., on Fort Point Channel. ☏ **617/426-6500.** www. bostonchildrensmuseum.org. Admission $14 adults, seniors, and children 1–15, free for children under 1; Fri 5–9pm $1 for all, Sat–Thurs after 4pm $7 for all. Sat–Thurs 10am–5pm; Fri 10am–9pm. Closed Thanksgiving, Dec 25, and until noon Jan 1. Discounted parking available; check website. T: Red Line to South Station; from South Station walk north on Atlantic Ave. 1 block (past Federal Reserve Bank), turn right onto Congress St., then walk 2 blocks (across bridge). Or Silver Line to Courthouse; walk toward downtown and turn left at Fort Point Channel.

Organized Tours

ORIENTATION TOURS

GUIDED WALKING TOURS   Even if you usually prefer to explore on your own, I heartily recommend a walking tour with **Boston By Foot ★★** (© 617/367-2345; www.bostonbyfoot.org). From April to October (the full schedule starts in May), the nonprofit educational corporation conducts historical and architectural tours that focus on particular neighborhoods or themes. Among them are the **Heart of the Freedom Trail, Beacon Hill,** the **North End,** and the **Dark Side of Boston.** The rigorously trained guides are volunteers who encourage questions. Buy tickets ($12 adults, $8 children 6–12) online or from the guide (cash only); reservations are not required. The 90-minute tours take place rain or shine. Check the website for details and meeting places. On the last Sunday of each month, a special tour ($15) covers a particular theme, such as Art Deco design or the architecture of Beacon Hill. In addition, the company offers themed holiday strolls and year-round group tours.

Trademark Tours (© 855/455-8747; www.trademarktours.com), the brainchild of some entrepreneurial Harvard grads, offer an insider's perspective on Harvard Square. Two student guides lead the 70-minute **Harvard Tour** ($10 per person). The company also offers group tours of MIT, the Freedom Trail, and other destinations.

For information about other guided walking tours of the **Freedom Trail** (with a costumed Freedom Trail Player, or free with a National Park Service ranger), see the section "The Freedom Trail," on p. 76.

"DUCK" TOURS   The most unusual and enjoyable way to see Boston is with **Boston Duck Tours ★★★** (© 800/226-7442 or 617/267-3825; www.bostonduck tours.com). The tours, offered from late March through November and on the first 3 weekends of December, are pricey but great fun. Sightseers board a "duck," a World War II–style amphibious landing craft, behind the Prudential Center on Huntington Avenue or at the Museum of Science for an 80-minute narrated tour. Excursions from the New England Aquarium (Apr–Oct) last 65 minutes. All start with a quick but comprehensive jaunt around the city. Then the duck lumbers down a ramp, splashes into the Charles River, and goes for a spin around the basin. Fun!

Tours from the Prudential Center and Museum of Science cost $35 for adults, $29 for seniors and students, $24 for children 3 to 11, and $11 for children 2 and under. From the New England Aquarium, children under 3 pay the same $11, and everyone else gets a $3 discount. Tours run every 30 or 60 minutes from 9am to 30 minutes before sunset, and they usually sell out. Timed tickets go on sale 30 days ahead online, in person, and by phone; same-day in-person sales start at 8:30am (9am at the aquarium). Reservations are accepted only for groups of 20 or more. No tours late December through mid-March.

TROLLEY TOURS   The ticket vendors who clamor for your business wherever tourists gather will claim that no visit is complete without a day on a trolley. Sometimes that's true. If you're unable to walk long distances, are short on time, or are traveling with children, a narrated tour on a trolley (actually a bus chassis with a trolley body) can be a good idea. You can get an overview of the city before you focus on specific attractions, or use the all-day pass to hit as many places as possible in 8 hours or so. In some neighborhoods, notably the North End, trolleys stop some distance from the attractions—don't believe a ticket seller who tells you otherwise. Because Boston is so pedestrian-friendly, a trolley tour isn't the best choice for the able-bodied and unencumbered making a long visit, but it can save time and effort, especially in extreme weather. For those who are physically able, I can't say this enough: ***Climb down and look around.***

The business is very competitive, with various firms offering different stops and add-ons in an effort to distinguish themselves from the rest. All cover the major attractions and offer informative narratives and anecdotes in their 90- to 120-minute tours; most offer free reboarding if you want to visit the attractions. Each tour is only as good as its guide, and quality varies widely—every few years a TV station or newspaper runs an "exposé" of the wacky tales a tour guide is passing off as fact. If you have time, you might chat up guides in the waiting area and choose the one you like best.

Trolley tickets cost $25 to $44 for adults, $16 or less for children. Most companies offer online discounts and reservations, and you may find discount coupons at visitor information centers and hotel-lobby brochure racks. Boarding spots are at hotels, historic sites, and tourist information centers. Busy waiting areas are near the New England Aquarium, the Park Street T stop, and the corner of Boylston Street and Charles Street South, across from Boston Common. Each company paints its cars a different color. They include orange-and-green **Old Town Trolley Tours** (☎ 888/910-8687 or 617/269-7010; www.trolleytours.com/boston), red **Beantown Trolley** vehicles (☎ 800/343-1328 or 617/720-6342; www.brushhilltours.com, click "Beantown Trolley"), silver **CityView Trolleys** (☎ 617/363-7899; www.cityviewtrolleys.com), and yellow-and-green **Upper Deck Trolley Tours** (☎ 877/343-8257 or 617/742-1440; www.bostonsupertrolleytours.com).

SIGHTSEEING CRUISES

Take to the water for a taste of Boston's rich maritime history or a daylong break from walking and driving. You can cruise around the harbor or go all the way to Provincetown. The **sightseeing cruise ★★** season runs from **April through November,** with spring and fall offerings often restricted to weekends. Check websites for discount coupons before you leave home. If you're traveling in a large group, call ahead for information about reservations and discounted tickets. And if you're prone to seasickness, check the size of the vessel for your tour before buying tickets; larger boats provide more cushioning and comfort than smaller ones.

Note: The **MBTA Inner Harbor ferry** runs year-round between Long Wharf and the Charlestown Navy Yard and costs just $3. See "Getting Around," earlier in this chapter.

The largest cruise company is **Boston Harbor Cruises,** 1 Long Wharf (☎ 877/SEE-WHALE [733-9425] or 617/227-4321; www.bostonharborcruises.com). Ninety-minute **historic sightseeing cruises,** which tour the Inner and Outer harbors, depart from Long Wharf May through August daily and on weekends in September at 11am, 1pm, and 3pm, with extra excursions at busy times. Tickets are $25 for adults, $23 for seniors, and $21 for children 3 to 11; tickets for the sunset cruise (6 or 7pm) cost $1 more. The 45-minute **USS *Constitution* cruise** takes you around the Inner Harbor and docks at the Charlestown Navy Yard so that you can go ashore and visit "Old Ironsides." Tours leave Long Wharf daily April through November hourly from 10:30am to 4:30pm, and on the hour from the Navy Yard from 11am to 5pm. The cruise is $20 for adults, $18 for seniors, and $16 for children. Check the website for other offerings, including dining cruises and a 5-hour excursion that passes a dozen lighthouses.

The **Charles Riverboat Company** (☎ 617/621-3001; www.charlesriverboat.com) offers 60-minute narrated cruises from the CambridgeSide Galleria mall daily May through October. Tours of the **lower Charles River basin** start six times daily between 10am and 4:15pm. Tickets cost $15 for adults, $13 for seniors and students, and $8 for children under 12. The company's other offerings include architectural tours of Boston Harbor and the river basin, and sunset cruises on the river. Check the website for details and reservations.

DAY TRIPS   Two companies serve **Provincetown,** at the tip of Cape Cod (see chapter 5).

Bay State Cruise Company (© **877/783-3779** or 617/748-1428; www.province townfastferry.com) operates high-speed and conventional service to Provincetown. High-speed service takes half as long and costs almost twice as much as the conventional excursion. Trips leave from the Seaport World Trade Center Marine Terminal, 200 Seaport Blvd. To get to the pier, take the Silver Line bus from South Station to the World Trade Center stop, the $10 water taxi (© **617/422-0392;** www.citywatertaxi. com) from locations around the harbor, or a regular taxi (when you reserve your cruise, ask the clerk for the best way to reach the pier from your hotel).

Fast ferry service on the *Provincetown III* takes 90 minutes and operates three times a day from mid-May to mid-October. The round-trip fare is $88 for adults, $76 for seniors, and and $65 for children 3 to 12, plus $6 each way for your bike. Reservations are recommended. **M/V *Provincetown II*** sails Saturday only from July through early September. It leaves at 9am for the 3-hour trip to Provincetown. The return leg departs at 3:30pm, giving you 3½ hours for shopping and sightseeing in P-town. The same-day round-trip fare is $46 for adults, free for children under 12 (reservations are required). Bringing a bike costs $6 extra each way.

Boston Harbor Cruises, 1 Long Wharf (© **877/733-9425** or 617/227-4321; www. bostonharborcruises.com), operates catamarans that make the trip in just 90 minutes. They operate from mid-May through mid-October, two or three times a day between early June and Labor Day weekend, and less often early and late in the season. The round-trip fare is $88 for adults, $76 for seniors, $65 for children 4 to 12, $33 for children 3 and under.

WHALE-WATCHING

The **New England Aquarium** (© **617/973-5206;** www.neaq.org; p. 74) and Boston Harbor Cruises (see above) run **whale watches** ★★ on weekends in early April and daily from mid-April through late October. You'll travel several miles out to sea to Stellwagen Bank, the feeding ground for the whales as they migrate from Newfoundland to Provincetown. Enthusiastic naturalists narrate and identify the whales, many of which they call by name. Allow 3 to 4 hours. Tickets are $47 for adults, $42 for seniors, $36 for children 3 to 11, $16 for children 2 and under, $140 for families (two adults, two kids 4–12). Reservations are strongly recommended; you can buy tickets online, subject to a service charge.

SPECIALTY TOURS

Two excellent resources to investigate before you leave home are the **Boston Center for Adult Education** (© **617/267-4430;** www.bcae.org) and the **Cambridge Center for Adult Education** (© **617/547-6789;** www.ccae.org). Multiple-week courses are the norm, but both schools also schedule single-day classes that last 2 hours or longer. The expert-led offerings include walking tours (often with a focus on local architecture), cooking classes and wine tastings, and workshops about topics such as poetry and gardening. Prices start at $30, and preregistration is required.

FOR HISTORY BUFFS   **Historic New England** ★ (© **617/994-5920;** www.historic newengland.org) offers a 2-hour walking tour of Beacon Hill on Saturday afternoons, plus excursions that concentrate on other areas and topics—surf ahead for specifics

A VACATION IN THE islands

Majestic ocean views, hiking trails, historic sites, rocky beaches, nature walks, campsites, and picnic areas abound in New England. To find them all together, head east of Boston to the **Boston Harbor Islands** (© 617/223-8666; www.bostonharborislands.org). The national park area's unspoiled beauty is a welcome break from the urban landscape, and the islands are not well known, even to many longtime Bostonians. Of the 34 islands and peninsulas that dot the Outer Harbor, at least a half dozen are open for exploring, camping, swimming, and more. Bring a sweater or jacket. Plan a day trip or even an overnight trip, but note that only Georges and Spectacle islands have fresh water, and management strongly suggests bringing your own.

Ferries run to **Georges Island** and **Spectacle Island.** Georges Island has a visitor center, museum, refreshment area, fishing pier, picnic area, and wonderful views of Boston's skyline. It's home to Fort Warren (1833), which held Confederate prisoners during the Civil War and may have a resident ghost. You can investigate on your own or take a ranger-led tour. **Spectacle Island,** which opened to the public in 2006, holds more than 3 million cubic yards of material dug up during the Big Dig—then sealed, covered with topsoil, and landscaped to allow recreational use. It has 5 miles of hiking trails, a beach, and a visitor center with a cafe. (**Thompson Island,** home of Thompson Island Outward Bound, is accessible to the public by ferry on summer Sun only.)

Allow at least half a day, longer if you plan to take the inter-island shuttle (summer only) to **Bumpkin, Grape, Lovells,** or **Peddocks Island,** all of which have picnic areas and campsites.

Admission to the islands is free. **Boston Harbor Cruises** (© 877/SEE-WHALE [733-9425] or 617/227-4321; www.bostonharborcruises.com) runs ferries to Georges Island (30 min.) and Spectacle Island (20 or 45 min.) from Long Wharf. Tickets are for sale online and at the **Boston Harbor Islands Pavilion** visitor center, on the Rose Kennedy Greenway across from Faneuil Hall Marketplace. Round-trip tickets cost $15 for adults, $11 for seniors, $9 for children 4 to 11, free for children 3 and under, $43 for families (two adults, two kids); the inter-island shuttle is free. Cruises depart daily on the hour from 9am to 5pm (6pm on weekends) from mid-June through Labor Day weekend, with shorter hours in the spring and fall. In the off season, check ahead for winter wildlife excursions (scheduled occasionally).

A public-private National Park Partnership administers the **Boston Harbor Islands National Recreation Area** (www.nps.gov/boha). For more information, chat up the park rangers at the Boston Harbor Islands Pavilion from May through October (it's not staffed in the winter). Or contact the **Friends of the Boston Harbor Islands** (© 617/740-4290; www.fbhi.org). The Friends coordinate a variety of cruises on and around the harbor throughout the summer and fall, including one that visits **Boston Light,** in Boston Harbor; check ahead for details.

and schedules. Beacon Hill tours begin at the Otis House, 141 Cambridge St. Prices start at $12, which includes a house tour, and reservations are recommended.

The **Cambridge African American Heritage Trail** focuses on significant sites in the history of the city's large black community. To buy the guide ($2), visit the office on the second floor of 831 Massachusetts Ave., or go to the website of the **Cambridge Historical Commission** (© 617/349-4683; www.cambridgema.gov/historic, click "History and Links").

A map of the self-guided tour created by the **Boston Irish Tourism Association** (℡ **617/696-9880**; www.irishheritagetrail.com) is available at the Boston Common and Prudential Center visitor centers. Check the website for an interactive map with pop-ups describing the sites, and information about guided tours.

BY BICYCLE A group bicycle tour covers more in 2½ to 3 hours than you could ever see on foot. Among the numerous and diverse offerings of **Urban AdvenTours,** 103 Atlantic Ave. (℡ **855/249-11950** for reservations, or 617/670-0637 for info; www.urbanadventours.com), are a tour that focuses on historic neighborhoods and landmarks and another that traces the harbor and the Charles River. You can also request a customized special-interest excursion. Prices for daytime tours begin at $50 per person and include bicycle and helmet rental. You can also rent bikes, which can be picked up at the North End shop (off the Rose Kennedy Greenway near Faneuil Hall Marketplace) or delivered to your hotel or any other location.

FOR SHUTTERBUGS The unusual offerings of **PhotoWalks** (℡ **617/851-2273**; www.photowalks.com) combine narrated walking tours with photography tips. On a 90-minute stroll around Beacon Hill, the Back Bay, or another picturesque area, visitors learn to look at Boston from (literally) a different angle—that of a creative photographer. Adults pay $40, youths 10 to 17 (with a paying adult) $20. Tours run several times a week from April through October, and by appointment during the winter. Call or surf ahead for specifics and tickets.

FOR MOVIE & TV FANS On Location Tours (℡ **212/683-2027**; www.screentours.com) are walking tours and bus excursions that look at Boston on the silver and small screens—a busy undertaking now that there's film production going on all over the place. Guides offer regularly updated info about numerous movies and TV shows, always including (of course) "Cheers." Passengers on the 3-hour bus tours ($40), which run daily from June to September, can watch clips on TV screens in the vehicle. On Saturdays in the spring, summer, and fall, 90-minute Boston Movie Mile walking tours ($24) concentrate on Beacon Hill and the Back Bay. Check start times and meeting points when you make reservations, which are strongly recommended.

FOR HORROR-MOVIE FANS Ghosts & Gravestones (℡ **617/269-3626**; www.ghostsandgravestones.com) covers burial grounds and other shiver-inducing areas in a trolley and on foot, with a guide dressed as a gravedigger. The 90-minute tour starts at dusk on weekends in April, May, and early November, and nightly from Memorial Day weekend through October. It costs $40 for adults, $37 for seniors and students, $25 for children 4 to 12. Children 3 and under are not allowed, and the company cautions that the tour might not be suitable for kids 12 and under. Reservations are required.

FOR FOODIES A neighborhood resident offers **North End Market Tours ★** (℡ **617/523-6032**; www.bostonfoodtours.com), 3-hour excursions that stop at many of the shops in the legendary Italian-American stronghold. Tours ($54) include product tastings, cooking tips, and plenty of local lore. The same company offers 3½-hour **Chinatown Market Tours;** the price ($69) includes a dim sum lunch. Visit the website to register and pay in advance.

SHOPPING

Boston-area shopping offers an irresistible blend of classic and contemporary. Boston and Cambridge teem with tiny boutiques and sprawling malls, esoteric bookshops and national chain stores, exclusive galleries and snazzy secondhand-clothing outlets.

The listings in this section focus on only-in-Boston businesses. But first, I'll point you to areas that are great for shop-hopping, where it's great fun to wander in and out of the shops and wait for inspiration to strike.

Note: The United States has no national **sales tax,** but most states impose their own. Tags and labels show pretax prices. Massachusetts does not charge sales tax on food items or on clothing priced below $175. The state taxes all other items at 6.25 percent. Most stores will handle domestic shipping for a fee, but if the store is part of a chain that operates in your home state, you'll probably have to pay that sales tax.

Great Shopping Areas
DOWNTOWN & VICINITY
The best shopping in this area is on Charles Street, the main drag of **Beacon Hill,** where you'll find numerous gift and antiques shops. The largest retail concentration downtown is at **Faneuil Hall Marketplace** and nearby **Downtown Crossing,** where you'll find numerous chain outlets. In the **North End,** boutiques crop up among the omnipresent restaurants on Hanover and Salem streets.

BACK BAY & VICINITY
The **Back Bay** is Boston area's premier shopping district. Dozens of upmarket art galleries, shops, and boutiques make **Newbury Street** the top destination in New England for fine art and high-end designer fashion. On parallel **Boylston Street**—like Newbury, a hotbed of retail chains—there's an entrance to the swanky **Shops at Prudential Center.** An enclosed walkway across Huntington Avenue links the Pru to the even more upscale **Copley Place.** The adjacent **South End**—focus on **Tremont Street** and **Washington Street**—is home to numerous independent retailers and chic boutiques.

CAMBRIDGE
Harvard Square, with its bookstores and boutiques, is about 15 minutes from downtown Boston by subway. Despite the neighborhood association's efforts, chain stores have swept over "the Square," where you'll also find some persistent independent retailers. For a less generic experience, stroll from Harvard Square along shop-lined **Massachusetts Avenue** toward **Porter Square** to the north or **Central Square** to the southeast. About 10 minutes up Prospect Street from Central Square is **Inman Square,** home to a number of vibrant independent retailers. In **East Cambridge** is the only suburban-style mall in the immediate Boston area, the **CambridgeSide Galleria** (see below).

Malls & Markets
Boston Public Market   While the permanent 28,000-sq.-ft. market is under construction—it's scheduled to open in 2015—the Boston Public Market Association offers shoppers a preview in the form of seasonal farmers' markets. One is on the Rose Kennedy Greenway side of the market building on Monday and Wednesday from 11am to 6pm, late May through the day before Thanksgiving. The association also runs the **Dewey Square** market, on the Rose Kennedy Greenway at Atlantic Avenue and Summer Street (T: Red Line to South Station). It operates from 11:30am to 6:30pm on Tuesday and Thursday from late May through late December. 136 Blackstone St., on the Rose Kennedy Greenway (at Hanover St.). ℂ **617/997-8669.** www.bostonpublicmarket.org. T: Orange or Green Line to Haymarket.

CambridgeSide Galleria   Here you'll find **Macy's** (ℂ **617/621-3800**), **Sears** (ℂ **617/252-3500**), dozens of other chain outlets, and hundreds of local teens.

Strollers and wheelchairs are available. Open Monday through Saturday from 10am to 9pm, Sunday from noon to 7pm. 100 CambridgeSide Place (btw. Edwin H. Land Blvd. and First St.), Cambridge. ℂ 617/621-8666. www.shopcambridgeside.com. T: Green Line to Lechmere, or Red Line to Kendall/MIT and free shuttle bus (every 20 min.). Garage parking from $2/hr.

Copley Place ★ The indoor counterpart to Newbury Street—without the art galleries—Copley Place is packed with designer boutiques and anchored by **Barneys New York** (ℂ 617/385-3461) and **Neiman Marcus** (ℂ 617/536-3660).

Open Monday through Saturday from 10am to 8pm, Sunday from noon to 6pm. Some establishments keep longer or shorter hours. 100 Huntington Ave. (at Dartmouth St.). ℂ 617/262-6600. www.simon.com. Discounted validated parking with purchase. T: Orange Line to Back Bay or Green Line to Copley.

Farmers' Markets The state **Department of Agricultural Resources** coordinates farmers' markets, which are proliferating throughout Massachusetts. At many, you'll also find vendors selling meat, fish, poultry, eggs, honey, maple syrup, and specialty foods such as fresh pasta and artisan bread. In Boston, visit **Copley Square** (St. James Ave. at Dartmouth St.) on Tuesday or Friday (T: Green Line to Copley or Orange Line to Back Bay); or the **Shops at Prudential Center** (Boylston St. near Gloucester St.) on Thursday (T: Green Line E to Prudential). The Boston Public Market Association (see above) runs its own markets. In Cambridge, several locations around **Harvard Square** (T: Red Line to Harvard) have markets throughout the week; a larger, more diverse market takes over Parking Lot 5, Norfolk Street and Bishop Allen Drive (1 block from Mass. Ave.), in **Central Square** on non-holiday Mondays (T: Red Line to Central). Multiple locations. ℂ 617/626-1700. www.mass.gov/massgrown and www.massfarmersmarkets.org.

Greenway Open Market ★ A spinoff of the SoWa Open Market (see below), the Greenway market features a similar, smaller variety of crafts, jewelry, art, specialty foods, and more. It operates from late May through October on Saturday only from 11am to 5pm, rain or shine. Rose Fitzgerald Kennedy Greenway, along Atlantic Ave. btw. State and High sts. ℂ 800/403-8305. www.greenwayopenmarket.com. T: Blue Line to Aquarium or Orange Line to State.

The Shops at Prudential Center ★ With a few exceptions, the shops and boutiques at the Pru are outlets of upscale chains, but it's a fun destination with a pleasant outdoor courtyard at its center. The main level of the city's second-tallest tower houses a large **Barnes & Noble** (p. 101) and one of the few retail outlets for the office and home accessories of **Levenger** (ℂ 800/667-8934 or 617/536-3434; www.levenger. com). The Greater Boston Convention & Visitors Bureau operates the **information booth.** Hours are Monday through Saturday from 10am to 9pm, Sunday from 11am to 6pm. Restaurant hours vary. 800 Boylston St. (at Fairfield St.); back entrance off Huntington Ave. at Belvidere St. ℂ 800/746-7778. www.prudentialcenter.com. Discounted validated parking with purchase. T: Green Line E to Prudential; Green Line to Copley; or Orange Line to Back Bay.

SoWa Open Market ★★ What seems to be the whole South End is here in good weather, shopping for art, crafts, jewelry, clothing, home accessories, and more from enthusiastic vendors. The SoWa (short for "South of Washington") market is also a red-hot place to check out local food trucks. Summer (May to mid-Nov) hours are 10am to 5pm on non-holiday-weekend Sundays; in winter, fewer vendors set up, and hours are 10am to 2pm. 460 Harrison Ave. (at Thayer St.). ℂ 800/403-8305. www.sowaopen market.com. T: Silver Line SL4/SL5 bus to E. Berkeley St.; or Orange Line to Tufts Medical Center or Back Bay, then 15-min. walk.

SHOPPING A TO Z

Here I've singled out establishments that I especially like and neighborhoods that suit shoppers interested in particular types of merchandise. Addresses are in Boston unless otherwise indicated.

Antiques & Collectibles

Bromfield Pen Shop ★   The fountain-pen collector in your life will be so mad if you visit Boston and don't at least stop in here. This shop repairs pens and sells new high-end writing instruments, Swiss army knives, watches, and business gifts. Closed Sunday. 5 Bromfield St. (off Washington St.). ℂ **617/482-9053.** www.bromfieldpenshop.com. T: Red or Orange Line to Downtown Crossing.

Cambridge Antique Market ★★   Scores of dealers fill the five floors of this East Cambridge treasure trove, hawking items of all sizes and descriptions. They make their own hours and are most likely to be open on Saturday. Prices are better than in Boston, but you may have to do some digging. Closed Monday. 201 Monsignor O'Brien Hwy. (at Third St.), Cambridge. ℂ617/868-9655. www.marketantique.com. T: Green Line to Lechmere.

Danish Country European & Asian Antiques ★   Eighteenth-century and younger Scandinavian antiques are the headliner here, alongside antique Chinese furniture and home accessories, folk art, Mora clocks, and Royal Copenhagen porcelain. 138 Charles St. (btw. Revere and Cambridge sts.). ℂ617/227-1804. www.europeanstyleantiques. com. T: Red Line to Charles/MGH.

Upstairs Downstairs Antiques ★★   The modest facade conceals a cavernous shop (keep walking) packed with antiques, collectibles, and irresistible gift items. The staff is exceptionally helpful. 93 Charles St. ℂ617/367-1950. www.upstairsdownstairsboston. com. T: Red Line to Charles/MGH.

Art Galleries

Art galleries dot the city and suburbs, with the greatest concentrations in Boston's Back Bay and South End. Time (yours) and space (mine) preclude listing galleries in outlying neighborhoods and suburbs, but if your travels take you off the beaten path, look around—soaring rents have driven savvy proprietors to some unexpected locations.

The **SoWa Artists Guild** (www.sowaartistsguild.com) website makes a good introduction to the South End community. On the first Friday of each month, guild members with spaces in 450 Harrison Ave. (at Thayer St.) throw open their doors to visitors from 5 to 9pm for **First Friday Open Studios.**

An excellent way to see artists at work is to visit during neighborhood **open studio** days. Artists' communities throughout the Boston area stage the weekend events once or twice a year. You might be asked for a contribution to a charity in exchange for a map of the studios. Check listings in the "Globe," "Herald," and "Improper Bostonian" or visit **www.cityofboston.gov/arts** for information.

Acme Fine Art   Come here—to the South End, not the original Newbury Street location—to see 20th-century American art, mostly abstract work in numerous media and styles. Closed Sunday and Monday. 1 Thayer St. (at Harrison Ave.). ℂ **617/585-9551.** www.acmefineart.com. T: Silver Line SL4/SL5 to East Berkeley.

Alpha Gallery ★★   The Alpha Gallery is a family business—the director is the founder's daughter—and a must-see destination if you appreciate contemporary paintings, sculpture, and prints. Closed Sunday and Monday. 37 Newbury St. (btw. Arlington and Berkeley sts.), 4th floor. ✆ **617/536-4465.** www.alphagallery.com. T: Green Line to Arlington.

Barbara Krakow Gallery ★★★ Barbara Krakow is a force of nature, and her gallery, which opened in 1964, is a rigorously curated showcase. The focus is minimalist, reductivist, and conceptual art—paintings, sculptures, drawings, and prints. Closed Sunday and Monday; closed August. 10 Newbury St. (btw. Arlington and Berkeley sts.), 5th floor. ✆ **617/262-4490.** www.barbarakrakowgallery.com. T: Green Line to Arlington.

Galería Cubana ★★ Only a few businesses have American government clearance to travel to and trade with Cuba, and Galería Cubana is one. Visit the website for a preview of some amazing work by contemporary Cuban artists. Closed Monday through Wednesday except by appointment. 460 Harrison Ave. (at Thayer St.). ✆ **617/292-2822.** www.lagaleriacubana.com. T: Silver Line SL4/SL5 bus to E. Berkeley St.; or Orange Line to Tufts Medical Center or Back Bay, then 15-min. walk.

Gallery NAGA ★★ The specialties here are contemporary paintings, photography, and studio furniture, often by New England artists. But the contemporary space in the neo-Gothic Church of the Covenant is best known for showing remarkable works in holography. Closed Sunday and Monday. 67 Newbury St. (at Berkeley St.). ✆ **617/267-9060.** www.gallerynaga.com. T: Green Line to Arlington.

International Poster Gallery ★★★ My favorite Boston art gallery—I can't pass by without stopping in—specializes in French, Swiss, Soviet, and Italian vintage posters. Pieces from elsewhere, including original works, round out the massive collection, which the gracious staff can help you explore. Be sure to check out the website. Poster prices start at $100, with most between $500 and $2,500. 205 Newbury St. (btw. Exeter and Fairfield sts.). ✆ **617/375-0076.** www.internationalposter.com. T: Green Line to Copley.

Martha Richardson Fine Art ★ Representational art is something of an oddity on abstraction-happy Newbury Street. Come here for a refreshing look at 19th- and 20th-century American and European landscapes, still lifes, and portraits. Closed Sunday and Monday; open Tuesday by appointment. 38 Newbury St. (btw. Arlington and Berkeley sts.), 4th floor. ✆ **617/266-3321.** www.martharichardsonfineart.com. T: Green Line to Arlington.

Robert Klein Gallery ★★★ The brightest lights in international fine-art photography show here—in 2014 alone, Chema Madoz (Spain), Formento & Formento (American-British), and Iranian Rana Javadi (presented at Ars Libri; see "Books," below). The gallery also represents the biggest names in 19th- and 20th-century photography. Closed Sunday and Monday. 38 Newbury St. (btw. Arlington and Berkeley sts.), 4th floor. ✆ **617/267-7997.** www.robertkleingallery.com. T: Green Line to Arlington.

Vose Galleries of Boston ★ This family business, which opened in 1841 (that's six generations), represents some contemporary American realists, but the gallery's calling card is 18th-, 19th-, and early-20th-century American paintings. You might see works of the Hudson River School, the Boston School, and American Impressionists. Closed Sunday and Monday. 238 Newbury St. (off Fairfield St.). ✆ **617/536-6176.** www.vosegalleries.com. T: Green Line to Copley, or Green Line B, C, or D to Hynes Convention Center.

Arts, Crafts & Museum Stores

Museum shops are a wonderful source of unique items, including crafts and games. Particularly good outlets include those at the **Museum of Fine Arts,** the **Museum of Science,** the **Isabella Stewart Gardner Museum,** and the **Institute of Contemporary**

Art (see listings earlier in this chapter). See "Jewelry," later in this chapter, for information about **Boston Bead Company.**

Cambridge Artists' Cooperative Craft Gallery ★ Three levels of display space—great for browsing—make this artist-owned and -operated gallery a great stop while you're exploring Harvard Square. Prices are high, but so is quality. 59A Church St. (off Brattle St.), Cambridge. ✆ **617/868-4434.** www.cambridgeartistscoop.com. T: Red Line to Harvard.

Society of Arts and Crafts ★★ Founded in 1897, the oldest nonprofit craft organization in the country is on a mission. Its gallery and retail shop could be in a less prominent—and cheaper—location, but that's the point: Craft artists are artists, and their wonderful work belongs on prestigious Newbury Street. Open Monday by appointment only. The society also sponsors **CraftBoston,** an internationally renowned juried show that takes place in the spring and before the holidays; check the website for dates and locations. 175 Newbury St. (btw. Dartmouth and Exeter sts.). ✆ **617/266-1810.** www.societyofcrafts.org. T: Green Line to Copley.

TistiK The name is Maya for "a warm welcome," and the work is by artisans from Latin America and other developing regions. The focus is on women's jewelry, home accessories, and gift items. Turnover is high and prices reasonable—if you see a piece you like, grab it. 54 Church St. (off Brattle St.), Cambridge. ✆ **617/661-0900.** www.shoptistik. com. T: Red Line to Harvard.

Books, Maps & Stationery

The Boston area is an important stop on most author tours; check the local papers or stop by any store that sells new books for details on **readings and book signings.**

Ars Libri Ltd. ★ Ars Libri ("the art of the book"), which only carries rare and out-of-print art books, boasts that it has the largest stock of such books in the country. That means all eras, all formats, all languages, and the next thing you know, you've spent an hour walking around—and you're not even an art historian. Closed Sunday year-round and Saturday in August. 500 Harrison Ave. (at Perry St.). ✆ **617/357-5212.** www. arslibri.com. T: Silver Line SL4/SL5 to East Berkeley St.

Barnes & Noble ★ Anchoring the Huntington Avenue side of the Prudential Center's main retail floor, Barnes & Noble is the best bookstore in the Back Bay. Come here for the large selections of magazines, children's books (and events), and gift items along with bestsellers and lots of popular fiction and nonfiction. Shops at Prudential Center, 800 Boylston St. (enter from Huntington Ave. at Belvidere St.). ✆ **617/247-6959.** www. barnesandnoble.com. T: Green Line E to Prudential or Green Line to Copley.

Barnes & Noble at Boston University ★ Abundant BU-logo merchandise complements a sprawling full-service bookstore. The author series schedules talks by writers year-round. 660 Beacon St. (at Commonwealth Ave.). ✆ **617/267-8484.** http:// bu.bncollege.com. T: Green Line B, C, or D to Kenmore.

Bob Slate Stationer The selection of greeting cards is so huge that you might have to remind yourself that all you needed was a nice pen. Bob Slate also carries writing paper, art supplies, and office accessories. 30 Brattle St. (btw. John F. Kennedy and Mount Auburn sts.), Cambridge. ✆ **617/547-1230.** www.bobslate.com. T: Red Line to Harvard.

Brattle Book Shop ★★ Bibliophiles from around the world find this little side street in their search for used, rare, and out-of-print titles. You'll find good deals on the carts and shelves arranged on the lot next door (in good weather). And owner Kenneth

Gloss, son of the founder, does free appraisals. Closed Sunday. 9 West St. (btw. Washington and Tremont sts.). ℂ **800/447-9595** or 617/542-0210. www.brattlebookshop.com. T: Red or Orange Line to Downtown Crossing, or Green Line to Park St.

Brookline Booksmith ★★★ The expanded toy and gift section reflects the realities of the modern book business, and the employee recommendations posted all over the large store reflect the old-school hand-selling philosophy. Head downstairs for used books and frequent author events. 279 Harvard St. (btw. Beacon and Green sts.), Brookline. ℂ **617/566-6660.** www.brooklinebooksmith.com. T: Green Line C to Coolidge Corner.

Grolier Poetry Book Shop In business since 1927, this tiny shop holds an incredible 15,000 volumes as well as a nice selection of spoken-word CDs. Closed Sunday and Monday. 6 Plympton St. (off Mass. Ave.), Cambridge. ℂ **617/547-4648.** www.grolierpoetrybookshop.org. T: Red Line to Harvard.

Harvard Book Store ★★★ The staff here will help you find a book or help you make your own—the contraption opposite the entrance is a print-on-demand Espresso Book Machine that draws on a 3.6-million-title catalog. The ground floor is a well-stocked general-interest store; the basement is packed with reasonably priced remainders and dirt-cheap used paperbacks. 1256 Mass. Ave. (at Plympton St.), Cambridge. ℂ **800/542-7323** or 617/661-1515. www.harvard.com. T: Red Line to Harvard.

The Harvard Coop ★★ The Harvard Cooperative Society (say *coop*, not *co-op*) is an enormous general-interest bookstore—as at BU, run by Barnes & Noble—and a purveyor of gifts, games, stationery, prints, and posters. The rear building, which opens onto Brattle and Palmer streets, carries an incredible selection of Harvard insignia merchandise. 1400 Massachusetts Ave. (at Brattle St.), Cambridge. ℂ **617/499-2000.** www.thecoop.com. T: Red Line to Harvard.

Porter Square Books ★★ Readers in this academic neighborhood want both "New York Times" bestsellers and obscure volumes the newspaper's columnists mention in passing—and Porter Square Books keeps them happy. The children's selection is great, as are the literary-themed gift items. Check ahead for author events. In the Porter Square Shopping Center, 25 White St. (off Mass. Ave.), Cambridge. ℂ **617/491-2220.** www.portersquarebooks.com. T: Red Line to Porter.

Raven Used Books Academic titles are the focus at these shops, filling a surprising gap in the local used-book market. Turnover is brisk, so move quickly if you (or the knowledgeable staff) turn up the book you think you need. 52B John F. Kennedy St. (near Winthrop St.), Cambridge. ℂ **617/441-6999.** www.ravencambridge.com. T: Red Line to Harvard. 263 Newbury St. (btw. Fairfield and Gloucester sts.). ℂ **617/578-9000.** T: Green Line B, C, or D to Haynes Convention Center.

Schoenhof's Foreign Books ★ In business since 1856, Schoenhof's stocks instructional materials for more than 700 languages and dialects as well as literature for adults and kids in 50-plus languages. It's worth a stop even if you're not in the market for a book—the gift selection is terrific. Closed Sunday except at the beginning of the semester (early Sept and late Jan). 76A Mt. Auburn St. (at Holyoke St.), Cambridge. ℂ **617/547-8855.** www.schoenhofs.com. T: Red Line to Harvard.

WardMaps LLC ★ Come here for the enormous variety of gift items printed with maps. Stick around to learn about the sources of the images: government "ward maps" (which show municipal divisions) and other maps of all descriptions. The maps and prints, available in various sizes, make great wedding presents. 1735 Massachusetts Ave. (at Prentiss St.), Cambridge. ℂ **617/497-0737.** www.wardmaps.com. T: Red Line to Porter.

Clothing & Accessories

ADULTS

Bodega ★★ Follow the hipster clotheshorses into the little convenience store, stand in front of the Snapple machine, and stroll into this hidden den of next-gen streetwear. This is one of the top places in New England to buy limited-edition and vintage sneakers. 6 Clearway St. (off Mass. Ave.). © **617/421-1550.** www.bdgastore.com. T: Green Line B, C, or D to Hynes Convention Center or Green Line E to Symphony.

Crush Boutique ★ This boutique was so successful on Charles Street that it expanded to Newbury Street—and I'm pretty sure it's because the staff is so pleasant (sadly, not always the case on either street). The eagle-eyed owners stock Crush with trendy but accessible women's clothing and accessories. 131 Charles St. (btw. Cambridge and Revere sts.). © **617/720-0010.** www.shopcrushboutique.com. T: Red Line to Charles/MGH. 264 Newbury St. (btw. Fairfield and Gloucester sts.). © **617/424-0010.** T: Green Line B, C, or D to Hynes Convention Center.

Injeanius ★★ The restaurant-choked North End doesn't have many stores, but it does have this fantastic boutique, which specializes in designer denim. Trust owner Alison Barnard and her staff to tell you the truth about whether those pants make you look fat, then check out the accessories and tops, many from brands you won't see elsewhere in Boston. Under the same ownership, **Twilight,** 12 Fleet St. (off Hanover St.; © **617/523-8008;** www.twillightboutique.com), specializes in lovely party dresses and accessories. 441 Hanover St. (at Salutation St.). © **617/523-5326.** www.injeanius.com. T: Green or Orange Line to Haymarket.

Looks ★★ Women's clothes that look good and feel great? Check. Helpful staff? Check. Excellent prices (especially during sales) for pieces—including accessories and jewelry—you'll wear over and over? Check. Looks inspires devotion in its repeat customers, and you'll see why. 11–13 Holyoke St. (btw. Mass. Ave. and Mount Auburn St.), Cambridge. © **617/491-4251.** www.looksclothing.com. T: Red Line to Harvard.

Louis Boston Since moving from the Back Bay to the Seaport District, Louis (say "Louie's") has only gotten more adventurous. Much of the super-high-end men's and women's fashions here aren't available anywhere else in the Boston area, making it worth a trip to this retail-deprived neighborhood. Stick around for a haircut at the on-premises salon or a meal at the restaurant. Fan Pier, 60 Northern Ave. (off Seaport Blvd.). © **617/262-6100.** www.louisboston.com. T: Silver Line SL1/SL2 to Court House.

Mint Julep ★ In keeping with the name, Mint Julep is the perfect place to outfit yourself for a classy cocktail party. In addition to the well-edited selection of casual and dressy designer duds, it carries lovely jewelry and handbags. Be sure to check the sale section. 6 Church St. (at Mass. Ave.), Cambridge. © **617/576-6468.** www.shopmintjulep.com. T: Red Line to Harvard.

CHILDREN

Mulberry Road ★ Fashionable children and their adult enablers come here for the latest in high-end clothing and accessories. The gift selection is small but choice, the staff welcoming and knowledgeable. 128 Newbury St. (btw. Clarendon and Dartmouth sts.). © **617/859-5861.** www.mulberryroad.com. T: Green Line to Copley.

The Red Wagon ★ This good-size boutique may just be the reason that the children who frequent Beacon Hill playgrounds look so put-together. You'll see American and European brands as well as plenty of fun toys. 69 Charles St. (off Mount Vernon St.). © **617/523-9402.** www.theredwagon.com. T: Red Line to Charles/MGH.

JEWELRY

Boston Bead Company You can make your own jewelry or select from preassembled pieces at this little shop, which is worth a peek just for the colorful selection of raw materials. Check ahead to see whether a jewelry-making workshop is taking place while you're in town. 23 Church St. (btw. Mass. Ave. and Palmer St.), Cambridge. ✆ **617/868-9777.** www.bostonbeadcompany.com. T: Red Line to Harvard.

John Lewis, Inc. ★★★ John Lewis himself designs the brilliant women's and men's jewelry that's made right here and displayed in dramatic style throughout the lovely space. He works in silver, gold, and platinum items, sometimes incorporating colored stones. The signature line consists of hammered metal secrets artfully formed into earrings, necklaces, and bracelets—often imitated, never duplicated. Closed Sunday and Monday. 97 Newbury St. (off Clarendon St.). ✆ **800/266-4101** or 617/266-6665. www.johnlewisinc.com. T: Green Line to Arlington.

SHOES & ACCESSORIES

Berk's Shoes ★ Casual shoes are this shop's bread and butter, but some trendy dress-up styles find their way in. Berk's gets extremely busy on weekends; come on a weekday if you want to browse in (relative) peace. 50 John F. Kennedy St. (at Winthrop St.). ✆ **888/462-3757** or 617/492-9511. www.berkshoes.com. T: Red Line to Harvard.

Converse ★★ If head-to-toe Converse sounds fashionable, this is the place to make it happen. This store also has an entire floor of shoes and a customization bar that lets shoppers design the perfect Chuck Taylors. 348 Newbury St. (btw. Hereford St. and Mass. Ave.). ✆ **617/424-5400.** www.converse.com. T: Green Line to B, C, or D to Hynes Convention Center.

Helen's Leather Shop ★ Beacon Hill is a tweedy place, but somehow Helen's has thrived here for 3 decades of selling Western boots and accessories. The big brand names are here, along with clothing for kids and adults, belts and buckles, hats (including Stetsons), and a lot of items with fringe on them. Closed Tuesday in the summer. 110 Charles St. (at Pinckney St.). ✆ **617/742-2077.** www.helensleather.com. T: Red Line to Charles/MGH.

Moxie ★★ Here you'll find one of the best women's designer shoe selections in the Boston area, along with jewelry and accessories. The unpretentious staff members can help outfit you for any occasion. 51 Charles St. (btw. Chestnut and Mount Vernon sts.). ✆ **617/557-9991.** www.moxieboston.com. T: Red Line to Charles/MGH.

Sudo Shoes If you eschew leather, then join the true believers who flock to this little shop in (of course) Cambridge for men's, women's, and kids' vegan footwear. 1771 Massachusetts Ave. (at Forest St.), Cambridge. ✆ **617/354-1771.** www.sudoshoes.com. T: Red Line to Porter.

VINTAGE & SECONDHAND CLOTHING

Bobby From Boston ★★ Men's vintage clothing is a very particular niche, and Bobby From Boston—tucked away among the South End's art galleries—is one of the best places in the country to find it. The focus is the 1940s through '70s, the clientele everyone from local chefs to Hollywood costume designers. Closed Sunday and Monday. 19 Thayer St. (off Harrison Ave.). ✆ **617/423-9299.** T: Silver Line SL4/SL5 bus to E. Berkeley St., or Orange Line to Tufts Medical Center and 10-min. walk.

Boomerangs ★★ Far nicer than a typical charity thrift store, this "Special Edition" of Boomerangs benefits the AIDS Action Committee. Come here for the well-edited selection of men's and women's vintage and "gently used" fashion. The larger space in Central Square has room for furniture and home accessories. The Special Edition is closed on Monday. 1407 Washington St. (btw. Union Park and Pelham sts.). ℰ **617/456-0996.** www.shopboomerangs.com. T: Silver Line SL4/SL5 bus to Union Park St. or Orange Line to Tufts Medical Center and 10-min. walk. 563 Massachusetts Ave. (at Pearl St.), Cambridge. ℰ **617/758-6128.** T: Red Line to Central.

The Closet ★★★ The best consignment shop in the Back Bay—maybe in all of Boston—is this jam-packed space below the Society of Arts & Crafts' retail gallery. In business since 1979, it charges incredibly reasonable prices for "gently worn" (not vintage) high-end designer clothing and accessories for women and men. 175 Newbury St. (btw. Dartmouth and Exeter sts.). ℰ **617/536-1919.** www.closetboston.com. T: Green Line to Copley.

The Garment District ★ Every teenager in my life *loves* the Garment District, which carries an amazing selection of inexpensive contemporary and vintage clothing, costumes, and accessories. Also amazing is the amount of effort sometimes required to unearth just the right item, which may be why you don't see a lot of adults here. "By the pound" merchandise (actually $1.50 a pound; not available Fri) is on the first floor. Also on the premises, Boston Costume is the area's best source of rental, retail, and vintage costumes, which are available year-round. 200 Broadway (at Davis St.), Cambridge. ℰ **617/876-5230.** www.garmentdistrict.com. T: Red Line to Kendall/MIT.

Oona's Experienced Clothing ★★★ The focus here is not just on "experienced" clothing but on craftsmanship: The eagle-eyed staff rejects anything flimsy or poorly made. This isn't the dirt-cheap junk you sometimes run across at so many vintage shops, but the prices are surprisingly reasonable considering the quality of the merchandise—women's and men's clothing, funky accessories, and lovely costume jewelry. 1210 Massachusetts Ave. (near Bow St.), Cambridge. ℰ **617/491-2654.** www.oonas boston.com. T: Red Line to Harvard.

Food & Drink

Beacon Hill Chocolates An acquaintance shared the name of this shop like a bootlegger mentioning a speakeasy. Right on Beacon Hill's main drag, it's no secret—but it is worth telling people about. If you can't spring for a handmade box of the delectable confections, try a hot chocolate. 91 Charles St. (at Pinckney St.) ℰ **617/725-1900.** www.beaconhillchocolates.com. T: Red Line to Charles/MGH.

J. Pace & Son ★★ If Salumeria Italiana (see below) doesn't have it, Pace's might. A North End landmark, Pace's (say "*pah*-chay's") carries imported Italian foodstuffs, including meats and cheeses, pasta and grains, and vinegars and oils. As long as you're here, grab a sandwich and a seat on the patio out front, which faces the Greenway. 42 Cross St. (off Salem St.). ℰ **617/227-9673.** www.jpaceandson.com. T: Green or Orange Line to Haymarket.

Salumeria Italiana ★ Dry goods imported from Italy line the shelves of this small, well-stocked grocery. The pastas, vinegars, olive oils, and condiments make great souvenirs. If you're picnicking, check out the meats, cheeses, olives, and fresh bread. 151 Richmond St. (btw. Hanover and North sts.). ℰ **617/523-8743.** www.salumeriaitaliana. com. T: Green or Orange Line to Haymarket.

Gifts & Souvenirs

Black Ink ★★★ Clever office accessories, retro toys, cute hostess gifts, kewpie dolls, clever greeting cards, gorgeous paper to wrap it all in—and that's just scratching the surface. Budget some time and some money. 101 Charles St. (btw. Revere and Pinckney sts.). ℰ **617/723-3883.** blackinkboston.squarespace.com. T: Red Line to Charles/MGH. 5 Brattle St. (off John F. Kennedy St.), Cambridge. ℰ **866/497-1221** or 617/497-1221. T: Red Line to Harvard.

Joie de Vivre ★★★ Joie de Vivre carries everything from games you haven't seen since childhood to bedroom slippers shaped like animal feet. The countless inventive gifts—two specialties are kaleidoscopes and salt-and-pepper shakers—and always-helpful service have helped this little shop thrive since 1984. 1792 Massachusetts Ave. (at Arlington St.), Cambridge. ℰ **617/864-8188.** www.joiedevivre.net. T: Red Line to Porter.

Lannan Ship Model Gallery ★ It's more than just ship models—there are also framed nautical charts, seagoing memorabilia, and home accessories, like sconces in the shape of ship figureheads. On any trip to South Station, make time to cross the Greenway and check this place out. Closed Sunday except by appointment. On the Rose Kennedy Greenway, 99 High St. (entrance at 185 Purchase St., at Congress St.). ℰ **617/451-2650.** www.lannangallery.com. T: Red Line to South Station.

Shake the Tree ★ Come here for trendy home accessories, great-smelling soaps and candles, lovely jewelry and baby gifts, kitchen-related items (including cookbooks), and a small but lovely women's fashion selection. It's a nice break from North End sightseeing. Check ahead for details of the monthly cocktail party. 67 Salem St. (off Cross St.). ℰ **617/742-0484.** www.shakethetreeboston.com. T: Green or Orange Line to Haymarket.

Home Design, Furnishings & Housewares

Boutique Fabulous ★★ Head to Inman Square to check out Boutique Fabulous's vintage clothing, home items, tabletop accessories, offbeat gifts, and antique furniture. Open until 9 or 10pm on weekends. 1309 Cambridge St. (at Oak St.), Cambridge. ℰ **617/864-0656.** www.boutiquefabulous.com. T: Red Line to Central, 10-min. walk on Prospect St.

Lekker ★ Lekker (Dutch for "tempting") doubled the size of its showroom when it moved a few doors down in late 2013, adding upholstered furniture to its fantastic selection of sleek home appointments and accessories. The gifts for all ages are the real find here. 1313 Washington St. (at Waltham St.). ℰ **877/7-LEKKER** (753-5537) or 617/542-6464. www.lekkerhome.com. T: Silver Line SL4/SL5 to Union Park St., or Orange Line to Back Bay and 10-min. walk.

Simon Pearce ★ This place looks almost like a museum of exquisite blown glass and gorgeous pottery. Simon Pearce is a real person—he trained in glassblowing in his native Ireland—and his Vermont-based company is one of a kind. Need a wedding present? You know what to do. 103 Newbury St. (at Clarendon St.). ℂ **617/450-8388.** www.simonpearce.com. T: Green Line to Copley.

Twelve Chairs Twelve Chairs relocated here from Fort Point in late 2013 and fits perfectly in the stylish South End. The owners are also interior designers, and the furniture, accessories, and gifts on display reflect their superb taste. Closed Sunday and Monday. 581 Tremont St. (btw. Upton and Union Park sts.). ℂ **617/982-6136.** www.twelvechairsboston.com. T: Orange Line to Back Bay, 10-min. walk.

Music

Cheapo Records Founded in 1954, Cheapo specializes in vinyl and stock plenty of CDs, DVDs, and even cassettes. Browse till you drop, or test the staff's encyclopedic knowledge. 538 Massachusetts Ave. (at Norfolk St.). ℂ **617/354-4455.** www.cheaporecords.com. T: Red Line to Central.

In Your Ear Records ★★ With some 100,000 items in stock, the Boston University location of In Your Ear is the perfect place for an audiophile to spend an afternoon. The Harvard store is about half the size but equally enticing. 957 Commonwealth Ave. (at Harry Agganis Way). ℂ **617/787-9755.** www.iye.com. T: Green Line B to Pleasant St. 72 Mount Auburn St. (btw. Mill St. and Holyoke Pl.), lower level. ℂ **617/491-5035.** T: Red Line to Harvard.

Stereo Jack's ★ Stereo Jack's opened in 1982 and has survived the transformation of the music business thanks to its combination of fantastic location and exceptionally knowledgeable staff. 1686 Massachusetts Ave. (at Sacramento St.). ℂ **617/497-9447.** www.stereojacks.com. T: Red Line to Porter.

Toys & Games

Also check out most of the shops listed under "Gifts & Souvenirs," the children's specialists in the "Fashion" section, and the gift shops at the **Boston Children's Museum, Museum of Science,** and **New England Aquarium.**

The Games People Play ★ From Scattergories to Sorry! to Dungeons & Dragons, this is the place for games of all descriptions. And if you're looking for an heirloom chess set, a challenging puzzle, unusual playing cards, or another offbeat gift, you're in luck. 1100 Massachusetts Ave. (at Putnam Ave.), Cambridge. ℂ **888/492-0711** or 617/492-0711. www.thegamespeopleplaycambridge.com. T: Red Line to Harvard.

Magic Beans ★ Magic Beans has a few suburban locations that carry a lot of baby items, but the real magic is the presence of a well-stocked toy store for older kids in the upscale, adult-focused Pru. Shops at Prudential Center, 800 Boylston St. (at Fairfield St.). ℂ **617/383-8296.** www.mbeans.com. T: Green Line to Copley or Green Line E to Prudential.

Stellabella Toys ★★ The best thing about the selection at these bustling shops isn't just how big it is (very). It's the fact that the helpful staff can help you pick just right item—game, toy, musical instrument, puppet, costume, crafting accessory, whatever—for the age group you specify. 196 Elm St. (at Tenney St.), Davis Sq., Somerville. ℂ **617/864-6290.** www.stellabellatoys.com. T: Red Line to Davis. 1360 Cambridge St. (btw. Oak and Springfield sts.), Inman Sq., Cambridge. ℂ **617/491-6290.** T: Red Line to Central, then 10-min. walk on Prospect St.

4

BOSTON | Shopping A to Z

ENTERTAINMENT & NIGHTLIFE

Boston has enough beloved cultural institutions—from a world-class symphony orchestra to Broadway-bound theater to a bear-costumed street musician playing a keytar—to keep you busy throughout your visit. "Nightlife" is a different story. Dance and music clubs close early, late-night hours on the T are only an experiment (a 1-year pilot program that started in 2014), and there are students *everywhere*. Adjust your expectations: Find a convivial bar, seek out a decades-old jazz club, take in some improv comedy, and have fun with the locals.

For up-to-date entertainment information online, "The Boston Globe" offers suggestions at **www.boston.com/thingstodo/nightlife** and on Twitter (**@bostoncalendar**). "Boston Magazine" (**@BostonMagazine**) also tweets about events. The tourist offices listed under "Visitor Information," earlier in this chapter, post event listings on their websites, and the websites of the agencies listed under "Getting Tickets," below, let you view events by date and location (don't forget to check Cambridge as well as Boston).

You'll find nightlife listings in **"The Weekly Dig"** and the biweekly **"Improper Bostonian,"** available free at newspaper boxes around town.

The Performing Arts

Classical music and pre–Broadway theater are Boston's big stars, but just about everyone and everything that isn't a Vegas-style extravaganza—rock and pop stars, established and up-and-coming comedians, world-music legends, avant-garde cabaret, and much, much more—originates or eventually plays in the area.

As a rule, the bigger the name, the larger the venue, the pricier the tickets, and the longer the lead time. For an international superstar playing Symphony Hall or the TD Garden, tickets are expensive and sell out weeks or even months ahead. At the other end of this broad spectrum, student performances in campus spaces are free or cheap, and you can decide to attend moments before they begin. Evening performances of all

---

Getting Discount Tickets

Some of the best bargains in town are available at the **BosTix** (⟨⟩ **617/262-8632;** www.bostix.org) booths at **Faneuil Hall Marketplace** (T: Green or Blue Line to Government Center, or Orange Line to Haymarket) and in **Copley Square** at the corner of Boylston and Dartmouth streets (T: Green Line to Copley or Orange Line to Back Bay). Check the board or the website for the day's offerings.

Both locations sell half-price (plus a service charge) same-day tickets to musical and theatrical performances, subject to availability. There are no refunds or exchanges. The booths are also Ticketmaster outlets. Both are open

Tuesday through Saturday from 10am to 6pm, Sunday from 11am to 4pm. BosTix also offers full-price advance tickets; discounts on more than 100 theater, music, and dance events; and tickets for trolley tours. *Tip:* Sign up for e-mail updates (you can always unsubscribe after you return home).

An actor friend turned me on to **Goldstar** (www.goldstar.com), which delivers daily emails about discounts on events. Act quickly when you see something you like—tickets can sell out fast. Your favorite daily-deal sights may also offer Boston-area discounts and special-event tickets.

types usually start at 7, 7:30, or 8pm, and curtain time for matinees ordinarily is 1 or 2pm; *always* double-check.

Three neighborhoods—the Theater District and the Fenway in Boston, and Harvard Square in Cambridge—are home to many prominent performing-arts venues, but don't write off an event taking place elsewhere. You might miss out on something great.

GETTING TICKETS

Some companies and venues sell tickets online or over the phone; many will refer you to a ticket agency. Two major agencies serve Boston: **Ticketmaster** (© **800/745-3000** or TDD 800/943-4327; www.ticketmaster.com) and **Telecharge** (© **800/432-7250** or TTY 888/889-8587; www.telecharge.com). Many smaller venues use independent companies that charge lower fees than their big rivals. Two popular firms are **Brown Paper Tickets** (© **800/838-3006;** www.brownpapertickets.com) and **Eventbrite** (© **888/810-2063** or www.eventbrite.com).

To avoid fees—and possible losses if your plans change and you can't get your money back—visit the box office in person. *Tip:* If you wait until the day before or day of a performance, you'll sometimes have access to tickets that were held back for some reason and have just gone on sale.

CLASSICAL MUSIC, OPERA & DANCE

Founded in 1815, the **Handel and Hayden Society** (© **617/266-3605;** www.handel andhaydn.org) uses period instruments and techniques in its "historically informed" orchestral, choral, and opera performances. Tickets cost $20 to $90. H&H gave the American premiere of Handel's **"Messiah"** in 1818 and has made it a holiday tradition since 1854. If you'll be in town in December, check for tickets as soon as you start planning your trip.

Boston Baroque (© **617/987-8600;** www.bostonbaroque.org) is a Grammy-nominated period orchestra with a chamber chorus. Semi-staged opera complements orchestral and choral performances, which often feature international guest artists. Tickets cost $30 to $80.

The **Boston Philharmonic Orchestra** (© **617/236-0999;** www.bostonphil.org) is a semiprofessional ensemble with a strong educational component; conductor Benjamin Zander introduces each performance with a talk that includes input from the audience. Tickets run $15 to $90.

The **Boston Lyric Opera** (© **617/542-6772;** www.blo.org) mounts one or two classical and one or two contemporary productions per season. Expect to pay at least $35.

Best known for its annual production of "The Nutcracker," **José Mateo Ballet Theatre** (© **617/354-7467;** www.ballettheatre.org) focuses on "culturally relevant" works by the artistic director and choreographer Mateo, who founded the company in 1986.

Boston Ballet ★★ Under the direction of Mikko Nissinen, Boston Ballet performs modern works, new commissions, and classic story ballets. But the company is best known for "The Nutcracker," which runs from Thanksgiving to New Year's. Tickets go on sale in early July; sales for the rest of the season (Oct–May) start in September. Performing at the Boston Opera House, 539 Washington St. (at Ave. de Lafayette). © **617/695-6955.** www.bostonballet.org. Tickets $34–$142. Senior, student, and child rush tickets (2 hr. before most performances) $20 cash; not available for "Nutcracker." T: Orange Line to Chinatown or Green Line to Boylston.

Boston Symphony Orchestra ★★★ One of the "Big Five" American orchestras (with Chicago, Cleveland, New York, and Philadelphia), the BSO has been the pride of the city since 1881. Best known for its great classical repertoire, the BSO also shines with contemporary works. You can plan for months to enjoy a certain composer, piece, or guest musician—or just show up and see whether rush or rehearsal tickets are available.

Performances take place on most Tuesday, Thursday, and Saturday evenings; Friday afternoons; and some Friday evenings. Check the website for information about interpretive talks and numerous other activities—including family programs—available throughout the season (Oct–Apr). If you can't buy tickets in advance, check at the box office for returns from subscribers 2 hours before show time. Except on Saturday, a limited number of same-day **rush tickets** (one per person, cash only) are available. Some Wednesday evening and Thursday morning rehearsals are open to the public. Symphony Hall, 301 Massachusetts Ave. (at Huntington Ave.). © **617/266-1492**, 617/266-2378 (concert info), or 888/266-1200 (tickets). www.bso.org. Tickets $30–$155. Rush tickets $9 (cash only; on sale Fri 10am and Tues, Thurs, Fri 5pm). Rehearsal tickets $20. T: Green Line E to Symphony or Orange Line to Massachusetts Ave.

Boston Pops ★★ Festive and audience-friendly performances are the calling card of the Boston Pops, who turn Symphony Hall into a sort of giant cabaret after the BSO season. Chairs and tables cover the floor of Symphony Hall (balcony seats are available), and light refreshments are served. Conductor Keith Lockhart is a local celebrity, and big stars of stage, screen, and especially musical theater join the fun. Performances ($24–$108) take place Tuesday through Sunday evenings during the season (early May to early July), plus holiday shows in December.

The regular season ends with two **free outdoor concerts at the Hatch Shell** on the Esplanade along the Charles River. The traditional **Fourth of July** concert is a mob scene; the rehearsal the night before is merely very crowded. Both are great fun. Symphony Hall, 301 Massachusetts Ave. (at Huntington Ave.). © **617/266-1492**, 617/266-2378 (concert info), or 888/266-1200 (tickets). www.bso.org. T: Green Line E to Symphony or Orange Line to Massachusetts Ave.

THEATER

Local and national companies, professional and amateur actors, and classic and experimental material combine to animate the local theater scene. To see what's on, surf or call ahead, or check the papers or BosTix (see "Getting Discount Tickets," above) after you arrive. With rare exceptions, performances are in English.

Boston is one of the last cities for pre-Broadway tryouts, allowing an early look at a classic (or a catastrophe) in the making. It's also a popular destination for touring companies of established hits. The dominant promoter is **Broadway in Boston** (© **866/523-7469** or 617/451-2345; http://boston.broadway.com). You'll find most of the shows headed to or coming from Broadway in the Theater District, at the **Boston Opera House,** 539 Washington St. (at Ave. de Lafayette; © **617/259-3400;** www.bostonoperahouseonline.com); the **Citi Wang Theatre,** 270 Tremont St. (½ block from Stuart St.); the **Colonial Theatre,** 106 Boylston St. (off Tremont St.); and the **Shubert Theatre,** 265 Tremont St. (½ block from Stuart St.). The Citi Performing Arts Center (© **617/482-9393;** www.citicenter.org) operates the Colonial, the Shubert and the Wang.

The **American Repertory Theater,** or ART (say "A-R-T"), makes its home at Harvard University's **Loeb Drama Center,** 64 Brattle St. (at Hilliard St.), Cambridge (© **617/547-8300;** www.americanrepertorytheater.org). The artistic director, Diane Paulus, won the 2013 Tony Award for Best Direction of a Musical for "Pippin," which

Entertainment & Nightlife

The **Commonwealth Shakespeare Company** ★★★ (℃ 617/426-0863; www.commshakes.org) performs free on Boston Common Tuesday through Sunday nights in late July and early August. Bring a picnic and blanket, rent a chair (less than $10) if you don't want to sit on the ground, and enjoy the sunset and a high-quality performance. The sets, lighting, and costumes are spectacular.

played here before heading to Broadway—as did Tony winner "The Gershwins' Porgy and Bess." Anything goes on the mainstage and in the programming of nearby **Club Oberon,** 2 Arrow St. (at Mass. Ave.; ℃ **617/496-8004;** www.cluboberon.com). It co-created the off-Broadway hit "Sleep No More" and regularly schedules "The Donkey Show," a Shakespeare-disco mash-up co-written by Paulus. The ART's main local rival for innovative theater and other performances is the **Boston Center for the Arts** (see "Major Theaters & Companies," below).

A lower-profile proving ground for Broadway productions—though you're equally likely to see a revival—is the **Huntington Theatre Company,** which performs at the Boston University Theatre, 264 Huntington Ave. (btw. Massachusetts Ave. and Gainsborough St.; ℃ **617/266-0800;** www.huntingtontheatre.org).

Emerson College's **ArtsEmerson: The World on Stage** (℃ **617/824-8400;** www.artsemerson.org or www.aestages.org [tickets]) oversees the college's audience outreach and is the central source for event information. It programs six performance spaces in the Theater District, including the **Emerson/Cutler Majestic Theatre,** 219 Tremont St. (btw. Boylston and Stuart sts.), and the **Emerson/Paramount Center,** 559 Washington St. (btw. West and Avery sts.)

The **Lyric Stage,** 140 Clarendon St. (at Stuart St.; ℃ **617/585-5678;** www.lyricstage.com), mounts contemporary and modern works in an intimate second-floor setting.

COLLEGE CONCERTS & THEATERS

See "Theater," above, for information about the diverse programming of BU's **Huntington Theatre Company,** Emerson College's **ArtsEmerson,** and Harvard's **American Repertory Theater.** See "Major Theaters & Companies," below, for information about New England Conservatory's **Jordan Hall,** Harvard's **Sanders Theatre,** and Berklee College of Music's **Berklee Performance Center.**

Students and faculty members at two prestigious musical institutions perform frequently during the academic year; admission is usually free. For information, contact the **New England Conservatory of Music,** 290 Huntington Ave. (at Gainsborough St.; ℃ **617/585-1260;** www.necmusic.edu/concerts-events), or the **Longy School of Music of Bard College,** 1 Follen St. (at Garden St.), Cambridge (℃ **617/876-0956,** ext. 1500; www.longy.edu, click "About," then "Events Calendar").

CONCERT & PERFORMANCE SERIES

Make your first stop the website of the **Celebrity Series of Boston** (℃ **617/482-2595** [info] or 617/482-6661 [tickets]; www.celebrityseries.org). The subscription series offers single-ticket sales for the biggest names in music, dance, theater, performance art, opera, literature, and more. **World Music** (℃ **617/876-4275;** www.worldmusic.

4

BOSTON

Entertainment & Nightlife

org) showcases top-flight musicians, dance troupes, and other performers from around the globe.

The **Museum of Fine Arts** (☏ **800/440-6975**; www.mfa.org/programs/music) and the **Isabella Stewart Gardner Museum** (☏ **617/278-5150**; www.gardnermuseum. org/music) schedule concerts year-round. Check ahead for schedules and tickets, which include museum admission. See p. 86 and p. 81 for full museum listings.

Free (& Almost Free) Concerts

Radio stations sponsor free outdoor music all summer at numerous venues, including City Hall Plaza, Copley Square, and the Hatch Shell, at lunch, after work, and in the evening. Check the papers when you arrive, visit the website of a station that sounds good to you, or just follow the crowds.

Four long-running concert series fill historic churches with music at least once a week. Admission to the first two is by free-will offering. At the **Old South Church,** 645 Boylston St. (off Dartmouth St.; ☏ **617/536-1970**; www.oldsouth.org), the choir sings or the handbell choir performs at the 11am Sunday service, accompanied by a 7,625-pipe Skinner organ, and a 1-hour jazz service begins at 6pm every Thursday. Across the square, **Trinity Church,** 206 Clarendon St. (btw. Boylston St. and St. James Ave.), in Copley Square (☏ **617/536-0944**; www.trinitychurchboston.org), features 30-minute organ recitals by local and visiting artists on Friday at 12:15pm. And **King's Chapel,** 58 Tremont St. (at School St.), on the Freedom Trail (☏ **617/227-2155**; www.kings-chapel.org), schedules 30- to 40-minute performances at 12:15pm on Tuesday ($3 donation requested) and full-blown concerts one Sunday a month at 5pm ($15).

Emmanuel Music ★★ Bach cantatas fill the sanctuary of Emmanuel Church, a Gothic Revival landmark, during the 10am service every Sunday in the fall, winter, and spring. Emmanuel Music schedules evening and chamber-music events, including occasional performances in the lovely Lindsey Chapel. Emmanuel Church, 15 Newbury St. (btw. Arlington and Berkeley sts.). ☏ **617/536-3356.** www.emmanuelmusic.org. Free-will offering. T: Green Line to Arlington.

MAJOR VENUES & COMPANIES

Two impressive college venues share the bulk of Boston's classical bookings with **Symphony Hall** (see below): New England Conservatory's **Jordan Hall,** 30 Gainsborough St. (at Huntington Ave.; ☏ **617/585-1270**; www.necmusic.edu/concerts-events), and Harvard University's **Sanders Theatre,** 45 Quincy St. (at Cambridge St.), Cambridge (☏ **617/496-4595**; www.fas.harvard.edu/~memhall).

The **Hatch Shell** on the Esplanade (☏ **617/626-4970**; www.mass.gov/eea; search "Hatch"; T: Red Line to Charles/MGH or Green Line to Arlington) is an amphitheater best known as the site of the Boston Pops' Fourth of July concerts. On many summer nights, free music and dance performances and films take over the stage, to the delight of crowds on the lawn.

Berklee Performance Center The Berklee College of Music has as many famous dropouts as it has famous alumni—maybe more—and incredibly talented instructors and students from around the world. Most of them eventually wind up onstage here. 136 Massachusetts Ave. (at Boylston St.). ℂ **617/747-2261.** www.berklee.edu/bpc. T: Green Line B, C, or D to Hynes Convention Center.

Blue Hills Bank Pavilion On the edge of the harbor in the Seaport District, this enormous white tent, formerly the Bank of America Pavilion, seats 5,000 for touring shows—adult contemporary, oldies, and more—on evenings from May through September. 290 Northern Ave. (at Congress St.), South Boston. ℂ **617/728-1600** or 800/745-9000 (Ticketmaster). www.livenation.com. T: Silver Line SL1/SL2 to Silver Line Way or water taxi to Liberty Wharf.

Boston Center for the Arts This South End complex is the Boston area's largest destination for contemporary theater, music, dance, and visual art, staged in a variety of performance spaces. The BCA and the Huntington Theatre Company (see "Theater," earlier in this chapter) book the 350- and 200-seat theaters in the Calderwood Pavilion. 539 Tremont St. (at Clarendon St.). ℂ **617/426-5000.** www.bcaonline.org. T: Orange Line to Back Bay.

Orpheum Theatre With 2,700 seats, the Orpheum occupies the middle ground between clubs and arenas. The 1852 theater, which has great sight lines, books music, comedy, and other performances by local, national, and international acts, recently including Lorde, Bryan Ferry, and the Shaolin Warriors. 1 Hamilton Place (off Tremont St., across from Park Street Church). ℂ **617/482-0106** or 800/745-3000 (Ticketmaster). www.crossroads presents.com. T: Red or Green Line to Park St.

Symphony Hall The **Boston Symphony Orchestra** and the **Boston Pops** (see above) share their home with performing artists—including comedians as well as musicians—from around the world. The acoustically perfect space opened in 1900. 301 Massachusetts Ave. (at Huntington Ave.). ℂ **617/266-1492** or 888/266-1200 (tickets). www.boston symphonyhall.org. T: Green Line E to Symphony or Orange Line to Massachusetts Ave.

TD Garden New England's premier arena, the Garden (often pronounced "Gah-den") seats 19,600. It books rock and pop artists, skating shows, and the circus, and is the home court of the Celtics and the home ice of the Bruins. Concerts are in the round or the arena stage format. 100 Legends Way (Causeway St.). ℂ **617/624-1000** (event info) or 800/745-3000 (Ticketmaster). www.tdgarden.com. T: Orange or Green Line to North Station.

Wilbur Theatre In its current incarnation, the 1914 Wilbur is effectively the city's largest comedy club. It seats 1,200 for high-profile comics—generally TV and/or movie stars—as well as touring musical acts. 246 Tremont St. (at Stuart St.). ℂ **617/248-9700** or 800/745-3000 (Ticketmaster). www.thewilbur.com. T: Green Line to Boylston or Orange Line to Tufts Medical Center.

LONG-RUNNING SHOWS

Extensively renovated in 2014, the 1839 **Charles Playhouse,** 74 Warrenton St. (off Stuart St.), is home to two beloved long-running shows. Performances take place Tuesday through Sunday; check BosTix (see above) for discounted tickets before you pay full price.

The off-Broadway sensation **Blue Man Group** ★ (© **800/BLUE-MAN** [258-3626]; www.blueman.com) has run on the theater's mainstage since 1995 and still regularly sells out. The blue-painted entertainers use live rock music and percussion, food, and audience members in their ever-changing performances. It's not recommended for children under 8, but older kids will love it. Tickets ($70 and $122; student rush $30) are available at the box office and through the website.

The audience-participation classic **"Shear Madness"** ★ (© **617/426-5225;** www.shearmadness.com), downstairs on the Second Stage, is the longest-running nonmusical play in theater history. Running since January 1980, the "comic murder mystery" takes place in a hair salon that's also the crime scene. The show changes with every performance as audience members conduct the investigation and name the murderer. Tickets ($50; $25 student rush) are available at the box office and online.

The Bar Scene

Bostonians had quibbles with the TV show "Cheers," but no one complained that the concept of a neighborhood bar where everybody knows your name was implausible. The bar scene tends to be fairly insular—as a stranger, don't assume that you'll get a warm welcome (except at Cheers itself, which is full of tourists!)—but you won't be unwelcome, either.

BARS & LOUNGES

Beat Hôtel ★   A subterranean den of cool, Beat Hôtel serves food but is better known as a nightclub and lounge with a great sound system and drink menu. The original hipster era inspired the faux-bohemian decor as well as the decision to book live jazz, blues, and world music. Check out the weekend brunch (you'll need a reservation). 13 Brattle St. (at Palmer St.), Cambridge. © **617/499-0001.** www.beathotel.com. T: Red Line to Harvard.

The Beehive   The Beehive is a throwback to the days when the South End overflowed with top-notch jazz clubs. It's a two-level lounge and restaurant with live music nightly in a suitably creative location: underneath the Boston Center for the Arts (p. 113). 541 Tremont St. (at Clarendon St.). © **617/423-0069.** www.beehiveboston.com. T: Orange Line to Back Bay.

Brick & Mortar ★   Like its stellar drinks and beer list, Brick & Mortar balances esoteric and accessible. A cavernous space with exposed-brick walls, it's an after-work destination for cocktail aficionados, who appreciate the staff's encyclopedic knowledge and laid-back attitude. Look for the unmarked door to the left of Central Kitchen. Open daily at 5pm. 567 Massachusetts Ave. (at Pearl St.), 2nd floor, Cambridge. © **617/491-0016.** T: Red Line to Central.

The Bristol Lounge ★★★   Boston's premier hotel bar—a competitive category—is a large, sophisticated room with a working fireplace and great martinis. The Bristol Lounge is also a top-notch restaurant. Food is available until 10:30pm (Fri–Sat until 11:30am). In the Four Seasons Hotel, 200 Boylston St. (at Hadassah Way, btw. Arlington St. and Charles St. S.). © **617/351-2037.** www.fourseasons.com/boston/dining. T: Green Line to Arlington.

Cheers (Beacon Hill)   Then known as the Bull & Finch Pub, this bar inspired the classic sitcom "Cheers" and now attracts tourists almost exclusively. They pose in front of the street-level entrance and the bar downstairs, a replica of the one on the show. Food is available starting at 11am, souvenirs all day every day (except Christmas). 84 Beacon St. (at Brimmer St.). © **617/227-9605.** www.cheersboston.com. T: Green Line to Arlington.

Cheers (Faneuil Hall Marketplace) Like the Beacon Hill original, the "Cheers" bar holds a faithful replica of the bar on the TV show, with lots of extra seating for international patrons yelling "Norm!" Memorabilia on display includes Sam Malone's Red Sox jacket. Bring a camera. You must be 21 to enter after 9pm. Quincy Market Building, South Canopy, Faneuil Hall Marketplace. ℭ **617/227-0150.** www.cheersboston. com. T: Green or Blue Line to Government Center, or Orange Line to Haymarket.

Drink ★★ One of the foremost cocktail bars in the country, Drink has no menu: You brainstorm with the bartender, who makes something just for you. Whether you fancy yourself a mixologist or can't tell elderflower liqueur from house-made milk punch, you'll leave happy. Open daily at 4pm. 348 Congress St. (near A St.). ℭ **617/695-1806.** www.drinkfortpoint.com. T: Red Blue Line to South Station.

Eastern Standard In the heart of Kenmore Square, Eastern Standard is a European-style all-day dining and drinking destination with a phenomenal cocktail list. It has a brasserie menu, patio seating in fine weather, and pro–Red Sox crowds throughout baseball season. In the Hotel Commonwealth, 528 Commonwealth Ave. (at Kenmore St.). ℭ **617/532-9100.** www.easternstandardboston.com. T: Green Line B, C, or D to Kenmore.

Grafton Street Grafton Street (named after a Dublin thoroughfare) attracts a cross-section of Harvard Square with a convivial bar, better-than-average food, and not-just-students clientele. In good weather, there's seating on the sidewalk. Open weeknights until 1am, weekends until 2am. 1230 Massachusetts Ave. (at Bow St.), Cambridge. ℭ **617/497-0400.** www.graftonstreetcambridge.com. T: Red Line to Harvard.

Grendel's Den ★ Opened in 1971, Grendel's is one of the few vestiges of Harvard Square's bohemian heyday. The underground space is indeed denlike, with a cozy fireplace and sometimes-spacey service. A young crowd flocks here for the half-price, vegetarian-friendly food menu (daily 5–7:30pm and Mon–Thurs 9–11:30pm)—but note that it's not available on the pleasant patio, which faces a small park. 89 Winthrop St. (at John F. Kennedy St.), Cambridge. ℭ **617/491-1160.** www. grendelsden.com. T: Red Line to Harvard.

The Hong Kong ★ The second-floor lounge is the headliner at this beloved Harvard Square restaurant and nightspot, in business since 1954. It draws a young crowd for brewskis and scorpion bowls—rum, fruit juice, and fun served with long straws and perfect for sharing (single portions are available). The first floor is a retro Chinese-American restaurant all day, and the third floor has a small dance floor but is better known as the home of the **Comedy Studio** (p. 121). 1238 Massachusetts Ave. (at Bow St.), Cambridge. ℭ **617/864-5311.** www.hongkongharvard.com. T: Red Line to Harvard.

The Littlest Bar ★★ A block from the Greenway, the Littlest Bar is unexpectedly spacious—the name comes from the closet-size original (now closed). On the edge of the Financial District, it attracts a not-particularly businesslike crowd with its excellent beer and whisky menus. There's outdoor seating on a relatively peaceful side street in good weather. 102 Broad St. (at Wharf St.). ℭ **617/542-8469.** www.littlestbar.com. T: Blue Line to Aquarium.

Miracle of Science Bar + Grill ★★ On the edge of Central Square, this friendly spot is obviously an MIT bar—the food menu (chalked on the wall) looks like the periodic table of the elements. Miracle of Science has a rare 8am liquor license, a holdover from the days when this was a factory neighborhood, which makes it popular with tech types who've been up all night doing … tech stuff. 321 Massachusetts Ave. (at State St.), Cambridge. ℭ **617/686-ATOM** [2866]. www.miracleofscience.us. T: Red Line to Central.

Silvertone Bar & Grill ★ A longtime Downtown Crossing favorite, Silvertone cultivates a "Mad Men"–era vibe and gets raucous after work on weekdays. If you stick around for dinner (not a bad move), be sure someone in your party orders macaroni and cheese. Closed Sunday. 69 Bromfield St. (off Tremont St.). ℂ **617/338-7887.** www. silvertonedowntown.com. T: Red or Green Line to Park St.

Sonsie A fashionable destination for chic locals and Newbury Street shoppers, Sonsie hops from midday till after midnight. It's perfect for a glass of wine and some people-watching when you've been boutique- and gallery-hopping. In good weather, the French doors turn the space into a see-and-be-seen scene. 327 Newbury St. (off Hereford St.). ℂ **617/351-2500.** www.sonsieboston.com. T: Green Line B, C, or D to Hynes Convention Center.

Top of the Hub ★★★ The 52nd-floor view from this classy lounge entrances legions of out-of-towners and even the most jaded Bostonians. A special-occasion standby, Top of the Hub offers live jazz as well as an excellent cocktail menu and wine list. Dress is casual but neat (no jeans). Open nightly until 1am. For a great view without the dress-up atmosphere, the Skywalk Observatory (p. 86) is two stories down. Prudential Center, 800 Boylston St. ℂ **617/536-1775.** www.topofthehub.net. $24 minimum at tables after 8pm. Validated parking available. T: Green Line to Copley or Green Line E to Prudential.

SPORTS BARS

Bleacher Bar ★ Follow the outside wall of Fenway Park, find the door, and step inside. Yes, you're *under* the bleachers. This is an unremarkable bar with one great big selling point: Many seats have a view of the outfield. During games, one-way glass separates the patrons from the Red Sox and their opponents; when the park isn't in use, the huge window is open, weather permitting. 82A Lansdowne St. (btw. Brookline Ave. and Ipswich St.). ℂ **617/262-2424.** www.bleacherbarboston.com. T: Green Line B, C, or D to Kenmore.

Cask 'n Flagon ★ Across the street from Fenway Park, "the Cask" draws thousands of people on Red Sox game days—and plenty of others throughout the year. If an important game or match is on TV, you'll find it on at least a few of the dozens of sets in this sprawling establishment, liberally decorated with sports memorabilia. 62 Brookline Ave. (at Lansdowne St.). ℂ **617/536-4840.** www.casknflagon.com. T: Green Line B, C, or D to Kenmore.

The Fours ★★ A stone's throw from the TD Garden, the Fours is a winter sports powerhouse—"Sport Illustrated" has named it the best sports bar in the country—that becomes an all-purpose fun watering hole when the Bruins and Celtics are out of season. There's sidewalk seating in good weather. 166 Canal St. (off Causeway St.). ℂ **617/720-4455.** www.thefours.com/boston. T: Green or Orange Line to North Station.

IRISH BARS

The Black Rose Less than a block from Faneuil Hall Marketplace, you'll see lots of other tourists at the Black Rose—but also real-deal Irish musicians (nightly) who encourage singing along. Come during the day or head to the second floor to enjoy the atmosphere without quite as much crowd noise. 160 State St. (at Commercial St.). ℂ **617/742-2286.** www.blackroseboston.com. Cover for music $5–$10. T: Blue Line to Aquarium or Orange Line to State.

The Burren ★   Davis Square is a bit of a trip on the Red Line—but it's faster than going to Ireland. The Burren is so authentic that Irish expats who have flocked here since 1996. Check the website for the music calendar, which is heavy on traditional artists with plenty of other options. 247 Elm St. (at Chester St.), Somerville. ✆ **617/776-6896.** www.burren.com. Cover (back room only) $5–$10. T: Red Line to Davis.

Mr. Dooley's Boston Tavern ★★   In a sea of wannabe Irish bars, Mr. Dooley's is as close as downtown Boston gets to the real deal. Gracious bartenders who know their way around a Guinness tap preside over a low-ceilinged room that draws Financial District types at lunch, congenial after-work crowds, and fans of live music at night. 77 Broad St. (at Custom House St.). ✆ **617/338-5656.** www.mrdooleys.com. Cover (Fri–Sat only) $3–$5. T: Orange Line to State or Blue Line to Aquarium.

The Plough & Stars ★★   On a nondescript corner between Central and Harvard squares, this pub and restaurant is a small space that attracts improbably large crowds with one of the best music calendars in the area. On weekdays, it's a neighborhood bar with good food; at night and on weekends, it's a tiny but top-notch music club. 912 Massachusetts Ave. (at Hancock St.), Cambridge. ✆ **617/576-0032.** www.ploughandstars.com. Cover free to $7. T: Red Line to Central or Harvard.

BREWPUBS

Boston Beer Works   Boston Beer Works originated in the shadow of Fenway Park and expanded to the shadow of what's now the TD Garden. But these aren't sports bars—they're serious brewpubs that happen to get earsplittingly loud before, during, and after games. Come during road trips or off hours to explore the extensive and excellent selection of draft brews. 61 Brookline Ave. (at Lansdowne St.). ✆ **617/536-BEER.** www.beerworks.net. T: Green Line B, C, or D to Kenmore. Also at 110 Canal St. (btw. Causeway St. and Valenti Way). ✆ 617/896-BEER. T: Green or Orange Line to North Station.

Cambridge Brewing Company ★   The tech hotbed of Kendall Square is also a destination for beer connoisseurs—there seems to be a lot of overlap—who come here for the outstanding selection of year-round and seasonal brews. In fine weather, it's worth waiting for a seat on the patio. 100 Kendall Sq., Building 100 (Hampshire St. and Cardinal Medeiros Ave.), Cambridge. ✆ **617/494-1994.** www.cambrew.com. T: Red Line to Kendall/MIT; 10-min. walk.

John Harvard's Brewery & Ale House ★★   A tweedy Harvard crowd flocks here for the ever-changing selection of traditional craft beers brewed in-house. The expert waitstaff can help you match a brew (or brews) to the beer-friendly food menu. The stained-glass windows—decorative, in this subterranean space—feature local sports legends. 33 Dunster St. (off Mount Auburn St.), Cambridge. ✆ **617/868-3585.** www.johnharvards.com. T: Red Line to Harvard.

The Club & Music Scene

As a rule, Boston's live-music scene is considerably more compelling than the action at dance clubs, but somewhere out there is a good time for almost everyone, regardless of age, musical taste, or budget. Check the sources listed in the introduction to this chapter for ideas; if you prefer to wait for inspiration to strike after you reach Boston, ask the staff at your hotel and check the daily "Globe," the Friday "Herald," or "Improper Bostonian." If you run across a venue that shares your taste, follow it on Twitter and friend it on Facebook, and you may get advance notice about special bookings and deals.

Dance clubs cluster in the **Theater District.** The center of the sprawling live-music universe is **Central Square** in Cambridge. Rowdy college bars and clubs abound near the intersection of Harvard and Brighton avenues in **Allston** (T: Green Line B to Harvard Ave.). That makes club-hopping easy, but it also means dealing with swarms of teenagers, students, and recent college grads. To steer clear, stick to slightly more upscale and less centrally located nightspots. If you do like teenagers (or you are one), seek out a place where admission is 18- or 19-plus. Policies change regularly, sometimes from night to night; check ahead.

A night on the town in Boston and Cambridge is brief: Most bars close by 1am, and clubs close at 2am. Under a pilot program instituted in 2014—and subject to being canceled after a 1-year trial—the T shuts down around 2:30am on weekends (and btw. 12:30 and 1am on weeknights). The **drinking age** is 21; a valid driver's license or passport is required as proof of age, and the law is strictly enforced, especially near college campuses.

LIVE MUSIC

Rock & Pop

Great Scott ★★ What appears to be a neighborhood bar with a student-heavy clientele is actually one of the Boston area's best destinations for live music—usually rock, usually local. Check ahead for the nightly schedule, which also includes comedy (the early show on Fri) and DJs. You can use a credit card for advance tickets (subject to a service fee), but bring cash for the bar. 1222 Commonwealth Ave. (at Harvard Ave.). ©**617/566-9014** or 800/745-3000 (Ticketmaster). www.greatscottboston.com. Cover $5–$20 (usually $12 or less). T: Green Line B to Harvard Ave.

The Middle East ★★★ For live music in the Boston area, there's the Middle East, and then there's everywhere else. The club enjoys a well-deserved reputation for booking the best local, national, and international performers in every genre—rock, hip-hop, ska, reggae, jazz, blues, funk, you name it—and attracting large, savvy crowds every night of the week. Also here are the **Corner,** which books acoustic shows and belly dancers, and **ZuZu** (www.zuzubar.com), a Middle Eastern restaurant with a separate calendar. Most shows are 18-plus; ZuZu is 21-plus. 472–480 Massachusetts Ave. (at Brookline St.), Central Sq., Cambridge. ©**617/864-3278** or 866/777-8932 (TicketWeb). www.mideastclub.com. Cover $8–$25 (usually $15 or less; ZuZu cover free to $7). T: Red Line to Central.

Paradise Rock Club ★ Although it's surrounded by Boston University buildings, the Paradise is more than just a student destination. It holds 900-plus for national and international artists who appreciate the relatively small space as well as local bands and stand-up comics. Most shows are 18-plus. 967–969 Commonwealth Ave. (½ block from Pleasant St.). ©**617/562-8800** or 877/598-8497 for tickets. www.crossroadspresents.com. T: Green Line B to Pleasant St.

The Sinclair ★ With its two-level performance space, cocktail bar, and restaurant, the Sinclair has been a Harvard-student magnet since 2012. It books an impressive variety of musical acts—most for 18-plus audiences, some for all ages—and the occasional comedy show. The box office accepts cash only. 52 Church St. (btw. Palmer and Brattle sts.), Cambridge. ©**617/547-5200** or 800/745-3000 (Ticketmaster). www.sinclaircambridge.com. Tickets $10–$35, most $12–$20. T: Red Line to Harvard.

Toad ★★ A small bar with a tiny stage, Toad is a neighborhood hangout with a great beer list (and a full bar) and a brilliant entertainment philosophy. There's live music—rock, rockabilly, blues, soul, and more—every night, and no cover charge. 1912

Massachusetts Ave. (at Porter Rd.), Cambridge. ✆ **617/497-4950** (info line). www.toadcambridge. com. T: Red Line to Porter.

T.T. the Bear's Place ★★   The Middle East (see above) and "T.T.'s" are the main reasons for Central Square's well-deserved reputation for great live music. This little club books mostly local rock, pop, alternative, and indie acts—as many as four per night, every night—and draws enthusiastic 20-, 30-, and even 40-somethings. Saturday is '80s dance party night, and there's a monthly Goth night. The box office accepts cash only. 10 Brookline St. (at Massachusetts Ave.), Cambridge. ✆ **617/492-0082,** 617/492-BEAR [2327] (concert line) or 866/468-7619 (TicketWeb). www.ttthebears.com. Cover $7–$17. T: Red Line to Central.

Eclectic

Lizard Lounge ★★   Rock, folk, and jazz music draws a lively crowd to the Lizard Lounge, a snug space that's a favorite with local acts who want to get up close and personal with the audience. The basement space adds to the sense that you wandered into the neighbors' rec room just as their incredibly talented friends started jamming. Food is available until 1am on weekends, midnight on weekdays. Sunday is poetry night; Monday is open-mic night. At Cambridge Common restaurant, 1667 Massachusetts Ave. (at Wendell St.), Cambridge. ✆ **617/547-0759** (show listings) or 800/838-3006 (Brown Paper Tickets). www.lizardloungeclub.com. Cover $5–$15. T: Red Line to Harvard.

The Red Room @ Cafe 939 ★   The Red Room is a student-run all-ages (in other words, alcohol-free) live-music club inside a Berklee College of Music coffeehouse. It might be the best deal in town if you want to be able—eventually—to say that you saw the senior recital of a breakout star. The 200-capacity venue has top-notch acoustics and books professionals as well as students. To buy advance tickets without a service fee, or to use your student discount, visit the Berklee Performance Center box office at 136 Massachusetts Ave. Closed Sunday; coffeehouse closed Saturday except during shows. 939 Boylston St. (off Hereford St.). ✆ **617/747-2261** (tickets) or 617/747-6038 (coffeehouse). www.cafe939.com. Tickets free to $30; most $12 or less. T: Green Line B, C, or D to Hynes Convention Center.

Folk

Boston is one of the only American cities where folk musicians consistently sell out large venues that usually book rock and pop performers. If an artist you want to see is touring, check ahead for Boston-area dates. Even post-gentrification, the streets around **Harvard Square** play host to a consistently promising roster or artists.

Also see the **Lizard Lounge** (above).

Club Passim ★★★   One of the folk-music world's legendary venues, Passim helped launch the careers of countless artists, including Joan Baez, Shawn Colvin, and Tom Rush. In a cramped basement near the Harvard Coop (its third location since opening in 1958), the all-ages coffeehouse spotlights promising new performers and welcomes international stars with equal passion. There's live music nightly, beer, wine, and, of course, coffee. Tuesdays without other bookings are open-mic nights. Shows nightly, usually at 8pm; on two-show nights, starting times are 7 and 10pm. 47 Palmer St. (at Church St.), Cambridge. ✆ **617/492-7679.** www.passimcenter.org. Cover $5–$40 (most shows $20 or less). T: Red Line to Harvard.

Jazz & Blues

Jazz Week (www.jazzboston.org) is a 10-day event in late April and early May at multiple venues. Surf around the website for an introduction to the local scene. The

Berklee Beantown Jazz Festival (www.beantownjazzfestival.com), in late September, draws tens of thousands of aficionados to Columbus Avenue in the South End for a full weekend afternoon of free outdoor music. Check the website for details.

On summer Thursdays at 6pm, the **Boston Harbor Hotel** (🕾 **617/491-2100;** www.bhh.com) sponsors free performances on the "Blues Barge," behind the hotel.

Cantab Lounge ★ Neighborhood dive bar by day, unbelievably loud music club by night, this Central Square standby is well into its fourth decade of bridging the town-gown divide. It books blues, bluegrass, rock, and jazz in a decent-sized street-level space and cramped basement. Both floors schedule bluegrass on Tuesday; Wednesday is poetry slam night downstairs. Cash only. 738 Massachusetts Ave. (at Pleasant St.), Cambridge. 🕾 **617/354-2685.** www.cantab-lounge.com. Cover $3–$10. T: Red Line to Central.

House of Blues Boston ★★ The chain originated in a little house in Cambridge and now encompasses 13 locations, including this state-of-the-art venue across the street from Fenway Park. It holds nearly 2,500 but feels almost clublike thanks to the layout and the enthusiasm of the crowds that turn out for high-profile blues, rock, and pop acts. The kitchen serves above-average Southern food on show nights (4–10pm) and starting 2 hours before Red Sox home games. 15 Lansdowne St. (btw. Brookline Ave. and Ipswich St.). 🕾 **888/693-2583.** www.houseofblues.com./boston Tickets $23–$55 (most shows $40 or less). T: Green Line B, C, or D to Kenmore.

Regattabar ★★ The second-best jazz club in the Boston area—my top pick is Scullers (see below)—Regattabar plays host to an impressive variety of acts. The large, relatively flat room has no real stage, which means some problematic sight lines. Buy tickets in advance or at the door at least 30 minutes before show time. Open Tuesday through Saturday and some Sundays, with one or two performances per night. In the Charles Hotel, 1 Bennett St. (at Eliot St.), Cambridge. 🕾 **617/395-7757** for tickets. www.regattabarjazz.com. Tickets $15–$35. T: Red Line to Harvard.

Scullers Jazz Club ★★★ The Boston area's best jazz club, Scullers has first pick of high-profile touring artists—recently, Will Downing, Cassandra Wilson, Delfeayo Marsalis, and the Manhattans—and local favorites. Patrons tend to be more hardcore than the crowds at the Regattabar (see above), but it depends on who's performing. Shows begin at 8pm (and, usually, 10pm) Tuesday through Saturday; the box office is open weekdays from 11am to 6pm. Ask about supper club–style dinner packages ($60–$100 per person). In the DoubleTree Suites by Hilton Hotel Boston, 400 Soldiers Field Rd. (at Cambridge St.). 🕾 **617/562-4111.** www.scullersjazz.com. Tickets $20–$60. Validated parking available.

Wally's Cafe ★★ In business since 1947, Wally's is a family-owned bar that just happens to book fantastic jazz, blues, funk, and more. It's legendary as much for its history—this is the lone holdover from the days when the South End was an internationally renowned jazz destination—as for its music-first philosophy and incredibly diverse clientele. Live music begins nightly at 9pm. Open daily until 1:30am. 427 Massachusetts Ave. (off Columbus Ave.). 🕾 **617/424-1408.** www.wallyscafe.com. No cover; 1-drink minimum. T: Orange Line to Massachusetts Ave.

COMEDY CLUBS

The **Wilbur Theatre** (p. 113) books high-profile comics on national tours as well as music acts. The annual **Boston International Comedy & Movie Festival** (🕾 **860/712-5093;** www.bostoncomedyfestival.com) attracts big-name national performers, local up-and-comers, and films. The weeklong event takes place all over town in November; check ahead for schedules and venues.

The Comedy Studio ★★ The Comedy Studio offers "serious" comedy fans the thrill of seeing little-known talents finding their voices—and offers casual fans more than a few hearty laughs. Standup, improv, sketches, and even magic shows, booked by experts with an uncanny ability to find talents on the verge of taking off, make this a great place to kick off a fun evening. Shows are Tuesday (magicians) through Sunday at 8pm. At the Hong Kong restaurant, 1238 Massachusetts Ave. (at Bow St.), Cambridge. *C* **617/661-6507.** www.thecomedystudio.com. Cover $10–$12. T: Red Line to Harvard.

Improv Asylum Right on the Freedom Trail, this subterranean venue livens up the North End with improv and sketch comedy. Performances are nightly in the summer (check for Sun and Mon winter schedules), and year-round on Saturday afternoon and at midnight on weekends. Management suggests buying tickets in advance. Recommended for people over 16. 216 Hanover St. (off Cross St.). *C* **617/263-6887.** www.improvasylum.com. Tickets $5–$25. Validated parking available. T: Green or Orange Line to Haymarket.

ImprovBoston ★ This longtime favorite—it opened in 1982—offers something for everyone, including families (who have their own show at 6pm on Sat). Professional and amateur performers, numerous classes, and two performance spaces make ImprovBoston a consistently entertaining destination for fans of standup and storytelling as well as improv and sketch comedy. Regular shows run Wednesday through Sunday, and the lobby bar serves beer and wine. 40 Prospect St. (off Mass. Ave.). *C* **617/576-1253.** www.improvboston.com. Tickets free to $18 (most shows $12). T: Red Line to Central.

Laugh Boston One of the Seaport District's few entertainment options, this 300-seat venue books comics who aren't yet big enough names to play the Wilbur Theatre (p. 113), including local up-and-comers in a weekly showcase called Boston Accents. Thank goodness for online videos, which can help you decide whether a particular comic is worth the trip to convention center–land. Shows Wednesday through Sunday. In the Westin Boston Waterfront hotel, 425 Summer St. (at D St.). *C* **617/725-2844.** www.laughboston.com. Tickets $5–$35 (most shows $10–$25). Validated parking available. T: Silver Line SL1/SL2 to World Trade Center.

DANCE CLUBS

Most clubs enforce a **dress code** that forbids athletic wear (including game jerseys), sneakers, jeans, Timberland boots, and ball caps—or some combination thereof—on everyone, as well as tank tops or collarless shirts on men. Check ahead if you have your heart set on a glitzy night out; a savvy concierge can help you avoid lines and let you know if you need to wear a jacket. *Tip:* While you're visiting websites, note that some clubs will let you put your name on the VIP list online. Can't hurt, might help.

The Estate A decent fallback if Royale (see below) isn't an option, this good-sized venue packs large crowds of 20-somethings into its two levels. Management instructs patrons to "dress like you mean it"; the secret to evading the long line that forms on weekends is to take that advice to heart—and maybe reserve a table. Open Thursday (gay night) through Saturday; check ahead for specifics. 1 Boylston Place (off Boylston St., near Tremont St.). *C* **617/351-7000.** www.theestateboston.com. Cover $10–$25. T: Green Line to Boylston.

Royale Boston ★★ By a wide margin, Royale is Boston's best dance club. The huge two-level space, a former hotel ballroom, attracts top-notch local DJs, international guest stars, and large crowds. Head to the balcony for a break from the action and great people-watching. The Bowery Presents books the excellent live music, which includes some early-evening all-ages shows. In the Courtyard Boston Downtown hotel, 279 Tremont St. (½ block from Stuart St.). © **617/338-7699.** www.royaleboston.com. Cover $15–$25. T: Green Line to Boylston or Orange Line to Tufts Medical Center.

The Gay & Lesbian Scene

Boston and Cambridge—especially the places where out-of-towners are likely to spend time—are gay friendly. The South End is the area's highest-profile gay neighborhood, and lesbians gravitate toward Porter Square in Cambridge and Jamaica Plain in Boston, but LGBT Bostonians and Cantabrigians live, work, and play everywhere. Throughout eastern Massachusetts, gay couples are no longer remarkable, and families with two mommies or two daddies fit right in. When you're out on the town, do remember that over-the-top PDA probably won't win you many friends—but the same is true for handsy straight couples.

One long-term result of all this inclusion is that bricks-and-mortar non-nightlife businesses catering more or less exclusively to gay and lesbian customers are vanishing. Here are some nightlife options.

BARS & CLUBS

In addition to the clubs listed here, some mainstream venues schedule a weekly or monthly gay night. The particulars are current at press time, but always check ahead.

The Estate (p. 121) plays host to Glamlife on Thursday, and the **House of Blues Boston** (p. 120) is home to Epic Saturdays. The promoter of both events is **Chris Harris Presents** (www.chrisharrispresents.com/gay-mafia). On Tuesdays, Zuesday! Queer Dance Party takes over **ZuZu** in Cambridge (p. 118). Once a month, **Great Scott** (p. 118) plays host to Don't Ask Don't Tell, an "unbridled experience of the senses."

The **Midway Cafe,** 3496 Washington St., Jamaica Plain (© **617/524-9038;** www. midwaycafe.com), schedules women's dance night, featuring Queeraoke, every Thursday.

The **Welcoming Committee** (http://thewelcomingcommittee.com) stages occasional flash mob–style takeovers of straight bars and clubs just for the night. Visit the website to sign up for a notification e-mail.

Worthwhile websites include www.edgeboston.com, www.queeragenda.org, http:// boston.gaycities.com, and www.dykenight.com. For listings, check the print and online versions of "Bay Windows" (www.baywindows.com) and "Improper Bostonian" (www.improper.com).

Club Café ★★   One of Boston's highest-profile gay clubs is also a good restaurant that draws a mixed crowd to the Back Bay–South End border for lunch, dinner, and the popular Sunday buffet brunch. Chic men and some women come here for conversation (the noise level is reasonable), live music, cabaret performers, and video entertainment. Thursday is the busiest night. Open daily until 2am. 209 Columbus Ave. (at Berkeley St.). © **617/536-0966.** www.clubcafe.com. Cover (after 11pm) $10 and up. T: Green Line to Arlington or Orange Line to Back Bay.

Jacques Cabaret ★   Boston's only drag venue, this little place draws its share of congenial regulars, both gay and straight patrons, who mingle with the "girls." The schedule encompasses live music (on weekends), performance artists, and, of course, drag shows. Open daily from noon to midnight. Cash only, but you'll need a credit card to reserve a table. 79 Broadway (at Piedmont St.), Bay Village. © **617/426-8902.** www.jacques cabaret.com/jacquesweb.asp. Cover $6–$10. T: Green Line to Arlington.

Machine A holdout in a rapidly gentrifying neighborhood, Machine is an old-school subterranean club with a good-size dance floor. Thursday is karaoke night, and the second Saturday of every month is Dyke Night. Upstairs, the space once known as the **Ramrod** (© 617/266-2986) has shed its reputation as a hard-core leather bar but has its own entertainment calendar. 1254 Boylston St. (at Ipswich St.). © **617/536-1950.** www. machine-boston.com. Cover free to $10. T: Green Line B, C, or D to Kenmore, then a 10-min. walk.

Paradise The only gay dance club in Cambridge draws men of all ages, shows plenty of porn, and schedules at least one go-go boy—sorry, *dancer*—nightly. Open Sunday through Wednesday until 1am, Thursday through Saturday until 2am. Cash only. 180 Massachusetts Ave. (at Albany St.), Cambridge. © **617/868-3000.** www.paradise cambridge.com. Cover $5. T: Red Line to Central, then a 10-min. walk.

Rise Straitlaced Boston has a single after-hours club, on the second and third floors of a nondescript building at the edge of the Back Bay. There's no alcohol, and DJs keep the 18-plus gay-friendly crowd moving till 6am. Though it's technically members only, Rise does admit guests—check the website. Open Saturday and Sunday, plus some Fridays, 1 to 6am. 306 Stuart St. (at Columbus Ave.). © **617/423-7473.** www.riseclub.us. T: Green Line to Arlington.

Alternative Entertainment
MOVIES

Two superb local revival houses feature lectures and live performances in addition to foreign and classic films: the **Brattle Theatre,** 40 Brattle St., Cambridge (© **617/876-6837;** www.brattlefilm.org; T: Red Line to Harvard), and the **Coolidge Corner Theatre,** 290 Harvard St., Brookline (© **617/734-2500;** www.coolidge.org; T: Green Line C to Coolidge Corner). The Coolidge also schedules midnight shows. Classic and foreign films are the tip of the iceberg at the quirky **Harvard Film Archive,** 24 Quincy St., Cambridge (© **617/495-4700;** http://hcl.harvard.edu/hfa; T: Red Line to Harvard), which also shows student films.

COFFEEHOUSES

As in most other American cities, you won't get far without seeing a Starbucks, but for coffee and hanging out, the Boston area offers plenty of less generic options. At all of them, hours are long and loitering is encouraged—these are good places to bring your laptop or journal.

Algiers Café & Restaurant ★ One of Harvard Square's original coffeehouse hangouts, Algiers is a longtime favorite for excellent plain and flavored coffees—try the mint—and decent Middle Eastern food. Lingering is encouraged, the service friendly (but sometimes forgetful), and the clientele of wannabe intellectuals and moguls unintentionally hilarious. Even with half of the patrons staring at screens, the eavesdropping here is great. 40 Brattle St. (btw. Brattle Sq. and Church St.), Cambridge. © **617/492-1557.** T: Red Line to Harvard.

Boston Common Coffee Co. ★★ This small local chain made its debut in the big leagues: the **North End.** Having held its own with the Italian-American neighborhood's espresso bars, Boston Common Coffee branched out. Comfortable and not too brightly lit—the vibe is almost lounge-y—all four locations are neighborhood hangouts. In addition to a wide selection of hot, cold, and frozen drinks, they serve good baked goods and even better sandwiches and salads. The High Street branch closes on weekends. 97 Salem St. (off Parmenter St.). © **617/725-0040.** www.bostoncommoncoffee.com.

T: Green or Orange Line to Haymarket. 515 Washington St. (at West St.). ℂ **617/542-0595.** T: Green Line to Boylston. 10 High St. (off Summer St.). ℂ **617/695-9700.** 89 Canal St. (at Valenti Way). T: Green or Orange Line to North Station.

Caffè Nero ★   The first U.S. location of the British chain is a glass-walled refuge that faces the increasingly interesting neighborhood where Downtown Crossing meets Chinatown. The view, the classy yet comfortable space, and the friendly service are all wonderful, but the big question is, How's the coffee? Even better. Open daily 7am to 9:30pm. 560 Washington St. (at Avery St.). ℂ **617/936-3432.** www.caffenero.com. T: Orange Line to Chinatown or Green Line to Boylston.

Equal Exchange Cafe   A stone's throw from North Station and the TD Garden, this place is a real find in a neighborhood choked with sports bars. Even better, the fair-trade coffee, tea, and hot chocolate are terrific. The cafe offers veggie-friendly food and baked goods prepared by local vendors. 226 Causeway St. (off N. Washington St.). ℂ **617/372-8777.** www.equalexchangecafe.com. T: Green or Orange Line to North Station.

Thinking Cup   Thinking Cup originated near **Boston Common** before branching out to two of the most competitive caffeine markets in Boston: the **North End** and **Newbury Street.** All three branches are thriving. They serve cult favorite Stumptown coffee, organic tea, superb house-made French pastries, and great sandwiches. 165 Tremont St. (near Avery St.). ℂ **617/482-5555.** www.thinkingcup.com. T: Green Line to Boylston. 236 Hanover St. (btw. Cross and Parmenter sts.). ℂ **857/233-5277.** T: Green or Orange Line to Haymarket. 85 Newbury St. (btw. Berkeley and Clarendon sts.). ℂ **617/247-3333.** T: Green Line to Arlington.

1369 Coffee House ★   The people-watching at these Cambridge standbys is almost as good as the hot and cold drinks, tasty baked goods, and menu of light fare (sandwiches, salads, and soups). Many patrons are transfixed by their computers, but enough are unplugged to make the 1369 a fun place for a pit stop. The Central Square location has a pleasant outdoor seating area; the equally enjoyable but less convenient original is at 1369 Cambridge St. (at Springfield St.), Inman Square (ℂ **617/576-1369**). 757 Massachusetts Ave. (at Pleasant St.), Central Sq., Cambridge. ℂ **617/576-4600.** www.1369coffeehouse.com. T: Red Line to Central.

Trident Booksellers & Café ★★   A longtime Back Bay favorite with a great book selection, terrific veggie-friendly food (including breakfast served all day), and free Wi-Fi, Trident is my go-to place at the friendlier end of Newbury Street. In good weather, ask to sit on the patio. Open 8am to midnight daily. 338 Newbury St. (btw. Hereford St. and Mass. Ave.). ℂ **617/267-8688.** www.tridentbookscafe.com. T: Green Line B, C, or D to Hynes Convention Center.

Spectator Sports

Tickets for pro teams can be tough or impossible to get, but before you resort to paying a reseller or scalper, try the following: Ask your **hotel concierge** for suggestions; sign up for **TixList** (www.tixlist.com); and visit the **team website** to see whether season ticket-holders' returns are available to the public. Then grit your teeth and check **StubHub** (ℂ **866/788-2482;** www.stubhub.com) and **Ace Ticket** (ℂ **800/697-3287;** www. aceticket.com)—or, if you're feeling lucky and don't mind the possibility of being scammed, **Craigslist.**

PRO & COLLEGE SPORTS
Baseball

On October 30, 2013, the **Boston Red Sox** won their third World Series in 10 years—and their first at legendary **Fenway Park ★★★** since 1918. The 2004 championship had ended an 86-year drought, and the baseball world was still pinching itself when the team brought home the 2007 crown. Fenway consistently sells out, and when the team is playing well, tickets are a precious commodity.

The season runs from early April to early October, later if the Sox make the playoffs. The quirkiness of the oldest park in the major leagues (1912), rich with history and atmosphere, only adds to the mystique. Most seats are narrow and uncomfortable, but also gratifyingly close to the field. A hand-operated scoreboard fronts the 37-foot left-field wall, or "Green Monster." Watch carefully during a pitching change—the left fielder might suddenly disappear into a door in the wall to get out of the sun.

Practical concerns: Compared with its modern brethren, Fenway is tiny. Tickets are the most expensive in the majors—and getting pricier, thanks to a "dynamic pricing" plan that takes demand into account. A few upper bleacher seats for games against less popular opponents cost $10, but most are in the $35-to-$129 range, with the best dugout boxes topping $600 (that's *if* you pay face value). They go on sale in December; try to order early. Given a choice between seats in a low-numbered grandstand section—say, 10 or below—and in the bleachers, go for the bleachers. They can get rowdy during night games, but the view is better from there than from deep right field. "Monster" seats cost at least $175 (standing room $45) and are sold in batches throughout the season; check the website. A limited number of same-day standing-room tickets ($20–$35) are available before each game, and fans sometimes return presold tickets, especially if a rainout causes rescheduling. It can't hurt to check, particularly if the team isn't playing well; cross your fingers and visit the ticket office. *Tip:* The Game Day Ticket Sales office, near Gate E on Lansdowne Street, offers tickets that went unsold for some reason. The doors open 2 hours before game time; lining up is permitted 3 hours before that (but not earlier).

The **Fenway Park ticket office** (*C* **877/REDSOX9** [733-7699]; www.redsox.com/tickets; T: Green Line B, C, or D to Kenmore, or D to Fenway) is at 4 Yawkey Way, near the corner of Brookline Avenue. Tickets for people with disabilities and in no-alcohol sections are available. Smoking is not allowed in the park.

Play Ball!

Fenway Park tours (*C* **617/226-6666**; www.redsox.com/tours) give visitors an inside look at the beloved ballpark. This is an excellent alternative if your budget or schedule doesn't allow for attending a game. The 50-minute tour may include a walk on the warning track, a stop in the press box, and a visit to the Red Sox Hall of Fame. During the season, tours start on the hour daily from 9am to 5pm (or 3 hr. before game time, whichever is earlier). There are no tours on holidays or before day games. In the winter, hours are shorter and tours may be truncated because of construction (but also cheaper than in the summer); check ahead to avoid disappointment. Admission is $17 for adults, $14 for seniors, $12 for students and children 3 to 15. Advance individual sales aren't available.

Basketball

With 17 National Basketball Association titles, the **Boston Celtics** are one of the highest-profile American sports franchises, but you can sometimes land surprisingly good (and pricey) seats without much notice. The Celtics play from early October until at least mid-April, later if they make the playoffs. When a top contender or a star player is visiting, getting tickets is especially tough. Prices are as low as $10 for some games and top out around $600 (more for floor seats). For information, visit **www.nba.com/celtics**—where you can sign up for same-day ticket alerts—or call the TD Garden (© **617/624-1000**); for tickets, contact Ticketmaster (© **800/745-3000;** www.ticket master.com). To reach the Garden, take the MBTA Green or Orange Line or commuter rail to North Station. *Note:* Spectators may not bring any large bags, including backpacks and briefcases, into the arena.

Football

The **New England Patriots** (© **800/543-1776;** www.patriots.com) play to standing-room-only crowds from August through December or January at Gillette Stadium on Route 1 in Foxboro, about a 45-minute drive south of Boston. Tickets ($75–$211) sell out well in advance, often as part of season-ticket packages. Call or check the website for information on individual ticket sales and resales as well as public-transit options.

Boston College is the state's only Division I-A team. The Eagles, who compete in the Atlantic Coast Conference, play at Alumni Stadium in Chestnut Hill (© **617/552-GoBC** [552-4622]; www.bceagles.com). The area's FCS (formerly Division I-AA) team is Ivy League power **Harvard University,** Harvard Stadium, North Harvard Street, Allston (© **617/495-2211;** www.gocrimson.com).

Hockey

Tickets to see the 2011 Stanley Cup champion **Boston Bruins,** one of the NHL's original six teams, are expensive ($25–$340) but worth it for hard-core fans. For information, visit **www.bostonbruins.com** or call the TD Garden (© **617/624-1000**); for tickets, contact Ticketmaster (© **800/745-3000;** www.ticketmaster.com). To reach the Garden, take the MBTA Green or Orange Line or commuter rail to North Station. *Note:* Spectators may not bring large bags, including backpacks and briefcases, into the arena.

A VISIT TO PLYMOUTH

45 miles SE of Boston

Even though visitors jam the downtown area and waterfront in the summer, Plymouth is large enough to feel more like the working community it is than like a touristy day-trip destination. It's a manageable 1-day excursion from Boston, and particularly enjoyable if you're traveling with children. Plymouth also makes an excellent stop between Boston and Cape Cod.

Everyone educated in the United States knows at least a little of the story of Plymouth—about how the Pilgrims, fleeing religious persecution, left Europe on the *Mayflower* and landed at Plymouth Rock in December 1620 after a stop at Provincetown (see chapter 5). Many also know that the Pilgrims endured disease and privation, and that just 53 people from the original group of 102 celebrated what we now call "the first Thanksgiving" in 1621.

What you won't know until you visit is how small everything was. The *Mayflower* (a reproduction) seems perilously tiny, and when you contemplate how dangerous life was at the time, it's hard not to marvel at the settlers' accomplishments. One of their descendants' accomplishments is this: Plymouth is in many ways a model destination, where the 17th century coexists with the 21st, and most historic attractions are both educational and fun.

Essentials

GETTING THERE   By car, follow the Southeast Expressway (I-93) south from Boston to Route 3. Take exit 6A to Route 44 east and follow signs to the historic attractions. The trip from Boston takes 45 to 60 minutes if it's not rush hour. Take exit 5 for the state **Tourist Information Center** (© **508/746-1150**; www.massvacation.com), where you can get maps, brochures, and information. To go directly to **Plimoth Plantation,** take exit 4. There's metered parking throughout town; visit **www.park plymouth.com** for information.

Plymouth and Brockton **buses** (© **508/746-0378**; www.p-b.com) serve Plymouth from South Station. The trip takes about 1 hour. Buses run more often than the train—and operate on weekends, which the commuter rail to Plymouth doesn't—and cost a little more ($15 one-way, $27 round-trip). Buses drop off and pick up passengers at the park-and-ride lot at Route 3, exit 5. The **commuter rail** (© **617/222-3200**; www.mbta. com) serves Cordage Park, on Route 3A north of downtown, from Boston's South Station four times a day on weekdays only. The round-trip fare is $20. The **Plymouth Area Link** bus (© **800/483-2500** or 508/732-6010; www.gatra.org) connects downtown with the park-and-ride lot and the train station. The fare is $1, free for children 6 and under.

VISITOR INFORMATION   If you haven't visited the Tourist Information Center (see above), pick up a map at the **Destination Plymouth Information Center** (© **508/ 747-7525**), open seasonally at 130 Water St., across from Town Pier. To plan ahead, contact **Destination Plymouth,** 134 Court St., Plymouth, MA 02360 (© **508/747-7533**; www.seeplymouth.com). The staff can help you plan your day and offer suggestions for booking accommodations if you decide to spend the night en route from Boston to Cape Cod or vice versa.

GETTING AROUND   The downtown attractions are easily accessible on foot. A shallow hill slopes from the center of town to the waterfront.

The **America's Hometown Shuttle** trolley (© **508/746-0378**; www.p-b.com/ahs. html) covers a loop throughout the town. It operates from late June through Labor Day weekend, daily from 9:45am to 5pm. The fare ($15 adults, $7.50 children 6–18) includes a narrated tour and unlimited reboarding. Check ahead for the schedule and route, which includes Plimoth Plantation.

Exploring Plymouth

The logical place to begin (good luck talking children out of it) is where the Pilgrims first set foot—at **Plymouth Rock ★★**. The rock, accepted as the landing place of the *Mayflower* passengers, was originally 15 feet long and 3 feet wide. It was moved on the eve of the Revolution and several times thereafter. In 1867, it assumed its present permanent position at tide level. The rock itself isn't much to look at, but the accompanying descriptions are interesting, and the atmosphere is curiously inspiring.

The Colonial Dames of America commissioned the portico around the rock, designed by McKim, Mead & White and erected in 1920. This property's formal name is **Pilgrim Memorial State Park,** 79 Water St. (© **508/747-5360**; www.mass.gov/eea/ agencies/dcr/massparks); it's the smallest state park in Massachusetts.

GUIDED TOURS   To walk in the Pilgrims' footsteps, take a **Colonial Lantern Tour ★** (℃ **774/454-8126;** www.lanterntours.com). Participants carry pierced-tin lanterns on a 1-mile, 90-minute walking tour of the original settlement, conducted by a knowledgeable guide. It might seem hokey at first, but it's fascinating. Tours run nightly at 7:30pm from April to Thanksgiving, rain or shine. The "Ghosts & Legends" tour starts at 8pm Thursday through Saturday June to October. Tickets are $12 for adults; $10 for seniors, AAA members, and children 6 to 16; free for children 5 and under. Check the meeting place when you make reservations. Check ahead for information about Halloween and Thanksgiving tours.

Native Plymouth Tours (℃ **774/454-7792;** www.nativeplymouthtours.com) are guided walking tours that look at town history from the perspective of the original residents. The 90-minute excursions are available from May through November on Friday and Saturday at 5:30pm, otherwise by reservation only. They cost $15 for adults, $12 for seniors, $10 for children 5 to 18.

Narrated cruises run from April or May through November from State Pier and Town Wharf; check the departure point when you make reservations, which are always recommended and imperative at busy times. **Pilgrim Belle Cruises** (℃ **508/747-3434;** www.pilgrimbellecruises.com) offers 75-minute narrated **harbor tours** on a paddle wheeler ($19 adults, $16 seniors, $12 children 5–12) as well as sunset and dining cruises. The offerings of **Plymouth Cruises** (℃ **508/746-5342;** www.plymouthcruises. com) include **pirate cruises** ($19 per person), which allow kids aged 4 to 11 to don hats and face paint and "defend" the boat against marauding buccaneers, and **lobster excursions** ($16 adults, $14 seniors, $12 children 11 and under), which give passengers the chance to haul up traps and observe marine life. **Capt. John Boats** (℃ **800/242-2469** or 508/746-2643; www.captjohn.com) offers **whale watches** ($47 adults, $39 seniors, $29 children 4–12, free for kids 3 and under).

Mayflower II ★★ HISTORIC SITE   Berthed a few steps from Plymouth Rock, the *Mayflower II* is a full-scale reproduction of the type of ship that brought the Pilgrims from England to America in 1620. Although little technical information about the original *Mayflower* survives, designer William A. Baker incorporated the few references in Governor Bradford's account of the voyage with other research to re-create the ship as authentically as possible. To modern eyes, the 106½-foot vessel, constructed in England from 1955 to 1957, seems dangerously small.

This is a self-guided experience, with costumed guides on hand to provide interesting first-person narratives about the vessel and voyage, and other interpreters giving a contemporary perspective. Displays describe and illustrate the journey and the Pilgrims' experience. They include exhibits about 17th-century navigation techniques, stocking the ship with food and other provisions, and the history of the *Mayflower II*. Plimoth Plantation (below) owns and maintains the vessel and offers combined admission discounts. Alongside the ship are museum shops that replicate early Pilgrim dwellings.

State Pier, opposite 174 Water St. ℃ **508/746-1622.** www.plimoth.org. Admission $10 adults, $9 seniors, $7 children 6–12. Plimoth Plantation (good for 2 consecutive days) and *Mayflower II* admission $30 adults, $27 seniors and students, $19 children 6–12. Free for children 5 and under. Late Mar to late Nov daily 9am–5pm (until 7pm July–Sept). Closed Dec to mid-Mar.

Plimoth Plantation ★★ HISTORIC SITE   Allow at least half a day to explore this re-creation of a 1627 English village and 17th-century Native American extended-family home. Children and adults find the experience equally interesting. The

"Pilgrims" are role-players who, in speech, dress, and manner, assume the personalities of members of the original community. The interpreters who staff the Wampanoag Homesite are actually Wampanoags and members of other tribes; they show visitors native foodstuffs, agricultural practices, and crafts. Staff members throughout the plantation eagerly welcome questions.

The exhibits are as accurate as research can make them, constructed with careful attention to historical detail. The planners combined accounts of the original colony with archaeological research, centuries-old records, and the history written by the Pilgrims' leader, William Bradford (who often used the spelling "Plimoth"). You can watch the "Pilgrims" framing a house, splitting wood, shearing sheep, preserving foodstuffs, or cooking a pot of fish stew over an open hearth, all as it was done in the 1600s and using only the tools and cookware available then. Sometimes you can join the activities—depending on the time of year, perhaps planting, harvesting, witnessing a trial, or visiting a wedding party. There are daily militia drills with matchlock muskets that are fired to demonstrate the community's defense system. In fact, little defense was needed, because the Native Americans were friendly. *Note:* Wear comfortable shoes, because you'll be walking a lot.

At the main entrance are two modern buildings that house exhibits, a gift shop, a bookstore, a cafeteria, and an auditorium where visitors can view a film produced by the History Channel. There's also a picnic area. Call or surf ahead for information about the many special events, lectures, tours, workshops, theme dinners, and children's and family programs offered throughout the season.

137 Warren Ave. (Rte. 3). © **508/746-1622.** www.plimoth.org. Admission (good for 2 consecutive days) $26 adults, $24 seniors, $15 children 6–12. Plimoth Plantation and *Mayflower II* admission $30 adults, $27 seniors and students, $19 children 6–12. Free for children 5 and under. Late Mar to late Nov daily 9am–5pm. Closed Dec to mid-Mar. From Rte. 3, take exit 4, Plimoth Plantation Hwy.

Where to Eat

Plimoth Plantation (p. 128) has a cafeteria and a picnic area, and it occasionally schedules theme dinners. Should you reach the "seafood again?" stage (it happens), a good destination downtown is **Sam Diego's,** 15 Main St. (© **508/747-0048;** www. samdiegos.com), a cheerful Tex-Mex restaurant and bar in a renovated firehouse. It has a kids' menu and seasonal outdoor seating. Hours are 11:30am to midnight daily.

Lobster Hut ★★ SEAFOOD   The place to be at this longtime Plymouth favorite is on the deck, watching boats on the harbor and keeping an eye out for greedy seagulls. It's not fancy—you order at a simple counter and wait for a staffer to call your number—but it's too busy for the food to be anything but very fresh. Although the location means the clientele includes lots of tourists, the numerous patrons from Plymouth, Mass., are as satisfied as diners from Plymouth, England. Stick with super-fresh fried or broiled seafood; for chicken or a burger, there are better places. Note that you must order food if you want beer or wine.

25 Town Wharf (off Court St. at Samoset St.). © **508/746-2270.** www.lobsterhutplymouth.com. Lunch specials (available Mon–Fri until 4pm) $9–$12, main courses $8–$21, sandwiches $3–$12 (most under $10), clams and lobster market price. Summer daily 11am–9pm; winter daily 11am–7pm. Closed Jan.

Persy's Place ★ AMERICAN   This is my go-to breakfast recommendation for families, because the menu is so huge that everyone likes something on it. From the nine kinds of pancakes to the eight eggs Benedicts to omelets, waffles, and multiple meat options (including chouriço sausage, big with southeastern Massachusetts' large Portuguese-American community), this local hangout has it all. If you can't decide, a friendly server can help you narrow down the choices. They're all good: Unlike a lot of places that boast about selection, this branch of a local mini-chain has no weak spots that I've been able to find. I'll keep trying, though—you know, in the name of research.

35A Main St. (at Middle St.). ✆ **508/732-9876.** www.persysplace.com. Breakfast items $4–$16, lunch items $6–$16. Daily 7am–3pm.

Shopping

Water Street, along the harbor, boasts an inexhaustible supply of souvenir and T-shirt shops. If you already have enough refrigerator magnets, a less kitschy destination, just up the hill, is Route 3A, known as Court, Main, and Warren Street as it runs through town. Heading south, you'll come to **Pilgrim's Progress,** 13 Court St. (✆ **508/746-6033;** www.pilgrimsprogressclothing.com), which carries stylish women's and men's clothing and accessories, then **British Imports of Plymouth,** 1 Court St. (✆ **877/264-8586** or 508/747-2972; www.britishsupplies.com), which specializes in English food and attracts homesick Marmite fans from miles around. A great place to explore, **Main Street Antiques,** 46 Main St. (✆ **508/747-8887**), is home to dozens of dealers; closed Tuesday in winter. **Lily's Apothecary,** 6 Main St. extension, in the old post office (✆ **508/747-7546;** www.lilysapothecary.com), stocks a big-city-style selection of skin- and hair-care products for women and men. Closed Sunday and Monday except by appointment.

CAPE COD

At only 75 miles long, Cape Cod is a curving peninsula that encompasses miles of beaches, hundreds of freshwater ponds, more than a dozen richly historic New England villages, scores of classic clam shacks and ice cream shops—and it's just about everyone's idea of the perfect summer vacation spot.

More than 13 million visitors flock to the Cape to enjoy summertime's nonstop carnival. In full swing, the Cape is, if anything, perhaps a bit too popular for some tastes. Connoisseurs are discovering the subtler appeal of the off-season, when prices plummet along with the population. For some travelers, the prospect of sunbathing en masse on sizzling sand can't hold a candle to a long, solitary stroll on a windswept beach with only the gulls as company. For that experience, you'll have to come in the springtime, or even better, the fall.

UPPER CAPE: SANDWICH & NEARBY

3 miles E of Sagamore; 16 miles NW of Hyannis

Essentials

VISITOR INFORMATION Contact the **Cape Cod Chamber of Commerce,** routes 6 and 132, Hyannis, MA 02601 (© **888/332-2732** or 508/362-3225; www.capecodchamber.org), open year-round, mid-April to mid-November daily 9am to 5pm and mid-November to mid-April Monday to Saturday 10am to 4pm. Stop in at the **Route 25 Visitor Center** (© **508/759-3814**), open daily 9am to 5pm; call for off-season hours. The **Sandwich Chamber of Commerce** (© **508/833-9755;** www.sandwich chamber.com) puts out a handy Sandwich booklet. The **Cape Cod Canal Region Chamber of Commerce,** 70 Main St., Buzzards Bay, MA 02532 (© **508/759-6000;** www.capecodcanalchamber.org), open year-round Monday to Friday 9am to 5pm, can provide literature on both Sandwich and Bourne. A consortium of Sandwich businesses has put together an excellent walking guide and map, available at most inns in town.

Where to Stay

In addition to the lodging places listed below, Sandwich has a number of motels along Route 6A, but the one with the best location is **Sandy Neck Motel,** at 669 Rte. 6A, East Sandwich (© **800/564-3992** or 508/362-3992; www.sandyneck.com), which sits at the entrance to the road leading to Sandy Neck, the best beach in these parts. Rates for the 12 units are $129 to $139 double and $199 to $299 for one- and two-room efficiencies. It's closed November to mid-April.

Cape Cod

Race Point
Beach
Race Pt.
PROVINCETOWN
Pilgrim L.
Head of the Meadow
6A
Herring Cove Beach
Provincetown
Provincetown Har.
Long Pt.
Truro
6
Corn Hill Beach
TRURO
ATLANTIC

OCEAN

CAPE COD

NATIONAL

SEASHORE

WELLFLEET
Wellfleet
Cahoon Hollow Beach
Mayo Beach
White Crest Beach
*Wellfleet
Harbor*
Marconi Beach
Jeremy Pt.
Lieutenant I.

North
Eastham
EASTHAM
Eastham

C A P E   C O D

B A Y

Rock
Harbor
ORLEANS
Skaket Beach
Orleans
Nauset Beach
East
Breakwater Beach
Brewster
Linnells Landing
Beach
Paines Creek Beach
Flax Pond
Pilgrim Beach
Brewster
Cliff
South
Corporation Beach
East
6A
Orleans
Mayflower Beach
Dennis
NICKERSON S.P.Pd.
124
South
Chapin
Scargo
B R E W S T E R
Brewster
Beach
Lake Upper
Pleasant' Bay
Grays Beach
Mill Pd.
Long Pd.
39
Barnstable Har.
Yarmouth
DENNIS
East
28
Chatham
Port
Yarmouth
134
Harwich
Port
Barnstable
6
137
North Beach
YARMOUTH
South
HARWICH
C H A T H A M
Barnstable
Dennis
Oyster
Mun. Airport
West
Pond Chatham
E
South
Harwich
Chatham
32
Yarmouth
Harwich
Chatham Light Beach
West
West Dennis
Port
Forest
Hardings
Yarmouth
Beach
Beach
Beach
South Beach
Hyannis
28
Bass River Beach
West
Parker's River Beach
Dennis
Veterans Beach
Seagull Beach
Port
Hyannis
Kalmus Beach
ort
Pt. Gammon
Orrin
Keyes Beach
Monomoy I.

N A N T U C K E T

*MONOMOY
NATIONAL
WILDLIFE
REFUGE*

S O U N D

Monomoy Pt.

0   5 mi

0   5 km

EXPENSIVE

The Dan'l Webster Inn and Spa ★★   Centrally located on Main Street in the Cape's oldest town, the Dan'l Webster Inn is named for the prominent 19th-century attorney and US senator, who who used to frequent a tavern on the site. The main building contains most of the rooms, as well as the restaurant and tavern and the full-service Beach Plum Spa. A heated outdoor pool and whirlpool tub is in the courtyard. There is an adjacent fully renovated historic home that contains additional upscale rooms. The rooms range from somewhat plain to luxuriously appointed suites complete with canopy beds, reproduction antiques and working fireplaces, a style fit for honeymooners. Besides the convenience of staying at a full-service inn, the Dan'l Webster is also within walking distance or a short drive to almost all the Sandwich attractions. Because it can accommodate groups, this hotel is popular with tour buses.

149 Main St. (in the center of town). ℂ **800/444-3566** or 508/888-3622. www.danlwebsterinn.com. 48 units. Summer $168–$224 double; $337–$374 suite. Rate includes $15 breakfast voucher. **Amenities:** Restaurant; tavern/bar; access to health club (2 miles away); small outdoor heated pool; room service; spa. Free Wi-Fi.

MODERATE

The Belfry Inn & Bistro ★★   What do a converted church, a pink "painted lady" Victorian rectory and a 19th-century Greek revival house have in common? They all make up the lodging accommodations of the unique Belfry Inn and Bistro in Sandwich center. The converted church, called the Abbey, makes full winking use of its dramatic space, using an elaborate stained glass window as a headboard, for example, and intricate gothic woodwork as room accents. The six rooms are done in a dark and bolder palette than the rooms in the other two buildings. They have vaulted ceilings and two-person whirlpool bathtubs. The 11 rooms in the Victorian are more feminine, relying on pastels and a crisper look. The third inn building, called the Village House, offers more casual accommodations and, for the most part, smaller and less expensive rooms. It has a long porch extending across the front of the building with rocking chairs positioned perfectly for guests to watch the world going by.

8 Jarves St. (in the center of town). ℂ **800/844-4542** or 508/888-8550. www.belfryinn.com. 22 units (in 3 properties). Summer $189–$299 double. Rates include full breakfast. **Amenities:** Restaurants and bar. Wi-Fi (free).

INEXPENSIVE

Spring Hill Motor Lodge ★   Great for families with children, this motel has a lot of extras on the property to keep a family entertained. From the outdoor heated pool and tennis court, to the basketball hoop and picnic area, families will be able to settle in to the property without worrying about driving to find activities. But because the motel is in East Sandwich, it is a relatively short trip either to Sandwich center or to Hyannis.

351 Rte. 6A (about 2½ miles east of the town center). ℂ **800/647-2514** or 508/888-1456. www. springhillmotorlodge.com. 24 units, 20 with tub/shower, 4 with shower only. Summer $99–$185 double; $229 1-bedroom cottage; $350 2-bedroom cottage. **Amenities:** Elegantly landscaped heated outdoor pool; night-lit tennis court. Wi-Fi (free).

Where to Eat

EXPENSIVE

The Belfry Bistro ★★ NEW AMERICAN   The premier fine-dining spot in Sandwich, the Belfry also gets an A for atmosphere. The setting is a converted church.

You enter through a majestic arched doorway and once inside you see the raised floor where the altar used to be and plenty of pretty stained glass windows. This is a roomy space, so couples will find it a good spot; no chance of a neighboring table eavesdropping. The chef takes his cues from the season, revising ingredients to feature the freshest local and regional ingredients. Start the meal with a lovely slow-roasted beet salad or chilled Wellfleet oysters. The main courses include a small but quality selection in the areas of fish, poultry and meat, be it spring lamb loin with sheep's milk yogurt or day boat sea scallops with Madras curry.

8 Jarves St. (in the center of town). © **508/888-8550.** Main courses $14–$33. Feb–April, Oct–Dec Wed–Sun 5–9pm.; May–Sept Wed–Sat 11:30am–3pm, 5–9pm, Sun 11am–3pm, 5–9pm, Closed Jan.

The Dan'l Webster Inn ★★ AMERICAN   Three meals a day in four dining rooms plus the tavern makes the Dan'l Webster Inn a real operation. But despite the volume, the chef does a top-notch job delivering from a wide-ranging menu that has items to please all manner of eaters. The menu mixes old New England favorites like prime rib with more delicate offerings An on-site pastry chef means dessert is also freshly made. The "green" menu includes vegetarian selections, uses organic ingredients, including free-range chicken. The tavern menu has soups, sandwiches, pizzas and burgers. There is fireside dining in the Music or Webster rooms, garden-side dining in the sky-lit Conservatory, more casual dining in the tavern or you can dine outside in season.

149 Main St. (in the center of town). © **508/888-3622.** Main courses $18–$39; tavern menu $10–$18. June–Aug daily 8–11am, 11:30am–3pm, and 4:30–9pm.

MODERATE

The Chart Room ★★ SEAFOOD   Great sunset views over Red Brook Harbor and fresh fish are reason enough to visit this dockside restaurant, housed in a former railroad barge at a busy marina. A piano bar lends a bit of elegance, as does the well-heeled clientele. The only downside is the noise level, due to this restaurant's ongoing popularity. The younger crowd likes to gather at the bar for the mudslides, said to be the best in the region.

1 Shipyard Lane (in the Kingman Yacht Center, off Shore Rd.), Cataumet. © **508/563-5350.** Dinner reservations strongly recommended. Main courses $12–$25. Mid-June to early Sept daily 11:30am–3pm, 5-10pm; mid-May to mid-June and early Sept to mid-Oct Thurs–Sun. 11:30am–3pm, 5-10pm. Closed mid-Oct to mid-May.

Lobster Trap Fish Market & Restaurant ★ CLAM SHACK   Since it's just a few miles from the Bourne Bridge, many people make their stop at the Lobster Trap either on the way on Cape or off Cape. After all, why not have one final plate of fried clams instead of sitting in all that traffic? This seafood shack has the benefit of being in a very scenic setting, overlooking the Back River in Monument Beach. All your standard fried fish plates are on the menu, plus some healthier grilled options and more unusual choices like spicy crab sliders or beef Thai sticks. Go early or late to avoid crowds.

290 Shore Road (take the first exit from the Bourne Bridge Rotary, toward the Tedeschi's; left on Shore Rd.), Bourne. © **508/759-7600.** www.lobstertrap.net. Reservations not accepted. Main courses $12–$25. May–Oct daily 11am–9pm. Closed Nov–April.

Pilot House ★★ SEAFOOD   Every town on the Cape has the requisite fish house overlooking the water, and this is Sandwich's version. Almost every seat here has a view of the Cape Cod Canal, the Sandwich marina or both. The only minus here is the less than scenic view of the Sandwich coal-fired power plant. Best bets are the Sonoran Style fish tacos or dig right in to a 2-pound boiled lobster. There is also fried seafood, sandwiches, and lots of burger options, which are among many reasonably priced options on this large menu.

14 Gallo Rd. (next to Sandwich Marina). *(C)* **508/888-8889.** www.pilothousecapecod.com. Main courses $9–$26. Late Apr to Oct Wed–Sat 11:30am–9pm; Sun 11:30am–5pm. Closed Nov to mid-Apr.

INEXPENSIVE

The Dunbar Tea Shop ★★ BRITISH   In this authentic tea room in a historic house overlooking Shawme Pond, you're likely to feel very coddled and leave with a full belly after trying any of the hearty lunches or the afternoon tea. You'd better come early if you want to get a table, though. Besides the cozy indoor seating, there is also an outdoor patio.

1 Water St. (in the center of town). *(C)* **508/833-2485.** www.dunbartea.com. Main courses under $10. May–Oct daily 8am–5pm; Nov–April Wed–Mon 11am–5pm.

Marshland Restaurant on 6A DINER   A proven formula of friendly service and comfort food and reasonable prices keeps this joint jumping all year long. Belly up to the counter on one of the old-fashioned diner stools and rub elbows with the locals as you dig into homemade meatloaf, Yankee pot roast, or a steaming plate of fried fish.

109 Rte. 6A. *(C)* **508/888-9824.** www.marshlandrestaurant.com. Main courses $9–20. Daily 6am–8pm.

Café Chew SANDWICH SHOP   When in Sandwich, why not have a sandwich? For that, consider Café Chew, which specializes in organic and natural ingredients for its menu items. Choose a classic, like a roast beef sandwich, or something a little more adventurous, like the Bavarian, ham and brie cheese with sliced Granny Smith apples. Great coffee and breakfast sandwiches here too.

4 Merchant's Road *(C)* **508/888-7717.** www.cafechew.com. All items under $11. Daily 8am–3pm.

SWEETS

Stop by Sandwich's appropriately named **Ice Cream Sandwich** ★, at 66 Rte. 6A, across from the Stop & Shop (*(C)* **508/888-7237;** www.icecreamsandwich.net), for a couple of scoops of the best local ice cream. Try the Cape Cod chocolate chunk. It's closed November through March. Sandwich's most classic ice cream shop is **Twin Acres Ice Cream Shoppe** ★, 21 Rte. 6A, Sandwich (*(C)* **508/888-0566**), which specializes in soft-serve. With its red, white, and blue bunting, this place is right out of a Norman Rockwell illustration.

A COFFEE BAR & WI-FI HOTSPOT

A great place to check your emails and enjoy some coffee or a sandwich is the **Daily Brew Coffee Bar and Café** ★, Cataumet Square, 1370 Rte. 28A, Cataumet (*(C)* **508/564-4755;** www.thedailybrewcoffeehouse.com), where you can get delicious espressos, cappuccinos, and baked goods, as well as soups, salads, and sandwiches. Several computers are available for public use upstairs. There is outside seating on a covered patio in back. The cafe is open year-round Monday to Saturday 6am to 3pm and Sunday 7am to 2pm.

Exploring: Beaches & Recreational Pursuits

BEACHES   For the Sandwich beaches listed below, nonresident parking stickers—$90 for the length of your stay—are available at **Sandwich Town Hall Annex,** 145 Main St. (*(C)* **508/833-8012**). *Note:* No swimming is allowed within the Cape Cod Canal because the currents are much too swift and dangerous. The Army Corps' **Cape Cod Canal Visitors Center,** at the Sandwich Marina (℃ **978/318-8816;** www.capecodcanal.us), is open daily 10am to 5pm in season. It displays exhibits about the canal, and rangers lead walks in the area.

o **Sandy Neck Beach ★★★**, off Sandy Neck Road, in East Sandwich (www.town.barnstable.ma.us/sandyneckpark/default.aspx): This 6-mile stretch of silken barrier beach with low, rounded dunes is one of the Cape's prettiest and most unspoiled. It is somewhat isolated, with no commercial businesses or accommodations on the beach. Because it is a Cape Cod Bay beach, the water tends to be warmer than the open ocean, and the waves are never too high. That makes it popular with families. The fact that the beach stretches out for miles makes it a magnet for endangered piping plovers—and their nemesis, off-road vehicles (ORV). That means that the ORV trails are closed for much of the summer while the Piping Plover chicks hatch. Parking for the beach in the upper parking lot costs $15 per day in season. Up to 4 days of camping in self-contained vehicles is permitted at $10 per night, plus an ORV permit. Tent camping costs $20 per night.

o **Town Neck Beach,** off Town Neck Road, in Sandwich: A bit rocky but ruggedly pretty, this narrow beach offers a busy view of passing ships, plus restrooms and a snack bar. Parking costs $10 per day, or you could hike from town (about 1½ miles) via the community-built boardwalk spanning the salt marsh.

o **Wakeby Pond,** Ryder Conservation Area, John Ewer Road (off South Sandwich Rd., on the Mashpee border): The beach, on the Cape's largest freshwater pond, has lifeguards, restrooms, and parking ($10 per day).

BICYCLING The **U.S. Army Corps of Engineers** (℃ **508/759-5991** for hotline with weather, tides, and current info; www.capecodcanal.us) maintains a flat, 14-mile loop along the **Cape Cod Canal ★★★**, equally suited to bicyclists, skaters, runners, and strollers. The most convenient place to park (free) is at the Bourne Recreation Area, north of the Bourne Bridge, on the Cape side. You can also park at the Sandcatcher Recreation Area at the end of Freezer Road in Sandwich.

FISHING So plentiful are herring, as they make their spring migration up the **Bournedale Herring Run ★★** (℃ **508/759-5991;** Rte. 6 in Bournedale, about 1 mile southwest of the Sagamore Bridge rotary), you can net them once they've reached their destination, Great Herring Pond. You can obtain a shellfish permit from **Bourne Town Hall,** at 24 Perry Ave., Buzzards Bay (℃ **508/759-0600**). Also plentiful here are pickerel, white perch, walleye, and bass. For freshwater fishing at Flax Pond and Red Brook Pond in Pocasset, you'll need a license from the Bourne Town Hall. You can also obtain a freshwater fishing license at **Red Top Sporting Goods,** at 265 Main St., in Buzzards Bay (℃ **508/759-3371;** www.redtoptackle.com). The Cape Cod Canal is a great place to try surf-casting, though the state now requires a $10-per-year permit. To get one online, go to www.mass.gov/marinefisheries or call 866/703-1925.

GOLF The **Sandwich Hollows Golf Club,** 1 Round Hill Rd., in East Sandwich (℃ **508/888-3384;** www.sandwichhollows.com), is a 6,200-yard, par-71 town-owned course. In season a round costs $30 to $62, depending on the day and time. The 18-hole, par-3 **Holly Ridge Golf Course,** at 121 Country Club Rd., in South Sandwich (℃ **508/428-5577;** www.hollyridgegolf.com), is, at 2,900 yards, shorter and easier. A round costs $34 in season, with afternoon discounts.

Sandwich Historical Sights

Green Briar Jam Kitchen ★★★   This sweet (in more ways than one) little spot is what is called a "living museum" where visitors can watch and learn how to make homemade jam using old school recipes in a turn-of-the-century kitchen. But that's not all. The kitchen is attached to the Green Briar Nature Center, which offers natural history programs for children and adults year-round. The property is a sanctuary located on the shores of Smiling Pool.

6 Discovery Hill Rd., East Sandwich. 🕾 **508/888-6870.** Open mid-Apr through Dec Mon–Sat 10am–4pm, Sun 1–4pm; Jan to mid-Apr Tues–Sat 1–4pm. Admission by donation.

Heritage Museums and Gardens ★★★   One of the Cape's top attractions, Heritage Museums and Gardens, which sprawls across an exquisitely landscaped 76-acre property, is a particularly good find for families with young children, gardening buffs, and collectors. The newest attraction among many at Heritage is the Hidden Hollow, a children's play area housed in a 2-acre dry kettle hole that teaches about the outdoors while encouraging creative play. But the showpiece of this property will always be the grounds, rolling acres perfect for a stroll, particularly in the spring when the rhododendrons are in bloom, a riot of blooms in all possible shades. (The Rhododendron festival is in May.) Most visitors begin their visit with the collection of cars, from Model T's to a sleek Delorean, all housed in a round Shaker barn. Walk along paths through the grounds to reach the Special Exhibition Building along with the American Art and Carousel Gallery on the far end of the property to explore the museum's permanent collections of toy soldiers, Native American artifacts and American Folk art. An indoor antique carousel offers unlimited rides, and a labyrinth on the grounds is perfect to sap the energy of boisterous children. A free trolley cruises the grounds in the summer for those who would prefer not to walk.

67 Grove St. (about ½ mile southwest of the town center). 🕾 **508/888-3300.** www.heritagemuseums andgardens.org. Admission $18 adults, $8 children 4–12, free for children 2 and under. mid-Apr to late May, Sept–Oct daily 10am–5pm; late May–Aug 10am–6pm. No tickets sold after 1 hour before closing. Closed Nov–mid-April.

Hoxie House ★   Hoxie House, circa 1675, is the oldest house on Cape Cod that is open for visitors to tour and is also one of the Cape's best preserved historic homes. It was the home of the town's second minister, Rev. John Smith, who lived here with his wife, Susanna, and their 13 (!) children. It is named for Abraham Hoxie, a Sandwich whaling captain, who purchased it in the 1850s. The house was lived in by families up until the 1950s without electricity, central heating, or plumbing, so its authenticity was never "ruined" by those modern conveniences. It is decorated with a few choice pieces appropriate to the period so visitors can see more precisely how its early occupants lived. Nearby is the **Dexter Grist Mill,** one of the earliest water mill sites in the country, worth a look to see how they did it in the olden days. You can take away a bag of freshly ground cornmeal for $3.50.

18 Water St. (on Shawme Pond, about ¼ mile south of the town center). 🕾 **508/888-1173.** Admission $3 adults, $2 children 5–15, free for children 4 and under; combination ticket ($5 adults, $3 children) available here for Hoxie House and Dexter Grist Mill (see above). Mid-June to mid-Oct Mon–Sat 10am–5pm; Sun 1–5pm. Closed mid-Oct to mid-June.

Sandwich Glass Museum ★★   The highlight of this museum is seeing the sunshine from outside glance off the dozens of brightly colored glass displays, refracting multicolored lights. That alone is worth the price of admission. But there is so much more, including glass-blowing demonstrations, which last 20 minutes and take place every hour on the hour.

Sandwich used to be known as Glasstown and to see why, you'll have to visit this museum, which gives a history not only of the glass industry on the Cape but also of the town itself. Sandwich was primarily a farming community until 1825 when Deming Jarves, a Boston businessman, came to town and changed everything. Because of its proximity to a shallow harbor, Jarves chose Sandwich as the base for his Boston and Sandwich Glass Company. The surrounding forest was cut and used to fuel the furnaces and the marsh hay on the coast was used to pack the fragile wares. He brought master glassblowers to the Cape and recruited workers from England and Ireland for his glass factory. The company mass-produced glass products and was very successful. Jarves eventually left the company and started a rival firm called Cape Cod Glass Works, also in Sandwich. The glass industry died down after the Civil War when cheaper glass could be made using coal furnaces down south and in the Midwest. In the 1880s, a union strike led to the closing of Sandwich's glass companies. Today, the town is embracing its glass history in the form of a newly formed Glasstown Cultural District (you can take a self-guided walking tour starting at the museum). There are also several art glassblowers in town whose studios are open to the public. Their works are sold in the museum's gift shop.

129 Main St. (in the center of town). ✆ **508/888-0251.** www.sandwichglassmuseum.org. Admission $8 adults, $2 children 6–14, free for children 5 and under. Apr–Dec daily 9:30am–5pm; Feb–Mar Wed–Sun 9:30am–4pm. Closed Jan, Thanksgiving, and Christmas.

Kid Stuff

The 18-hole **Sandwich Mini Golf,** 159 Rte. 6A, at the corner of Main Street (✆ **508/833-1905**), is a grassy 1950s classic that encapsulates Cape Cod history. Built on a former cranberry bog, it has an unusual floating green. Hours are Monday to Saturday from 10am to 9pm and Sunday from noon to 9pm. Admission is $8 for adults, $6 for children 12 and under. Add $4 and play two rounds, or 36 holes.

Shopping

Most shops are concentrated in the town center, and several of the museums (see "Sandwich Historical Sights," above) also have worthwhile gift shops.

ANTIQUES & COLLECTIBLES The **Sandwich Antiques Center,** 131 Rte. 6A, at Jarves Street (✆ **508/833-3600**), showcases wares from over 100 dealers in 6,000 square feet of rooms. It's headed by a congenial auctioneer and offers virtual one-stop shopping for the likes of Sandwich glass, primitives, country furnishings, and other items. The center is open daily year-round.

BOOKS **Titcomb's Bookshop** ★, 432 Rte. 6A, East Sandwich, about 4 miles east of the town center (✆ **508/888-2331;** www.titcombsbookshop.com), has a terrific selection of new and used books relating to Cape Cod and much more. Look for the life-size statue of English Renaissance dramatist Ben Jonson out front.

FOOD & WINE **Crow Farm** ★, 192 Rte. 6A, ¼ mile east of the town center (✆ **508/888-0690;** www.crowfarm.net), is a picture-perfect farm stand purveying such as sweet corn, tomatoes, peaches, apples, and other produce, as well as flowers. It's closed Sunday in summer but open daily in spring and fall. It's closed late December through April. **The Brown Jug,** 155 Main St., in Sandwich (✆ **508/888-4669;** www. thebrownjug.com), is stocked with delicacies from around the corner and around the world, from fine cheeses and olive oils to rich baked goods and hearty homemade breads. **Momo's Food Emporium,** 598 Rte. 6A, East Sandwich (🕾 **508/888-3633;** www.momosfoodemporium.com), has the best of the best cookies, cakes and other baked goods, along with sandwiches and soups to take home.

GLASS For the finest in art glass and a souvenir of your trip to Sandwich, visit **The Glass Studio ★★**, 470 Rte. 6A, East Sandwich (🕾 **508/888-6681;** www.capecod glass.net), where master glass blower Michael Magyar crafts such one-of-a-kind pieces as his "sea bubbles" series and Venetian-style goblets. Watch glass blowing Thursday through Sunday from 10am to 1pm and 2 to 5pm.

At **McDermott Glass Studio & Gallery ★★**, 272 Cotuit Rd., Sandwich (🕾 **508/ 477-0705;** www.mcdermottglass.com), Dave McDermott creates exquisite hand-blown art glass, from vases to stemware. Glass blowing takes place Thursday to Saturday from 10am to 5pm.

GIFTS/HOME DECOR The **Weather Store ★**, 146 Main St. (🕾 **800/646-1203;** www.theweatherstore.com), has a fascinating collection of meteorological paraphernalia old and new, ranging from antique instruments to coffee-table books. Although technically open year-round, from January through April it's open by chance or appointment.

Visit a Museum

Aptucxet Trading Post Museum Aptucxet is where to go to learn about shopping, Pilgrim-style. The Algonquin name means "little trap in the river," and the site is where the Manamet and Scusset rivers met making it a convenient trading place for Native Americans. Historical records indicate that in 1627, the Pilgrims began using the site for early trade with the Wampanoag tribe and the Dutch. The building used for the small museum here is a replica of the Pilgrim trading post and is erected on the original foundation. The site was excavated in the 1920s and the foundation is considered the earliest remains of a Pilgrim building. This is the site of one of the oldest trading posts in America. The building is surrounded by 12 acres of land used for recreation.

On the museum grounds is a replica **salt works** built by students at the nearby Upper Cape Regional Technical School. Salt-making was a big early industry on the Cape. The first salt-making on Cape Cod was done by evaporating seawater placed in large boilers over fire. After the Revolutionary War, the process was refined and salt-works were built using large wooden vats and solar evaporation. The vats had lids to protect the product from rain. Saltworks used to line the shores of Cape Cod. On Buzzards Bay, the first one was said to be on the southeast side of Eel Pond near Monument Beach. The most extensive saltworks were on Mashnee Island, but those were destroyed by hurricane in 1835. The **windmill** here houses an art studio that hosts exhibits and painting classes throughout the season.

Also on the grounds of the museum is the tiny Victorian-style **Gray Gables Train Depot,** which was built as the personal station for President Grover Cleveland during his second term in the White House from 1893 to 1896. Cleveland had a summer home at Gray Gables in Bourne, which he chose because of its proximity to rich fishing grounds. Because of its use for the President, the train depot was outfitted with a direct telegraph line to Washington, D.C. The depot was moved to the trading post grounds in 1976.

The Aptucxet Museum is also a good starting spot to explore the Cape Cod Canal bike path, which takes riders along the canal and past the Railroad Bridge, an unusual vertical lift structure that is used summer weekends for a train, the Cape Flyer, that travels to and from Boston, as well as a daily train between 5 and 6pm carrying garbage to a landfill off-Cape.

24 Aptucxet Rd., off Perry Ave. (about ½ mile west of the town center), Bourne Village. ℂ **508/ 759-9487.** www.bournehistoricalsociety.org. Admission $5 adults, $4 seniors, $2 children 6–18, free for children 5 and under. Families do not pay more than $10 in total. Open Memorial Day to Columbus Day weekend July and August Tues–Sat 11am–4pm; open Memorial Day–June and Sept–Columbus Day 11am–3pm. Closed mid-Oct–late May.

Take a Cruise

Cape Cod Canal Cruises ★★ You have three ways to get a gander at the wonder that is the Cape Cod Canal: Take a quick look around for the 10 seconds you are driving over the Bourne or Sagmore Bridge; bike along the Cape Cod Canal or take a canal cruise. The second two options are strongly recommended. The 17.5-mile Cape Cod Canal is the gateway to Cape Cod and it has a fascinating history. There is only one company that operates canal sightseeing cruises and that is Hy-Line, the same company that runs ferries to and from Martha's Vineyard and Nantucket. During the 2- or 3-hour cruise, you'll learn about the history of how in 1914 a ditch was transformed through the wonders of engineering into a canal that serves as the shortcut between Boston and New York for about 14,000 boats per year. Building a canal offered economic, life-saving and military benefits, and the conversation about the possibility of constructing a canal is said to have begun in about 1620. The first known Cape Cod Canal feasibility study, if you will, was commissioned by none other than George Washington. The project was finally undertaken by a wealthy industrialist August Belmont II, who paid for it himself through his Boston, Cape Cod and New York Canal Company, and operated it as a private toll waterway. In 1927, he sold the Cape Cod Canal to the US government for $11.5 million. To improve navigation, the canal was widened to 480 feet and deepened to 32 feet. If you want to learn more, the Army Corps of Engineers operates a free canal visitor center May through October from 10am to 5pm on 60 Moffitt Drive in Sandwich.

Onset Bay Town Pier (on the northern side of the canal, about 2 miles west of the Bourne Bridge), Onset. ℂ **508/295-3883.** www.hy-linecruises.com. Tickets $14–$19 adults, half-price or free for children 12 and under. Mid-June to Sept departures Mon 10am, 1:30pm, and 4pm; Tues–Thurs 10am, 1:30pm, 4pm, and 7pm; Fri–Sat 10am, 1:30pm, 4pm, and 8pm; Sun 10am and 2pm. Call for off-season schedule. Closed mid-Oct to Apr.

Take Yourself Out to a Ballgame

Sports fans of all ages will enjoy taking in nine innings of the Grand Old Game. The elite-amateur **Cape Cod Baseball League** (ℂ **508/432-6909;** www.capecodbaseball. org) plays all up and down the Cape, in July and August. Games are free.

After Dark

On weekends local bands draw a crowd of young adults to the **Courtyard Restaurant and Pub,** 1337 County Rd., Cataumet (ℂ **508/563-1818;** www.courtyardcapecod. com). Usually, there is no cover charge. From here you can barhop to the **Parrot Bar and Grille,** 1356 Rte. 28A (see "Where to Eat," above), which has live music Thursday to Saturday in season.

FALMOUTH ★★★

18 miles S of Sagamore; 20 miles SW of Hyannis

Essentials

VISITOR INFORMATION Contact the **Falmouth Chamber of Commerce,** 20 Academy Lane, Falmouth, MA 02540 (② **800/526-8532** or 508/548-8500; www. falmouthchamber.com), which is open year-round Monday to Friday 9am to 5pm, Saturday 10am to 4pm, and Sunday 11am to 3pm; or the **Cape Cod Chamber of Commerce** (see "Visitor Information," under "Sandwich," above).

Where to Stay

For a basic motel with a great location, try the **Tides Motel** (② **508/548-3126;** www. tidesmotelcapecod.com), on Clinton Avenue, at the far west end of Grand Avenue in Falmouth Heights. The 1950s-style no-frills motel (no air-conditioning, no phone) sits on the beach at the head of Falmouth Harbor facing Vineyard Sound. Rates in season for the 29 rooms are $165 to $175 double, $220 suite. It's closed late October to mid-May.

The **Seaside Inn,** at 263 Grand Ave., Falmouth Heights (② **800/827-1976;** www. seasideinnfalmouth.com), is a reasonably priced motel in a superb location, across the street from Falmouth Heights Beach. The 23 rooms, with air-conditioning, TVs, phones with free calls, and some with kitchenettes and decks, are priced at $155 to $199 for a double, $234 to $249 for a deluxe room. Open year-round.

EXPENSIVE

Inn on the Sound ★★ If a charming waterfront B&B is what you are looking for, look no further. Inn on the Sound sits on a bluff in Falmouth Heights—on a clear day, you can see to Martha's Vineyard. The inn is in a neighborhood made up of Victorian shingle-style homes, many of them beautifully restored. The beach, just a short walk from the inn, is one of Falmouth's best. The 10-room inn itself is small enough to provide a lot of privacy as well as a personal touch. Rooms are decorated in an elegant and crisp style that avoids anything too frilly.

313 Grand Ave., Falmouth Heights. ② **800/564-9668** or 508/457-9666. www.innonthesound.com. 10 units, 8 with tub/shower, 2 with shower only. Summer $245–$395 double. Rates include full breakfast. No children 11 and under.

MODERATE

Beach Breeze Inn ★ The big plus of the Beach Breeze is that you are within walking distance—a very pleasant walk at that—to Surf Drive beach and to Falmouth's lively Main Street. The beach is good for children or people who like to swim, because the water's fairly placid here. The rooms, which are in a converted mid-19th-century house, vary in size; they're humble but homey. A few have kitchenettes. There's nothing fancy here, giving you more of an old-fashioned Cape Cod experience.

321 Shore St. (about ¼ mile south of Main St.), Falmouth. ② **800/828-3255** or 508/548-1765. www. beachbreezeinn.com. 21 units. Summer $219–$279 double; $1,500–$1,700 weekly efficiencies. **Amenities:** Unheated pool; Wi-Fi (free).

Coonamessett Inn ★★ The Coonamessett, set on 7 acres overlooking Jones Pond, has been a reliable lodging choice since the 1950s. Guest are no doubt drawn to

Falmouth

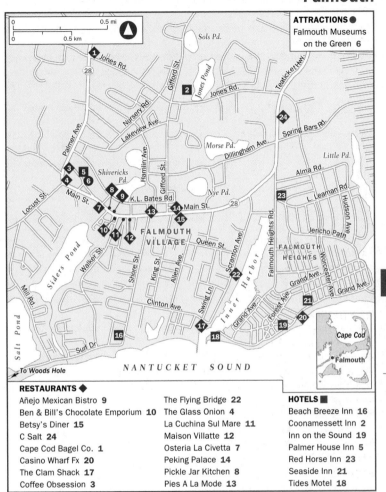

ATTRACTIONS ●

Falmouth Museums on the Green 6

0   0.5 mi
0   0.5 km

FALMOUTH VILLAGE

FALMOUTH HEIGHTS

NANTUCKET SOUND

To Woods Hole

Cape Cod

Falmouth

5

CAPE COD | Falmouth

RESTAURANTS ◆

Añejo Mexican Bistro 9	The Flying Bridge 22
Ben & Bill's Chocolate Emporium 10	The Glass Onion 4
Betsy's Diner 15	La Cuchina Sul Mare 11
C Salt 24	Maison Villatte 12
Cape Cod Bagel Co. 1	Osteria La Civetta 7
Casino Wharf Fx 20	Peking Palace 14
The Clam Shack 17	Pickle Jar Kitchen 8
Coffee Obsession 3	Pies A La Mode 13

HOTELS ■

Beach Breeze Inn 16
Coonamessett Inn 2
Inn on the Sound 19
Palmer House Inn 5
Red Horse Inn 23
Seaside Inn 21
Tides Motel 18

the folksy charm of the place, the historic red clapboard farmhouse exterior and gardens resplendent with flowers, and, inside, the large function rooms. Most of the rooms are suites that include a sitting room, which comes in handy if you (or your partner) are an early riser. The decor is mostly soothing blues, and the location is perfect as a base to explore Falmouth. The tavern is open for guests only for lunch and dinner and an elaborate Sunday brunch. It serves traditional New England fare, like seafood stew and roasted chicken.

311 Gifford St. (about ½ mile north of Main St.), Falmouth. ⓒ **508/548-2300**. www.capecod restaurants.org. 27 units, 1 cottage. Summer $160–$350 double; $250–$325 2-bedroom suite; $200–$350 cottage. Rates include continental breakfast. **Amenities:** Restaurant; Wi-Fi (free).

Palmer House Inn ★ The Palmer House has a terrific location steps from Falmouth's Village Green and a short walk to Main Street. Of the many B&Bs in the area, this one also rises above the rest by virtue of its warm and welcoming hosts and the amenities, which include sumptuous linens and a top-notch hot breakfast. Rooms are beautifully decorated with an old-world appeal appropriate to this 1879 home. There is one room accessible for those with disabilities and one room that allows pets.

81 Palmer Ave. (on Falmouth Village Green), Falmouth. ✆ **800/472-2632** or 508/548-1230. www.palmerhouseinn.com. 17 units. Summer $209–$289 double. Rates include full breakfast. Free Wi-Fi.

Sands of Time Motor Inn & Harbor House ★★ Sure, the rooms may be a tad dated here, but the location can't be beat. It's across the street from where ferries leave in the summer for Martha's Vineyard. It is also a short walk to Woods Hole, a fishing village with lots of terrific restaurants and shops. There are two very different choices for rooms: a no-frills 1950s vintage motel and a 19th-century shingled house, which definitely feels more like a B&B. Both have rooms with wonderful views of Little Harbor. Lying between the two buildings is a small heated pool.

549 Woods Hole Rd., Woods Hole. ✆ **800/841-0114** or 508/548-6300. www.sandsoftime.com. 35 units, 2 with shared bathroom. Summer $179–$269 double. Rates include continental breakfast. Closed Nov–Mar. **Amenities:** Small outdoor heated pool; free Wi-Fi.

Where to Eat
EXPENSIVE

C Salt Wine Bar & Grille ★★ NEW AMERICAN This restaurant, inside a cozy house that's on a busy commercial stretch of Route 28, is a respite from all the commotion outside. The menu, American cuisine with French and Asian influences, includes two standouts: Thai pork coconut cashew stir-fry, served over jasmine rice; and the braised short rib, which comes with crispy bacon and Brussels sprouts. As an inexpensive option, the menu includes a couple of choices of flat bread pizzas, including a Portuguese version with spicy chorizo sausage. There is also a vegetarian tasting menu offered for $22.

75 Davis Straits, Falmouth. ✆ **774/763-2954.** www.csaltfalmouth.com. Main courses $22–$32. Wed and Thurs 5–9pm, Fri and Sat 5–10pm, Sun 11am–2:30pm and 5–9pm.

Casino Wharf FX ★ SEAFOOD The Casino is the place to go for those looking for a meal with views out across Vineyard Sound to Martha's Vineyard. Dining is on two levels, but the best bet is to get a table out on one of the decks overlooking the beach. Seafood dishes like the tuna with citrus couscous are the featured items on the menu but there are plenty of choices for meat lovers, including BBQ ribs and filet mignon. The Casino doubles as a nightclub, with live music several nights a week in season.

286 Grand Ave. (next to Falmouth Heights Beach), Falmouth Heights. ✆ **508/540-6160.** www.casinowharffx.com. Main courses $19–$28. Daily 11:30am–3:30pm and 4:30–10pm; call for off-season hours.

The Glass Onion ★★★ NEW AMERICAN Regularly cited as Falmouth's top upscale restaurant, the Glass Onion is a labor of love, and it shows. It's very popular: Try it on an off night if you don't want a long wait for a table. The formal touches here manage to make it feel friendly, if not exactly casual. Have no fear when choosing from this menu; there are no losers. But among the favorites are the poached lobster, shrimp and mussels with a spinach risotto or the grilled pork chop with creamy polenta. The menu relies heavily on local ingredients, such as Barnstable oysters and Coonamessett Farm greens. There is also homemade gnocchi and fresh pasta.

37 N. Main St./Rte. 28 (in the Queen's Buyway), Falmouth. ℰ **508/540-3730.** www.theglassonion dining.com. Main courses $19–$36. Tues–Sat 5–9pm. Open year-round.

Osteria La Civetta ★★★ NORTHERN ITALIAN "The Little Owl" is unique on the Cape for serving food the way they do in Italy, not an Americanized version of it—you could almost imagine you have wandered into this place from a side street in Rome. The dining room, which has a small bar, feels cozy but sophisticated. On the first-course *(primi)* menu, there are the homemade pastas, such as the wild boar pappardelle and tortellini filled with butternut squash and nutmeg. As for the *secondi,* you may have a hard time choosing between the pork tenderloin with fontina pasta and the polenta-encrusted chicken with oven-roasted potatoes. For dessert, a *salame di cioccolato* ("chocolate salami"), a rich chocolate log of goodness, awaits.

133 Main St. (across from the post office), Falmouth. ℰ **508/540-1616.** www.osterialacivetta.com. Reservations recommended. Main courses $16–$28. Wed–Sat noon–2:30pm and 5:30–10pm, Sun–Tues 5:30-10pm. Closed Mon off-season.

Phusion Grille ★★ NEW AMERICAN Set on a dock over Eel Pond in Woods Hole, this upscale restaurant is well worth the trip. It's the perfect spot to come on a clear night: All the doors and windows—two sides of almost floor-to-ceiling glass here—can be swung open (there's also ample seating on the deck). The menus change each year, but in general the operative word is "fusion," with a focus on Asian influences, just as the name implies. Expect unusual flavors and combinations. Appetizers might include tempura asparagus fries or pan-seared pork dumplings. The main course menu might include red Thai curry grilled salmon or vanilla seared scallops with couscous.

71 Water St., Woods Hole. ℰ **508/457-3100.** www.phusiongrille.com. Reservations not accepted. Main courses $21–$27. Daily 11:30am–2:30pm and 5–10pm. Closed mid-Oct to early May.

MODERATE

Añejo Mexican Bistro & Tequila Bar ★ MEXICAN People love the hip vibe and affordable prices at this popular Mexican restaurant on Falmouth's Main Street. Although the menu features house specials like *pescado encornflecado* (cornflake-crusted cod) and carne asada (Mexican-style grilled skirt steak), the best part of the menu is inspired by Mexican taquerias: enchiladas, burritos, tacos and tostadas served with Mexican rice and refried beans for great prices ($12–$16). Anejo's popularity (and lack of reservations) means you will often see people standing outside waiting for a table: The wait can be over an hour. Best to try it either early or on the late side.

188 Main St. (center of town), Falmouth. ℰ **508/388-7631.** www.anejomexicanbistro.com. Main courses $12–$28. Mon–Sat 11:30am–3pm and 4–10pm; Sun 10:30am–3pm and 4–10pm.

The Flying Bridge ★★ AMERICAN/CONTINENTAL This dockside cafe is the place to go for traditional Cape cod cuisine with a water view. It's also a great place for boaters who want to step right off the docks of Falmouth Harbor and onto the restaurant's ample decking. You'll want to go on a sunny day and sit outside under the blue and white awnings, but with two floors and a capacity of 600, there is no shortage of seating. The large menu is focused on traditional club sandwiches and lobster rolls, but you'll also find the occasional unusual offering, like shrimp tacos.

220 Scranton Ave. (about ½ mile south of Main St., on Falmouth Inner Harbor). ℰ **508/548-2700.** www.capecodrestaurants.org/flyingbridge. Main courses $8–$20. Mid-Apr to mid-Oct daily 11:30am–9pm. Closed mid-Oct to mid-Apr.

La Cucina Sul Mare Italian Ristorante ★★ ITALIAN   It's no wonder this friendly restaurant is so popular that it doubled in size a few years back. It all resembles a European bistro, with ceilings elaborately decorated in tin, and 19th-century-style light fixtures. The chef-owner Mark Cilfone will often wander out of the kitchen to chat with customers and find out what they ordered. The classically inclined dishes include lasagna, braised lamb shanks, osso bucco, and lobster fra diavolo over linguine. You'll often see diners waiting outside to get into this popular place, so call ahead to put your name on the list before coming.

237 Main St. (in the center of town), Falmouth. © **508/548-5600.** www.lacucinasulmare.com. Main courses $17–$27. AE, MC, V. Daily 11:30am–2pm and 5–10pm; call for off-season hours.

Landfall ★★ AMERICAN   Falmouth's longest standing restaurant to still be in the same family, Landfall brings to mind old Cape Cod. Buoys, lobster pots, oars, and other flotsam and jetsam hang from the rafters; the huge Gothic window came out of a library, and the stained glass window came from a mansion on nearby Penzance Point. At a place where you can dip your feet into the water while eating, it's no surprise that fish is the focus, with lobsters, swordfish, clams, scallops and seasonal finfish. The seafood can be ordered fried, broiled, or grilled.

Luscombe Ave. (½ block south of Water St.), Woods Hole. © **508/548-1758.** www.woodshole. com/landfall. Reservations recommended. Main courses $9–$38. AE, MC, V. Mid-May to Sept daily 11:30am–9:30pm; call for off-season hours. Closed late Nov to early Apr.

Quicks Hole Tavern ★★★ NEW AMERICAN   Close to the ferry terminal, the Quicks Hole Tavern serves upscale tavern food. The burgers come with truffle fries, and the lobster roll is served on a croissant, with basil and lemon. There are a wide array of sandwiches and salads for those looking for a quick bite before catching the ferry, but there are also house specialties for those who want to linger over some like a quinoa succotash soba noodle cake, or chocolate-braised short ribs with wild mushrooms. Climb up to the second floor for a 180-degree view of Vineyard Sound.

29 Railroad Ave., Woods Hole. © **508/495-0048.** www.quicksholewickedfresh.com. Main courses $7–$38. Daily 11am–10pm.

INEXPENSIVE

Betsy's Diner ★ AMERICAN   The neon sign out front of this vintage diner says "eat heavy," and I guess that's one way to sum up diner food. But a more apt phrase for Betsy's might be "comfort food." That includes wonderful meatloaf and macaroni and cheese, and breakfast served all day. The booths have individual jukeboxes, and the counter seats can twirl three times with a good spin. The waitresses are sassy and the service is speedy. That's what this diner is all about.

457 Main St. (a couple blocks east of the center of town), Falmouth. © **508/540-0060.** All items under $11. Mon–Sat 6am–8pm; Sun 7am–2pm; call for off-season hours.

The Clam Shack SEAFOOD   Sitting near the entrance to Falmouth harbor, this is a slice of old Cape Cod as well as a great place for fried seafood. Climbing up to the second floor to sit on the roof of the Clam Shack with a steaming plate of fried fish just feels like summer. The cool breeze blows across Falmouth Harbor as the boats pass by: There's nothing else like it. Keep in mind: This one is a good-weather choice only. If it rains, there are only a couple of tables inside.

227 Clinton Ave. (off Scranton Ave., on Falmouth Inner Harbor, about 1 mile south of Main St.), Falmouth. © **508/540-7758.** Main courses $5–$25. No credit cards. Daily 11:30am–7:30pm. Closed early Sept to late May.

Moonakis Cafe ★★ DINER   On summer mornings, people line up to get into this friendly, folksy diner. Don't bother if you are running late; the line will have already formed. They come for the creative and delicious omelets, like the one with lobster, asparagus, and Swiss cheese. The specials also include special pancakes (lemon–poppy seed, cranberry-pecan, and chocolate chip among them) as well as lots of French toast options.

460 Waquoit Hwy./Rte. 28, Waquoit. ℂ **508/457-9630.** Reservations not accepted. All items under $10. MC, V. Mon–Sat 7am–1:30pm; Sunday 7am–noon.

Peking Palace ★★ CHINESE/JAPANESE/THAI   A voluminous menu of all manner of Asian cuisine, including Chinese, Japanese, and Thai, awaits you at Peking Palace, easily the best restaurant of its kind on Cape Cod. The featured items include Peking duck and Thai clay pot curry. Seafood choices include the delectable Hunan spicy Chilean sea bass and the lobster with ginger and scallion. Another plus here are the hours: It's the only restaurant in Falmouth, and one of the only ones on all of Cape Cod, to serve food until midnight.

452 Main St. (a few blocks east of the center of town), Falmouth. ℂ **508/540-8204.** www.peking palacefalmouth.com. Main courses $5–$15. Daily 11:30am–midnight.

The Pickle Jar Kitchen ★★★ CAFE   This charming cafe is that rare place where after a big meal you feel like you had something healthy, not a belly bomb. So a marathon scrambler is egg whites sautéed with garden fresh veggies and kale served with homemade toasted bread and home fries. The lunch menu also has unusual offerings, like the open-faced BBQ boneless pork sandwich. The namesake house pickles, including the Mexi-Cali with carrot and jalapeno, are available to purchase by the pound.

170 Main St., Falmouth. ℂ **508/540-6760.** Breakfast mostly under $10. Lunch $9–$14. Wed–Mon 7am–3pm.

COFFEE & SWEETS

Coffee Obsession, 110 Palmer Ave., in the Queen's Buyway Shops (ℂ **508/540-2233;** www.coffeeobsession.com), is a hip coffee bar open from 6am to 7pm Monday through Saturday and 7am to 6:30pm on Sunday. You'll see slackers, suits, and surfers all lined up for the best coffee in town. **Coffee O.,** as it's known to locals, has a branch in **Woods Hole,** at 38 Water St. (ℂ **508/540-8130**). The Woods Hole location has several computers with Internet access and a play area for children; it's open daily 6:30am to 9pm.

The line sometimes extends out the door of **Maison Villatte,** an authentic French bakery on 267 Main St., Falmouth (ℂ **774/255-1855**). Chef Boris Villatte knows just what he's doing, with a dozen kinds of bread in addition to wonderful patisseries, all lined up in a long glass bakery case. Do not miss a stop here.

Locals know to get to **Pie in the Sky Dessert Café and Bake Shop** ★★, 10 Water St., Woods Hole (ℂ **508/540-5475**), by 9am for the best sticky buns anywhere. Those bound for Martha's Vineyard stop at this small bakery near the ferry terminal for treats before hopping on the boat.

Falmouth residents are the beneficiaries of a struggle for ice cream bragging rights: **Ben & Bill's Chocolate Emporium** ★, at 209 Main St., in the center of town (ℂ **508/548-7878;** www.benandbills.com), draws crowds even in winter, late into the evening. They come for the homemade ice cream, not to mention the hand-dipped candies showcased in a wraparound display. It's the only place on Cape Cod where you can get surprisingly yummy lobster ice cream, and customers can watch the ice cream being made. Open 9am to 11pm.

Pies A La Mode ★★, 352 Main St., unit 4, Falmouth (© **508/540-8777;** www. piesalamode.com), sells delicious homemade ice cream and gelato, plus wonderful baked goods, including homemade quiches. Open Monday to Saturday 10am to 10pm and Sunday noon to 9pm in season; call for off-season hours.

There's also **Smitty's Homemade Ice Cream** ★, at 326 E. Falmouth Hwy., East Falmouth (© **508/457-1060**), whose proprietor, the cheerful, blond Smitty, is an ice cream man straight out of central casting.

Exploring: Beaches & Recreational Pursuits

BEACHES Although Old Silver Beach, Surf Drive Beach, and Menauhant Beach sell 1-day passes, most other Falmouth public beaches require a parking sticker instead. Day passes to Old Silver are $20, and day passes to Surf Drive and Menauhant are $10. Renters can obtain temporary beach parking stickers, for $60 per week or $70 for 2 weeks, at **Falmouth Town Hall,** 59 Town Hall Sq. (© **508/548-7611**), or at the **Surf Drive Beach bathhouse** in season (© **508/548-8623**), which is open 9am to 4pm daily. The town beaches that charge a parking fee all have lifeguards, restrooms, and concession stands. Some of Falmouth's more notable public shores are as follows:

o **Falmouth Heights Beach** ★★★, off Grand Avenue, in Falmouth Heights: At this family-oriented beach, the parking is sticker-only; some local inns will provide stickers to guests. This neighborhood supported the Cape's first summer colony; the grand Victorian mansions still overlook the beach. The beach has lifeguards and bathroom facilities.

o **Grews Pond** ★★, in Goodwill Park, off Palmer Avenue, in Falmouth: This freshwater pond in a large town forest stays fairly uncrowded, even in the middle of summer. While everyone else is experiencing beach rage, trying to find parking at Falmouth's popular beaches, here you park for free and can wander shady paths around the pond. You'll find picnic tables, a playground, barbecue grills, a lifeguard, and restrooms.

o **Menauhant Beach** ★★, off Central Avenue, in East Falmouth: A bit off the beaten track, Menauhant is a little less mobbed than Falmouth Heights Beach and better protected from the winds. There are lifeguards, bathroom facilities, and a bathhouse. A 1-day parking pass costs $10.

o **Old Silver Beach** ★★★, off Route 28A, in North Falmouth: Western-facing (great for sunsets) and relatively calm, this warm Buzzards Bay beach is a popular, often crowded, choice. This is the spot for the college crowd and other rowdy young folk. Mothers and their charges cluster on the opposite side of the street, where a shallow pool formed by a sandbar is perfect for toddlers. The beach provides several amenities, including a bathhouse with showers and bathrooms, food concessions, and lifeguards. Sailboards are available to rent in season. A 1-day parking pass costs $20.

o **Surf Drive Beach** ★★★, off Shore Street in Falmouth: About a half-mile from downtown, this beach is easily accessible (it's a 10-min. walk from Main St.) but with limited parking. It's an appealing beach for families: The shallow, calm area between the jetties is called "the kiddie pool." You'll find an outdoor shower, bathrooms, a food concession, and lifeguards. A 1-day parking pass costs $10.

BICYCLING The **Shining Sea Bikeway** ★★★ (© **508/548-7611**) is a 12-mile beauty that runs along an old railroad right-of-way from North Falmouth past cranberry bogs, farmland, and the Great Sippewissett Marsh, and then skirts Vineyard Sound from Falmouth center to Woods Hole. This is one of the Cape's most scenic bike paths and one of the few that travels alongside a beach. There is free parking on Locust Street; on Depot Avenue; in West Falmouth, on Old Dock Road; and at the trailhead on County Road, in North Falmouth. The Falmouth Chamber of Commerce offers a map and brochure about the bike path.

The path's name is a nod to Falmouth's own Katharine Lee Bates (1859–1929), who wrote the lyrics to "America the Beautiful," with its verse, "And crown thy good with brotherhood, from sea to shining sea!"

The closest bike shop—convenient to the main cluster of B&Bs, some of which offer loaners—is **Corner Cycle,** at 115 Palmer Ave., at North Main Street (© **508/540-4195;** www.cornercycle.com). A half-day bike rental is $17 ($12 for children), a 24-hour rental $25 ($18 for children). For a broad selection of vehicles—from six-speed cruisers to six-passenger "surreys"—and good advice on routes, visit **Holiday Cycles,** at 465 Grand Ave., in Falmouth Heights (© **508/540-3549**), where a half-day (4-hr.) bike rental is $20, a 1-day rental $25, and a week rental $75. The surreys rent for $20 to $30 an hour. Holiday Cycles does not accept credit cards.

BOATING Cape Cod Kayak (© **508/563-9377;** www.capecodkayak.com) rents kayaks (free delivery in North Falmouth or West Falmouth) by the day or week and offers lessons and ecotours on local waterways. Kayak rentals are $35 to $60 for 8 hours ($5 more for tandems). Lessons are $52 to $65 per hour. Four-hour trips are $49 to $75.

FISHING To go after bigger prey, head out with a group on one of the **Patriot Party Boats,** based in Falmouth's Inner Harbor (© **800/734-0088** or 508/548-2626; www.patriotpartyboats.com). Boats leave twice daily, at 8am and 1pm, in season. The *Patriot Too,* with an enclosed deck, is ideal for family-style "bottom fishing" (4-hr. trips $45 adults, $30 children 12 and under; full-day trips $65 adults, $45 children; equipment and instruction provided).

GOLF Falmouth has four public golf courses. The most notable is the challenging 18-hole championship course at **Ballymeade Country Club,** 125 Falmouth Woods Rd. (© **508/540-4005;** www.ballymeade.com). Greens fees are $65 (Mon–Thurs) and $80 (Sat–Sun) and include carts; there are reduced afternoon rates.

NATURE & WILDLIFE AREAS Ashumet Holly and Wildlife Sanctuary ★★, operated by the Massachusetts Audubon Society, at 186 Ashumet Rd., off Route 151, in East Falmouth (© **508/362-1426;** www.massaudubon.org), is an intriguing 49-acre collection of more than 1,000 holly trees, representing 65 species culled from around the world. Preserved by the state's first commissioner of agriculture, who was concerned that commercial harvesting might wipe out native species, they flourish here, along with more than 130 species of birds and a carpet of Oriental lotus blossoms, which covers a kettle pond come summer. The trail fee is $4 for adults and $2 for seniors and children 15 and under.

Named for its round shape, **The Knob ★★** (13 acres of trails at Quissett Harbor, at the end of Quissett Road) provides a perfect short walk and lovely views of Buzzards Bay. There's very limited parking at this small, secluded harbor, so try it early or late in the day. The Knob, owned by the nonprofit group Salt Pond Areas Bird Sanctuaries, is free and open to the public.

The 2,250-acre **Waquoit Bay National Estuarine Research Reserve (WBNERR),** at 149 Waquoit Hwy., in Waquoit (© **508/457-0495;** www.waquoitbayreserve.org), maintains a 1-mile, self-guided nature trail. The reserve also offers a number of walks and interpretive programs, including the popular "Evenings on the Bluff," on Tuesday nights at 6:30pm, which are geared toward families. The visitor center is open Monday to Saturday from 10am to 4pm. You'll find several interesting exhibits especially for children. On Saturday in season, WBNERR hosts a free 20-minute cruise over to **Washburn Island ★★**. Once on the island, visitors can explore its wooded trails or relax on its pristine beaches. The 12-passenger motorboat leaves at 9am and returns by 12:30pm. The reserve also manages 11 primitive campsites on Washburn Island. Permits cost $10 a night. Advance reservations for the cruise and camping are required and can be made by calling ✆ **877/422-6762.** (The campsites book up 6 months in advance for summer weekends; you'll have better luck with a late-spring or early fall booking.)

WATERSPORTS Sailboarders prize Falmouth for its unflagging southwesterly winds. Although Old Silver Beach in North Falmouth is the most popular spot for windsurfing, it's only allowed there before 9am and after 5pm. You can rent gear from **Cape Cod Windsurfing** (✆ 508/801-3329; www.capecodwindsurfing.com), located on Old Silver Beach. There are windsurfers ($70 for a half-day; 2-hr. lessons $75); kayaks ($50 for a half-day); sailboats (a Sunfish costs $150 for a half-day; lessons are $75 an hour); and stand-up paddleboards ($50 for a half-day). There are also jet skis and bikes for rent. The Trunk River area on the west end of Falmouth's Surf Drive Beach and a portion of Chapoquoit Beach are the only public beaches where windsurfers are allowed during the day.

5 Sea Science in Woods Hole

Woods Hole Oceanographic Institution Ocean Science Exhibit Center and Gift Shop The high point at this small visitor's center is a climb aboard a life-size replica of the DSV *Alvin,* the deep-submergence vehicle that discovered the *Titanic*. But there are a range of other interactive exhibits here that will intrigue children and their parents, including a computer program about whale and dolphin sounds, a hydrothermal vent exhibit, and a presentation about toxic algae. The Woods Hole Oceanographic Institution (called WHOI—rhymes with phooey) is a world-class research organization and a $100 million operation mostly funded by the federal government. It, along with the Marine Biological Laboratory and the National Oceanic & Atmospheric Administration (NOAA) helped make this little fishing village into a world-renowned science community.

15 School St. (off Water St.), Woods Hole. ✆ **508/289-2663.** www.whoi.edu. $2 donation requested. Mid-Apr to Oct Mon–Fri 11am–4pm; Nov–Dec Tues–Fri 11am–4pm.

Woods Hole Science Aquarium ★ The country's oldest marine aquarium, having been established in 1885, makes for a nice little 45-minute visit. Young children will particularly appreciate its charms. Time your visit to coincide with feeding time for the two seals in a special pool out in front of the museum. Their injuries—one is blind—make them unable to be released, so the aquarium is their permanent home. Feeding time is 11am and 4pm most days. The best parts of the aquarium are the touch tanks with lobsters, quahogs, horseshoe crabs, spider crabs, starfish, and hermit crabs. The tanks contain 140 marine animals, mainly fish of the Northeast and Middle Atlantic waters. There are also displays about marine environments, endangered species, and marine science.

166 Water St., at Albatross St. (off the western end of Water St.), Woods Hole. ✆ **508/495-2001.** http://aquarium.nefsc.noaa.gov. Free admission; donations accepted. Mid-June to early Sept daily 11am–4pm; early Sept to mid-June Mon–Fri 10am–4pm. Adults need a picture ID to enter.

Falmouth Historical Sights

Falmouth Museums on the Green ★★ Across the street from the Village Green, where Colonial militia used to train, stand these historically focused museums. The two main museum buildings, inside 18th-century houses display period furniture, fine art, textiles, and temporary exhibits. The 1790 Dr. Francis Wicks House is set up to show what a doctor's office was like 200 years ago. The Conant House, built about 1730, has revolving exhibits covering topics such as Victorian Life in Falmouth. The museum's visitors' center is inside the reconstructed Hallett Barn, first built in the 18th century. Walking tours of Falmouth depart from the barn at 10am on Tuesday, Wednesday and Thursday mornings in season. Behind the barn is the Cultural Center where many of the museum's activities take place. The gardens—a Colonial-style flower garden, an herb garden and a Memorial Park—are particularly exquisite.

55 and 65 Palmer Ave. (at the Village Green). ⓒ **508/548-4857.** www.falmouthhistoricalsociety. org. Admission $5 adults, free for children 12 and under. Late June to early Oct Tues–Fri 10am–4pm, Sat 10am–1pm; by appointment early Oct to late June.

Woods Hole Historical Museum ★★ The Woods Hole Museum is a small lively museum that celebrates this fishing village's unique history. The main building, the Bradley House, contains a diorama of the village; revolving exhibits focus on local history, such as old Woods Hole businesses or the Woods Hole Science School. The Swift Barn, built in 1877 by E. E. Swift for $80.71, now houses a small boat museum. Displays include an 1890s Woods Hole Spritsail, a Herreshoff 12½ sailboat, and other maritime artifacts and models. In summer there's a boat-building class for families. The Yale Workshop houses a re-creation of the workshop of a local pediatrician, Dr. Leroy Milton Yale Jr., who was an accomplished artist and fly fisherman who made his own rods and flies. The museum hosts walking tours on Tuesdays at 3:30pm in July and August.

579 Woods Hole Rd. (eastern edge of town), Woods Hole. ⓒ **508/548-7270.** www.woodshole museum.org. Free admission; donations welcome. Mid-June to mid-Sept Tues–Sat 10am–4pm; by appointment during the off-season.

Shopping

Falmouth's spiffy Main Street has a number of stores selling good clothing, home goods, and gifts.

BOOKS **Eight Cousins Books,** 189 Main St., Falmouth (ⓒ **508/548-5548;** www. eightcousins.com), specializes in books for children and young adults but also sells books for adults, as well as games, and toys for kids.

FASHION Don't be too intimidated to browse in **Maxwell & Co.,** 200 Main St. (in the center of town), Falmouth (ⓒ **508/540-8752;** www.maxwellandco.com), which may be the highest-end clothier on the Cape. Comfortable Italian fashions for men and women are displayed here in an elegant setting. Its end-of-summer sale in mid-August offers up to 70 percent off the prices of these exquisite goods.

The clothing at **Caline for Kids,** 149 Main St. (in the center of town), Falmouth (ⓒ **508/548-2533;** www.calineforkids.com), ranges from practical to elegant, and sometimes manages to be both. Sizes from newborn to 14 are available.

FOOD & WINE "Pick your own" is the watchword at the long-established **Tony Andrews Farm and Produce Stand ★★**, 394 Old Meeting House Rd. (about 1½ miles north of Rte. 28), East Falmouth (ⓒ **508/548-4717;** www.tonyandrewsfarmstand.com), where it's strawberries early in the summer and tomatoes, sweet corn, squash, sunflowers, and more as the season progresses. Of course, you can just buy them here without picking, though the Puritans wouldn't have approved. Open daily 10am to 6pm. **Coonamessett Farm** ★★, 277 Hatchville Rd. (about 1 mile east of Sandwich Rd.), East Falmouth (© **508/563-2560;** www.coonamessettfarm.com), runs a full farm stand of vegetables grown in the fields out back. You can pick your own vegetables, look at the farm animals (including two cute llamas), or rent a canoe for a quick paddle in the on-site pond.

TOYS One of the best toy shops on the Cape is **Kaleidoscope Toys,** 208 Main St., Falmouth, © **508/548-5635,** a colorful shop filled with all manner of gewgaws for "children" from 0 to 99 years old. Among the shop's specialties are a variety of arts and crafts projects and a menagerie of stuffed animals.

Falmouth After Dark

DRINKS Grab a stool at the **British Beer Company** ★, 263 Grand Ave., Falmouth Heights (© **508/540-9600;** www.britishbeer.com/local/falmouth), and choose from a revolving selection of more than 18 drafts from the British Isles as you ponder views of the beach across the street.

Who knows whom you'll meet in the rough-and-tumble old **Captain Kidd Bar** ★, 77 Water St., in Woods Hole (© **508/548-9206;** www.thecaptainkidd.com): maybe a lobsterwoman, maybe a Nobel Prize winner. Good grub, too.

Everyone heads to **Liam Maguire's Irish Pub** ★, at 273 Main St., in Falmouth (© **508/548-0285;** www.liammaguire.com), for a taste of the Emerald Isle. Live music is performed on weekends year-round, often by Liam. No cover.

Grumpy's Pub, at 29 Locust St. (© **508/540-3930;** www.grumpyspub.blogspot. com), is a good old bar/shack with live music (rock, blues, and jazz) Thursday to Saturday nights. Cover is typically $5. Look for free passes on the counter at Coffee Obsession (110 Palmer Ave.) nearby.

The great menu with lots of intriguing appetizers at **RoöBar,** 285 Main St., in Falmouth (© **508/548-8600;** www.theroobar.com), draws a hip crowd.

PERFORMANCE **Falmouth Theatre Guild** performs on the historic Highfield Theater stage, offering family-friendly musicals and comedies from September through May. Find out what's playing and buy tickets at www.falmouththeatreguild. org. **The Woods Hole Folk Music Society** ★ (© **508/540-0320;** www.arts-cape.com/ whfolkmusic) mounts concerts October through May (first and third Sun of each month), attracting a grassroots crowd to Community Hall on Water Street, by the Eel Pond drawbridge. General admission is $8; discounts are available for members, seniors, and children.

The top talent from college drama departments across the country form the **College Light Opera Company** ★ (© **508/548-0668;** www.collegelightopera.com), which puts on a fast-paced summer repertory from late June through August at the Highfield Theatre. The venue, a former horse barn, has been a terrific summer-stock theater for the past half-century. Shows often sell out, so call well ahead or keep your fingers crossed for a scattering of single tickets.

THE MID CAPE: HYANNIS, BARNSTABLE & ENVIRONS ★★

15 miles E of Sagamore; 44 miles S of Provincetown

Essentials

VISITOR INFORMATION   For information contact the **Hyannis Area Chamber of Commerce,** 397 Main St., Hyannis, MA 02601 (© **508/775-2201;** www.hyannis. com), which is open Mon through Sat 9am to 5pm, Sun 10am to 2pm. The handsome chamber building on Main Street, which used to be the town hall, also contains the John F. Kennedy Hyannis Museum and the Cape Cod Baseball League Hall of Fame. The **Cape Cod Chamber of Commerce,** routes 6 and 132 (just off the exit 6 eastbound ramp), Centerville, MA 02632 (© **888/332-2732** or 508/362-3225; www. capecodchamber.org), is open year-round: mid-Apr to mid-Nov daily 9am to 5pm, and mid-Nov to mid-Apr Mon through Sat 10am to 4pm.

Where to Stay

IN HYANNIS, HYANNIS PORT & CENTERVILLE

There are a variety of large, generic, but convenient hotels and motels in Hyannis.

Anchor In, 1 South St. (on Hyannis Inner Harbor), Hyannis (© **508/775-0357;** www.anchorin.com), has a great location on the harbor and is a short walk to the center of town. There are numerous decks and a heated pool, all with harbor views. During the high season, the 42 rooms are priced at $289 to $309, including continental breakfast.

Heritage House Hotel, 259 Main St. (in the center of town), Hyannis (© **508/775-7000;** www.heritagehousehotel.com), is on Main Street, within walking distance of restaurants, shops, and the ferries to Nantucket and Martha's Vineyard. There is an indoor and an outdoor pool, a hot tub and saunas, and a restaurant/lounge on-site with entertainment. During the high season, the 143 rooms are $132 on weekdays and $188 on weekends, for double occupancy.

If you prefer more amenities, there's the **Resort and Conference Center at Hyannis,** at 35 Scudder Ave., at the West End Circle just off Main Street (© **866/828-8259;** www.capecodresortandconference.com). Summer rates are $220 to $230 double. Out the back door is an 18-hole, par-3 golf course. There are also two restaurants, a fitness center, and indoor-outdoor pools.

A great choice for families is the **Cape Codder Resort & Spa,** 1225 Iyannough Rd./Rte. 132 (at the intersection of Bearse's Way), Hyannis (© **888/297-2200** or 508/771-3000; www.capecodderresort.com). It features two restaurants (Grand Cru Wine Bar, and Hearth 'n Kettle for families) and a spa. Kids love the indoor wave pool, with two water slides. Summer rates for the 260 rooms are $179–$239 for a double, $350–$389 for a suite.

Moderate

Long Dell Inn ★★   Built in 1849 as a home for Captain Reuben Jones, who made his wealth in the Gold Rush, this pretty Greek Revival is now one of the few B&Bs in this pretty corner of the mid-Cape—it's welcomed lodgers for over 80 years. The terrific Centerville location means you'll be close to the village's cute general store and a very good ice-cream shop. From the inn it's just a short walk or drive to Craigville Beach, one of the best in the area.

436 S. Main St., Centerville. ℭ **508/775-2750.** www.longdellinn.com. 7 units. Summer $150–$210. Rates include full breakfast. Free Wi-Fi.

Simmons Homestead Inn ★★ If you prize uniqueness and informality over routine, this former captain's house may be your B&B of choice. Fun is the buzzword here. Your host, Bill Putnam, has amassed an unusual collection of red sports cars, 55 at last count. As for the B&B itself, it feels like old Cape Cod, except with modern niceties. The rooms are decorated with whimsy in mind, with animal themes reflected in the bedding, artwork, and knickknacks. The interior also reflects the historic nature of the property, with antique reproductions and four-poster beds, for example. There is a billiard room and a backyard with some well-placed hammocks. The inn allows dogs; Putnam has a large number of cats.

288 Scudder Ave. (about ¼ mile west of the West End rotary), Hyannis Port. ℭ **800/637-1649** or 508/778-4999. www.simmonshomesteadinn.com. 14 units. Summer $180–$280 double; $300 2-bedroom suite. Rates include full breakfast. Dogs welcome. **Amenities:** Bikes; Wi-Fi (free).

Inexpensive

Hostelling International–Hyannis This former historic house on the harbor is now a youth hostel with a stellar location, overlooking Aselton Park on Hyannis Harbor and a short walk to Main Street's stores and restaurants, as well as the docks for ferries to the islands. Use of a fully equipped kitchen as well as breakfast are included in the rate.

111 Ocean St., Hyannis. ℭ **877/683-7990** or 508/775-7990. http://capecod.hiusa.org. 37 beds. Summer $35–$39 bed; $99–$125 private room. Rates include continental breakfast. Closed Nov-Apr. Wi-Fi (free).

IN BARNSTABLE VILLAGE

To check on the availability at 17 bed-and-breakfasts along Route 6A from Sandwich to Brewster, head to www.historiccapecodbay.com. Being on Route 6A means most of these inns are walking distance to a bayside beach and the shops and restaurants in Barnstable Village.

Moderate

The Acworth Inn In the tiny village of Cummaquid on the Old King's Highway, this historic little B&B is a find. Guests can enjoy a stroll along the old stagecoach route to a placid beach or a charming gallery. A short drive brings you to Barnstable Village or Yarmouthport, with a variety of restaurants, or you can take a 5-minute drive to get to Hyannis, the Cape's hub. Some rooms have extra amenities like a minifridge or a whirlpool tub; all are romantically decorated.

4352 Rte. 6A/Old King's Hwy. (near the Yarmouth Port border), Cummaquid. ℭ **800/362-6363** or 508/362-3330. www.acworthinn.com. 5 units. Summer $159–$179 double; $239 suite. Rates include full breakfast. **Amenities:** Bikes, Wi-Fi (free).

Ashley Manor Inn This historic B&B is a step up from some of the others along Route 6A by virtue of the size of the rooms and the amenities. With fancy linens and antique furnishings, it also feels more luxurious, and it's within walking distance of Barnstable Harbor, Millway Beach, and Barnstable Village. The inn was built in 1699, making it one of the oldest B&B buildings on the Cape. Its rich heritage can be seen in the wide-board floors, huge hearth fireplaces, and a secret passageway connecting the upstairs to the downstairs. The theory is this is where the Tories hid during the

Hyannis

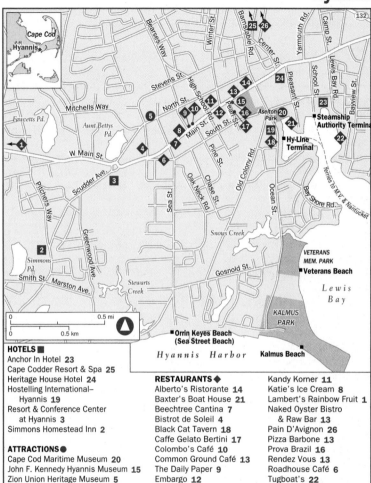

HOTELS ■
Anchor In Hotel **23**
Cape Codder Resort & Spa **25**
Heritage House Hotel **24**
Hostelling International–
Hyannis **19**
Resort & Conference Center
at Hyannis **3**
Simmons Homestead Inn **2**

ATTRACTIONS ●
Cape Cod Maritime Museum **20**
John F. Kennedy Hyannis Museum **15**
Zion Union Heritage Museum **5**

RESTAURANTS ◆
Alberto's Ristorante **14**
Baxter's Boat House **21**
Beechtree Cantina **7**
Bistrot de Soleil **4**
Black Cat Tavern **18**
Caffe Gelato Bertini **17**
Colombo's Café **10**
Common Ground Café **13**
The Daily Paper **9**
Embargo **12**

Kandy Korner **11**
Katie's Ice Cream **8**
Lambert's Rainbow Fruit **1**
Naked Oyster Bistro
& Raw Bar **13**
Pain D'Avignon **26**
Pizza Barbone **13**
Prova Brazil **16**
Rendez Vous **13**
Roadhouse Café **6**
Tugboat's **22**

Revolutionary War. The patio is a particularly nice place to enjoy the ample hot breakfasts, served here on sunny mornings.

3660 Rte. 6A (just east of Hyannis Rd.), Barnstable. © **888/535-2246** or 508/362-8044. www.ashleymanor.net. 6 units. Summer $180 double; $280 suite. Rates include full breakfast. No children 13 and under. **Amenities:** Bikes; Har-Tru tennis court, Wi-Fi (free).

Beechwood Inn ★★ This exquisite B&B gets its name from the two stately beech trees on the property. The house, a Queen Anne–style Victorian, has a three-sided veranda on the outside and handsome woodwork within. Guest rooms are decorated with period antiques; some have fireplaces. Cape Cod Bay is a short walk away down a country lane, and Barnstable Village is also close. In the morning, the three-course breakfast is served outside or in the wood-paneled dining room. The innkeepers, the Traugots, also breed golden retrievers.

2839 Rte. 6A (about 1½ miles east of Rte. 132), Barnstable Village. ℂ **800/609-6618** or 508/362-6618. www.beechwoodinn.com. 6 units, 4 with tub/shower combination, 2 with shower only. Summer $189–$229 double. Rates include full breakfast. No children 12 or under. Wi-Fi (free).

Lamb and Lion Inn ★   The Lamb and Lion has a lot to recommend it., but most of its laurels stem from the fact that its owners Tom Dott and Ali Pitcher understand hospitality. They also understand fun (Dott is an Elvis impersonator), and they will ensure that you have it. The rooms, which are all different, include some with wood-burning fireplaces or with kitchenettes. From the outside, this is a classic antique Cape house with a beautiful lawn and gardens, with lots of colorful flowerboxes and flower beds. Inside, you'll be surprised to see the guest rooms surround a courtyard with a saltwater pool and large hot tub. There is also a converted 1700s horse stable the size of a small cottage. Also on site is a spa where you can have a massage, facial or other treatment. The owners are fans of small dogs, and they have several.

2504 Main St./Rte. 6A, Barnstable. ℂ **800/909-6923** or 508/362-6823. www.lambandlion.com. 10 units, 6 with tub/shower combination, 4 with shower only. Summer $229–$295 double, $299–379 suite. Rates include continental breakfast. Well-behaved dogs allowed (30-lb. limit). **Amenities:** Hot tub; pool; Wi-Fi (free).

Where to Eat

IN HYANNIS & CENTERVILLE
Expensive

Alberto's Ristorante ★★★ NORTHERN ITALIAN   When Alberto's opened in 1984, it was said to be the first Northern Italian in the region. Many other local restaurants have come and gone since then, but Alberto's, run by the suave Felisberto Barreiro, has remained a consistent choice. It is an elegant venue, with crisp white tablecloths and chandeliers providing romantic lighting, but there's also a lively bar scene, particularly in the summer. The best deal is the three-course prix-fixe dinner, served daily from 4 to 6pm for $22. Favorites include the cannelloni and other house-made pastas. There's also a sublime roasted duck, and the signature "Alberto," a delicate veal cutlet with peppers, artichoke hearts, pesto, and a fresh tomato sauce. There's also a good children's menu.

360 Main St., Hyannis. ℂ**508/778-1770.** www.albertos.net. Main courses $16–$27. Daily 11:30am–9:30pm.

Bistrot de Soleil Restaurant and Bar ★★ FRENCH   This hidden gem is on a side street on the west end of Hyannis's main street. The dining room is a roomy mix of tables and booths, with one side airy with a high ceiling, the other more intimate. The sophisticated menu is a pleasing mix of old and new, so we have beef Wellington and coquilles Saint Jacques as well as a variety of gluten-free and vegetarian options. Among the least expensive menu items are the various burgers, served on a locally baked bun with seasoned fries. There is also a list of unusual risottos, such as one with salmon, sweet peas, gorgonzola, and grilled zucchini. A well-chosen wine list and homemade desserts complete the picture.

350 Stevens St., Hyannis. ℂ**508/534-9308.** www.bistrotdesoleil.com. Main courses $9–$29. Daily 11:30am–9pm.

Black Cat Tavern ★ NEW AMERICAN Tourists love this traditional restaurant across the street from Hyannis Harbor. The interior is very "mid-century yacht club," with polished brass, sailboat models, and framed nautical flags. The menu hits all the basics, with burgers, steaks and seafood. Four nights a week, the restaurant doubles as a piano lounge with live music. The patio out front is ideal on warm nights or for a quick bite, the **Black Cat Harbor Shack** next door can handle to-go order, and the **Shack Out Back** is an outdoor patio and raw bar.

165 Ocean St. (opposite the Ocean St. Dock), Hyannis. ☏ **508/778-1233.** www.blackcattavern. com. Main courses $20–$43. Apr–Oct daily 11:30am–10pm. Closed Jan.

The Naked Oyster Bistro & Raw Bar ★★★ FRENCH BISTRO Chef Florence Lowell, from Bordeaux, France, runs the show at the Naked Oyster, one of the Cape's top restaurants. Lowell has her own oyster beds in nearby Barnstable Harbor, so the sweet, salty shellfish comes straight from the sea to the table, served, ideally, with the mignonette (sauce) of the day. In addition to oysters, served dressed or naked, you might want to start with the French onion soup or the oyster stew, then move on to the seared diver scallops that are served over a roasted-shitake-mushroom risotto. Another winner is the duck confit with thyme gnocchi. A number of items on the menu are gluten-free. Desserts are extra-special here, and the wine list is unrivaled in the region. This bistro is pleasantly cozy and romantically lit, with vibrant paintings shown off the brick walls.

410 Main St. (next to Puritan Clothing Co., in the center of town), Hyannis. ☏ **508/778-6500.** www. nakedoyster.com. Main courses $24–$35. May–Oct daily 11:30am–9:30pm; Nov–April Mon–Sat 11:30am–9:30pm.

Pain D'Avignon ★★★ FRENCH CAFE You'd be hard-pressed to accidentally find this place, located as it is on a side street off Route 132 near the airport. It's well worth the trip. Despite the industrial surroundings, stepping into Pain D'Avignon is really like entering a European cafe. It's very stylish, all blacks and whites, including the photos on the walls. Pain D'Avignon began as a wholesale bread business, and breakfast and lunch both feature their exquisite bread, be it a croissant, bagel, brioche, or baguette. The more extensive dinner menu includes as starters Dennis Bay View Oysters, grilled Spanish octopus, and foie gras with a buttered brioche. As a main course, you might try the dish of the day, perhaps the coq au vin or the steak frites, with house-made fries and watercress salad. Desserts are made in-house.

15 Hinckley Rd. (just north of the airport rotary), Hyannis. ☏ **508/778-8588.** www.paindavignon. com. Main courses $16–$34. Mon and Tues 7am–6pm; Wed–Sun 7am–10pm.

Prova Brazil Steakhouse & Italian Cuisine ★ BRAZILIAN/ITALIAN At this modern interpretation of a Brazilian steakhouse, a large statue of a bull on the patio makes it very clear what its priorities are. "Prova" means "to taste" in Portuguese and "to try" in Italian, so it is an apt name for a restaurant offering both styles of cuisine. Diners can choose from the regular menu, or go for the *rodizio*, a traditional Brazilian restaurant style in which waiters come to the table with slices of different types and cuts of meats. If you choose this, your table is equipped with a little flag that tells the waiters whether you want more meat. As is typical of Brazilian-style restaurants, there is also a large self-serve salad bar. The prices may seem a little high, but meals come with a side salad or cup of soup, and a choice of pasta or vegetable. The Prova fillet, a 10-ounce cut of grilled tenderloin, is the signature dish. During the warmer months, the outside patio and bar area is a great place to people-watch and enjoy the hustle and bustle of Main Street.

415 Main St., Hyannis. © **508/827-4341.** www.provabrazil.com. Main courses $15–$29. Daily 11am–11pm.

Roadhouse Café ★★ AMERICAN/NORTHERN ITALIAN   This stalwart has been in business for more than 30 years, winning accolades for its clubby atmosphere and a menu that combines the best of Northern Italian cuisine with New American flair. The best room in the place is in the room with the glorious mahogany bar, high-backed booths, and a fireplace that warms the room all winter. The front dining rooms are more formal; the Back Door Bistro, which has a special pizza menu, is where the entertainers play 5 nights a week in season. The Monday Night Jazz Ensemble plays from 7 to 10pm year-round. Special dishes include the cioppino, which is a lovely seafood stew, and the lobster ravioli.

488 South St. (off Main St., near the West End rotary), Hyannis. © **508/775-2386.** www.roadhouse cafe.com. Main courses $17–$35. Daily 4–10pm.

Moderate

Baxter's Boat House ★ SEAFOOD   For waterfront dining in Hyannis, you can't do much better than Baxter's, set on a pier on Hyannis Harbor. It's fun to sit out on the deck and watch the ferries, sailboats, fishing boats, and even a pirate cruise come and go from the harbor. The fare here is standard clam-shack cuisine, including fried fish with all the fixings. But you can't argue with success; they've been doing their thing here since 1957, when the Baxter family ran a fish market out of the building. There is a lively bar scene here on summer nights; live entertainment starts at 9:30pm.

177 Pleasant St. (near the Steamship Authority ferry), Hyannis. © **508/775-4490.** www.baxters capecod.com. Main courses $11–$25. Late May to early Sept daily 11am–9:30pm; hours may vary at beginning and end of the season. Closed mid-Oct to early Apr.

Beech Tree Cantina ★★ MEXICAN   One highlight here is the magnificent English weeping beech tree, said to have been planted in 1776 and given to the town for its loyalty to the British Crown. The tree is not only the namesake of the restaurant, but the focal point of the popular outdoor bar area, which includes comfy couches that make it feel like an outdoor living room. Visit on a sunny summer day, when you can see and be seen in this one-of-a-kind venue. Otherwise, you can eat inside the restaurant, a hip venue with a large bar. The guacamole, made at the table, is particularly good and is made at the table.

599 Main St. (at the west end of Main St.), Hyannis. © **508/534-9876.** www.beechtreecantina.com. $6–$24. Mon–Fri 4–10pm, Sat 11:30am–10pm, Sun noon–9pm.

Embargo ★★ NEW AMERICAN   The bar is where most of the action is here, but it also happens to have yummy and sophisticated food. Delectables like pan-seared scallops over truffle Parmesan basmati compete with baby-back ribs with a mango salsa. Come between 4:30 to 6pm, when there are half-price oysters and tapas. There's a lots of other nibble food on the menu, such as pizza, sushi, sliders, spring rolls, and tacos, prepared with style and pizzazz.

453 Main St., Hyannis. © **508/771-9700.** $13–$30. Mon–Thurs 4:30–9pm, Fri–Sun 11:30am–9pm.

Tugboats at Hyannis Marina ★ SEAFOOD   Those looking for a lunch overlooking Hyannis Harbor will find this former sail loft to be a good choice; it's informal enough for large parties and children. Large decks overlooking the harbor provide great views of the comings and goings of boats and ferries. The menu is heavy on burgers, salads, and fried seafood—it's a good place to come if you are craving lobster with all the fixings. There is a kids' menu, too.

21 Arlington St., Yarmouth. ℂ**508/775-6433.** www.tugboatscapecod.com. $12–$29. Late May to early Sept daily 11am–9pm.

Inexpensive

Common Ground Cafe ★ AMERICAN   This deli, run by members of a Northern Vermont commune, serves wholesome soups, salads and baked goods in what looks like a mysterious tree fort. The booths are made out of carved-out trunks and seem to be tucked into the walls. The menu changes with the seasons, but favorites include the tomato soup, the tuna melt, and the turkey burrito. Smoothies are a specialty; a retail shop in the back sells natural soaps and similar products.

420 Main St., Hyannis. ℂ**508/778-8390.** Most items under $6. Mon–Thurs 10am–9pm; Fri 10am–3pm; Sun noon–9pm.

The Daily Paper ★ DINER   Sit at the counter on a swivel stool and chat with your neighbor or grab a booth or a table at this chef-owned and -operated diner. Serving good honest comfort food has been a winning formula, and now there is a second Daily Paper just about a mile east on Main Street. The menu has all the diner classics, plus some special offerings, such as lobster Benedict for breakfast and a warm ham-and-brie sandwich for lunch.

644 W. Main St., Hyannis. ℂ**508/790-8800.** www.dailypapercapecod.com. Most items under $10. MC, V. Mon–Sat 6am–2pm; Sun 7am–1pm.

Pizza Barbone ★★ PIZZA   The competition is over. The best pizza on the Cape is at this small shop on Main Street Hyannis. The Neopolitan wood-fired pizza oven, a 6,000-pound beauty made by third generation oven-makers, was imported from Italy complete with hand-painted glass tiles. The pizza is makes is sublime, a delicate thin crust topped with fresh, unusual ingredients like crushed potato with garlic cream and bacon; pistachio pesto; or the more traditional sweet sausage. The pasta, dressings, sauces, and gelato are all made in-house, and the restaurant even has a roof garden for the organic vegetables used in salads and on the pizzas. As for the flour, it's imported from Italy. The business started as a mobile pizza shop that turned up at parties, and thus the name, which means "vagabond" in Italian.

390 Main St., Hyannis. ℂ**508/957-2377.** www.pizzabarbone.com. Pizzas $9–$14. Daily 11am–9pm.

Rendez Vous Café & Creperie ★★★ CREPERIE   Rendezvous's signature dish, whether sweet or savory, is a buttery delight. You haven't lived until you've had a portobello crepe with blue cheese and baby spinach. Live on the wild side and finish your meal with a wonderfully sweet bananas-Foster crepe. The menu also features hot and cold panini. Coffee is a specialty here, and all manner of cappuccinos made with fair-trade coffee are available. There are open-mic nights and other entertainments scheduled some evenings.

394 Main St., Hyannis. ℂ**508/827-4449.** www.rendezvouscapecod.com. Most crepes and sandwiches $8–$10. Daily 8am–5pm.

Coffee & Desserts

Rich and creamy gelato made one batch at a time from a secret Florentine recipe can be found slightly off the beaten track at **Caffè Gelato Bertini** at 20R Pearl St., Hyannis (ℂ **508/778-0244;** www.capecodgelato.com). Open May to Oct; hours vary.

Since 1934 several generations of summer-goers—including enthusiastic Kennedys—have fed their ice cream cravings at **Four Seas Ice Cream** ★★, 360 S. Main St., at Main Street, in the center of Centerville (✆ **508/775-1394;** www.fourseasicecream.com). This place had exotic flavors long before they became the norm: Specialties include rum-butter toffee, cantaloupe, and—at the height of the season—Cape Cod beach plum. Open late May to early Sept.

Look for the big stuffed bear sitting on a bench to find **Kandy Korner** ★★, 474 Main St., Hyannis (✆ **508/771-5313;** www.kandykorner.com), an old-fashioned candy store and ice cream shop that's been pleasing strollers on Hyannis's Main Street for decades. The ice cream, chocolates, fudge and saltwater taffy are all made in-house. Open 10am to 6pm daily.

Another excellent ice cream shop is **Katie's Homemade Ice Cream,** a little farther west on Main Street at 568 Main St., Hyannis (✆ **508/771-6889;** www.katiesicecreamcapecod.com), in the big pink house. All the ice cream (hard and soft serve plus frozen yogurt) is made here in small batches. There is a deli and lots of outside seating attached. Open late May to Sept daily 10:30am to 11pm.

Takeout & Picnic Fare
Lambert's Rainbow Fruit ★ (✆ **508/790-5954**), at 1000 W. Main St., Centerville, has the best produce selection in the area, bar none. This is also a great place pick up such picnic fixings as breads and spreads.

5 IN BARNSTABLE VILLAGE & OSTERVILLE
Moderate
The Barnstable Restaurant and Tavern ★★ NEW AMERICAN/ITALIAN/PUB   You can almost hear the echoes of horse-drawn carriages at this former stage-coach stop, its wide-board floors and antiques left over from colonial days. A tavern has been on this property for at least 200 years. These days, the popular restaurant is chef-owned and notable not just for its New American cuisine but also for very reason-able prices. A grilled tavern burger, thin-crust pizzas, deli sandwiches, and fried sea-food are always available, as are Italian specialties like the mushroom ravioli and more upscale offerings like the grilled tuna steak with wasabi or the Mediterranean seafood stew with a garlic-aioli crouton. There is a kids' menu and gluten-free offerings, too.

3176 Main St./Rte. 6A (in the center of Barnstable Village). ✆ **508/362-2355.** www.barnstablerestaurant.com. Main courses $10–$20. Daily 11:30am–9pm.

Mattakeese Wharf ★ SEAFOOD   This is the ultimate mid-Cape restaurant to go to for a sunset view, sitting as it does in Barnstable Harbor, with lovely views out to Cape Cod Bay and Sandy Neck. Seafood—have it on the half shell or fried, broiled, or baked—makes up most of the menu. Many people indulge in the lobster dinner with all the trimmings. Prices are high here, since you're paying for that spectacular view. There is entertainment on summer weekends beginning at sunset.

273 Millway (about ½ mile north of Rte. 6A), Barnstable Village. ✆ **508/362-4511.** www.mattakeese.com. Main courses $16–$37. May to mid-Oct daily 11am–9:30pm; call for off-season hours.

Takeout & Picnic Fare
Earthly Delights ★★ (✆ **508/420-2206**), at 15 W. Bay Rd., Osterville, specializes in natural foods to go. There are different specials prepared every day, but expect to find delicious pizzas and quiches that use organic ingredients. **Fancy's** ★ (✆ **508/428-6954**), at 699 Main St., Osterville, is a family-owned market specializing in meats, produce, and breads. The deli here is a great place to pick up a picnic lunch. Treat

The Mid Cape: Hyannis, Barnstable & Environs

CAPE COD

yourself to a panini. **Nirvana Coffee Company ★** (℃ **508/744-6983**), at 3206 Main St., Barnstable Village, is centrally located across from the courthouse. Some say it has the best coffee on Cape Cod.

Exploring: Beaches & Recreational Pursuits

BEACHES Barnstable's primary bay beach is Sandy Neck Beach, accessed through East Sandwich (p. 137). Most of the Nantucket Sound beaches are fairly protected and thus not big in terms of surf. Beach parking costs $15 a day, usually payable at the lot; for a weeklong parking sticker ($50), visit the Recreation Department at 141 Bassett Lane, at the **Hyannis Youth & Community Center** (℃ **508/790-6345**), open daily (Mon–Sat 7am–10pm, Sun noon–9pm). The center also has an elevated walking track and an elaborate teen center, in addition to two skating rinks and basketball courts. Day passes cost $5. *Note:* There is a smoking ban on beaches in the town of Barnstable during the summer.

o **Craigville Beach ★★★**, off Craigville Beach Road, in Centerville: Once a magnet for Methodist camp meetings (conference centers still line the shore), this broad expanse of sand has lifeguards and restrooms. A destination for the bronzed and buffed, it's known as "Muscle Beach."

o **Kalmus Beach ★★**, off Gosnold Street, in Hyannis Port: This 800-foot spit of sand stretching toward the mouth of the harbor makes an ideal launching site for wind-surfers, who sometimes seem to play chicken with the steady parade of ferries. The surf is tame, the slope shallow, and the conditions ideal for little kids. There are lifeguards, a snack bar, and restrooms.

o **Orrin Keyes Beach ★★** (also known as Sea Street Beach), at the end of Sea Street, in Hyannis: This little beach at the end of a residential road is popular with families.

o **Veterans Beach,** off Ocean Street, in Hyannis: A small stretch of harborside sand adjoining the John F. Kennedy Memorial, this spot is not tops for swimming, unless you're very young. Parking is usually easy to find, though, and it's walkable from town. The snack bar, restrooms, and playground will see to a family's needs.

FISHING The township of Barnstable has 11 ponds for freshwater fishing; for information and permits, visit **Town Hall,** at 367 Main St., Hyannis (℃ **508/862-4044**); or **Sports Port,** 149 W. Main St., Hyannis (℃ **508/775-3096**). Shell-fishing permits are available from the **Department of Natural Resources,** at 1189 Phinney's Lane, Centerville (℃ **508/790-6272**). Surf-casting, which now requires a $10 license, is permitted on Sandy Neck (p. 132).

Among the charter boats berthed in **Barnstable Harbor** is Capt. Justin Zacek's *Drifter* (℃ **774/836-7292;** www.driftersportfishing.com), a 36-foot boat available for half- and full-day trips costing $550 to $775, depending on the length of the trip and the number of people. **Hy-Line Cruises** offers seasonal sonar-aided "bottom" or blues fishing from its Ocean Street dock in Hyannis (℃ **508/790-0696;** www.hylinecruises. com). The cost for a half-day bottom-fishing trip is $35 to $38 per adult, $25 to $38 for kids ages 5 to 12 (children 4 and under are prohibited). **Helen H Deep-Sea Fishing,** at 137 Pleasant St., Hyannis (℃ **508/790-0660;** www.helen-h.com), offers daily expeditions aboard a 100-foot boat with a heated cabin and full galley. Choose whether you want to fish for porgies and black sea bass or fluke and bluefish. Adults pay $35, children $24.

GOLF The **Hyannis Golf Club,** 1840 Rte. 132 (© **508/362-2606**), offers a 46-station driving range, as well as an 18-hole championship course. High-season greens fees are $61. At the scenic 9-hole **Cotuit High Ground Country Club,** at 31 Crockers Neck Rd., Cotuit (© **508/428-9863;** www.cotuithighground.com), an 18-hole round costs $20; it's $15 for juniors and seniors, and for everyone after 4pm.

HARBOR CRUISES For a fun and informative introduction to the harbor, take a leisurely, 1-hour, narrated tour aboard one of Hy-Line Cruises' 1911 steamer replicas, **MV *Patience*** or **MV *Prudence*.** There are five 1-hour family cruises a day in season, but for a real treat, take the Sunday 3pm "Ice Cream Float," which includes a design-your-own Ben & Jerry's ice-cream sundae. Hy-Line Cruises depart from the Ocean Street Dock (© **508/790-0696;** www.hy-linecruises.com), and you should call for a reservation and schedule. Tickets are $16 for adults and free to $8 for children 12 and under. (The ice-cream cruises are $1 more.) There are 16 departures daily from late June to September; it's closed November to mid-April. Credit cards are accepted. Parking is $5 per car.

NATURE **Long Pasture Wildlife Sanctuary ★★**, 345 Bone Hill Rd., Barnstable Village (© **508/362-7475;** www.massaudubon.org), a 110-acre Audubon sanctuary, offers easy-to-walk trails out to a meadow with a view of Barnstable Harbor. Wildlife spottings are likely to include numerous butterflies, dragonflies, and red-tailed hawks. Admission $4 for adults, $3 children.

WATERSPORTS **Eastern Mountain Sports,** 1513 Iyannough Rd./Rte. 132 (© **508/362-8690;** www.ems.com), rents kayaks, tents, and sleeping bags, and sponsors free clinics and walks, such as a full-moon hike. Kayaks rent for $50 a day, $100 for 3 days.

WHALE-WATCHING Although Provincetown is about an hour closer to the whales' preferred feeding grounds, it would take you at least an hour (possibly hours on a summer weekend) to drive all the way down-Cape. If your time and itinerary are limited, hop aboard **Hyannis Whale Watcher Cruises,** Barnstable Harbor (about ½ mile north of Rte. 6A, on Mill Way), Barnstable (© **800/287-0374** or 508/362-6088; www. whales.net), for a 4-hour voyage on a 100-foot high-speed cruiser. Naturalists provide the narration, and if you fail to spot a whale, your next trek is free. Tickets cost $47 for adults, $40 for seniors (62 and older), and $28 for children 4 to 12 from April through mid-October.

Kid Stuff

The top-of-the-line **Hyannis Youth & Community Center,** has a teen center and kids activities. It's at 141 Bassett Lane, Hyannis (© **508/790-6345;** www.town.barnstable. ma.us/hycc), and opens at 7am daily; closing times are Sunday to Thursday at 9pm, Fridays and Saturdays at 10pm. Day passes are $5. Check the website for public skating times and special events. The **Lightning Falls** mini-golf course, 455 W. Main St. (© **508/771-3194**), is a nice diversion for young children or for the young at heart. A round costs $8 for adults, $7 for children. Open in season 10am to 11pm. Call for off-season hours. On Wednesday mornings in summer, the **Cape Cod Melody Tent,** at the West End rotary (© **508/775-5630;** www.melodytent.com), offers children's theater productions. Tickets are $8.50 ($11 the day of performance) and can be ordered from **Ticketmaster** (© **800/745-3000;** www.ticketmaster.com).

Shopping

Hyannis is undoubtedly the commercial center of the Cape, and you'll find a number of unique shops on Main Street. In Osterville and along the Old King's Highway (Rte. 6A) to the north, you're also likely to find some real gems. On weekends from late May to mid-June, and daily from mid-June through September, art enthusiasts may want to visit **Harbor Your Arts Artist Shanties ★**, Ocean Street, along Hyannis Harbor (www.harboryourarts.com). In its seven artists' shacks, you can watch the artists at work and buy directly from them. Nearby on **Pearl Street,** the town of Barnstable has set up a small arts district. There are several art galleries and studios clustered together, including the Hyannis Harbor Arts Center at **Guyer Art Barn** (250 South St.; open noon–4pm weekends), giving a chance for the public to see artists at work. The first Thursday of the month in the summer is an **Arts Stroll** in Hyannis, in which galleries offer open houses and musicians serenade strollers on Main Street.

ARTS & CRAFTS Richard Kiusalas and Steven Whittlesey salvage antique lumber and turn it into cupboards, tables, and chairs, among other things; old windows are turned into mirrors. Most of their stock at **West Barnstable Tables ★**, 2454 Meetinghouse Way (off Rte. 149, near the intersection of Rte. 6A), West Barnstable (*©* **508/362-2676;** www.westbarnstabletables.com), looks freshly made, albeit with wood of unusually high quality. Pieces are priced accordingly: A dining-room set—a pine trestle table with six bow-back chairs—runs more than $4,000. When the wood still bears interesting traces of its former life, it's turned into folk-art furniture.

BOOKS & EPHEMERA Named for the Revolutionary printer who helped foment the War of Independence, **Isaiah Thomas Books & Prints,** 4632 Falmouth Rd./Rte. 28 (near Rte. 130), Cotuit (*©* **508/428-2752;** www.isaiahthomasbooks.com), has a 60,000-volume collection, housed in an 1850 home. The shop is full of treasures, clustered by topic. The owner, James S. Visbeck, is happy to show off his first editions, rare miniatures, and maps; you get the sense that sales are secondary to sheer bibliophilic pleasure. You should be able to find just about any book you're looking for at the big chain bookstore **Barnes & Noble,** 769 Iyannough Rd. (at the Cape Cod Mall, on Rte. 132), Hyannis (*©* **508/862-6310**).

FOOD **Cape Cod Potato Chips,** 100 Breed's Hill Rd. (at Independence Way, off Rte. 132), Hyannis (*©* **508/775-7253;** www.capecodchips.com), really are the world's best. Long a local favorite—they're chunkier than the norm—they originate right here. Free 15-minute factory tours are offered Monday to Friday from 9am to 5pm in July and August. Call for off-season hours. **Cape Cod Beer** (*©* **508/790-4200;** www.capecodbeer.com), at 1336 Phinney's Lane, in Hyannis, gives free tours of its brewery on Saturdays at 1pm and Tuesdays at 11am.

Maritime Museums

The **Cape Cod Maritime Museum ★**, at 135 South St., in Hyannis, on the eastern end of Aselton Park (*©* **508/775-1723;** www.capecodmaritimemuseum.org), is small but interesting. The museum displays artifacts from shipwrecks off the shore of Cape Cod and exhibits a collection of items from the United States Lifesaving Service, the precursor to the Coast Guard. The museum is open mid-March to mid-December Tuesday through Saturday 10am to 4pm, Sunday noon to 4pm. Admission is $5 for adults, $4 for students and seniors, and free for children 6 and under. On the north side of town, the **Coast Guard Heritage Museum ★** (*©* **508/362-8521;** www.coastguardheritagemuseum.org) is in a former U.S. Custom House that's also the former Trayser

CAMELOT ON CAPE COD: THE KENNEDYS
IN hyannis port

It's been more than 60 years since those days of Camelot, when JFK was in the White House and America seemed rejuvenated by the Kennedy style, but the Kennedy sites on Cape Cod still attract record numbers of visitors every summer.

The Kennedys always knew how to have fun, and they had it in Hyannis Port. And ever since Hyannis Port became JFK's summer White House, Cape Cod has been inextricably linked to the Kennedy clan. Although the current Kennedys spend time elsewhere—working in Washington or wintering in Palm Beach—when they go home, they go to Cape Cod.

Meanwhile, much has changed since the early 1960s on Cape Cod, especially in the mid-Cape area. Since then, a mall was built in Hyannis, and urban sprawl infested routes 132 and 28. Yet much, thankfully, remains the same. The Kennedy compound, with its large, gabled Dutch Colonial houses, still commands the end of Scudder Avenue in Hyannis Port.

To bask in the Kennedys' Cape Cod experience, visit the **John F. Kennedy Hyannis Museum ★**, 397 Main St., Hyannis (℡ **508/790-3077;** www.jfk hyannismuseum.org). Admission is $9 for adults, $5 for children 8 to 17, and $6 for seniors; the hours are June through October Monday to Saturday 9am to 5pm and Sunday noon to 5pm; mid-April through May and November Monday to Saturday 10am to 4pm, and Sunday noon to 4pm. The museum shows a documentary on Kennedy, narrated by Walter Cronkite, and contains several rooms featuring photos of the Kennedys on Cape Cod. (In the basement of the museum is the Cape Cod Baseball Hall of Fame & Museum, which is free with admission to JFK Museum.)

Busloads of tourists visit the **Kennedy Memorial** just above Veterans Beach on Ocean Avenue; it's a moving tribute, beautifully maintained by the town, but crowds in season can be distracting. Finally, you may want to drive by the simple white clapboard church, St. Francis Xavier, on South Street; JFK's mother, Rose, attended Mass there daily, and Caroline Kennedy and several other cousins got married here.

As Rose once told a reporter, "Our family would rather be in Hyannis Port in the summer than anyplace else in the world." And yours?

Museum building (3353 Main St./Rte. 6A, Barnstable Village). The main museum building houses displays of pre–Coast Guard groups, such as the lighthouse service, the lightship service, and the lifesaving service. The village blacksmith shop gives demonstrations daily. Also on the property is the oldest wooden jail in the country, built in the 1600s. The museum is open May through October, Tuesday through Saturday 10am to 3pm. Admission is $5.

A Celebration of African-American History

Displaying artwork and memorabilia reflecting the region's African-American and Cape Verdean heritage, the **Zion Union Heritage Museum ★** at 276 North St., Hyannis (℡ **508/790-9466;** www.zionunionheritagemuseum.org), is in the former Zion Union Church, a historic African-American church. People of color were very important to the whaling and cranberry industries on Cape Cod, and the museum contains a range of historic documents about well-known community leaders. There are revolving art shows and other exhibits about the African-American community. The museum is open from May through October, Tuesday through Saturday 11am to 5pm; November through December, Thursday to Saturday 10am to 4pm; and February through April, Thursday through Saturday 11am to 5pm. Admission is $5 adults, $4 for seniors, $3 for ages 10 to 17.

A Historic Art Museum

Located in an 18th-century red clapboard house, the **Cahoon Museum of American Art** ★ at 4676 Falmouth Rd./Rte. 28 (just east of the intersection of Rte. 28 and Rte. 130), Cotuit (ⓒ **508/428-7581;** www.cahoonmuseum.org), has long been a popular site for art lovers. The museum is in the former home of Ralph and Martha Cahoon, whose whimsical folk-art paintings featuring mermaids remain popular years after the death of the artists (Ralph in 1982 and Martha in 1999). The museum sponsors frequent gallery talks and other special events. It is open Tuesday through Saturday 10am to 4pm and Sunday 1 to 4pm. Admission is $8 for adults, $7 for seniors, and $6 for students.

Hyannis & Environs After Dark

LOW-KEY EVENINGS

Roadhouse Café Duck into this dark-paneled bar, decorated like an English gentlemen's club in burgundy leather, if you're looking for sophisticated entertainment and company. The bistro area next to the bar has live jazz piano. Insiders know to show up Monday nights to hear local jazz great Lou Colombo. 488 South St., Hyannis. ⓒ **508/775-2386.** www.roadhousecafe.com.

Trader Ed's This summer-only hangout at the Hyannis Marina attracts sailors, yachting types, fishermen, and other sea lovers. Besides the location on the harbor, there's also a large pool. On weekends a DJ spins tunes for dancing under the stars. 21 Arlington St., Hyannis. ⓒ **508/790-8686.** www.tradereds.com. No cover.

LIVE & LOUD

House of Bud's Fans of live blues, R&B, pop, and funk all head to this year-round bar. There are local bands here several nights a week. Mondays is karaoke; Wednesdays is Latin Dance Night; and Open Mic Funk Jam is on Sundays. 959 Bearse's Way, Hyannis. ⓒ **508/771-2505.** Cover $5.

The Island Merchant This hip cafe on Main Street in Hyannis feels a little Greenwich Village. Live entertainment nightly, with jazz, rock, and blues. From 10pm to 1am, burgers are $2. Mondays, Wednesdays, and Thursdays, half-price appetizers are served at the bar from 5:30 to 7:30pm. Closed Tuesdays. 302 Main St., Hyannis. ⓒ **508/771-1337.** www.theislandmerchant.com. No cover.

PERFORMANCES, MOVIES, READINGS & LECTURES

The Cape Cod Melody Tent ★ Built as a summer theater in 1950, this billowy, blue big-top proved even better for variety shows. A nonprofit venture since 1990 (proceeds fund other cultural initiatives Cape-wide), the Melody Tent has hosted the major performers of the past half-century, from jazz greats to comedians, crooners to rockers. Every seat is a winner in this grand oval, only 20 banked aisles deep. Curtains open 8pm nightly from July to early September. There's also a children's theater program Wednesday mornings at 11am; tickets are $8. Call for a schedule. 21 W. Main St. (West End rotary), Hyannis. ⓒ **508/775-5630.** ⓒ 800/745-3000 for Ticketmaster. www.melodytent. org. Admission $18–$45.

Cotuit Center for the Arts Offering a rich variety of plays, musical performances, art exhibits, and cultural happenings, the Cotuit Center for the Arts, with consistently professional and sophisticated programming, has become the go-to place for those passionate about the arts. 4404 Rte. 28 (½ mile east of intersection of rtes. 28 and 130), Cotuit. ℂ **508/428-0669.** www.cotuitcenterforthearts.org. Admission $22 adults, $20 seniors, $10 students. Gallery Tues–Fri 10am–4pm; Sat 10am–2pm.

YARMOUTH ★

19 miles E of Sandwich; 38 miles S of Provincetown

Essentials

VISITOR INFORMATION Contact the **Yarmouth Area Chamber of Commerce,** 424 Rte. 28, West Yarmouth, MA 02673 (ℂ **800/732-1008** or 508/778-1008; www. yarmouthcapecod.com), or the **Cape Cod Chamber of Commerce** (see "Visitor Information," under "Hyannis, Barnstable & Environs," above). The Yarmouth chamber is open in-season Monday through Friday 9am to 5pm and Sunday 10am to 3pm; off-season the hours are Monday through Friday 9am to 5pm.

Where to Stay Nearby on Nantucket Sound

So many hotels and motels line Route 28 and the shore in West and South Yarmouth that it may be hard to make sense of the choices. The following are some that offer clean rooms and cater to families looking for a reasonably priced beach vacation. All are either within a few miles of the beach or right on the beach. For those staying on Route 28, the town runs frequent beach shuttles in season.

The **Tidewater Inn,** 135 Main St./Rte. 28, West Yarmouth (ℂ **800/338-6322** or 508/775-6322; www.tidewater-capecod.com), is a short walk (½ mile) from a small beach on Lewis Bay, and a not-so-short walk (about a mile) from Hyannis's Main Street and the ferries to Nantucket. Summer rates in the 100 rooms are $110 to $118 for double occupancy. One of the more attractive motels along this strip, it's a white clapboard double-decker with green shutters and doors. The Tidewater also has an indoor and an outdoor pool and a restaurant that's open for breakfast.

Ocean Mist Motor Lodge ★, 97 S. Shore Dr., South Yarmouth (ℂ **508/398-2633**), is a large motel right on the beach. There's also an indoor pool, just in case it rains. Summer rates for the 63 rooms are $199 to $229 double, $259 suite. It's a good choice if you have kids.

EXPENSIVE

Captain Farris House ★★ This 1849 house, listed on the prestigious National Register of Historic Places, has been done up to the nines. It's located in the very scenic Bass River area, steps from the wide river that divides Yarmouth and Dennis and in the middle of a historic district of other 19th-century homes. The rooms are notable for being extra roomy compared to most B&Bs in the region; some have been remodeled to accommodate Jacuzzi tubs. Luxurious linens and fluffy towels, afternoon tea and cookies, and evening cordials are all among the niceties awaiting guests here.

308 Old Main St. (west of the Bass River Bridge), Bass River. ℂ **800/350-9477** or 508/760-2818. www.captainfarris.com. 9 units, 8 with tub/shower combination, 1 with shower only. Summer $210–$249 double; $299 suite. Rates include full breakfast. Closed Dec to mid-Feb. **Amenities:** Wi-Fi (free).

Red Jacket Beach Resort ★★   This resort has two really exceptional qualities: the location, between the Parkers River and Nantucket Sound, and the activities, which include a free kids' program and numerous family and adult and activities. In addition, the same company owns four other nearby resorts (Blue Rock Golf, which has a championship golf course; Green Harbor, Blue Water, and Riviera) and guests get to take advantage of the activities, beaches, and golf at any of the five. The private beach (in addition to indoor and outdoor pools) is a nice plus, also. Particularly for families with young children, this resort is a good choice. The focus for the staff is ensuring guests have a great time and want to come back. And that works well for everyone.

1 S. Shore Dr., South Yarmouth. 📞 **800/672-0500** or 508/398-6941. www.redjacketresorts.com. 170 units, 14 cottages. Summer $299–$450 double; $780–$905 cottages, plus a $15 resort fee per day added to all bills. Closed Nov to mid-Apr. **Amenities:** Restaurant; bar/lounge; concierge; day spa; exercise room; ice cream shop; indoor and outdoor heated pools; putting green; sauna; tennis court; whirlpool; Wi-Fi (free).

WHERE TO STAY NEARBY ON THE OLD KING'S HIGHWAY

The Inn at Cape Cod ★   Though it resembles a southern plantation house with its towering ionic columns, this B&B was built in 1820 for the Sears family. It is well situated in the village of Yarmouth Port, a pleasant walk to shops, museums, restaurants and nature trails; and with the bayside beaches not far away. Inside, a grand curving staircase leads up to five of the nine guestrooms. The others are on the ground floor. All are decorated with fine reproductions and outfitted for comfort, from the mattresses to the seating.

4 Summer St., Yarmouth Port. 📞 **800/850-7301** or 508/375-0590. www.innatcapecod.com. 9 units, 2 with tub/shower combination, 7 with shower only. Summer $275–$339 double; $285 suite. Rates include full breakfast. Closed Dec–Feb. No children 8 and under. **Amenities:** Wi-Fi (free).

Where to Eat
EXPENSIVE

Lyric Restaurant ★★ NORTHERN ITALIAN   Under different owners and different names, this has long been a reliable choice for fine dining in the mid-Cape area. New chefs seem to come and go with great regularity here, they have all put their own stamp on the menu. Inside, the house is divided into small dining rooms, making the experience feel extra intimate. The decorations are very modern, and the service is somewhat format, making it all seem more big city than small town. The Italian menu, made up of small courses, features *primi* (mostly pasta) and *secondi* (meat and fish). Highlights are the beet ravioli with truffle butter sauce and the fish stew. The wine list, which has some hard-to-find vintages, is a highlight.

43 Main St./Rte. 6A (take exit 7 off Rte. 6), Yarmouth Port. 📞 **774/330-0000.** www.lyriccapecod. com. Main courses $12–$38. Mid-May to early Sept Wed–Sun 4:30–9pm.

MODERATE

Old Yarmouth Inn ★ NEW ENGLAND   This is the real deal, a stagecoach stop dating from 1686. Today ye olde atmosphere remains, and there's also good food. Burgers and pizzas and similar items are on the tavern menu. The regular dinner menu is more upscale (and more costly), with dishes like roasted panko-and-Parmesan-crusted haddock and roasted duck with vanilla bean, strawberry, and rhubarb compote. It's good place to come off-season, when there's a fire crackling in the hearth.

223 Rte. 6A (in the center of town), Yarmouth Port. 📞 **508/362-9962.** www.oldyarmouthinn.com. Reservations recommended. Main courses $11–$46. June–Oct Mon 4:30–9pm; Tues–Sat 11:30am–2:30pm and 4:30–9pm; Sun 10am–1pm and 4:30–9pm. Call for off-season hours.

Optimist Cafe ★ AMERICAN   Optimism can take many forms, but this bright-pink gingerbread house on the Old King's Highway can certainly make a claim to one of them. Captain Frederick Howes built this beauty in 1849, and as one of the finest examples of Gothic Revival architecture in Yarmouth, it is listed on the National Historic Register. With breakfast served all day, excellent options for lunch, and an elegant high tea, this place holds its own in the little restaurant row along Route 6A. Though the menu has room for are standards like omelets and sandwiches, what elevates it are dishes like curries and fish tacos.

134 Main St./Rte. 6A, Yarmouth Port. ℂ **508/362-1024.** www.optimistcafe.com. All items under $15. Daily 8am–3pm; call for off-season hours. From Rte. 6, take exit 7 (Willow St.) toward Rte. 6A and take a right on 6A.

Ice Cream
Cape Cod Creamery   Supplying 40 Cape-inspired ice cream flavors wholesale all over the region, Cape Cod Creamery also runs a retail shop on the premises. Monomoy mud pie and Patti Page peppermint are favorites.

1199 Rte. 28 (next to the new Clarion Inn), South Yarmouth. ℂ **508/398-8400.** www.capecod creamery.com. Year-round Mon–Thurs noon–6pm; Fri–Sun noon–9:30pm.

Beaches & Recreational Pursuits

BEACHES   Yarmouth has 11 saltwater and 2 pond beaches open to the public. The body-per-square-yard ratio can be pretty intense along the sound, but so is the social scene, so no one seems to mind. The beachside parking lots charge $15 a day and sell weeklong stickers ($70).

○ **Bass River Beach** ★, off South Shore Drive, in Bass River (South Yarmouth): Located at the mouth of the largest tidal river on the eastern seaboard, this sound beach has restrooms and a snack bar, plus a wheelchair-accessible fishing pier. The beaches along the south shore (Nantucket Sound) tend to be clean and sandy, with comfortable water temps (kids will want to stay in all day), but they can also be crowded during peak times. You'll need a beach sticker or a day pass to park here.

○ **Gray's Beach,** off Center Street, in Yarmouth Port: This isn't much of a beach, but tame waters make this tiny spit of dark sand good for young children; it adjoins the Callery-Darling Conservation Area. The **Bass Hole boardwalk** ★★ offers one of the mid-Cape's most scenic walks. Parking is free, and there's a picnic area with grills.

○ **Parker's River Beach,** off South Shore Drive, in Bass River: The usual amenities are available, including restrooms and a snack bar, plus a 20-foot gazebo for the sun-shy. A beach sticker or day pass is required.

○ **Seagull Beach** ★, off South Sea Avenue, in West Yarmouth: Rolling dunes, a board-walk, and all the necessary facilities—such as restrooms and a snack bar—attract a young crowd. Bring bug spray, though: Greenhead flies (a kind of horsefly) get hungry in July. You'll need a beach sticker or day pass to park here.

GOLF   The township maintains two 18-hole courses: the seasonal **Bayberry Hills,** off West Yarmouth Road, in West Yarmouth (ℂ **508/394-5597;** www.golfyarmouth capecod.com/Bayberry.htm), and the **Bass River Golf Course,** off High Bank Road, in South Yarmouth (ℂ **508/398-9079**). The Bass River course is one of the Cape's most famous. It was founded in 1900 and redesigned by Donald Ross. It is open year-round.

5

CAPE COD | Yarmouth

A round at Bayberry costs $85; at Bass River, it costs $45 to $58 to walk and an additional $19 with a cart. Prices are reduced in the afternoon. Another 18-holer open to the public is the par-54 **Blue Rock Golf Course,** off High Bank Road, in South Yarmouth (© **508/398-9295**); it's open year-round, and a round costs $30 to $50.

Shopping

Driving Route 6A, the Old King's Highway, in Yarmouth Port, you'll pass a number of antiques stores and fine shops selling household items. Unless you have children in tow, you may want to bypass Route 28 entirely and stay on the pretty north side of Yarmouth.

BOOKS The most colorful bookshop on the Cape is **Parnassus Books ★**, 220 Rte. 6A (about ¼ mile east of the town center), Yarmouth Port (© **508/362-6420;** www.parnassusbooks.com). This jam-packed repository—housed in an 1858 Swedenborgian church—is the creation of Ben Muse, who has been collecting and selling vintage tomes since the 1960s. Relevant new stock, including the Cape-related reissues published by Parnassus Imprints, is sold alongside the older treasures. Don't expect much handholding on the part of the gruff proprietor. You'll earn his respect by knowing what you're looking for or, better yet, being willing to browse until it finds you. The outdoor racks, maintained on an honor system, are open 24 hours a day, for those who suffer from abibliophobia—fear of the lack of reading material.

Celebrating a Quirky Talent

The Edward Gorey House ★★ A museum that celebrates such a unique talent as the author/illustrator/playwright Edward Gorey should offer surprises, and this one, inside Gorey's 200-year-old sea captain's home, does just that. The house celebrates the author's passion for collectibles—potato mashers and sea glass were favorites—and animals (he usually had half a dozen cats). The annual exhibits focus on his rich body of work, the quirky and macabre illustrations that were also the basis of his plays, set designs, costume designs and even stuffed animal–making. This is a fun museum and a must for literary-minded travelers, who will also want to stop in the nearby Parnassus Bookstore, which was one of Gorey's favorite places.

8 Strawberry Lane (off Rte. 6A, on the Common), Yarmouth Port. © **508/362-3909.** www.edward goreyhouse.org. Admission $8 adults, $5 students and seniors, $2 children 6–12, free for children 5 and under. July to mid-Oct Wed–Sat 11am–4pm; Sun noon–4pm. Call for off-season hours. Closed Jan–March.

A Bustling Art Center

Cultural Center of Cape Cod In 2000, a group of Yarmouth residents set out to turn the decaying and abandoned Bass River Savings Bank in South Yarmouth into an arts and cultural center. They have transformed the center into a happening year-round venue. There are always new art exhibits in the center's galleries, including the "vault," which has the original bank vault door. In the evenings, even more fun can be had, as the center books local musicians as well as off-Cape musicians to perform.

307 Old Main St., South Yarmouth. © **508/394-7100.** www.cultural-center.org. Gallery hours Mon–Fri 9am–5pm; Sat 11am–5pm; Sun noon–5pm (and many evenings for art openings and performances). From Rte. 6, take exit 8 (Station Ave.) south toward Bass River to Old Main St.; center is on left.

DENNIS ★

20 miles E of Sandwich; 36 miles S of Provincetown

Essentials

VISITOR INFORMATION Contact the **Dennis Chamber of Commerce,** 238 Swan River Rd., West Dennis, MA 02670 (© **508/398-3568;** www.dennischamber. com), or the **Cape Cod Chamber of Commerce** (see "Visitor Information," under "Hyannis, Barnstable & Environs," above). The Dennis chamber is open May to October Monday through Saturday 10am to 4pm, and November to April Monday through Friday 10am to 2pm.

Where to Stay

EXPENSIVE

Lighthouse Inn ★★ The third generation is now running the Stone family's inn, a slice of old Cape Cod if ever there was one. The inn sits on a placid stretch of Nantucket Sound, its private beach guarded by the decommissioned lighthouse that Everett Stone had the foresight to purchase in 1938. Everett built an inn and cottage colony on the property, and families have been coming back for generations to enjoy this special spot. Lodging choices include the rather spartan rooms in the inn itself (great for singles!) as well as the more expensive cottages, which range from studios to three-bedrooms. One of the best parts about this 9-acre compound is there is really no need to leave if you don't want to. The inn's restaurant serves three meals a day. There is a heated outdoor pool, tennis court, volleyball, mini-golf, and shuffleboard also. A beach bar at the entrance has live entertainment on weekends in season.

1 Lighthouse Inn Rd. (off Lower County Rd., ½ mile south of Rte. 28), West Dennis. © **508/398-2244.** www.lighthouseinn.com. 44 units, 24 cottages. Summer $245–$320 double; $305–$335 1-bedroom cottage; $265–$340 2-bedroom cottage; $543–$624 3-bedroom cottage. Rates include full breakfast and all gratuities and parking. Closed mid-Oct to late May. **Amenities:** 2 restaurants; bar w/entertainment; free supervised kids' program (ages 3–11) offered July–Aug; mini-golf; outdoor heated pool; shuffleboard; outdoor tennis court; volleyball; Wi-Fi (free).

MODERATE

Isaiah Hall B&B Inn ★★ "Homey" is the word that comes to mind with this B&B, which has been welcoming guests since around 1948. The inn's namesake was a cooper (barrel-maker) whose grandfather Henry Hall is credited with cultivating the first cranberry bog in 1807. The bog, behind the inn, can be visited by guests. The building is an 1857 farmhouse in a quiet residential neighborhood off Route 6A. This B&B's location, just steps from the Cape Cod Playhouse, makes it an ideal base for seeing a show and exploring the area. It's also a short walk from the Cape Cinema, which plays art-house films, and the Cape Museum of. Breakfast is served communally on an antique 12-foot table.

152 Whig St. (1 block northwest of the Cape Playhouse), Dennis. © **800/736-0160** or 508/385-9928. www.isaiahhallinn.com. 12 units, 6 with tub/shower combination, 6 with shower only. Summer $120–$195 double; $250 suite. Rates include full breakfast. No children 7 and under. Free Wi-Fi in common rooms and most guest rooms.

Where to Eat
EXPENSIVE

Fin ★★ NEW AMERICAN   Using the best local ingredients, including local fish, is the focus of Fin, an upscale restaurant in a historic house in the Theater Marketplace, a short walk from the Cape Cinema, Cape Playhouse and Cape Museum of Art. Food is on the rich side and very good. You'll want to have an appetite to eat the likes of foie gras crème brûlée. Among the main courses, there are surprises: The seared peppered yellow-fin tuna comes with a soy-peanut dressing and cucumber-cilantro relish; the poached salmon comes with black-truffle butter.

800 Main St./Rte. 6A (Theater Marketplace; in the center of Dennis Village), Dennis Village. ⓒ **508/385-2096.** www.fincapecod.com. Main courses $25–$32. June to late Aug Tues–Sat 5–9:30pm. Call for off-season hours.

Norabella ★ SOUTHERN ITALIAN   Attention to detail is the operative phrase at this tiny and romantic chef-owned restaurant. The restaurant looks like a modest road-house from the outside, but the interior makes it clear that special care has gone into all aspects of dining here. The owner states that hospitality is as important as the meal, and it shows, from the moment you are welcomed upon arrival, to the end of the meal, when the chef may come out to ask how everything was. Special dishes include the house-made gnocchi with portobello, baby spinach, and gorgonzola; and the Tuscan veal chop, served with pancetta, cannellini beans, white wine, roasted-garlic sauce, and sautéed spinach.

702 Rte. 28, West Dennis. ⓒ **508/398-6672.** www.norabella.com. Main courses $18–$29. Tues–Sun 4:30–10pm. Take exit 9 off Rte. 6.

The Ocean House New American Bistro and Bar ★★★ NEW AMERI-CAN   A regular contender for the Cape's top restaurant, the Ocean House seems to have it all: attentive service, great food, and sensational views of the Sound. The res-taurant sits on the beach, with windows giving diners a 180-degree beachfront view. The thoughtful menu means that light bites, a couple of appetizers (spring rolls and calamari) and perhaps a gourmet pizza (artichoke and wild mushroom or lobster and asparagus), can take the place of a more expansive meal. But if you are steering toward the large plates, consider the lobster ravioli with champagne cream (you can order a half portion) or the Korean BBQ short ribs. Keep in mind that this place is very popular in the summer, so make a reservation unless you don't mind a very long wait.

3 Chase Ave. (at Depot St., on the beach), Dennisport. ⓒ **508/394-0700.** www.oceanhouse restaurant.com. Main courses $16–$36. June–Sept Tues–Sun 5–10pm (late-night menu to 11pm); call for off-season hours.

The Red Pheasant Inn ★★★ NEW AMERICAN   Restaurant patrons have been heading to this 200-year-old red barn on the Old King's Highway since 1977, when Bill Atwood Sr. converted the space into an elegant restaurant. His son, Bill Atwood Jr., now runs the show with his wife, Denise. Although the menu has its heart in French cuisine, its soul is in the farm-to-table movement. Barnstable oysters are outstanding, and so are the scallops with native oyster mushrooms and house-cured bacon. Desserts include a very special tiramisu.

905 Main St. (about ½ mile east of the town center), Dennis Village. ⓒ **508/385-2133.** www.red pheasantinn.com. Main courses $20–$38. Jan–Mar Wed–Sun 5–9pm; Apr–Dec daily 5–9pm.

5

CAPE COD | Dennis

Scargo Cafe ★ AMERICAN   When you emerge from the Cape Playhouse late at night and need a place to eat, there aren't many options. Fortunately, the Scargo Café is right across the street, in a beautifully restored captain's house. It's been satisfying hungry theatergoers for decades. The beauty of this place is the variety of the menu. You can have a burger (try the one on a pretzel roll) or a sandwich (like the caprese chicken) or a full on surf-and-turf meal, with steak and lobster. There's also a menu of gluten-free items.

799 Main St./Rte. 6A (opposite the Cape Playhouse), Dennis. ℂ **508/385-8200.** www.scargocafe. com. Main courses $11–$27. Mid-June to mid-Sept daily 11am–11pm; mid-Sept to mid-June daily 11am–10pm.

MODERATE

Gina's by the Sea ★★ SOUTHERN ITALIAN   Just steps from Chapin Beach, Gina's has been pleasing beachgoers for more than 60 years. The restaurant consists of a back room, which is dark and romantic if a little crowded, and the porchlike front room, which is more light and airy. This is old-fashioned Italian food like your mother might have made if she grew up in the old country. The menu is small but full of winners, such as the chicken parmigiana or the fettuccine Alfredo. Daily specials are on the blackboard, which might include one of the house specialties, clams casino. This place is very busy in the summer. Come early or late.

134 Taunton Ave. (about 1½ miles northwest of Rte. 6A), Dennis. ℂ **508/385-3213.** www.ginasby thesea.com. Main courses $10–$22. Apr–Nov Thurs–Sun 5–9pm. Closed Dec–Mar. Turn north across from the Dennis Public Market and follow the signs.

INEXPENSIVE

Captain Frosty's ★ SEAFOOD   The ultimate seafood shack is an institution in these parts. Somehow the fried food is not greasy, the breading is flavorful, and the fish is cooked perfectly. Most people sit outside on the picnic tables, but you can also sit inside or get the food to go and take it to nearby Corporation Beach for a sunset picnic.

219 Rte. 6A (about 1 mile west of the town center), Dennis. ℂ **508/385-8548.** www.captainfrosty. com. Most items under $18. No credit cards. June–Aug daily 11am–9pm; call for off-season hours. Closed late Sept to early Apr.

Sesuit Harbor Cafe ★ SEAFOOD   You'll feel like a local if you can find this place, located at harborside at Northside Marina just north of Dennis Village. Preferred seating is on picnic tables out on the deck under colorful umbrellas. This is a great place to come for drinks to partake of the raw bar, which besides shellfish also has chowder, crab cakes and sashimi. The dinner menu, served from 3:30 to sunset, is heavy on fried seafood, half and full plates of fried clams, scallops, oysters or shrimp. The lobster roll is a favorite and comes with homemade slaw, as is the tuna shrimp skewer.

357 Sesuit Neck Rd., Dennis. ℂ **508/386-5473** (summer) or 508/385-6134 (winter). www.sesuit harbor-cafe.com. Main courses $9–$30. Late May–Sept daily 7am–8:30pm; call for off-season hours. Closed mid-Oct to late Apr. Exit 9B off Rte. 6 to Rte. 6A and straight across to Bridge St.; take a right on Sesuit Neck Rd. and follow to the harbor.

Wee Packet ★ CLAM SHACK/IRISH   Packet ships used to ply the local waters, transporting goods from Boston to New York. A "wee packet," which gives this restaurant its name, was the colloquial name for a small ship. Cape Cod byways used to be lined with little family fish shacks like this. What's fun here is the traditional full Irish breakfast, complete with grilled tomato and baked beans. Lunch is perhaps the most popular meal of the day here; traditional fried-fish plates and lobster rolls are on the menu. For dinner, you can try a full-on clambake. There is a new outdoor patio here for seating, though I prefer the cute Formica tables inside. On Thursday nights in season, there is a raw bar with oysters from East Dennis Oyster Farm.

79 Depot St. (at intersection of Lower County Rd.), Dennisport. ℂ **508/394-6595.** www.wee packetrestaurant.com. Main courses $8–$20. July 4 to Labor Day daily 7:30am–9pm; call for off-season hours. Closed mid-Oct to May.

SWEETS

Buckies Bakery Cafe ★   With a large selection of bakery items plus sandwiches, soups, salads and wraps for lunch, this is a great place to stock up on picnic foods before a day at the beach. A sister bakery is at 554 Rte. 28 in Harwichport.

681 Main St., Dennisport. ℂ **508/398-9700.** www.buckysbiscotti.com. Daily 6:30am–6:30pm.

Ice Cream Smuggler ★   When choosing the best ice cream shop on Cape Cod, tradition counts, and so does ambiance. Ice Cream Smuggler, founded 35 years ago and inside a cute Cape Cod cottage, has both of those in spades. This place is popular with the beach-going crowds at Chapin, Corporation and Mayflower beaches, so time your stop to avoid the post-beach lines. It's hard to choose a favorite from the 31 plus flavors, but it's hard to go wrong with Junior Mint and Cookie Monster.

716 Rte. 6A, Dennis Village. ℂ **508/385-5307.** www.icecreamsmuggler.com. July–Aug daily 11am–10:30pm; Apr–June and Sept to mid-Oct noon–10:30pm. Closed mid-Oct to Mar.

Stage Stop Candy ★   Eighty years after Frederick E. Hebert began a family tradition of making fine candy, his grandson, Ray Hebert, with his wife, Donna, continue the tradition. The Cranberry Cordial has long been the signature candy here, but the white, dark, and milk chocolates here are all superlative. But the be-all, end-all has to be the Gold Coast truffles, made with special cocoas from around the world.

411 Main St./Rte. 28, Dennisport. ℂ **508/394-1791.** www.stagestopcandy.com. July–Aug Mon–Sat 9am–5pm, Sun 10:30am–6pm; call for off-season hours. Closed for 2 weeks in Jan.

Sundae School ★   This old-fashioned ice-cream parlor in a shingled barn with a bright red door is full of fun ice-cream memorabilia. The homemade flavors here are sensational, from the Amaretto Nut all the way down to the Turtle (chocolate and butterscotch ice cream with pecans).

381 Lower County Rd. (at Sea St., about ⅓ mile south of Rte. 28), Dennisport. ℂ **508/394-9122.** www.sundaeschool.com. Summer daily 11am–11pm; spring and fall Sat–Sun only (hours vary; call ahead). Closed mid-Sept to mid-Apr.

Exploring: Beaches & Recreational Pursuits

BEACHES   Dennis has more than a dozen saltwater and two freshwater beaches open to nonresidents. The bay beaches are charming and a big hit with families, who prize the easygoing surf, so soft it won't bring toddlers to their knees. The beaches on the sound tend to attract wall-to-wall families, but the parking lots are usually not too crowded, as so many beachgoers stay within walking distance. The lots charge $15 to $20 per day; for a weeklong permit ($60), visit **Town Hall,** at 485 Main St., in South Dennis (ℂ **508/394-8300**).

- **Chapin Beach ★★**, off Route 6A, in Dennis: This is a nice, long bay beach pocked with occasional boulders and surrounded by dunes. There is no lifeguard, but there are restrooms.

- **Corporation Beach ★★**, off Route 6A, in Dennis: Before it filled in with sand, this bay beach—with wheelchair-accessible boardwalk, lifeguards, snack bar, restrooms, and a children's play area—was once a packet landing for a shipbuilding corporation owned by area residents.

- **Mayflower Beach ★★**, off Route 6A, in Dennis: This 1,200-foot bay beach has the necessary amenities, plus an accessible boardwalk. The tide pools attract lots of children.

- **Scargo Lake,** in Dennis: This large kettle-hole pond (formed by a melting fragment of a glacier) has two pleasant beaches: Scargo Beach, accessible right off Route 6A, and Princess Beach, off Scargo Hill Road, where there are restrooms and a picnic area.

- **West Dennis Beach ★★**, off Route 28, in West Dennis: This long (½-mile) but narrow beach along the sound has lifeguards, a playground, a snack bar, restrooms, and a special kite-flying area. The eastern end is reserved for residents; the western end tends, in any case, to be less packed.

BICYCLING The 25-mile **Cape Cod Rail Trail ★★★** (© **508/896-3491**) starts—or, depending on your perspective, ends—here, on Route 134, a half-mile south of Route 6's exit 9. Once a Penn Central track, this 8-foot-wide paved bikeway extends all the way to Wellfleet (with a few on-road lapses), passing through woods, marshes, and dunes. Sustenance is never too far off-trail, and plenty of bike shops dot the course. At the trail head is **Barb's Bike Shop,** 430 Rte. 134, South Dennis (© **508/760-4723;** www.barbsbikeshop.com), which rents bikes and does repairs. Rates are $12 for 2 hours, and up to $24 for the full day. Another paved bike path runs along Old Bass Road, 3½ miles north to Route 6A.

GOLF The public is welcome to use two 18-hole championship courses: the hilly, par-71 **Dennis Highlands,** on Old Bass River Road, in Dennis, and the even more challenging par-72 **Dennis Pines,** on Golf Course Road, in East Dennis. For information on either course, call © **508/385-8347** or visit www.dennisgolf.com. Both charge $64 for a round in the morning, $25 to $39 in the afternoon.

Museums

Cape Cod Museum of Art ★★ This museum was founded in the 19890s to highlight outstanding artists of Cape Cod and the Islands. The founders felt that unless they began a repository for the Cape's art, it would migrate to museums all over the country, leaving little for locals to enjoy. The museum's several galleries regularly feature multiple exhibits of current and past Cape artists. There is also a fine outdoor sculpture garden with pieces from the museum's permanent collection. The museum is on the grounds of the Cape Cod Center for the Arts, which includes the Cape Playhouse and the Cape Cinema.

60 Hope Lane, Dennis Village. © **508/385-4477.** www.cmfa.org. Admission $9 adults, $8 seniors, $5 age 13-18, free for children 12 and under. Tues–Sat 10am–5pm; Sun noon–5pm. Take exit 8 off Rte. 6, left off exit ramp, and right onto Rte. 6A; museum is 2 miles on the left.

Kid Stuff

If kids get sick of all the miscellaneous go-carts and mini-golf concessions on Route 28, they can take in a show. On Thursday and Friday mornings in season, at 9:30 and 11:30am, the **Cape Playhouse,** at 820 Rte. 6A, in Dennis Village (🕽 **508/385-3911;** www.capeplayhouse.com), hosts various visiting companies that mount children's theater geared toward kids 4 and older; tickets ($11) go fast.

Shopping

You can pretty much ignore Route 28. There's a growing cluster of antiques shops in Dennisport, but the stock is flea-market level and requires more patience than most mere browsers—as opposed to avid collectors—may be able to muster. Save your time and money for the better shops along Route 6A, where you'll also find fine contemporary crafts.

ANTIQUES/COLLECTIBLES More than 136 dealers stock the co-op **Antiques Center of Cape Cod,** 243 Rte. 6A (about 1 mile south of Dennis Village center), Dennis (🕽 **508/385-6400;** www.antiquecenterofcapecod.com); it's the largest such enterprise on the Cape. You'll find all the usual "smalls" on the first floor; the big stuff—from blanket chests to copper bathtubs—beckons above.

Eldred's, 1483 Rte. 6A (about ¼ mile west of Dennis Village center), East Dennis (🕽 **508/385-3116;** www.eldreds.com), where the gavel has been wielded for more than 40 years, is the Cape's most prestigious auction house. Specialties include Asian art, American and European paintings, marine art, and Americana.

ARTS & CRAFTS The dramatic creations of **Ross Coppelman Goldsmith,** 1439 Rte. 6A (about ¼ mile west of the town center), East Dennis (🕽 **508/385-7900;** www. rosscoppelman.com)—mostly fashioned of lustrous 22-karat gold—seem to draw on the aesthetics of some grand, lost civilization.

Scargo Pottery, 30 Dr. Lord's Rd. S. (off Rte. 6A, about 1 mile east of the town center), Dennis (🕽 **508/385-3894;** www.scargopottery.com), is a magical place. Harry Holl set up his glass-ceilinged studio here in 1952; today his work, and the output of his four daughters, fills a glade overlooking Scargo Lake. Much of it, such as the signature birdhouses shaped like fanciful castles, is meant to reside outside. The other wares deserve a place of honor on the dining room table or perhaps over a mantel. The hand-painted tiles by Sarah Holl are particularly enchanting.

Dennis After Dark
PERFORMANCES

Cape Playhouse ★★ From the first performance at this summer theater ("The Guardsman," starring Basil Rathbone, 1927) to the years when soon-to-be Hollywood stars like Henry Fonda and Bette Davis plied the boards in summer stock, the Cape Playhouse has brought the quintessential summer theater experience to the area. The brainchild of Raymond Moore, who was close to stage star Gertrude Lawrence and moved an abandoned 1838 meetinghouse to the present spot off Route 6A, it's considered America's oldest professional summer theater. These days Broadway-caliber Equity actors perform in high-quality traveling shows, usually comedies and musicals. The shows run for about 2 weeks, and there are usually six per summer. So many people order a season pass that most of the performances sell out, so plan ahead. Friday mornings, there is children's theater at 9:30 and 11:30am. 820 Rte. 6A (in the center of town), Dennis Village. 🕽 **877/385-3911** or 508/385-3911. www.capeplayhouse.com. Admission $22–$81; children's theater $12.

LIVE MUSIC & ENTERTAINMENT

Cape Cod Chat House Gallery   A combo coffee shop, art gallery and entertainment venue, the Chat House is setting the new standard for Cape Cod's burgeoning hipster scene. Performances in a given week might include jazz, poetry and Middle Eastern dance. Located inside an 1853 farmhouse on 6A, it's all very eco-conscious, from its recycled granite walkway to the bamboo floors and walnut-shell countertops. 593 Main St., Dennis Village. ✆ **508/694-7187.** www.capecodchathouse.com. Open mid-May to Nov Wed–Sat 10am–5pm. No cover.

Harvest Gallery Wine Bar   Harvest has become a major destination venue for the 30- to 60-year-old crowd looking for some rootsy music on a Saturday night. The walls also serve as gallery space, brightening up the restaurant and bar areas. Music starts at 7:30pm. 776 Main St./Rte. 28, Dennis Village (behind the post office). ✆ **508/385-2444.** www.harvestgallerywinebar.com. No cover.

O'Shea's Olde Inne   At one of the Cape's best Irish venues, Celtic musicians can join the "seisiuns" on Sunday night, when musicians offering jigs, reels and sing-alongs. On other nights, there's jazz, blues, folk and even rockabilly. 348 Main St./Rte. 28, West Dennis. ✆ **508/398-8887.** www.osheasoldeinne.com. Cover varies.

Sand Dollar Bar and Grill   Entertainment is 7 nights a week from April through October at this fun and lively venue for the younger crowds. Weekends feature a raw bar, and bands start playing at 4pm. 244 Lower County Rd., Dennisport. ✆ **508/398-4823.** www.sanddollarbg.com. Cover varies.

Sundancers   Dancing on the decks overlooking the Bass River is de rigueur at this club, which has been going strong for more than 30 years. Entertainment, from karaoke to 80s night to reggae, is on weekends until Memorial Day and the nightly during the summer season. 116 Main St./Rte. 28, West Dennis. ✆ **508/394-1600.** www.sundancers capecod.com. Cover varies.

A RETRO MOVIE THEATER

Cape Cinema ★★   The Cape's only year-round art-house theater is a treasure, and it doesn't hurt that it's inside a 1930s Art Deco building complete with a colorful ceiling mural by the artist and book illustrator Rockwell Kent. There is just one large screen, and seating is on black leather armchairs. The cinema was built by Raymond Moore, the same man who started the nearby Cape Playhouse. 35 Hope Lane (off Rte. 6A, on the grounds of the Cape Playhouse), Dennis Village. ✆ **508/385-2503** or 385-5644. www.capecinema.com. Admission $8.50, seniors $6:50.

THE LOWER CAPE: BREWSTER ★★

25 miles E of Sandwich; 31 miles S of Provincetown

Essentials

VISITOR INFORMATION   Contact the **Brewster Chamber of Commerce Visitor Center,** behind Brewster Town Hall, 2198 Main St./Rte. 6A, Brewster (✆ **508/896-3500;** www.brewster-capecod.com); or the **Cape Cod Chamber of Commerce,** routes 6 and 132, Hyannis, MA 02601 (✆ **888/332-2732;** www.capecodchamber.org). The Brewster Visitor Center is open from June to early September daily from 9am to 3pm and is closed from October to late May. The Cape Cod Chamber of Commerce visitor center is open year-round Monday to Saturday from 9am to 5pm and Sundays and holidays from 10am to 4pm.

Where to Stay

EXPENSIVE

Ocean Edge Resort & Club ★★ Ocean Edge is for those who like a full-service vacation: The 429-acre property has a private Cape Cod Bay beach, tennis, and an 18-hole golf course designed by Jack Nicklaus. At the resort's center is a 1912 mansion that now houses guest rooms and a restaurant and more casual pub. In the guestrooms, particular attention has been paid to their design, bedding, and bathrooms. The result are modern and fresh, with soothing shades of seafoam, coral and wheat.

2907 Main St., Brewster. © 508/896-9000. www.oceanedge.com. 335 units. Summer $255–$559 double; $600–$1,050/night or $2,400–$7,500/week 2- to 3-bedroom villa. $20–$40 resort fee. **Amenities:** private beach, 3 restaurants; babysitting; bike trail and bike rentals; children's program for ages 4–12; concierge; fitness center; 18-hole championship golf course; 6 pools (2 indoor, 4 outdoor); room service; 11 tennis courts, Wi-Fi (free).

MODERATE

The Bramble Inn and Restaurant ★★ This is a sweet B&B, but its chief virtue is that one the Cape's top restaurants is on-site (see review below). The guestrooms are countrified and cozy, with four-poster beds draped with lace and laden with quilts and needlepoint pillows. The full breakfast served in the courtyard garden is a high point.

2019 Rte. 6A (about ⅓ mile east of the town center), Brewster.© 508/896-7644. www.brambleinn.com. 5 units, 2 with tub/shower combination, 3 with shower only. Summer $170–$198 double. Rates include full breakfast. Closed Jan to mid-Apr. **Amenities:** Restaurant, Wi-Fi (free).

Candleberry Inn ★ What a showpiece: This grand 1790 Georgian-style structure with its square-rigger design (two chimneys) is among the most regal sea captains' homes in town; it was once owned by the 19th-century author Horatio Alger. There are six rooms in the main house, all graciously decorated with antiques and heirlooms, and Oriental rugs over wide-pine floors. The two in the Carriage House are more modern in style and come with a little extra privacy. Four of the rooms have working fireplaces. Another big plus for this property are its innkeepers, Stu and Charlotte Fyfe, real Cape Codders who can fill you in on what's where while providing some historical context.

1882 Main St./Rte. 6A, Brewster. © 800/573-4769 or 508/896-3300. www.candleberryinn.com. 8 units, 1 with tub/shower combination, 7 with shower only. Summer $145–$190 double; $235–$250 suite. Rates include full breakfast and afternoon tea. From Rte. 6, take exit 9B; take a right on 6A; inn is 4½ miles on left. Children 10 and over welcome. **Amenities:** Wi-Fi (free).

Captain Freeman Inn ★★ Next to the beloved Brewster General Store, a short walk to two terrific restaurants, and down the street from Breakwater beach, the Captain Freeman Inn occupies an enviable spot in Brewster. Walking up to the inn, you might first notice the magnificent and welcoming wraparound front porch. The large size of this B&B makes it feel more like a small inn. There are three levels of rooms, the highest having romantic touches like a fireplace and Jacuzzi tub. Breakfast is served on the screened in porch overlooking the pool. The owners, Byron and Donna Cain, are consummate hosts who know their way around.

15 Breakwater Rd. (at the intersection of Main St./Rte. 6A), Brewster. © 508/896-7481. www.captainfreemaninn.com. 10 units. Summer $235–$285 double. Rates include full breakfast and afternoon tea. From Rte. 6, take exit 10 to Rte. 124 north to Rte. 6A; take first left to Breakwater Rd. Free Wi-Fi.

INEXPENSIVE

Old Sea Pines Inn ★★   This inn still has charm and personality, perhaps left over from when it was the Sea Pines School of Charm and Personality for Young Women. A lot has changed since then, but the inn offers an old-fashioned Cape vacation. Guest rooms are spread among three buildings on the 3½-acre property. Bickford Hall, the main building, holds the smallest of the rooms on its second and third floor; they don't have TVs, perhaps because of their proximity. The two cottages have rooms that are more modern, with TVs. The cottages also have the family suites, where children under 8 are welcome. The inn is the site of a dinner theater in season.

2553 Main St. (about 1 mile east of the town center), Brewster. ℭ **508/896-6114.** www.oldsea pinesinn.com. 24 units, 5 with shared bathroom. Summer $85 double with shared bathroom; $125–$170 double; $205 suite. Rates include full breakfast and afternoon tea. Closed Nov–May. **Amenities:** Wi-Fi (free).

Where to Eat
EXPENSIVE

The Bramble Inn and Restaurant ★★★ NEW AMERICAN   In any list of the best Cape restaurants, the Bramble is always at or near the top. The executive chef, Ruth Manchester, works with the seasons and local produce to create wonderful and creative meals. You might see an appetizer of Provincetown mussels with Portuguese sausage and banana pepper rings, or as a main course, Chatham jumbo sea scallops served over shiitake and crimini mushroom risotto. There is also a traditional four-course dinner menu. At the Bayside Bar, you can get small plates ($9–$15), as a way to get a hint of the lavish menu. Before 6pm, there's also an à la carte menu and cocktail-hour menu with less expensive choices available.

2019 Main St./Rte. 6A (about ⅓ mile east of Rte. 124), Brewster. ℭ **508/896-7644.** www.bramble inn.com. Main courses $25–$38. June to early Sept Wed–Sun 6–9pm; call for off-season hours. Closed Jan–Mar.

The Brewster Fish House ★★ NEW AMERICAN   If a restaurant's quality can be judged by how hard it is to get in, this one wins hands down. Patrons are so loyal to this lovely little restaurant in a cottage that they fill it night after night. The menu is very inventive—just when you think you have it figured out, you try something like seared foie gras with griddled cornbread, smoked shallot jam, and pink. As you'd expect, this is an excellent place to order fish. But, again, you might want to try something unusual, such as the pan-roasted skate wing with an almond puree and curry vinaigrette. Desserts are particularly good here, but there is no escaping the chocolate bread pudding.

2208 Main St./Rte. 6A, Brewster. ℭ **508/896-7867.** www.brewsterfish.com. Main courses $18–$32. May–Aug daily 11:30am–3pm and 5–9pm; call for off-season hours. Closed Dec–Apr. From Rte. 6, take exit 12 toward Brewster.

Chillingsworth ★★★ FRENCH   Two separate kitchens, two separate auras at this restaurant that's been a mainstay since 1976. One kitchen serves the fancy and formal main dining rooms, where guests can order à la carte or choose the 7-course prix-fixe option. The other kitchen serves the more relaxed bistro area, where you can get away with a couple of appetizers and call it a night. In the dining rooms, dishes like the lobster stew starter and the main course of pesto rack of lamb with a goat cheese, fig, and herb brûlée are favorites. As for the bistro, there are lots of good choices, but the gnocchi with a mushroom-butter fondue and the pan-seared sea scallops both stand out. House-made desserts are a specialty here, and you are wise to save room, however hard that may be. Three country-style rooms upstairs rent for $110 to $150 a night.

2449 Main St./Rte. 6A, Brewster. (© **508/896-3640.** www.chillingsworth.com. Fixed-price meals 7 courses) $65–$72; bistro $19–$36. Mid-June to Aug Sat–Sun noon–2pm and 6–9:30pm, Mon–Fri 6–9:30pm (bistro opens for dinner at 5pm; on Mon one seating only for fine-dining 7–7:30pm); call for off-season hours. Closed Dec to mid-May. From Rte. 6, take exit 10; take a right on 6A; 1½ miles up on the left.

MODERATE

Brewster Inn & Chowder House ★ SEAFOOD/AMERICAN Every town
has its tavern, and this is Brewster's. It's friendly and homey, serving reasonably priced chowder, burgers, and fish several ways (baked, broiled, and, of course, fried). Next door is the Woodshed, a busy bar with bands most nights in season.

1993 Rte. 6A (in the center of town), Brewster. (© **508/896-7771.** Main courses $12–$18. Late May to mid-Oct daily 11:30am–3pm and 5–10pm; call for off-season hours.

INEXPENSIVE

Cobie's ★ AMERICAN This roadside clam shack, in business since 1948, is a
stone's throw from the Rail Trail. Pack a picnic or just grab a table and settle in with a steaming plate of fried clams and French fries or onion rings, Cape Cod style.

3260 Rte. 6A (about 2 miles east of the town center), Brewster. (© **508/896-7021.** www.cobies. com. Most items under $15. No credit cards. Late May to early Sept daily 10:30am–9pm. Closed early Sept to late May.

SWEETS

The **Hopkins House Bakery,** 2727 Main St. ((© **508/896-3450**), is inside in a sweet little country gift shop. The hermit cookies (molasses, raisins, and nuts) here are a standout, as are the breads and muffins. Open Thursdays through Sundays 8am to 5pm in July and August, weekends only in June and September.

Exploring: Beaches & Recreational Pursuits

BEACHES Brewster's eight lovely bay beaches have minimal facilities. When the tide is out, the "beach" enlarges to as much as 2 miles, leaving behind tide pools to splash in and explore, and vast stretches of rippled, reddish "garnet" sand. On a clear day, you can see the whole curve of the Cape, from Sandwich to Provincetown. That hulking wreck midway, incidentally, is the USS *James Longstreet,* pressed into service for target practice in 1943 and used for that purpose right up until 1970; it's now a popular dive site. You can purchase a beach parking sticker ($15 per day, $50 per week) at the **Brewster Visitor Center,** behind Brewster Town Hall, at 2198 Main St./ Rte. 6A, a half-mile east of the General Store ((© **508/896-3701**).

o **Breakwater Beach ★★**, off Breakwater Road, Brewster: A brief walk from the center of town, this calm, shallow beach (the only one with restrooms) is ideal for young children. This was once a packet landing, where packet boats would unload tourists and load up produce—a system that became obsolete when the railroads came along.

o **Flax Pond ★★**, in Nickerson State Park (see "Nature & Wildlife Areas," below): This large freshwater pond, surrounded by pines, has a bathhouse and offers water-sports rentals. The park contains two more ponds with beaches—Cliff and Little Cliff. Access and parking are free.

o **Linnells Landing Beach ★**, on Linnell Road, in East Brewster: This is a half-mile, wheelchair-accessible bay beach.

○ **Paines Creek Beach** ★, off Paines Creek Road, West Brewster: With 1½ miles on which to stretch out, this bay beach has something to offer sun lovers and nature lovers alike. Your kids will love it if you arrive when the tide's coming in—the current will give an air mattress a nice little ride.

GOLF One of the most challenging courses in Brewster is **Captain's Golf Course** at 1000 Freemans Way (© **508/896-1716;** www.captainsgolfcourse.com). In season a round at Captain's is $69 to $76, with discounted rates in the afternoon.

NATURE & WILDLIFE AREAS The 1,955-acre **Nickerson State Park,** at Route 6A and Crosby Lane (© **508/896-3491;** www.mass.gov/dcr/parks/southeast/nick. htm), is the legacy of a vast, self-sustaining private estate that once generated its own electricity (with a horse-powered plant) and had its own golf course and game preserve; notable guests included President Grover Cleveland. Today it's a nature preserve encompassing 420 campsites (reservations pour in a year in advance to **Reserve America** at © **877/422-6762,** which charges $15 for Massachusetts residents, $17 for out-of-staters), eight kettle ponds (stocked year-round with trout), and 8 miles of bicycle paths. The rest is trees—some 88,000 evergreens, planted by the Civilian Conservation Corps during the 1930s and 40s. This is land that has been through a lot but, thanks to careful management, is bouncing back.

Brewster Historic Sights & Museums

Cape Cod Museum of Natural History ★★★ One of the top attractions on the Cape, this museum and nature education center is an ideal place to bring the kids, rain or shine. The extensive trails on this 80-acre property make learning about the natural world as easy as taking a walk. The varied varied habitats here include a salt marsh, a stretch of beach along the Bay between Quivett and Paine's creeks, and Wing's Island.

The museum's collection, which covers two floors, includes exhibits about whales and birds and live marine exhibits. In aquariums are fish, eels, turtles, shellfish and mollusks. Other topics include archeology, honeybees, sharks, and erosion. There are educational programs for adults and children as well as nature tours on- and off-site.

869 Rte. 6A (about 2 miles west of the town center), Brewster. © **508/896-3867.** www.ccmnh.org. Admission $10 adults, $7 seniors 65 and over, $5 children 3–12. June–Aug daily 9:30am–4pm; Sept daily 11am–3pm; Apr–May and Oct–Dec Wed–Sun 11am–3pm. Closed Jan–Mar (open for special programs only) and major holidays.

Stony Brook Grist Mill and Museum ★ There is perhaps no sight so welcome during a Cape Cod spring as that of the herring making their way up rivers to spawn in freshwater ponds. Watching the fish flip-flopping their way against the tide is nothing if not an analogy for the gumption needed to overcome life's trials. Most herring runs are deep in the wood, and if you don't know where they are, you won't find them. But Stony Brook, one of the Cape's most productive runs, is right off a main road and set up for visitors.

Beginning around 1660, this site was bustling with industry. Besides a mill for grinding corn, there was a fulling mill, a woolen mill, and a tannery. Later there was a cotton weaving mill, a carding mill, and a paper mill. The grist mill was built around 1873 and is powered by the waters of the brook. Inside the grist mill, a volunteer miller grinds corn into cornmeal that can be bought for $2. Upstairs in the mill, there are artifacts of Cape Cod in the 1800s, including an antique loom.

830 Stony Brook Rd. (at the intersection of Satucket Rd.), West Brewster. © **508/896-9521.** Free admission. July–Aug Sat 10am–2pm. Closed Sept–June.

Shopping

ANTIQUES/COLLECTIBLES Brewster's stretch of Route 6A has the best antiquing on the entire Cape. Die-hards would do well to stop at every intriguing shop; you never know what you might find. There are several reliable standouts.

ARTS & CRAFTS Clayton Calderwood's **Clayworks,** 3820 Main St./Rte. 6A, East Brewster (𝄞 **508/255-4937;** www.claytonsclayworks.com), is always worth a stop, if only to marvel at the famous mammoth urns. There's also a world of functional bowls, pots, and lamps, in porcelain, stoneware, and terra cotta.

Collectors from around the world converge at **Sydenstricker Glass,** 490 Main St., Brewster (𝄞 **508/385-3272;** www.sydenstricker.com), in which a 1960s-era kiln-fired process uses concepts from the art of enameling to yield unique glassware, especially dishes and stemware.

GIFTS/HOME DECOR Though quite a bit spiffier than a "real" general store, the **Brewster Store,** 1935 Main St./Rte. 6A, in the center of town (𝄞 **508/896-3744;** www.brewsterstore.com), an 1866 survivor that was fashioned from an 1852 Universalist church, is a fun place to shop for sundries and catch up on local gossip. The wares are mostly tourist-oriented these days, but include some handy kitchen gear (cobalt glassware, for example) and beach paraphernalia. Give the kids a couple of dimes to feed the Nickelodeon piano machine, and relax on a sunny church pew out front as you pore over the local paper.

Brewster After Dark

Performances at the **Cape Cod Repertory Theatre,** 3299 Rte. 6A, Brewster, about 2½ miles east of Brewster center (𝄞 **866/811-4111** or 508/896-1888; www.caperep.org or www.theatermania.com), are given Tuesday to Saturday at 8pm from early July to early September. In summer this shoestring troupe tackles the Bard, as well as serious contemporary fare, at an indoor theater as well as an outdoor theater on the old Crosby estate (now state-owned and undergoing restoration).

Hot local bands take the tiny stage seasonally at the **Woodshed,** at the Brewster Inn & Chowder House, 1993 Rte. 6A (𝄞 **508/896-7771**), a far cry from the glitzy discos on the southern shore. If your tastes run more to Raitt and Buffett than techno, you'll feel right at home in this dark, friendly dive. Cover charge $5.

A Special Resort on Pleasant Bay

Wequassett Resort and Golf Club ★★★ A secluded, full-service resort, Wequassett has long been in the running for the title of top lodging on Cape Cod. Improvements in recent years have brought the number of restaurants to four, improved the kids' play area, and added a lap pool and increased the size of the beach on Pleasant Bay. The resort's guest rooms and suites, spread out in six buildings, are exceptionally comfortable and stylish—and at these prices, they should be. Rooms without bay views are a cheaper but quite a bit less inviting. What guests are really paying for here are all the amenities. Besides the beach, the pools and the restaurants, there are four tennis courts and playing privileges at a nearby exclusive golf club (for $190 a round). The entire 27-acre property sits on a rise above the bay with eastward views beyond to the Atlantic Ocean. The inn's skiff is available to take guests out to the North Beach for a fee. Among the most special amenities here are the fine dining restaurant, 28 Atlantic, and the Outer Bar & Grill, by the pool. Both are exceptional.

2173 Rte. 28 (about 5 miles northeast of Chatham center, on Pleasant Bay), Harwich. ©**800/225-7125** or 508/432-5400. www.wequassett.com. 120 units. Summer $575–$835 double; $970–$1,455 suites. $15 per day resort charge. Closed Dec–Mar. **Amenities:** 4 restaurants); babysitting; bike rentals ($20–$40 per day); Children's Fun Club ($25 for half-day; $45 for full day); concierge; fitness room; 2 heated outdoor pools (one a lap pool); room service; 4 tennis courts ($15 an hour per person), plus a pro shop; watersports equipment/rentals; yoga and Pilates classes ($15); Wi-Fi (free).

A Standout for Wining & Dining

28 Atlantic ★★★ NEW AMERICAN   The wow factor starts when you enter the dining room at 28 Atlantic to see a 180-degree view of Pleasant Bay through a wall of 8-foot-tall windows. Chandeliers, snow-white tablecloths, and fine china hint of the elegant experience to come. The menu is rich with delicacies, such as foie gras, that are served in a non-traditional way—with grilled watermelon and smoked maple syrup, for instance. A playful twist on tradition continues with the main courses, which mght include butter-braised lobster with cashew curry, or duck breast with pistachio praline. With top-notch service to boot, it all adds up to a meal fit for a very special occasion. The dress code urges "smart casual" and prohibits jeans, T-shirts, or shorts. For casual dining, the **Outer Bar & Grill,** a hip bar overlooking the pool and the bay, is the perfect venue.

2173 Rte. 28 (at the Wequassett Resort and Golf Club, about 5 miles northwest of Chatham center, on Pleasant Bay), Harwich. ©**508/430-3000.** www.wequassett.com. Main courses $21–$44. May–Nov daily 6–10pm; call for off-season hours. Closed Dec to mid-Apr.

CHATHAM ★★★

32 miles E of Sandwich; 24 miles S of Provincetown

Essentials

VISITOR INFORMATION   Visit the **Cape Cod Chamber of Commerce** (see "Visitor Information," under "Brewster," earlier in this chapter); the **Chatham Chamber of Commerce,** 2377 Main St., South Chatham, MA 02659 (© **800/715-5567** or 508/945-5199; www.chathaminfo.com); or the **Chatham Chamber booth** (Bassett House Visitor Center), at 533 Main St., at the intersection of Rte. 137 and Rte. 28, in Chatham. Hours for both the Chatham chamber and the booth are July and August Monday to Saturday 10am to 5pm, Sunday noon to 3pm; call for off-season hours. It's closed late October to April.

Where to Stay

Chatham's lodging choices are more expensive than those of neighboring towns because it's considered a chichi place to vacation. But for those allergic to fussy, fancy B&Bs and inns, Chatham has several good motel options.

Practically across the street from the Chatham Bars Inn, the **Hawthorne ★**, 196 Shore Rd. (© **508/945-0372;** www.thehawthorne.com), is a no-frills motel with one of the best locations in town: right on the water, with striking views of Chatham Harbor, Pleasant Bay, and the Atlantic Ocean. An additional perk here is free phone calls (local and long distance) and Internet access. Rates for the 26 rooms are $240 to $305 for a double. The more expensive rooms are efficiencies with kitchenettes. Closed mid-October to mid-May.

Chatham Seafarer, 2079 Rte. 28 (about ½ mile east of Rte. 137), Chatham (© **800/786-2772** or 508/432-1739; www.chathamseafarer.com), is a lovely, personable, well-run motel. It's only about a half-mile from Ridgevale Beach, but there is also a pool here. Rates are $175 to $225 double.

EXPENSIVE

Captain's House Inn ★★★   The highest standards of hospitality have long been what has set the 1839 Captain's House apart from the many other B&Bs in Chatham. The 2-acre property includes not just the grand captain's home but the converted barn and stables now called the "Carriage House," with 5 units; the "Captain's Cottage," with 3 units; and the luxurious "Stables" building, also with 3 units. All the Stables rooms have fireplaces, and many have whirlpools.

369–377 Old Harbor Rd. (about ½ mile north of the rotary). © **800/315-0728** or 508/945-0127. www.captainshouseinn.com. 16 units, 14 with tub/shower combination, 2 with shower only. Summer $260–$380 double, $275-480 suite. Rates include full breakfast and afternoon tea. Children 9 and under not allowed. **Amenities:** Exercise room; outdoor heated pool; room service.

Carriage House Inn ★★   Carriage House is a small but well-run B&B in an 1890 house and renovated horse stables. All the rooms—3 in the main house, 3 in the carriage house—are cozy and decorated in a cheerful Cape Cod style. Room 6 is particularly nice, with a private entrance and outdoor sitting area. The inn is about a mile to downtown. Breakfast includes a hot entrée, such as like upside-down apple French toast.

407 Old Harbor Rd., Chatham. © **800/355-8868** or 508/945-4688. www.thecarriagehouseinn.com. 6 units. Summer $299–$349 double. Rates include full breakfast. Take Rte. 6 to exit 11; take Rte. 137 to Pleasant Bay Rd.; take a right on Rte. 28; go 3 miles to Old Harbor Rd. Children 9 and under not allowed. **Amenities:** Wi-Fi (free).

Chatham Bars Inn Resort & Spa ★★★   Generations of families return year after year here, because there is nothing else this grand on Cape Cod. The location couldn't be better: 25 acres overlooking a private beach and (just beyond a barrier beach) the Atlantic Ocean. Checking in is a treat as you traverse the veranda and enter the grand lobby to the front desk, the same one used in 1913. Rooms are in the main building or spread in cottages throughout the grounds, many with water views. To save some money, consider a less expensive room with a garden view. There is so much to do here, you won't be spending much time in your room anyway. The list of amenities on site is daunting: restaurants, spa, pools, tennis, and even a 9-hole golf course next door. The inn is a short walk to charming Chatham center.

297 Shore Rd. (off Seaview St., about ½ mile northwest of the town center), Chatham. © **800/527-4884** or 508/945-0096. www.chathambarsinn.com. 205 units. Summer $495–$725 double; $725–$1,350 1-bedroom suite; $790–$2,625 2-bedroom suite. **Amenities:** 4 restaurants; babysitting; children's program for ages 4 and over in summer; concierge; putting green, 9-hole public golf course; 2 pools; room service; fitness center; gym; 3 tennis courts ($15 an hour); Wi-Fi (free).

Cranberry Inn ★★   What's extra-nice about this small inn is there is a wide choice of size of room and price, so if you want to save some money but be centrally located, this is the place. It is down on the quiet end of Main Street, a short walk to both Lighthouse Beach and the center of Main Street. Many of the rooms have fireplaces and private balconies. The country breakfast is served in the dining room; there's also a small tavern on the premises.

359 Main St., Chatham. © **800/332-4667** or 508/945-9232. www.cranberryinn.com. 18 units. Summer $249–$379 double. Rates include full breakfast. Take Rte, 6 to exit 11; take Rte. 137 south to Rte. 28; take a right on Rte. 28; continue to Main St. Free Wi-Fi.

Chatham Wayside Inn ★★ Centrally located, this large hotel is popular with groups because of its size as well as its location. A former stagecoach stop, the inn has a completely modern interior. The rooms are comfortable and decorated in a somewhat generic style, though some have four-poster beds and fireplaces. The Wild Goose Tavern has a moderately priced menu with burgers, salads, pizza, and sandwiches.

512 Main St. (center of town), Chatham. (©**800/242-8426** or 508/945-5550. www.waysideinn.com. 56 units. Summer $360–$375 double; $400–$495 suite. **Amenities:** Restaurant/bar; outdoor heated pool; Wi-Fi (free).

Where to Eat
EXPENSIVE
Del Mar Bar & Bistro ★★ BISTRO This cool nightspot specializes in modern bistro cuisine, such as wood-fired thin-crust pizzas and substantial steaks, like the 14-ounce rib eye with mashed sweet potatoes and bourbon-soaked black cherries. Don't forget to check out the nightly blackboard specials where you might find BLT pizza or the native fluke baked in parchment, with couscous flavored with dry apricots. There's a lively bar scene, with a young crowd sipping cocktails.

907 Main St. (©**508/945-9988.** www.delmarbistro.com. Main courses $22–$32. Daily 5–10pm.

Pisces ★★ NEW AMERICAN This small chef-owned spot has an unpretentious homey feel, even though there is sophisticated cooking going on in the kitchen. The meal begins with homemade rosemary focaccia for dipping in garlicky white bean spread. With a name like Pisces, you might as well stick to the fish. Start with calamari from Point Judith, Rhode Island, which is sautéed with garlic and kalamata olives. For a substantial but special meal, try the Mediterranean fisherman's stew, which has cod and all manner of shellfish in a spicy lobster broth.

2653 Main St./Rte.28, South Chatham. (© **508/432-4600.** www.piscesofchatham.com. Reservations recommended. Main courses $22–$36. Tues–Sun 5–10pm.

MODERATE
Chatham Squire ★★ AMERICAN At some point, everyone in town ends up around the Squire's big bar. But don't be fooled into thinking a place this popular can't possibly serve good food. Besides the prize-winning chowder, the menu has dishes from much farther afield, including France (the sole), Asia (shrimp and chicken stir-fry), and Italy (cioppino—a fish stew).

487 Main St. (in the center of town), Chatham. (© **508/945-0945.** www.thesquire.com. Main courses $16–$26. May–Oct Mon–Sat 11:30am–10pm; Sun noon–10:30pm.

INEXPENSIVE
Red Nun Bar & Grill DINER This is a real fisherman's bar. The small menu has a few choice items, mainly fried fish, soup and salads: The fish tacos are great. The line forms around dinnertime here, so plan to arrive early if you want a bite before catching a Cape Cod Baseball League game at the field next door.

746 Main St. (near Monomoy Theatre and Veterans Field), Chatham. (© **508/348-0469.** www. rednun.com. Main courses $13–$17. May–Sept daily 11:30am–10pm; call for off-season hours. Closed Jan 15–Apr 1.

A PIE SHOP
Marion's Pie Shop ★ It all started in 1947, with Marion making chicken pot pies in her home. She built a bakery next door and was soon making fruit pies. Though

Marion is no longer at the stove, this place still churns out sublime sweet and savory pies using her special pastry crust recipe.

2022 Rte. 28 (about ½ mile east of Rte. 137), Chatham. (𝒞 **508/432-9439.** www.marionspieshop ofchatham.com. Mon–Sat 8am–6pm; Sun 8am–4pm.

Exploring: Beaches & Recreational Pursuits

BEACHES   Chatham has an unusual array of beach styles, from the peaceful shores of the Nantucket Sound to the treacherous, shifting shoals along the Atlantic. For information on beach stickers ($15 per day, $60 per week), call the **Permit Department,** at 283 George Ryder Rd., in West Chatham (𝒞 **508/945-5180**).

o **Chatham Lighthouse Beach ★★**: Directly below the lighthouse parking lot (where stopovers are limited to 30 min.), this narrow stretch of sand is easy to get to: Just walk down the stairs. Currents here can be tricky and swift, though, so swimming is discouraged. The beach has been closed occasionally over the past few years because of shark sightings in the harbor. Great white sharks are attracted to the area's large number of seals, their main source of food.

o **Cockle Cove Beach, Ridgevale Beach,** and **Hardings Beach ★★**: Lined up along the sound, each at the end of its namesake road, south of Route 28, these family-pleasing beaches offer gentle surf suitable for all ages, as well as full facilities, including lifeguards. Parking stickers are required.

o **Forest Beach ★**: With limited parking and no lifeguard, this sound landing near the Harwich border is still popular, especially among surfers.

o **North Beach ★★**: Extending all the way south from Orleans, this 5-mile barrier beach is accessible from Chatham only by boat; if you don't have your own, you can take the **Beachcomber,** a water taxi, which leaves from Chatham Fish Pier on Shore Road. Call 𝒞 **508/945-5265** (www.sealwatch.com) to schedule your trip, though reservations are not necessary. Round-trip costs $29 for adults, $25 for children 3 to 15. The water taxi makes the trip from 10am to 5pm daily in season on sunny days. Inquire about other possible drop-off points if you'd like to beach around.

o **Oyster Pond Beach,** off Route 28: Only a block from Chatham's Main Street, this sheltered saltwater pond (with restrooms) swarms with children. It's free to park here, and there is a lifeguard.

o **South Beach ★★**: A former island jutting out slightly to the south of the Chatham Light, this glorified sand bar can be dangerous, so heed posted warnings and content yourself with strolling or, at most, wading. A sticker is not required to park here.

NATURE & WILDLIFE AREAS   Chatham's natural bonanza lies to the south: The uninhabited **Monomoy Islands ★★**, 2,750 acres of brush-covered sand favored by some 285 species of migrating birds, is the perfect pit stop along the Atlantic Flyway. Harbor and gray seals are catching on, too: Hundreds now carpet the coastline from late November through May. If you go out during that time, you won't have any trouble seeing them—they're practically unavoidable.

Outermost Adventures (𝒞 **508/945-5858;** www.outermostharbor.com) runs boat shuttle service—basically water taxis—to South Beach and North Monomoy. The ride takes 10 minutes; once on the beach, passengers can walk for 2 minutes to the far side of the spit to see seals gathered along the coast. The shuttle begins at 8am, goes every 20 minutes, and is first-come, first-served. The last pickup is at 4:30pm. The cost is $20 for adults, $10 for children 12 and under. Trips run from Memorial Day to

Columbus Day. The boats leave from Outermost Harbor, just south of the lighthouse. Follow signs to Morris Island.

SEAL-WATCHING The *Beachcomber* ★★ (☎ **508/945-5265;** www.sealwatch. com) runs **seal-watching cruises** out of Chatham Harbor from mid-May to late September daily in season, weekends in the shoulder seasons. Parking is on Crowell Road, at Chatham Boat Company, near the bakery. There are typically four cruises a day—at 10am, noon, 2pm, and 4pm—depending on the weather. The 90-minute cruises cost $29 for adults, $27 for seniors, and $25 for children 3 to 15, and are free for children 2 and under. Where there are seals, there may also be their main predator, great white sharks. The large number of seals has attracted sharks in recent years, and passengers should stay alert for sightings.

Kid Stuff

The **Play-a-Round Park** ★★, on Depot Street, will keep kids entertained for hours on end. The weekly **band concerts** ★★ (☎ **508/945-5199**), at Kate Gould Park, held Friday nights in summer, are perfectly gauged for underage enjoyment: There's usually a bunny-hop at some point in the evening.

Every July, junior connoisseurs get a chance to enjoy some really fine music, when the Monomoy Chamber Ensemble puts on a free morning children's performance at the **Monomoy Theatre** (☎ **508/945-1589;** www.monomoytheatre.org). Musicals there are always fun.

Shopping

Chatham's tree-shaded Main Street, lined with specialty stores, offers a terrific opportunity to shop and stroll. The goods tend to be on the conservative side, but every so often, you'll happen upon a hedonistic delight.

BOOKS **Yellow Umbrella Books,** 501 Main St., in the center of town (☎ **508/945-0144**), sells both new and used books (from rare volumes to paperbacks perfect for a beach read). This full-service, all-ages bookstore invites protracted browsing.

FASHION Catering to fashionable parents and their kids, ages newborn well into the teens, the **Children's Shop,** 515 Main St., in the center of town (☎ **508/945-0234;** www.chathamchildrenshop.com), is the best children's clothing store in a 100-mile radius. While according a nod to doting grannies with such classics as hand-smocked party dresses, Ginny Nickerson also stays up-to-speed on what kids themselves prefer.

The flagship store of **Puritan Clothing Company** is at 573 Main St., Chatham (☎ **508/945-0326;** www.puritancapecod.com). This venerable institution, with stores all over the Cape, carries a wide range of quality men's and women's wear, including Polo, Nautica, Eileen Fisher, and Teva, at good prices.

Chatham After Dark

Although most towns host some comparable event, Chatham's free **band concerts**—40 players strong—are arguably the best on the Cape and attract crowds in the thousands. This is small-town America at its most nostalgic, as the band, made up mostly of local folks, plays those standards of yesteryear that never go out of style. Held in **Kate Gould Park** (off Chatham Bars Ave., in the center of town) from July to early September, it kicks off at 8pm every Friday. Better come early to claim your square of lawn (it's already a checkerboard of blankets by late afternoon), and be prepared to sing—or dance—along. Call ☎ **508/945-5199** for information.

PERFORMANCE ARTS

Monomoy Theatre   One of the Cape's best summer theater companies, the Ohio University Players steal the show with eight productions a summer in this small historic theater. Performances are mid-June to August, Tuesday to Saturday at 8pm and a Thursday matinee at 2pm. 776 Rte. 28 (about ¼ mile west of the rotary), Chatham. ℭ **508/945-1589.** www.monomoytheatre.org. Admission $25–$30.

ORLEANS ★★

31 miles E of Sandwich; 25 miles S of Provincetown

Essentials

VISITOR INFORMATION   Contact the **Orleans Chamber of Commerce,** 44 Main St. (P.O. Box 153), Orleans, MA 02653 (ℭ **508/255-1386;** www.capecodorleans.com), open year-round Monday through Friday from 10am to 3pm; or the **Cape Cod Chamber of Commerce** (see "Visitor Information," under "Brewster," earlier in this chapter).

Where to Stay

EXPENSIVE

A Little Inn on Pleasant Bay ★★   Part of the fun here are your hosts, made up of two British sisters and the German husband of one of them. They have extensively renovated this 1798 house and two adjacent buildings into a very modern and comfortable B&B. The property is beautifully landscaped, with flowers everywhere, and it sits high up on a knoll with exquisite views of Pleasant Bay—very peaceful. The 9 rooms are named after the kinds of boats you might see sailing by, such as Beetle Cat and Knockabout.

654 S. Orleans Rd., Orleans. ℭ**888/332-3351** or 508/255-0780. www.alittleinnonpleasantbay.com. 9 units. $295–$380 double. Extra person $30 per night. Rates include continental breakfast and evening sherry. No children under 10. Closed Oct to late May. **Amenities:** Wi-Fi (free).

MODERATE

The Cove ★   It's just a motel with nothing-fancy rooms, but it has a great location. There is a heated pool and lots of places to sit to look out on the cove, which is nearby. Some rooms are suites and have kitchenettes.

13 S. Orleans Rd./Rte. 28 (north of Main St.), Orleans. ℭ **800/343-2233** or 508/255-1203. www. thecoveorleans.com. 47 units. Summer $124–$169 double; $194 suite or efficiency. **Amenities:** Small heated pool; Wi-Fi (free).

Nauset Knoll Motor Lodge ★★   The only motel in the Cape Cod National Seashore, this one sits just above Nauset Beach. You are a guest of Uncle Sam in this no-frills motel, and you can't beat the views or the location, just steps from the Cape's largest beach. The rooms look like they haven't been updated since the 1950s, but with an 8-foot picture window looking out on the beach, who cares?

237 Beach Rd. (at Nauset Beach, about 2 miles east of the town center), East Orleans. ℭ **508/255-2364.** www.capecodtravel.com/nausetknoll. 12 units. Summer $190 double. Closed late Oct to early Apr.

The Orleans Inn ★   This eye-catching Victorian mansion on Town Cove has quite a rich history. Captain Aaron Snow built it in 1875; it soon became known as "Aaron's Folly" because of its large size. Today's owners, the Maas family, have brought the inn back to its glory as a big part of the community. It is a popular function and wedding site. The restaurant and bar on the first floor are convenient for guests. A short walk across a parking lot brings guests to Goose Hummock, which rents kayaks for exploring the Cove. Rooms are simple but adequate, and half have Cove views.

3 Old Country Rd./Rte. 6A (P.O. Box 188, just south of the Orleans rotary), Orleans. 📞 **800/863-3039** or 508/255-2222. www.orleansinn.com. 11 units. Summer $250–$275 double; $375–$450 suite. Rates include full breakfast. Closed Jan to mid-Feb. Dogs allowed. **Amenities:** Restaurant/bar; Wi-Fi (free).

INEXPENSIVE

Nauset House Inn ★★   This inn is a slice of old Cape Cod, a simple 1810 farmhouse that has been family owned and operated since 1982. The folksy rooms have hand-painted furniture, floral stencils and trompe l'oeil walls. This is one of the few inns on the Cape that has some rooms with shared bathrooms; these are significantly less expensive in-season than anything else around. The main house has 9 guest rooms including 6 with shared baths. An outbuilding, the Carriage House, has larger rooms, and the stand-alone Outermost House, set in the apple orchard is even more private. The inn is a short walk to Nauset Beach.

143 Beach Rd. (P.O. Box 774; about 1 mile east of the town center), East Orleans. 📞 **800/771-5508** or 508/255-2195. www.nausethouseinn.com. 14 units, 6 with shared bathroom, 4 with tub/shower combination, 4 with shower only. Summer $90 single; $99–$120 double with shared bathroom; $145–$210 double with private bathroom. Rates include full breakfast. Closed Nov–Mar. No children 12 and under.

Where to Eat
EXPENSIVE

Abba ★★★ MEDITERRANEAN   A French-cuisine-trained Israeli chef and a Thai line cook create the fusion cuisine at this popular spot. The mood, with candles in Moroccan tea glasses and colorful pillows, is sophisticated. The flavors found here are found in no other restaurants on Cape Cod. Dishes from North Africa, Spain, Italy and France are joined with Indian curries and Thai spices. It's an impressive combination. Start with Wellfleet oysters with Thai lemon sauce; move on to a rack of lamb with dried-fruit couscous, and end with the sticky black-rice pudding with fresh pineapple and coconut-pineapple ice cream. It's a whirlwind trip without leaving the Cape.

90 Old Colony Way, at West Rd. (2 blocks from Main St., toward Skaket Beach), Orleans. 📞 **508/255-8144.** www.abbarestaurant.com. Main courses $20–$27. June–Aug daily 5–10pm; call for off-season hours.

MODERATE

The Lobster Claw Restaurant ★ SEAFOOD   Your basic family fish shack, this big red barn of a restaurant has been at it for almost 50 years. You can get your seafood baked, broiled or steamed, but most people get it fried. This is also a good place to get a full-fledged lobster clambake. No problem if the kids get too loud here; everyone else's are, too. So pick a picnic table and settle in. We're all family.

42 Rte. 6A (just south of the rotary), Orleans. 📞 **508/255-1800.** www.lobsterclaw.com. Main courses $9–$26. Apr–Oct daily 11:30am–9pm. Closed Nov–Mar.

INEXPENSIVE

Land Ho! ★★ AMERICAN   John Murphy opened this pub, known as the Ho, in 1969, and it's been the social center of Orleans pretty much ever since. At this hangout, everyone feels welcome. It is always very busy, but the late-night service (serving food sometimes until 10pm) can be a godsend. Orleans business signs hang on every available space. Fried seafood, burgers, and salads are among the mainstays.

38 Rte. 6A (at Cove Rd.), Orleans. © **508/255-5165.** www.land-ho.com/orleans. Main courses $9–$25. Mon–Sat 11:30am–10pm; Sun noon–10pm.

The Yardarm ★ PUB GRUB   John Sully has been running this popular tavern since 1972. You can rub elbows with all manner of locals here: fishermen, lawyers from the Orleans courthouse, local politicians, and working people. The menu features the award-winning chowder, in addition knockwurst, homemade fish cakes, other tavern favorites.

48 Rte. 28 (just east of Main St.), Orleans. © **508/255-4840.** www.yardarmrestaurant.com. Main courses $8–21. Daily 11:30am–3pm and 5:30–10pm.

SWEETS
The Hot Chocolate Sparrow ★★   Opened in 1994, this cafe provides specialty coffee drinks, desserts, and hand-dipped chocolates to a community that embraces every single espresso, smoothie, and caramel turtle. There are also free-range egg sandwiches for breakfast and grilled sandwiches on focaccia for lunch. With the best community bulletin board in town, this is also a place to meet locals and find out what's going on.

5 Old Colony Way, Orleans. © **508/240-2230.** www.hotchocolatesparrow.com. Apr–Oct daily 6:30am–11pm; Nov–Mar Sun–Thurs 6:30am–9pm, Fri–Sat 6:30am–11pm.

Exploring: Beaches & Recreational Pursuits

BEACHES   From here on up, on the eastern side, you're dealing with the wild and whimsical Atlantic, which can be kittenish one day and tigerish the next. While storms may whip up surf you can actually ride, less confident swimmers should wait a few days until the turmoil and riptides subside. In any case, current conditions are clearly posted at the entrance. Weeklong parking permits ($50 for renters) may be obtained from **Town Hall,** at 19 School Rd., Orleans (© **508/240-3700**). Day-trippers who arrive early enough—before 10am on weekends in July and August—can pay at the gate (© **508/240-3780**).

○ **Crystal Lake** ★, off Monument Road, about ¾ mile south of Main Street: Parking—if you can find a space—is free, but there are no facilities.

○ **Nauset Beach** ★★★, in East Orleans (© **508/240-3780**): Stretching southward all the way past Chatham, this 10-mile-long barrier beach, which is part of the Cape Cod National Seashore but is managed by the town, has long been one of the Cape's gonzo beach scenes—good surf, big crowds, lots of young people. Full facilities, including a snack bar serving terrific fried fish, can be found within the 1,000-car parking lot; the in-season fee is $15 per car, which is also good for same-day parking at Skaket Beach. Substantial waves make for good surfing in the special section reserved for that purpose, and boogie boards are ubiquitous.

○ **Pilgrim Lake** ★, off Monument Road, about 1 mile south of Main Street: A beach parking sticker is necessary for this small freshwater beach, which has lifeguards.

○ **Skaket Beach** ★, off Skaket Beach Road to the west of town: This peaceful bay beach is a better choice for families with young children. When the tide recedes (as much as 1 mile), little kids will enjoy splashing about in the tide pools left behind. Parking costs $15, and you'd better turn up early.

BOATING The **Goose Hummock Outdoor Center,** at 15 Rte. 6A, south of the rotary (© 508/255-2620; www.goose.com), rents out canoes, kayaks, and more, and the northern half of Pleasant Bay is the place to use them; inquire about guided excursions. Canoe and kayak rentals are $50 to $75 per day.

FISHING Fishing is allowed in Baker Pond, Pilgrim Lake, and Crystal Lake; the latter is a likely spot to reel in trout and perch. For details and a license, visit **Town Hall,** at 19 School Rd. (Post Office Square), in the center of town (© 508/240-3700, ext. 305), or **Goose Hummock** (see "Boating," above). Surf-casting—no license needed—is permitted on Nauset Beach South, off Beach Road. **Rock Harbor ★★,** a former packet landing on the bay (about 1¼ miles northwest of the town center), shelters New England's largest sportfishing fleet: some 18 boats at last count. One call (© 508/255-9757) will get you information on them all. Or go look them over. Rock Harbor charter prices range from $550 for 4 hours to $750 for 8 hours. Individual prices are also available ($140 per person for 4 hr.; $150 per person for 8 hr.).

WATERSPORTS The **Pump House Surf Shop,** at 9 Cranberry Hwy./Rte. 6A (© 508/240-2226; www.pumphousesurf.com), rents and sells wet suits, body boards, and surfboards, while providing up-to-date reports on where to find the best waves. Surfboards rent for $20 to $30 a day. **Nauset Surf Shop,** at Jeremiah Square, Route 6A, at the rotary (© 508/255-4742; www.nausetsports.com), also rents surfboards, boogie boards, skim boards, kayaks, and wet suits.

5 Kid Stuff

The Nauset Regional Middle School, in Eldredge Park, has its own **skateboard park,** with four ramps and a "fun box"; helmets are required.

Shopping

Though shops are somewhat scattered, Orleans is full of great finds for browsers and grazers.

ANTIQUES/COLLECTIBLES Got an old house in need of illumination, or a new one in want of some style? You'll find some 400 vintage light fixtures at **Continuum Antiques,** 7 S. Orleans Rd./Rte 28, south of the junction with Route 6A (© 508/255-8513; www.oldlamp.com), from Victorian to colonial, along with a smattering of old advertising signs and duck decoys. Open Tuesday to Sunday 11am to 4:30pm, by chance or appointment.

BOOKS In the Skaket Corners shopping center, on Route 6A, is a branch of the large retailer **Booksmith/Musicsmith** (© 508/255-4590).

FASHION **Karol Richardson,** 47 Main St., in the center of town (© 508/255-3944; www.karolrichardson.com), is a preview of Richardson's main showroom in Wellfleet; stop in to see the latest from this gifted ex-Londoner.

GIFTS Birders will go batty over **Bird Watcher's General Store,** 36 Rte. 6A, south of the rotary (© 800/562-1512; www.birdwatchersgeneralstore.com). The brainchild of local aficionado Mike O'Connor, who'd like everyone to share his passion, it stocks virtually every bird-watching accessory under the sun, from basic binoculars to costly telescopes, modest birdhouses to birdbaths fit for a tiny Roman emperor; there's also a good selection of CDs and field guides.

Orleans After Dark

Joe's Beach Road Bar & Grille (✆ **508/255-0212**) is a big old barn of a bar that might as well be town hall: It's where you'll find all the locals exchanging juicy gossip and jokes. Live music ranges from jazz to rock to blues. There's never a cover.

There's often live music at **Land Ho!** (✆ **508/255-5165;** see "Where to Eat," above), the best pub in town. Performers are on the bill on Monday and Tuesday nights in season, and Thursday and Saturday off-season. There's usually no cover.

The Academy Playhouse, 120 Main St., about ¾ mile southeast of the town center (✆ **508/255-1963;** www.apacape.org), makes a fine platform for local talent in the form of musicals and drama, recitals, and poetry readings. The 162-seat arena-style stage is housed in the town's old town hall (built in 1873). Tickets are $22. Shows take place July through August Tuesday to Sunday at 8pm; call for off-season hours. A children's theater series runs from late June to early September on Friday and Saturday mornings. The cost is $10.

THE OUTER CAPE: WELLFLEET ★★★

42 miles NE of Sandwich; 14 miles S of Provincetown

Essentials

VISITOR INFORMATION   Contact the **Wellfleet Chamber of Commerce** (off Rte. 6), P.O. Box 571, Wellfleet, MA 02667 (✆ **508/349-2510;** www.wellfleetchamber. com). The Wellfleet information center is open mid-June to mid-September 9am to 6pm daily. Call for off-season hours.

Where to Stay

MODERATE

Even'tide ★   This motel in a pine forest off Route 6 ranks as one of the best on the Cape by virtue of its location—on the Cape Rail Trail bike path and a short walk to Marconi Beach—and also its amenities, which include a large pool and loads of kid-friendly stuff on site. There is a basketball court, five-hole mini-golf, horseshoe pit, badminton, shuffleboard, and table tennis. All the motel rooms have mini-fridges and coffeemakers and HBO on the TV, so you are all set if the weather is rainy. In addition to the motel rooms, there are 8 cottages and a 4-bedroom house for rent on the property. Ask for a cottage with an outdoor shower; those are a real treat.

650 Rte. 6, South Wellfleet. ✆ **800/368-0007** or 508/349-3410. www.eventidemotel.com. 40 units, 39 with tub/shower combination, 1 with shower only. Summer $149–$207 double; $215–$360 efficiency. $25 surcharge Sat–Sun for a 1-night stay. Closed Nov to early May. **Amenities:** Playground; large heated indoor pool; Wi-Fi (free).

Surf Side Cottages ★★   For fans of mid-century Cape Cod style, these cottages have it in spades, simple, boxlike clapboard-sided units with big windows and roof decks. Even better is the location, just steps from the dunes near LeCount's Hollow beach in South Wellfleet. With kitchens, barbecues and outdoor showers, these make the perfect base for a family vacation. Although it began as a cottage colony, the units are now individually owned condos, but they are still rented in much the same way. The managers of the property also rent out about a dozen additional houses in the area.

Ocean View Dr. (at LeCount Hollow Rd.), South Wellfleet. ℂ **508/349-3959.** www.surfside cottages.com. 24 cottages, showers only. Summer $1,400–$2,500 weekly; off-season $175–$250 per day. No credit cards. Closed Nov to March. Pets allowed in some cottages off-season. **Amenities:** Wi-Fi (some cottages).

INEXPENSIVE

Hostelling International–Truro   By far the most scenic of the youth hostels on the Cape, this Hopperesque house on a lonely bluff a short stroll from Ballston Beach was once a Coast Guard station; these days it's used as an environmental-studies center in the winter. During the summer, it's a magnet for hikers, cyclists, and surfers.

111 N. Pamet Rd. (1¼ miles east of Rte. 6), Truro, MA 02666. http://capecod.hiusa.org. ℂ **508/ 349-3889.** 42 beds. $32–$35 bed in dorm room; $125–$150 private room. Closed early Sept– late June.

Where to Eat

EXPENSIVE

Mac's Shack ★ SEAFOOD   Run by two brothers, Mac and Alex Hay, this upscale restaurant in a mammoth 19th-century house serves updated classics, like their grand-mother's cracker-crusted bluefish, or more experimental dishes, such as grilled oys-ters with absinthe and halibut in a saffron lobster broth. A sushi chef is on hand, and there's also a raw bar that's open 2 hours before the restaurant. This is a very popular place in the summer, and if you don't have reservations, you'll need to find a strategic off night to get in.

91 Commercial St. (a few blocks north of Wellfleet Center), Wellfleet. ℂ **508/349-6333.** www. macsseafood.com. Main courses $13–$32. Mid-June to early Sept daily 5–9:30pm (raw bar 3–9:30pm); call for off-season hours. Closed mid-Oct to mid-May.

Pearl Restaurant & Bar ★★★ SEAFOOD   The old Captain Higgins fried fish shack, was transformed in 2009 into Pearl, a glorious harbor-front restaurant (still serv-ing fish, fried as well as grilled, baked, and sautéed). Ample multi-level outdoor decks allow unobstructed views of boats going in and out of Wellfleet Harbor. Another deck faces the marsh in the back of the building, and that is where live music is performed from 3 to 5pm daily in summer. Fresh fish cooked to order in the open kitchen is the thing here. The oysters on the half-shell, set up at the raw bar made from an old fishing boat, come from a shellfish area you can see from the upper deck of the restaurant. Lobster and steaks, chicken and BBQ ribs are all popular menu items.

250 Commercial St., Wellfleet. ℂ **508/349-2999.** www.wellfleetpearl.com. Main courses $19–$34. Mid-May–mid-Oct daily 11am–9pm. Closed mid-Oct to mid-May.

The Wicked Oyster ★★★ NEW AMERICAN   Housed in a big red weathered building from 1750, this sophisticated bistro is a dependable choice for breakfast, lunch, or dinner. The best seats are on the enclosed porch, where summer breezes come free. No surprise that the small but creative menu has a focus on seafood. There are those Wellfleet oysters, a seafood stew, and pan-fried sole. On the less expensive side, there are fish-and-chips and fried oysters, as well as burgers, including a veggie burger that is among the best around.

50 Main St. (just off Rte. 6, close to Wellfleet Center), Wellfleet. ℂ **508/349-3455.** www.the wickedo.com. Main courses $11–$30. June–Aug daily 8am–2pm and 5–9:30pm; call for off-season hours. Closed Dec to mid-Jan.

Winslow's Tavern ★★ NEW AMERICAN   Brought to you by the Barry family, that same crew that has the insanely popular Moby Dick's clam shack out on Route 6,

Winslow's is a fancier option in the center of town. It's in an 1805 captain's house and former governor's mansion. Tables set out on the sloping lawn are the ideal places to sit on a pleasant summer day or night. The perfect appetizer would have to be Wellfleet oysters; they have them six ways. The beet salad is heaven. As for main courses, fish is a specialty, but there's also a very sophisticated crisp lamb belly dish with beluga lentils and pickled mustard.

316 Main St. (in the center of town), Wellfleet. ℃ **508/349-6450.** www.winslowstavern.com. Main courses $16–$27. Late May to Aug daily noon–3pm and 5:30–10pm; call for off-season hours. Closed late Oct to mid-May.

MODERATE

The Lighthouse AMERICAN   The only year-round restaurant in Wellfleet, this is where to rub elbows with locals at the bar. Breakfast is your best bet here (the blueberry pancakes are keepers) but come early if you want a table. Thursday is Mexican Night, when the usual New England fare gets a spicy shake-up. The place rocks with live music on some summer evenings.

317 Main St. (in the center of town), Wellfleet. ℃ **508/349-3681.** www.mainstreetlighthouse.com. Main courses $10–$25. May–Oct daily 8am–9pm; call for off-season hours. Closed mid-Feb to mid-April.

INEXPENSIVE

Moby Dick's Restaurant ★ SEAFOOD   The first codfish sandwich was made here in 1983, and it's been hopping ever since at this popular and family-friendly fish shack. Lines go out the door around dinnertime in the summer, so try to visit before 5pm or after 8pm. And if you see a full parking lot, keep on driving. The restaurant is set up for counter service. The way it works is you stand in line to place your order, then you find a seat among the picnic tables and a waitress brings your order when it is ready. Good grub. The restaurant is BYOB.

3225 Rte. 6, Wellfleet. ℃ **508/349-9795.** www.mobydicksrestaurant.com. Main courses $8–$20. May to mid-Oct daily 11:30am–9:30pm.

TAKEOUT & PICNIC FARE

Mac's on the Pier ★   This was the first restaurant for Wellfleet's Hay brothers, who have four fish markets and three restaurants. It is a no-fuss take-out clam shack, perfectly located on the Wellfleet pier. You order from the window and find a picnic table (there are only a few). It is dining al fresco, Cape Cod style. The usual fried fish dinners are here, but for there's also grilled tuna with summer vegetables, fish tacos, and even jambalaya. Ice cream, both soft-serve and hard, gets its own window.

265 Commercial St. (on the Wellfleet Town Pier), Wellfleet. ℃ **508/349-9611.** www.macsseafood. com. Mid-May to Sept daily 11am–7pm. Closed Oct to mid-May.

Exploring: Beaches & Recreational Pursuits

BEACHES   Though the distinctions are far from hard and fast, Wellfleet's fabulous ocean beaches tend to sort themselves demographically: LeCount Hollow is popular with families, Newcomb Hollow with high-schoolers, White Crest with the college crowd (including surfers and off-hour hang gliders), and Cahoon Hollow with 30-somethings. Only the latter two beaches permit parking by nonresidents ($15 per day). To enjoy the other two, as well as Burton Baker Beach, on the harbor, and Duck Harbor, on the bay, plus three freshwater ponds, you'll have to walk or bike in, or see if you qualify for a sticker ($35 for 3 consecutive days, $70 per week). Bring proof of residency to the seasonal Beach Sticker Booth, on the Town Pier, or call the **Wellfleet**

CAPE COD NATIONAL seashore

No trip to Cape Cod would be complete without a visit to the **Cape Cod National Seashore,** on the Outer Cape, and a barefoot stroll along "The Great Beach," where you see exactly why the Cape has attracted so many artists and poets. On August 7, 1961, President John F. Kennedy signed a bill designating 27,000 acres in the 40 miles from Chatham to Provincetown as the Cape Cod National Seashore, a new national park. Perhaps surprisingly, the Seashore includes 500 private residences, the owners of which lease land from the park service. Convincing residents that a National Seashore would be a good thing for Cape Cod was an arduous task back then, and Provincetown still grapples with Seashore officials over town land issues.

The Seashore's claim to fame is its spectacular beaches—in reality, one long beach—with dunes 50 to 150 feet high. This is the Atlantic Ocean, so the surf is rough (and cold), but a number of the beaches have lifeguards. Seashore beaches include **Marconi Beach,** in Wellfleet; **Head of the Meadow Beach,** in Truro; and Provincetown's **Race Point** and **Herring Cove beaches.** A $45 pass will get you into all of them for the season, or you can pay a daily rate of $15.

The Seashore also has a number of walking trails—all free, all picturesque, and all worth a trip. In Eastham, **Fort Hill** (off Rte. 6) has one of the best scenic views on Cape Cod and a popular boardwalk trail through a red-maple swamp. The **Nauset Marsh Trail** is accessed from the Salt Pond Visitor Center, on Route 6, in Eastham. **Great Island,** on the bay side in Wellfleet, is surely one of the finest places to have a picnic; you could spend the day hiking the trails. On **Pamet Trail,** off North Pamet Road, in Truro, hikers pass the decrepit old cranberry-bog building (restoration is in the works) on the way to a trail through the dunes. Don't try the old boardwalk trail over the bogs here; it has flooded and is no longer in use. The **Atlantic White Cedar Swamp Trail** is located at the Marconi Station site; **Small Swamp** and **Pilgrim Spring** trails are found at Pilgrim Heights Beach; and **Beech Forest Trail** is at Race Point, in Provincetown. The best bike path on Cape Cod is the Province Lands Trail, 5 swooping and invigorating miles, at Race Point Beach. Race Point is also a popular spot for surf-casting, which is allowed from the ocean beaches.

Getting There: Take Route 6, the Mid-Cape Highway, to Eastham (about 50 miles). Pick up a map at the Cape Cod National Seashore's **Salt Pond Visitor Center,** in Eastham (✆ **508/ 255-3421;** www.nps.gov/caco). Another visitor center is at **Race Point.** Both centers have ranger activities, maps, gift shops, and restrooms. Seashore beaches are all off Route 6 and are clearly marked. Additional beaches along this stretch are run by individual towns, and you must have a sticker or pay a fee.

Beach Sticker Office (✆ **508/349-9818**). Parking is free at all beaches and ponds after 4pm.

o **Marconi Beach** ★★, off Marconi Beach Road, in South Wellfleet: A National Seashore property, this cliff-lined beach (with restrooms) charges an entry fee of $15 per day, or $45 for the season. *Note:* The bluffs are so high that the beach lies in shadow by late afternoon.

o **Mayo Beach,** Kendrick Avenue (near the Town Pier): Right by the harbor, facing south, this warm, shallow bay beach (with restrooms) is very central; it will please young waders and splashers. This is one of the few beaches on the Cape with free parking. Make sure you go at high tide; at low tide, oyster farmers take over. You could grab a bite (and a paperback) at the Bookstore Restaurant across the street, which serves three meals a day and sells used books.

○ **White Crest & Cahoon Hollow beaches ★★★**, off Ocean View Drive, in Wellfleet: These two town-run ocean beaches—big with surfers—are open to all. As with all the oceanside beaches on the Outer Cape, large sand dunes border the beach, which is a wide-open and beautiful expanse. Both have snack bars and restrooms. What makes Cahoon Hollow Beach unique is the restaurant/nightclub, The Beachcomber, in the beach parking lot, so you can go straight from a day at the beach to an evening of live music and dancing. Parking costs $15 per day.

BOATING Jack's Boat Rental, on Gull Pond, off Gull Pond Road, about a half-mile south of the Truro border (② 508/349-7553; www.jacksboatrental.com), rents out canoes, kayaks, sailboards, and Sunfish, as well as sea cycles and surf bikes. Renting a kayak or canoe at Gull Pond for an hour and a half costs about $50. If you'd like to rent a boat for a few days, you'll need to go to the Jack's Boat Rental location on Route 6 in Wellfleet (next to the Cumberland Farms). There a kayak rents for $50 for a single, $65 for a tandem for 24 hours. Sunfish sailboats are $200 for 3 days. Rentals come with a roof rack if you need it. There are many wonderful places to canoe in Wellfleet—for example, a trip across the harbor from Wellfleet's Town Pier to Great Island.

WATERSPORTS Surfing is restricted to White Crest Beach, and sailboarding to Burton Baker Beach, at Indian Neck, during certain tide conditions; ask for a copy of the regulations at the Beach Sticker Booth on the Town Pier.

Eric Gustafson (② 508/349-1429; www.funseekers.org) offers windsurfing and surfing instruction ($120 for 2 hr.) and, for the most adventurous, kite-boarding lessons ($250 for 3 hr.). He also teaches stand-up paddleboarding ($60 per hour) in the ocean and estuaries of Wellfleet. SUP, which uses a surfboard and paddle, is gaining popularity in the United States as a full-body workout.

Kid Stuff

No conceivable nocturnal treat beats an outing to the **Wellfleet Drive-In Theater**—unless it's by a game of mini-golf at the adjacent course while you're waiting for the sky to darken. The restaurant on-site is the **Dairy Bar and Grill** (② 508/349-7176; www.wellfleetcinemas.com), which specializes in fried seafood and is open from 11:30am to 10pm daily in season. During the day, check out what's up at the Wellfleet Bay Wildlife Sanctuary (see "Beaches & Recreational Pursuits," above).

Shopping

ANTIQUES/COLLECTIBLES Wheeler-dealers should head for the **Wellfleet Flea Market,** 51 Rte. 6, north of the Eastham-Wellfleet border (② 508/349-0541; www.wellfleetcinemas.com/flea-market). A few days a week in summer and during the shoulder seasons, the parking lot of the Wellfleet Drive-In Theater "daylights" as an outdoor bazaar with as many as 300 booths. Though a great many vendors stock discount surplus, there are usually enough collectibles dealers on hand to warrant a browse through. An added bonus: Kids can kick loose in the little playground or grab a quick bite at the snack bar. Lookers are charged $2 to $3 per carload.

ARTS & CRAFTS One of the more distinguished galleries in town, the smallish **Cove Gallery,** 15 Commercial St., by Duck Creek (② 508/349-2530; www.cove gallery.com)—with a waterside sculpture garden—carries the paintings and prints of many well-known artists, including Barry Moser and Leonard Baskin. John Grillo's work astounds every summer during his annual show, which has featured boldly painted tango-themed paintings, watercolors, and prints. Closed mid-October through April.

Crafts make a stronger stand than art at **Left Bank Gallery,** 25 Commercial St., by Duck Creek (© **508/349-9451;** www.leftbankgallery.com), inside a 1933 American Legion Hall, that makes an optimal display space. Although the paintings occupying the former auditorium sometimes verge on hackneyed, the "Potter's Room" overlooking the cove is packed with sturdy, handsome, useful vessels, along with compatible textiles. Also worth hunting out are the curious collages of Kim Victoria Kettler. The **Left Bank Small Works & Jewelry Gallery,** 3 W. Main St., in the center of town (© **508/349-7939**), features the spillover from the Left Bank Gallery, and in some ways, it's better. There's also an irresistible sampling of new-wave jewelry designs, collected from more than 100 noted artisans across the nation and arrayed in clever thematic displays.

FASHION **Karol Richardson,** 11 W. Main St. (© **508/349-6378;** www.karol richardson.com), is owned and operated by its namesake, an alumna of the London College of Fashion and a refugee from the New York rag trade. She has a feel for sensual fabrics and a knack for lovely clothes that, in her own words, are "wonderfully comfortable but sophisticated at the same time and very flattering to the less-than-perfect body." Closed mid-October through April.

GIFTS **Jules Besch Stationers,** 15 Bank St. (© **508/349-1231**), specializes in papers, ribbon, gift cards, handmade journals and albums, desktop pen sets, guest books, and unusual gift items. This exquisite store is in a mansard-roofed former bank building. Closed January through March.

Wellfleet After Dark
CLUBS & WATERING HOLES
The Beachcomber ★★   The only nightclub on Cape Cod with an Atlantic Ocean view, the Beachcomber has since 1978 been the dance club for those in the know on the Cape. Built as a lifesaving station in 1897, the club, which also serves lunch and dinner, is in the parking lot of Cahoon's Hollow Beach. The food here is surprisingly good, with fish tacos a standby; frozen drinks and a great selection of draft beer complete the picture. As for the music, the acts have been mostly the same for years. It starts and ends with the Incredible Casuals, a rockabilly band. Parking is tricky here because the restaurant is on a busy beach, where parking costs $15. If you park in the Beachcomber lot before 5pm, the $15 cost can be put toward food or a T-shirt at the restaurant; after 5pm parking is free. It's open daily from late June to early September, noon to 1am. 1120 Old Cahoon Hollow Rd. (off Ocean View Dr., at Cahoon Hollow Beach), Wellfleet. © **508/349-6055.** www.thebeachcomber.com. Cover varies ($10–$25).

WHAT? W.H.A.T.
The principals behind the **Wellfleet Harbor Actors' Theatre (WHAT),** 2357 Rte. 6 (next to the post office; © **508/349-9428;** www.what.org), aim to provoke—and usually succeed, even amid this very sophisticated, seen-it-all summer colony. The company goes to great lengths to secure original work, some local and some by playwrights of considerable renown, with the result that the repertory rarely suffers a dull moment.

A Vineyard in the Dunes ★

Truro Vineyards of Cape Cod, 11 Shore Rd./Rte. 6A, North Truro (✆ **508/487-6200;** http://trurovineyardsofcapecod.com), one of the last working farms in the Outer Cape. The vineyard uncorked its first homegrown chardonnay and cabernet franc in the fall of 1996, and muscadet and merlot soon followed.

Inside the main house on this pastoral property, the living room, with its exposed beams, is decorated with interesting wine-related artifacts. From late May through October, free wine tastings are held every half-hour Monday to Saturday from 11am to 5pm, Sunday noon to 5pm.

PROVINCETOWN ★★★

56 miles NE of Sandwich; 42 miles NE of Hyannis

Essentials

GETTING THERE If you plan to spend your entire vacation in Provincetown, you don't need a car, because everything is within walking or biking distance. And because parking is a hassle in this tiny town, consider leaving your car at home and taking a boat from Boston or Plymouth. Another advantage is that you'll get to skip the horrendous Sagamore Bridge traffic jams.

Bay State Cruises (✆ **877/783-3779;** www.provincetownfastferry.com) makes round-trips from Boston, daily from May to early October.

The high-speed **Provincetown Express** boat takes 90 minutes and makes three round-trips daily from mid-May to mid-October. It leaves 200 Seaport Blvd., at Boston's World Trade Center, at 8:30am, 1pm, and 5:30pm. On the return trip, it leaves Provincetown at 10:30am, 3pm, and 7:30pm. Tickets on the high-speed boat cost $56 one-way, $88 round-trip for adults. Seniors are $51 one-way and $76 round-trip. Children ages 3 to 12 are $37 one-way, $65 round-trip. Reservations are recommended.

From late June to early September, the regular 3-hour boat, called **Provincetown II,** leaves from dockside at Boston's World Trade Center on Saturdays at 9am and arrives in Provincetown at noon. At 3:30pm the boat leaves Provincetown, arriving in Boston at 6:30pm. On the slow boat, round-trip fare is $46 for adults ($23 one-way) and free for children 11 and under.

Boston Harbor Cruises (✆ **877/733-9425** or 617/227-4321; www.bostonharbor cruises.com) runs fast ferries from Boston's Long Wharf, next to the aquarium, to Provincetown's MacMillan Wharf. It's a 90-minute trip. In high season, there are two or three round-trips a day from Boston, leaving at 9am and 2pm, with an additional 6:30pm trip Thursdays to Sundays. The boat leaves from Provincetown at 11am and 4pm, with an additional 8:30pm trip on Thursdays through Sundays. In the shoulder season, beginning in late May to mid-June and from early September to mid-October, there are one or two trips a day. Ferry tickets cost $88 round-trip for adults ($56 one-way). Tickets for seniors cost $76 round-trip; tickets for children cost $65 round-trip. Bikes cost $6 each way. Reservations are a must on this popular boat.

Provincetown

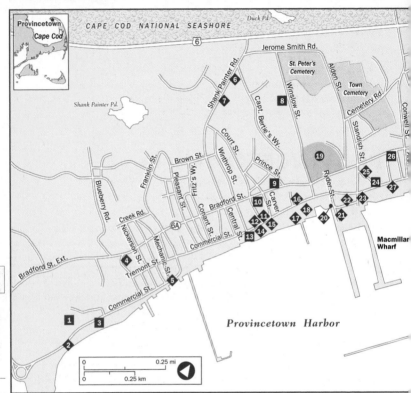

You can also fly into Provincetown (see chapter 8). **Cape Air/Nantucket Airlines** (© **800/352-0714** or 508/771-6944; www.flycapeair.com) offers flights from Boston in season. The trip takes about 25 minutes and costs $200 to $250 round-trip.

As far as getting around once you're settled, you can enjoy the vintage fleet of the **Mercedes Cab Company** (© **508/487-3333**). There's also **Jody's Taxi** (© **508/487-0265**). They charge only $8 per person to take passengers from MacMillan Pier to just about anywhere in town. Provincetown is such a funky place that it seems perfectly ordinary to use **Ptown Pedicabs** (© **508/487-0660;** www.ptownpedicabs.com), "chariots for hire," for your transportation needs. These cheerful bikers will ferry you up and down Commercial Street for whatever you want to pay. That's right: You pay what you think the ride was worth. If you need to get from a gallery opening in the East End to dinner in the West End, this is the best way to do it.

VISITOR INFORMATION   Contact the **Provincetown Chamber of Commerce,** 307 Commercial St., Provincetown, MA 02657 (© **508/487-3424;** www.ptown chamber.com), open late May to mid-September daily from 9am to 5pm (call for off-season hours); or the gay-oriented **Provincetown Business Guild,** 3 Freeman St., P.O. Box 421, Provincetown, MA 02657 (© **508/487-2313;** www.ptown.org), open Monday to Friday from 10am to 2pm.

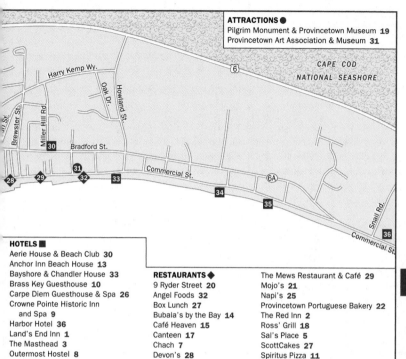

5

CAPE COD | Provincetown

Where to Stay

For last-minute availability, check out www.ptown.org to see a list of all available rooms in town.

EXPENSIVE

Anchor Inn Beach House ★★   This inn is in a historic waterfront house that's closer to the west end of town, not right in the middle of things but a 2-minute walk to the center. Decor in the rooms varies, from cottage-style, with wicker, to handmade furniture from the West Indies and classic English chintz. The suites have 2-person whirlpool tubs and balconies overlooking the harbor. The waterview rooms are more expensive and worth the price.

175 Commercial St. (in the center of town), Provincetown. ℂ **800/858-2657** or 508/487-0432. www.anchorinnbeachhouse.com. 23 units. Summer $275–$415 double. Rates include continental breakfast. **Amenities:** Wi-Fi (free).

Brass Key Guesthouse ★★★   This was the first hotel to bring luxury lodging to Provincetown, and it remains one of the top inns in town. The property consists of a number of historic homes, including the 1790s main inn building, that have been converted into hotel rooms. Rooms are spread out in 10 buildings, including 3 small cottages that have just one unit apiece. Just as the buildings in the compound are of different architectural styles, the rooms are all different, but the common denominator is comfort. From the beds to the seating areas to the amenities, every need has been anticipated. There are two dog-friendly rooms.

67 Bradford St. (in the center of town), Provincetown. ℂ **800/842-9858** or 508/487-9005. www. brasskey.com. 43 units. Summer $349–$469 double, $499–$729 suites. Rates include continental breakfast and afternoon wine-and-cheese hour. Closed late Nov to early Apr. No children 16 and under. **Amenities:** Bar; 17-ft. hot tub; outdoor heated pool, Wi-Fi (free).

Carpe Diem Guesthouse & Spa ★★★

The owners of this first-class inn in the heart of Provincetown are continually upgrading and improving. The 2006 addition of a second house to the property allowed the creation of a Zen garden between the two buildings. In 2007, the Namaste Spa, offering massage, aromatherapy, and wraps, opened. In 2013, the inn expanded again with a large yoga and meditation room. In the morning, the inn serves a German-style breakfast (the home country of the owners), complete with eggs cooked to order, Belgian waffles, and quiche.

12–14 Johnson St. (in the center of town), Provincetown. ℂ **800/487-0132** or 508/487-4242. www. carpediemguesthouse.com. 19 units. Summer $299–$319 double; $379–$419 suites; $419-489 cottage. Rates include full breakfast and wine-and-cheese hour. **Amenities:** 6-person hot tub; Wi-Fi (free).

Crowne Pointe Historic Inn and Spa ★★

A historic sea captain's house, restored and expanded, has been turned into this luxury hotel with a fine restaurant and a spa. Six buildings make up the compound; although all the rooms differ in size, and some have fireplaces and whirlpool tubs, they all have very comfortable beds with high-end linens. The decor is modern, with muted colors. There's one dog-friendly room.

82 Bradford St. (in the center of town), Provincetown. ℂ **877/CROWNE1** (276-9631) or 508/487-6767. www.crownepointe.com. 35 units. Summer $299–$419 double; $459-$499 suites. Rates include full breakfast, afternoon tea and cookies, and wine-and-cheese hour. **Amenities:** Restaurant (dinner only); bar; 2 10-person outdoor Jacuzzis; heated outdoor pool; spa; Wi-Fi (free). No children under 16.

Land's End Inn ★★★

Probably the most unique property in a town of unique properties, this house was originally built as a bungalow in 1904, high up on Gull Hill, which is on the far west end of Commercial Street. Subsequent owners turned it into a guest house and later an over-the-top valentine to Victoriana that straddled the line, and sometimes crossed over, into kitsch. The tower rooms (there are three), which have 360-degree views of the Cape's tip, are perhaps the most exceptional rooms on the Cape. It is a long walk into town from here. Consider renting a bike if you plan to make the trek often. Dogs are allowed in 7 rooms.

22 Commercial St. (in the West End), Provincetown. ℂ **800/276-7088** or 508/487-0706. www. landsendinn.com. 18 units. Summer $360–$590 double; $460–$570 tower rooms. Rates include continental breakfast and wine-and-cheese hour. **Amenities:** Wi-Fi (free).

Watermark Inn ★★

It is often hard to get a reservation at the Watermark in season, because those who discover it go back year after year. It is a find. The inn sits directly on the sand, the water sometimes lapping up to the stairs from your unit down to the beach. The interiors are light, breezy, and modern. Each unit is a suite with a kitchenette and a private deck. A couple of the suites do not face the water—you want one that does.

603 Commercial St. (in the East End), Provincetown. ℂ **508/487-0165.** www.watermark-inn.com. 10 units. Summer $220–$500 suite; weekly $1,410–$3,200. **Amenities:** Wi-Fi (free).

MODERATE

Aerie House & Beach Club ★★   There is a lot of variety in the rooms here: Those in the house on Bradford Street are less expensive and include rooms with shared baths. The four deluxe rooms at the Beach Club property at 425 Commercial Street are steps from the beach and have waterfront decks. There are also suites and efficiencies for those who prefer to have a kitchenette. In season, the inn provides a fleet of bicycles for guests.

184 Bradford St. (in the East End), Provincetown. ℂ **800/487-1197** or 508/487-1197. www.aeriehouse. com. 11 units, 3 with shared bathroom. Summer $150 double with shared bathroom; $180–$350 double. MC, V. Well-behaved dog allowed with prior permission. **Amenities:** Bikes; Jacuzzi. Free Wi-Fi.

Bayshore and Chandler House ★★   Twenty-five individually decorated apartments can be found at Bayshore (16 units) and Chandler House (6 units) on the east end of town and 77 Commercial Street (1 unit) on the far west end of town, perhaps the ideal place to stay if you want extra privacy and a water view. All the buildings are on the beach side of Commercial Street. The units all have separate entrances and complete kitchenettes. The Bayshore property is perhaps the prettiest with a courtyard full of flowers in season.

Bayshore: 493 Commercial St. (in the East End), Provincetown. Chandler House: 480 Commercial St., Provincetown. ℂ **508/487-9133.** www.bayshorechandler.com. 23 units, 20 with tub/shower combination, 3 with shower. Summer $1,450–$3,800 weekly; shoulder season daily $110–$275. Dogs allowed with advance notice. **Amenities:** Wi-Fi (free).

Harbor Hotel ★★   This is one jazzy motel. It is way off the main drag, though, so guests have to bike or take a free town shuttle bus, taxi, or pedicab to get to the center of town, where parking is almost impossible in season. The contemporary and primarily white rooms are enlivened with vibrant colors on the walls and bedding. The Whaler's Lounge serves three meals daily, and there's also a poolside bar.

698 Commercial St. (at Rte. 6A, in the East End), Provincetown. ℂ **800/422-4224** or 508/487-1711. www.harborhotelptown.com. 129 units. Summer $259–$309 double, $329–$359 suites. Rates include continental breakfast. Open year-round. Dogs allowed. **Amenities:** Restaurant; outdoor pool; Wi-Fi (free).

The Masthead ★★   The harborfront compound offers a wide range of lodging options, from singles with shared bathrooms to three-bedroom suites with water views. The property was popular with celebrities in decades past, which is why some rooms have names like the Isabella Rossellini Cottage, Mrs. Bob Hope room, Billy Joel efficiency, and Helena Rubenstein cottage. Hang out on the sun deck along the 450-foot private beach and you never know who you might meet.

31–41 Commercial St. (in the West End), Provincetown. ℂ **800/395-5095** or 508/487-0523. www. themasthead.com. 21 units, 2 with shared bathroom, 3 with tub/shower combination, 16 with shower; 4 cottages. Summer $125–$130 double with shared bathroom; $179–$379 double; $289–$359 efficiency and 1-bedroom; $422–$692 2-bedroom apt; $2,954–$4,844 cottage weekly.

Sage Inn & Lounge ★★   In a historic house set back from the street, this sleek, modern and hip hotel is in the heart of P'town's Commercial Street. In the off-season, the owners offer guest rooms to those affiliated with the town's art nonprofits.

336 Commercial St., Provincetown. ℂ **508/487-6424.** www.sageinnptown.com. 19 units. Summer $250 double. Dogs allowed. **Amenities:** Wi-Fi (free).

INEXPENSIVE

Outermost Hostel ★   If you feel like roughing it, head over to this tiny compound of tiny houses, P'town's version of a hostel. Rates are the best in town. There are five units with bunk beds, so you share those with other guests, as in a typical hostel. The bunks fill up fast.

28 Winslow St. (near the Pilgrim Monument), Provincetown. ℂ **508/487-4378.** www.outermost hostel.com. 40 beds. Summer $25 per bunk.

Where to Eat
EXPENSIVE

Devon's ★★★ NEW AMERICAN   This intimate 37-seat restaurant, a repurposed boat shack, turns out some of the best meals in town. The focus is on local and organic foods. Look for unusual combinations on the small but precise menu. For starters, the lobster cake contains strawberries. Among the main courses, the day boat scallops have a pineapple-dill-anchovy sauce. Dessert extravagances include the Callebaut chocolate pot au crème. This is also a popular place for breakfast; the prime seats are in the front patio.

401½ Commercial St. (in the East End). ℂ **508/487-4773.** www.devons.org. Main courses $18–$25. June–Sept daily 8am–1pm and 5:30–10pm; call for off-season hours. Closed Mid-Oct–mid-May.

The Mews Restaurant & Cafe ★★ INTERNATIONAL/AMERICAN FUSION   This granddaddy of the Provincetown restaurant scene can be counted on for great food and service. Downstairs is more formal, where the sandy beach is right out the window and the menu has the likes of filet mignon with béarnaise sauce. Upstairs is an upscale lounge, and the menu includes lower-priced bistro fare. This is where to find roasted chicken with lingonberry cream sauce and top-notch burgers.

429 Commercial St. ℂ **508/487-1500.** www.mews.com. Main courses $21–$37. Mid-June to early Sept daily 6–10pm, Sun brunch 11am–2:30pm; early Dec to mid-Feb daily 6–10pm; call for off-season hours.

Napi's ★★ INTERNATIONAL   Checking out Napi's art collection is one of the main reasons to come to this big barn of a restaurant. Antique stained glass, carousel horses, and even a gorgeous chimney are worth the trip. The menu is massive and hits almost every country worth its culinary salt, including Chinese, Greek, and Japanese, and that's just in the appetizer section. Fish served a variety of ways is a specialty. There is a large portion of the menu that's vegetarian.

7 Freeman St. (at Bradford St.). ℂ **800/571-6274.** www.napis-restaurant.com. Main courses $18–$36. May to mid-Sept daily 5–9:30pm; Oct to Apr daily 11:30am–4pm and 5–9pm.

9 Ryder Seaside Dining ★★★ ITALIAN   This is a real find, a harbor shack converted into an intimate little restaurant. Candles twinkle and historic photos of old Provincetown line the walls. Servers are a bit more professional than usual on the Cape, the better to explain the menu items and make educated recommendations. That's how I ended up eating the divine native littleneck clams in white wine sauce. Menu items are recognizable as traditional old-fashioned Italian cuisine—scampi and chicken parmigiana, for instance—but made with very high-quality ingredients that make them seem new. Gluten-free pasta is available on request.

9 Ryder St. (on the pier at Fisherman's Wharf/Cabral's Marina), Provincetown. ℂ **508/487-9990.** 9ryder.com. Main courses $17–$33. Open mid-May to mid-Oct.

The Red Inn ★★ NEW AMERICAN   It's a lovely expedition to go to the far west end of Commercial Street to this bright red restaurant, which is set on the harbor, covered with flowers, and looks like something out of a fairy tale. Dinner here is best done for very special occasions, when price is no object and its formality will be appreciated. The best part is the view; there are no bad seats. Be prepared for a substantial meal. The lobster and artichoke fondue, is very hard to resist, so don't even try. Sitting this close to the water, it's hard to pass up fish. The local scallops are served with orzo and a buttery citrus sauce. The warm bread pudding comes with a white-chocolate and Frangelico sauce.

15 Commercial St. ✆ **508/487-7334.** www.theredinn.com. Main courses $26–$38. Mid-May to early Oct daily 5:30–10:30pm, call for off-season hours.

Ross' Grill ★★★ NEW AMERICAN BISTRO

This is the most unabashedly urban restaurant in P'town, one that wouldn't be out of place in Boston or even New York. The restaurant is on the second floor of Whaler's Wharf, with terrific views out to the harbor. But in such a clubby atmosphere, you almost feel like turning your back to the view and focusing on the matters at hand, the fine food and the expert service. This is one for the meat-lovers, with filet mignon and over-roasted rack of lamb. The wine list is one of the most extensive in town. Tapas are served at happy hour, when a raw bar is also on hand.

237 Commercial St. (in the Whaler's Wharf). ✆ **508/487-8878.** www.rossgrillptown.com. Main courses $22–$40. May to mid-Sept Mon and Wed–Sat noon–2:30pm and 5:30–9:30pm, Sun noon–3pm and 5:30–9pm; call for off-season hours.

Sal's Place ★★ SOUTHERN ITALIAN

Sal's, begun in 1962 by the artist Sal Del Deo, has been a standby in recent years for an old-fashioned Italian meal. But a new young chef/owner has taken over and freshened up the space and the menu—there's now a Living Well menu section with healthier foods, for instance, as well as vegetarian, vegan and gluten-free offerings. Traditional dishes, remain, though, such seafood Fra Diavolo, with fresh shellfish and fish in a spicy marinara broth. Seating is inside or outside on the deck, which has harbor views.

99 Commercial St. (in the West End). ✆ **508/487-1279.** www.salsplaceofprovincetown.com. Main courses $25–$42. Apr–Oct daily 5:30–9:30pm; call for off-season hours.

Victor's ★★ NEW AMERICAN/TAPAS

Travel to the far west end of town to find this gem, which serves tapas in a dining room with a cathedral ceiling and a large stone fireplace that makes it a welcoming place to settle. The chef leans toward healthier offerings; menu innovations include a deconstructed ahi tuna "napoleon," dusted with chamomile; and the impossibly rich lobster and edamame (raw soybean) risotto with mascarpone. The raw bar from 4 to 6pm serves 99-cent oysters.

175 Bradford St. Ext. (in the West End, near W. Vine). ✆ **508/487-1777.** www.victorsptown.com. Tapas $12–$27. June–Sept daily 3–6pm (raw bar) and 5–10pm (Sun also 9am–2pm); call for off-season hours. Closed Nov to late April.

MODERATE

Bubala's by the Bay ★ INTERNATIONAL

People-watching is the name of the game here. There is really no better place to do it than the immense patio in the front of the restaurant. Inside, there is a large colorful wall mural that speaks to the light-heartedness of the whole enterprise. The international flavor is apparent on the menu where there are quesadillas next to Thai spring rolls. This isn't fine dining and if anything, it is a little overpriced for what it is, but it's good for lunch or a light snack.

185 Commercial St. (in the West End). ✆ **508/487-0773.** www.bubalas.com. Main courses $9–$29. Mid-Apr to late Oct daily 11am–11pm. Closed late Oct to mid-Apr.

Canteen ★★★ INTERNATIONAL   The three owners of this restaurant were inspired by summer dinner parties to create a twist on summer shack favorites like lobster rolls and fish-and-chips. This is a good place to try something you've never had, like kale and quinoa salad or the very unusual but delicious cod *bánh mì* (a saudwich with marinated cod, pickled diakon radishes, and carrots, cucumber, cilantro, mint, aioli and sriracha sauce). There are also more typical items like fish and chips, that for some reason taste much better here.

225 Commercial St. (center of town), Provincetown. ✆ **508/487-3800.** thecanteenptown.com. Main courses $10–$20. June-Aug daily 11am–9pm. Call for off-season hours. Closed Nov–April.

Local 186 ★★ BURGERS   Hands-down—the best burgers in town, and the house-made condiments, including the bacon jam, are wonderful, as are the fries. They may try to up-sell you to the Kobe burger; let them. They also have great veggie burgers. On the lower level, the Grotto Bar has wild local acts and DJ dance parties late at night on weekends. A guest house upstairs has 4 rooms available.

186 Commercial St. (in the West End). ✆ **508/487-7555.** www.enzolives.com. Reservations not accepted. Main courses $12–$21. July–Aug daily 11am–10pm; call for off-season hours. Closed Feb–May.

The Lobster Pot ★ SEAFOOD   Yes, it is an institution. And you could do a lot worse than making your way to the upper level of the Lobster Pot and ordering a steaming bowl of Tim's clam chowder while you watch the boats come and go from the harbor. Or make a meal of it and order one of the signature bouillabaisses and stews, including cioppino.

321 Commercial St. (in the center of town). ✆ **508/487-0842.** www.ptownlobsterpot.com. Main courses $13–$32. Mid-June to mid-Sept daily 11:30am–10:30pm; call for off-season hours. Closed Dec–March.

INEXPENSIVE

Cafe Heaven ★ AMERICAN   Café Heaven, a small storefront cafe in the west end of town, wins the prize for best breakfast in Provincetown. Big bold paintings adore the walls of this casual spot and the large windows look out on bustling Commercial Street. Freshly baked breads, omelets overstuffed with veggies, and stacks of pancakes with fruit toppings are all on the menu. In high season, get here early before all the tables fill up. Lunch features European-influenced sandwiches and salads, such as the avocado and goat cheese on a baguette.

199 Commercial St. (in the West End). ✆ **508/487-9639.** Most item under $15. Late June–Aug daily 8am–2pm; call for off-season hours. Closed Nov–May.

Chach ★ DINER   This new take on the classic diner is chef-owned (by Chach, natch)—everything is homemade. Breakfast options, like the French toast with blackberry crumble or the breakfast quesadilla, really are worth waking up for. For lunch, try the beer-battered crispy cod sandwich with homemade cole slaw, or the Reuben, piled high with corned beef. Chach is off the beaten path a bit, but those in the know fill the place up early in season.

73 Shank Painter Rd. (off Bradford St., a few blocks south of town). ✆ **508/487-1530.** Most items under $15. July and August 8am–2pm. Call for off-season hours. Closed Mar.

Spiritus Pizza ★ PIZZA/ICE CREAM   At one o'clock in the morning, this is the unofficial center of town, as bar habitués head here for late-night snack and the front patio becomes an after-hours meet-and-greet (a polite way of saying a hook-up joint).

The pizza here has a thin, chewy crust; it's a little greasy and pretty satisfying when you're hungry. Pizza is served until 1am and beyond, depending on demand. Emack and Bolio's ice cream finishes the meal.

190 Commercial St. (©) **508/487-2808.** www.spirituspizza.com. Pizzas $18–$25. No credit cards. Apr–Oct daily 11:30am–2am. Closed Nov–Mar.

TAKEOUT & PICNIC FARE

Angel Foods, 467 Commercial St., in the East End (© **508/487-6666;** www.angel foods.com), is an upscale takeout shop with Italian specialties and other scrumptious prepared foods to go. Open 7am to 8pm.

Many of the offerings at **Box Lunch,** 353 Commercial St. (© **508/487-6026;** www. boxlunch.com), especially the "rollwiches"—pita bread packed with a wide range of fillings—are ideal for a strolling lunch. Open 8:30am to 8pm.

One thing you absolutely have to do while in town is to sample the *pasties* (meat pies) and pastries at **Provincetown Portuguese Bakery,** 299 Commercial St., in the center of town (© **508/487-1803**). Point to a few and take your surprise package out on the pier for delectation. Open daily 7am to 11pm. Closed November to early April.

Some tasty pizza slices can be found at **Twist'd Sisters New York Pizza ★**, at 293 Commercial St. (© **508/487-6973;** www.twistdsisters.com), which is conveniently located near Macmillan Wharf. The creative toppings include breaded eggplant. Open 10am to 2am.

Exploring: Beaches & Recreational Pursuits

BEACHES   Provincetown has miles of beaches. The 3-mile bay beach that lines the harbor, though certainly swimmable, is not all that inviting compared to the magnificent ocean beaches overseen by the National Seashore. The two official access areas (see below) tend to be crowded; however, you can always find a less densely populated stretch if you're willing to hike.

Note: Local beachgoer activists have been lobbying for "clothing-optional" beaches for years, but the rangers, fearful of voyeurs trampling the dune grass, are firmly opposed and routinely issue tickets, so stand forewarned (and clothed).

o **Herring Cove ★★★** and **Race Point ★★★**: Both National Seashore beaches are spectacular, with long stretches of pristine sand, and they are very popular. Herring Cove, facing west, is known for its spectacular sunsets; observers often applaud. Race Point, on the ocean side, is rougher, and you might actually spot whales en route to Stellwagen Bank. Calmer Herring Cove is a haven for same-sex couples. Parking costs $15 per day, $45 per season.

o **Long Point:** Trek out over the breakwater and beyond by catching a water shuttle to visit this very last spit of land, capped by an 1827 lighthouse. Locals call it "the end of the earth." Shuttles run hourly from 9am to 5pm in July and August—$10 one-way, $15 round-trip; hourly in season, or by demand off-season—from Flyer's Boat Rental (see "Boating," below), located at slip 2 on MacMillan Wharf (© **508/487-0898**).

BICYCLING   North of town, nestled amid the Cape Cod National Seashore preserve, is one of the more spectacular bike paths in New England, the 7-mile **Province Lands Trail ★★**, a heady swirl of steep dunes (watch out for sand drifts on the path) anchored by wind-stunted scrub pines. With its free parking, the **Province Lands Visitor Center ★** (© **508/487-1256;** www.nps.gov/caco) is a good place to start: You can survey the landscape from the observation tower to try to get your bearings before

whale-watching: A PRIME P-TOWN PASTIME

In 1975, 4 years after the U.S. government—fearing the species' extinction—called an official halt to whaling, fisherman Al Avellar noticed that they seemed to be making a comeback in the Stellwagen Bank feeding area, 8 miles off Provincetown. Together with marine biologist Charles "Stormy" Mayo of the Center for Coastal Studies, he came up with the notion of a new kind of hunt, spearheaded by tourists bearing cameras. An immediate success, the **Dolphin Fleet/Portuguese Princess** ★★, which works with the Center for Coastal Studies and uses its naturalists on the trips, on MacMillan Wharf (✆ **800/826-9300** or 508/240-3636; www.whalewatch.com), was widely copied up and down the coast. These are still the prime feeding grounds, however, which is why all the whale-watching fleets can confidently "guarantee" sightings—they offer a rain check should the cetaceans fail to surface. Prices for whale-watching trips are $39 for adults, $36 for seniors, $29 for children 5 to 12, and free for children 4 and under. Discounts of $3 off are available for AAA memberships and by using coupons available at the chamber of commerce.

Another good Cape Cod whale-watch organization is **Capt. John Boats,** which operates 4-hour trips daily in season out of Plymouth Harbor in Plymouth, about 20 miles north of the Sagamore Bridge (✆ **800/242-2469** or 508/746-2643; www.captjohn.com). Prices are $43 for adults, $36 for seniors 62 and over, and $29 for children 12 and under.

On most cruises, running commentary is provided by naturalists with various qualifications. The naturalists aboard the *Portuguese Princess* are Center for Coastal Studies scientists who do research crucial to the whales' survival. Part of the proceeds go to the center's efforts. Serious whale aficionados can take a daylong trip to the Great South Channel, where humpbacks and finbacks are likely to be found by the dozen.

Some tips for first-timers: Dress very warmly, in layers (it's cold out on the water), and definitely take along a windbreaker, waterproof if possible. The weather is capricious, and if you stand in the bow of the boat, the best viewing point, you can count on getting drenched. Veteran whale-watchers know to bring a spare set of dry clothes, as well as binoculars—although if the whales seem to be feeling friendly and frisky, as they often are, they'll play practically within reach of the boat. And last but not least, if you're prone to seasickness, bring along some motion-sickness pills: It can get pretty rough out there.

setting off amid the dizzying maze. Signs point to spur paths leading to Race Point or Herring Cove beaches. The most centrally located bike rental store is **Arnold's Where You Rent The Bikes** (✆ 508/487-0844), at 329 Commercial St., near MacMillan Wharf. Bike rentals are also offered May through October at **Gale Force Bikes,** at 144 Bradford St. (✆ 508/487-4849; www.galeforcebikes.com), in the West End. The Province Lands Trail begins nearby. The Beach Market, on-site at Gale Force Bikes, offers delicious sandwiches and wraps and other picnic fare for your ride. It's also an easy jaunt from town, where you'll find plenty of good bike shops—such as **Ptown Bikes,** at 42 Bradford St. (✆ 508/487-8735; www.ptownbikes.com), where you should reserve several days in advance during high season. Bike rentals cost $22 to $25 for 24 hours.

BOATING In addition to operating a Long Point shuttle from its own dock (see "Beaches," above), **Flyer's Boat Rental,** at 131A Commercial St., in the West End (✆ **508/487-0898;** www.flyersboats.com)—established in 1945—offers all sorts of crafts, from kayaks ($30–$50 half-day for singles and tandems) to various sailboats ($60–$90 for a half-day).

Organized Tours

Art's Dune Tours ★★ In 1946, Art Costa started driving sightseers out to ogle the decrepit "dune shacks," where such transient luminaries as Eugene O'Neill, Jack Kerouac, and Jackson Pollock found their respective muses; in one such hovel, Tennessee Williams cooked up "A Streetcar Named Desire." The park service wanted to raze these eyesores, but luckily, saner heads prevailed: They're now National Historic Landmarks. The tours conducted by Art's son and others, via Chevy Suburban, typically take about 1 to 1½ hours and are filled with wonderful stories of local literati and other characters.

At the corner of Commercial and Standish sts. (in the center of town). ✆ **800/894-1951** or 508/487-1950. www.artsdunetours.com. Admission 1-hr. tour $26 adults, $17 children 6–11; sunset tours (2 hr.) $42 adults, $24 children. Call for schedule and reservations.

Bay Lady II ★★ In sightseeing aboard this 73-foot reproduction gaff-rigged Grand Banks schooner, you'll actually add to the scenery for onlookers on shore. The sunset trip is especially spectacular.

MacMillan Wharf (in the center of town). ✆ **508/487-9308.** www.sailcapecod.com. Admission $20–$25 adults, $12–$20 children 12 and under. Mid-May to mid-Oct 2-hr. sails daily at 10am, 12:30pm, 3:30pm, and 7pm; call for reservations. Closed mid-Oct to mid-May.

Provincetown Museums

Pilgrim Monument & Provincetown Museum ★★ The 252-foot Pilgrim Monument is the town's way of reminding everyone that the Pilgrims arrived here first. (Take that Plymouth.) It is the tallest all-granite structure in the country. A climb to the top is a must as you can appreciate the curl of the Cape's arm and how the Cape's tip is essentially a sandbar, between Cape Cod Bay and the Atlantic Ocean. The museum at the foot of the monument contains a variety of colorful exhibits. Is that a polar bear over there? Yes, Admiral Donald Macmillan, the first to the North Pole, was raised in Provincetown. There are playbills from the Provincetown Players, a group that had Eugene O'Neill as a member, and even a replica dune shack, of the type lived in by Harry Kemp, who was called "the poet of the dunes."

High Pole Hill Rd. (off Winslow St., north of Bradford St.). ✆ **508/487-1310.** www.pilgrim-monument.org. Admission $12 adults, $10 seniors 62 and up, $4 children 4–14. July to mid-Sept daily 9am–7pm; off-season daily 9am–5pm. Last admission 45 min. before closing. Closed Dec–Mar.

Provincetown Art Association & Museum ★★★ In 1914, a group of Provincetown artists and businesspeople who supported the arts came together to build a collection of works by Outer Cape artists. Now, a century that first group gathered, PAAM has collected 3,000 works and morphed into a pillar of the community, with exhibitions, lectures, workshops and cultural events. The contemporary wing, built onto the old captain's house in 2006, has given the museum more space for exhibits and classes, not to mention an air of contemporary sophistication.

460 Commercial St. (in the East End). ✆ **508/487-1750.** www.paam.org. Admission $10. July–Aug Mon–Thurs 11am–8pm, Fri 11am–10pm (free 5–10pm), Sat–Sun 11am–5pm; call for off-season hours.

Shopping

ART GALLERIES

Berta Walker is a force to be reckoned with, having nurtured many top artists through her association with the Fine Arts Work Center before opening her own gallery in 1990. At **Berta Walker Gallery,** 208 Bradford St., in the East End (*C* **508/487-6411;** www.bertawalker.com), the historic holdings span Charles Hawthorne, Milton Avery, and Robert Motherwell. Closed late October to late May.

The **Fine Arts Works Center** displays weekly shows that are always worth checking out in its **Hudson D. Walker Gallery,** 24 Pearl St., in the center of town (*C* **508/487-9960;** www.fawc.org). The center is the heart of creativity in town, as it supports a crew of creative artists and writers on fellowships in residence every year.

Ehva Gallery, 74 Shank Painter Rd., in the west end between Bradford St. and Rte. 6 (*C* **508/487-0011;** www.galleryehva.com), is way off the beaten track but worth a visit. The sculpture garden is a treat. Closed January to mid-February.

Julie Heller started collecting early P-town paintings as a child—and as a tourist at that. She chose so incredibly well that her roster at **Julie Heller Gallery ★★**, 2 Gosnold St., on the beach in the center of town (*C* **508/487-2166**), and at 465 Commercial St. (*C* **508/487-2169;** www.juliehellergallery.com), reads like a who's who of local art. Hawthorne, Avery, Hofmann, Lazzell, Hensche—all the big names from Provincetown's past are here, as well as some contemporary artists. Closed weekdays January to April. Open winter weekends by chance or appointment.

At the far east end of town at the corner of Howland Street is a former church building that houses two galleries. **Schoolhouse Gallery ★**, 494 Commercial St. (*C* **508/487-4800;** www.schoolhouseprovincetown.com), specializes in modern and contemporary painting, photography, and printmaking. The **ArtStrand Gallery ★** (*C* **508/487-1153;** www.artstrand.com), in the back of the building, shows the work of nine of the town's most prominent artists.

BOOKS

Provincetown Bookshop, 246 Commercial St. (*C* **508/487-0964**), has the most complete selection in town. You'll find all the bestsellers, as well as books about the region and local lore.

DISCOUNT SHOPPING

Marine Specialties ★, 235 Commercial St., in the center of town (*C* **508/487-1730;** www.marspec.net), is packed with useful stuff, from discounted Doc Martens to Swiss Army knives and all sorts of odd nautical surplus whose uses will suggest themselves to you eventually. Be sure to look up: Hanging from the ceiling are some real antiques, including several carillons' worth of ships' bells.

Provincetown After Dark

THE CLUB SCENE

The Atlantic House The "A-House" is the only year-round dance club in P'town. The three sections of the club are the Little Bar, which has a jukebox; the Macho Bar, a leather bar, and the Big Room, for dancing. The building is actually one of the oldest in town (1798) and some of the club's history can be seen from the photos on the walls, including a famous one of Tennessee Williams walking along in the buff along a Provincetown beach. Though the clientele is predominantly gay, everyone is welcome. 6 Masonic Pl. (off Commercial St., 2 blocks west of Town Hall). *C* **508/487-3821.** www.ahouse.com. Cover $5–$10 for the Big Room.

Crown & Anchor The Crown and Anchor is the biggest and most varied entertainment venue in town, plus it has hotel rooms and a restaurant. The massive complex in the center of town has six separate gay bars including the largest nightclub (The Paramount); a video bar (Wave); a cabaret venue, a poolside bar; a piano bar; and a leather bar (The Vault). Closed November to April. 247 Commercial St. (in the center of town). *C* **508/487-1430.** www.onlyatthecrown.com. Cover $20–$30 for shows.

Post Office Café and Cabaret No nightclub listing is complete without the Post Office, a small club that tends to have the top acts in town, particularly in the realm of drag and comedy. Closed November to April. 303 Commercial St. (in the center of town). *C* **508/487-0006.** Cover $22.

THE BAR SCENE

Governor Bradford A good old bar with pool tables, drag karaoke (summer nights at 9:30pm), and disco. 312 Commercial St. (in the center of town). *C* **508/487-2781.**

Harbor Lounge ★★ Walk through a long courtyard and pass some stores to find this modern, minimalist bar overlooking the beach. This is only drinks, no food. But what a terrific place to have a cocktail: You are essentially in a three-sided glass box (sliders that can open and let the breeze through) overlooking the beach. Seating is on leather sofas. A little pier sticks out the back. The bar is open noon to 10pm. 359 Commercial St. (in the center of town). *C* **508/413-9527.** www.theharborlounge.com.

Patio A large outdoor seating area on Commercial Street makes this a terrific place to sip summer cocktails and people-watch. Tasty appetizers, desserts, light fare, and even whole dinners are served until 11pm. The interior holds a sleek, attractive bar. 328 Commercial St. (in the center of town). *C* **508/487-4003.** www.ptownpatio.com.

Nor'East Beer Garden This open-air bar also features good food. There are 16 craft beers on draft, like Founders Curmudgeon out of Grand Rapids, and 26 more in bottles. 206 Commercial St. (on the west end of town). *C* **508/487-BEER.** Closed mid-Oct to mid-May.

The Squealing Pig ★ No, it's not a gay bar, but there are usually gay people here. It's not a sports bar either, but there is often sports on the TVs. It might be a pickup bar, but everyone seems to know everyone else. In a town of great bars, this is one of the best. Good food, too. 335 Commercial St. (in the center of town). *C* **508/487-5804.** www. squealingpigptown.com.

PERFORMANCE

Art House ★★ Art house films are just the beginning of the programming at this centrally located modern movie palace on Commercial Street. The summer season is packed with a parade of well-known performers, be they drag legends, like Varla Jean Merman, nationally known comedians, like Andrea Martin, or musicians, like Well Strung, a hunky classical quartet. Performances are given mid-May to mid-September from 7 to 10pm. Films are shown in the off-season. 214 Commercial St. (in the center of town). *C* **508/487-9222.** www.ptownarthouse.com. Admission $25–$30.

The Provincetown Theater ★★ Provincetown is considered the birthplace of modern American theater. Both Eugene O'Neill and Tennessee Williams spent time here. O'Neill even lived in the old coast guard station and staged his first plays in a shack on a P'town wharf. New plays and revivals are staged here in the summer; many are exciting works that may be bound for Boston or even New York. Other events take place here year-round including readings, movies, lectures and more. 238 Bradford St. (2 blocks east of Howland St.). *C* **800/791-7487** or 508/487-9793 (box office), 508/487-7487, or 866/811-4111 (Theatre Mania). www.provincetowntheater.org. Ticket prices vary.

MARTHA'S VINEYARD & NANTUCKET

New England sea captains' houses framed with white picket fences. Flying horses are alongside ice cream shops. Colorful gingerbread cottages on one end of the island and an authentic fishing village on the other. Lighthouses pierce the fog with their signals. A Native American community preserves its identity amid miles of pristine beaches and rolling farmland. Martha's Vineyard is a picturesque island indeed.

MARTHA'S VINEYARD

Essentials

VISITOR INFORMATION

Contact the **Martha's Vineyard Chamber of Commerce,** at 24 Beach St., Vineyard Haven, MA 02568 (© **800/505-4815** or 508/693-0085), or visit their website at www.mvy.com. Their office is just 2 blocks up from the ferry terminal in Vineyard Haven and is open Monday to Friday 9am to 5pm year-round, plus weekends in season. There are also information booths at the ferry terminal in Vineyard Haven; across from the Flying Horses Carousel, in Oak Bluffs; and on Church Street, in Edgartown.

GETTING THERE

BY FERRY   Most visitors take the ferry service connecting the Vineyard and the mainland. If you're traveling via car or bus, you will most likely catch the ferry from Woods Hole, in the town of Falmouth, on Cape Cod; however, boats do run from Falmouth Inner Harbor, Hyannis, New Bedford, Rhode Island, and Nantucket. On weekends in season, the Steamship Authority ferries make more than 25 trips a day to Martha's Vineyard from Woods Hole (two other companies provide an additional 12 passenger ferries a day from Falmouth Inner Harbor).

The state-run **Steamship Authority** (www.steamshipauthority.com) runs the show in Woods Hole (© **508/477-8600** early Apr to early Sept daily 8am–5pm, or 508/693-9130 daily 8am–5pm) and operates every day, year-round (weather permitting). It maintains the only ferries to Martha's Vineyard that accommodate cars in addition to passengers and makes about 20 crossings a day in season. The large ferries make the 45-minute trip to Vineyard Haven throughout the year; some boats go to Oak Bluffs from late May to late October (call for seasonal schedules). During the summer, you'll need a reservation to bring your car to the island, and you must reserve *months in advance* to secure a spot. If you plan to bring your car over to the island, plan to get to the Woods Hole terminal at least 30 minutes before your scheduled departure.

Many people prefer to leave their cars on the mainland, take the ferry (often with their bikes), and then rent a car, Jeep, or bicycle on the island. You can park your car at the Woods Hole lot (always full in the summer) or at one of the many lots in Falmouth and Bourne that absorb the overflow of cars during the summer months; parking is $10 to $12 per day. Plan to arrive at the parking lots in Falmouth at least an hour before sailing time to allow for parking, taking the free shuttle bus to the ferry terminal, and buying your ferry ticket. Free shuttle buses (some equipped for bikes) run regularly from the outlying lots to the Woods Hole ferry terminal.

The cost of a round-trip passenger ticket on the ferry to Martha's Vineyard is $16 for adults and $8.50 for children 5 to 12. (Kids 4 and under ride free.) If you bring your bike along, it's an extra $8 round-trip, year-round.

You do not need a reservation on the ferry if you're traveling without a car, and no reservations are needed for parking. The cost of a round-trip car passage from April through October is $137 to $157 (depending on the size of your car); in the off season, it drops to $87 to $107. Car rates do not include drivers or passengers; you must buy tickets for each person going to the island.

Note: The Steamship Authority charges different rates for cars of different lengths. You will need to specify the make and model of your car when you place your reservation.

From Falmouth, you can board the *Island Queen* at Falmouth Inner Harbor (*€* **508/548-4800;** www.islandqueen.com) for a 35-minute cruise to Oak Bluffs (passengers only). The boat runs from late May to mid-October; round-trip fare is $20 for adults, $10 for children 12 and under, and an extra $8 for bikes. There are seven crossings a day in season (eight on Fri and Sun), and no reservations are needed. Parking will run you $15 per calendar day. Credit cards are not accepted.

Tip: It pays to buy a round-trip ticket on the *Island Queen;* it's cheaper than two one-way tickets.

The **Falmouth–Edgartown Ferry Service,** 278 Scranton Ave. (*€* **508/548-9400;** www.falmouthferry.com), operates a 1-hour passenger ferry, called the *Pied Piper,* from Falmouth Harbor to Edgartown. The boat runs from late May to mid-October, and reservations are required. In season there are four crossings a day (more on Fri). Round-trip fares are $50 for adults and $30 for children 6 to 12. Bicycles are $10 round-trip. A second boat, the *Sandpiper,* goes from Falmouth Harbor to Vineyard Haven. It takes a half-hour and costs $25 round-trip for adults, $15 for children.

There are several options for parking. Parking is $25 per day on site. Parking is $15 per day at three satellite lots that are accessed by a trolley. Parking is $20 per day if the car is valet parked to the satellite lots.

From Hyannis, you can take the traditional **Hy-Line** ferry, Ocean Street Dock (*€* **800/492-8082;** www.hy-linecruises.com), to Oak Bluffs, late May through mid-October. They run one trip a day, and trip time is about 1 hour and 40 minutes; round-trip costs $45 for adults; children 12 and under are free ($14 round-trip for bikes).

Hy-Line also operates a year-round **fast ferry** from Hyannis to Martha's Vineyard. It departs five times daily in season and takes 55 minutes. Round-trip tickets cost $72 for adults, $48 for children.

Parking at the Hy-Line lot is $17 per calendar day in season ($10 off-season).

From Nantucket, Hy-Line (*€* **800/492-8082,** or 508/693-0112 from the Vineyard) runs one passenger-only ferries to Oak Bluffs on Martha's Vineyard from early June to

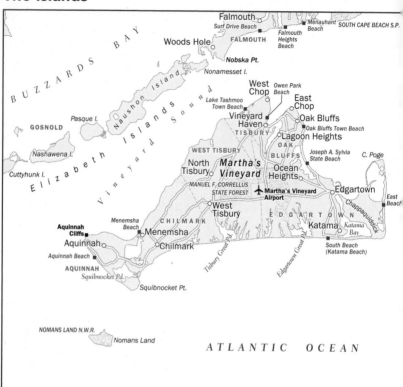

mid-September (there is no car-ferry service between the islands). The trip time is 2 hours and 15 minutes. The one-way fare is $35 for adults, $22 for children ages 5 to 12; kids 4 and under ride free; it's $7 extra for bikes. *Note:* This ferry is not for day trips, as the return boat leaves on the heels of the arriving vessel.

From New Bedford, Massachusetts, the fast ferry MV *Whaling City Express* travels to Martha's Vineyard in 1 hour. It makes six trips a day in season and is in service from late May through November. A ticket costs $35 one-way and $70 round-trip for adults; $30 one-way and $60 round-trip for seniors; and $20 one-way and $40 round-trip for children 12 and under. Contact **Seastreak Martha's Vineyard** for details (© **866/683-3779;** www.nefastferry.com).

Tip: Traveling to Martha's Vineyard from New Bedford is a great way to avoid Cape traffic and enjoy a scenic ocean cruise.

From **North Kingstown, Rhode Island,** to Oak Bluffs, Vineyard Fast Ferry runs its high-speed catamaran, *Millennium,* two to three round-trips daily from mid-June through October. The trip takes 90 minutes. The ferry leaves from Quonset Point, about 10 minutes from I-95, 15 minutes from T. F. Green Airport in Providence, and 20 minutes from the Amtrak station in Kingston. There is dockside parking. Rates are $79 round-trip for adults; $56 round-trip for children 4 to 12; and $16 round-trip for bikes. Parking next to the ferry port is $10 per calendar day. Reservations can be made by calling ✆ **401/295-4040** or by visiting www.vineyardfastferry.com.

From **New York City and New Jersey,** to Oak Bluffs, Seastreak Martha's Vineyard runs its high-speed catamaran, *Martha's Vineyard Express,* from late May to mid-October. Fares are $240 round-trip for adults, $135 round-trip for children. Bikes cost $30 round-trip. The catamaran leaves Thursdays and Fridays from New York with a stop to pick up passengers in New Jersey. It takes 6½ hours from New York to Oak Bluffs (comparable to driving and taking the ferry from Woods Hole). The ferry makes the return trip Sundays, Mondays, and Tuesdays. For more information, check out www.neferry.com or call ✆ **866/683-3779.**

BY AIR   You can fly into **Martha's Vineyard Airport,** also known as Dukes County Airport (✆ 508/693-7022), in West Tisbury, about 5 miles outside Edgartown.

Airlines serving the Vineyard include **Cape Air/Nantucket Airlines** (✆ 800/352-0714 or 508/771-6944; www.flycapeair.com), which connects the island year-round with Boston (trip time 34 min., hourly shuttle service in summer about $187 one-way); Hyannis (trip time 20 min.; $49 one-way); Nantucket (15 min.; $49 one-way); Providence, Rhode Island (trip time 25 min.; $124 one-way); and New Bedford (trip time

20 min.; $45 one-way). **US Airways** (✆ **800/428-4322;** www.usairways.com) flies from Boston for about $215 round-trip and also has seasonal weekend service from LaGuardia Airport, in New York City (trip time 1¼ hr.), which costs approximately $400 round-trip.

BY BUS **Peter Pan Bus Lines** (✆ **888/751-8800** or 508/548-7588; www.peterpan bus.com) connects the Woods Hole ferry port with South Station and Logan Airport, in Boston, as well as with New York City and Providence, Rhode Island. The trip from South Station takes about 1 hour and 35 minutes and costs about $27 one-way, $52 round-trip; from Boston's Logan Airport, the cost is $30 one-way, $55 round-trip; from Providence, the 2½-hr. trip to Woods Hole costs $30 one-way or $58 round-trip; from New York, the bus trip to Woods Hole takes about 6 hours and costs approximately $74 one-way or $123 round-trip.

BY LIMO **Falmouth Taxi** (✆ **508/548-3100**) also runs limo service from Boston and the airport. It charges $165 plus a gratuity.

GETTING AROUND

The down-island towns of Vineyard Haven, Oak Bluffs, and Edgartown are fairly compact, and if your inn is located in the heart of one of these small towns, you will be within walking distance of shopping, beaches, and attractions in town. Frequent shuttle buses can whisk you to the other down-island towns and beaches in 5 to 15 minutes. To explore the up-island towns, you will need to bike; it's possible to tour the entire island—60-some-odd miles—in a day. In season you can also take the shuttle bus up-island. Otherwise you will have to take a cab.

BY BICYCLE & MOPED You shouldn't leave without exploring the Vineyard on two wheels, even if only for a couple of hours. There's a little of everything for cyclists, from paved paths to hilly country roads (see "Beaches & Recreational Pursuits," below, for details on where to ride), and you don't have to be an expert rider to enjoy yourself. Plus, biking is a relatively hassle-free way to get around the island.

Mopeds are also a way to navigate Vineyard roads, but the number of accidents involving mopeds seems to rise every year, and many islanders are opposed to these vehicles. If you rent one, be aware they are considered quite dangerous on the island's busy, narrow, winding, sandy roads. Moped renting is banned in Edgartown.

Bike rental shops are clustered throughout all three down-island towns. Mopeds and scooters can be rented in Oak Bluffs and Vineyard Haven only, and you will need a driver's license. Bike rentals cost about $18 to $25 a day; mopeds cost $99 to $140 a day. For bike rentals in Vineyard Haven, try **Martha's Bike Rentals,** Lagoon Pond Road (✆ **800/559-0312** or 508/693-6593). For mopeds, try **Adventure Rentals,** Beach Road (✆ **508/693-1959;** www.islandadventuresmv.com). In Oak Bluffs, there's **Anderson's,** Circuit Avenue Extension (✆ **508/693-9346**), which rents bikes only; and **Sun 'n' Fun,** 26 Lake Ave. (✆ **508/693-5457;** www.sunnfunrentals.com), which also rents mopeds. In Edgartown you'll find bike rentals only at **R. W. Cutler Edgartown Bike Rentals,** 1 Main St. (✆ **800/627-2763;** www.edgartownbikerentals.com); and **Wheel Happy,** with two locations, at 204 Upper Main St. and 8 S. Water St., both in Edgartown (✆ **508/627-5928**).

BY CAR If you're coming to the Vineyard for a few days and you're going to stick to the down-island towns, it's best to leave your car at home, as traffic and parking on the island can be brutal in summer. Also, it's easy to take the shuttle buses (see "By Shuttle Bus & Trolley," below) from town to town, or you can simply bike your way around. If you're staying for a longer period of time or you want to do some exploring up-island, you should bring your car or rent one on the island—my favorite way to tour the Vineyard is by Jeep. Keep in mind that car rental rates soar during peak season, and gas is much more expensive on the island. Off-road driving on the beaches is a major topic of debate on the Vineyard, and the most popular spots may be closed for nesting piping plovers at the height of the season. If you plan to do some off-road exploration, check with the chamber of commerce to see if the trails are open to vehicles before you rent. To drive off-road at Cape Pogue or Cape Wasque on Chappaquiddick, you'll need to purchase a permit from the **Trustees of Reservations** (www.thetrustees.org); the cost is $180 for the car and $3 per person. Keep in mind that if you drive a rental car off-road without permission from the rental company, you could be subjected to a $500 fine.

There are representatives of the national car rental chains at the airport and in Vineyard Haven and Oak Bluffs. Local agencies also operate out of all three port towns, and many of them also rent Jeeps, mopeds, and bikes. The national chains include **Budget** (𝄐 **800/527-0700** or 508/693-1911; www.budget.com) and **Hertz** (𝄐 **800/654-3131;** www.hertz.com).

In Vineyard Haven, you'll find **Adventure Rentals,** Beach Road (𝄐 **508/693-1959;** www.islandadventuresmv.com), where a Jeep will run you about $199 to $249 per day in season, and a regular car costs about $140 per day. In Edgartown try **AAA Island Rentals,** 31 Circuit Ave. Ext. (𝄐 **508/627-6800**); they're also at Five Corners in Vineyard Haven (𝄐 **508/696-5300**).

BY SHUTTLE BUS & TROLLEY In season shuttle buses run often enough to make them a practical means of getting around. They are also cheap, dependable, and easy.

The **Martha's Vineyard Regional Transit Authority** (𝄐 **508/693-9440;** www.vineyardtransit.com) operates shuttle buses year-round on about a dozen routes around the island. The buses, which are white with purple logos, cost about $2 to $5 depending on distance. The formula is $1 per town. For example, Vineyard Haven to Oak Bluffs is $2, but Vineyard Haven to Edgartown (passing through Oak Bluffs) is $3. A 1-day pass is $7, and a 3-day pass is $15. The Edgartown Downtown Shuttle and the South Beach buses circle throughout town or out to South Beach every 20 minutes in season. They also stop at the free parking lots just north of the town center—this is a great way to avoid circling the streets in search of a vacant spot on busy weekends. The main down-island stops are Vineyard Haven (near the ferry terminal), Oak Bluffs (near the Civil War statue, in Ocean Park), and Edgartown (Church St., near the Old Whaling Church). From late June to early September, they run more frequently—from 6am to midnight every 15 minutes or half-hour. Hours are reduced in spring and fall. Buses also go out to Aquinnah (via the airport, West Tisbury, and Chilmark), leaving every couple of hours from down-island towns and looping about every hour through up-island towns.

For a 2½-hour bus tour of the island, call **Martha's Vineyard Siteseeing Bus Tours** (𝄐 **508/627-8687;** www.mvtour.com), or hop on one of the Island Transport buses that are stationed at the ferry terminals in Vineyard Haven and Oak Bluffs from late May to the end of September. Tours are $29 per adult, $10 for children.

BY TAXI Upon arrival you'll find taxis at all ferry terminals and at the airport, and there are permanent taxi stands in Oak Bluffs (at the Flying Horses Carousel) and Edgartown (next to the Town Wharf). Most taxi outfits operate cars as well as vans for larger groups and travelers with bikes. Cab companies on the island include **AdamCab** (𝄐 800/360-8629 or 508/627-4462), **Accurate Cab** (𝄐 508/627-9798; the only 24-hr.

service), **All Island Taxi** (𝄐 508/693-2929), **Vineyard Taxi** (𝄐 508/693-8660), **Patti's Taxi** (𝄐 508/693-1663), and **Atlantic Taxi** (𝄐 508/693-7110). Rates from town to town in summer are generally flat fees based on where you're headed and the number of passengers on board. A trip from Vineyard Haven to Edgartown would probably cost around $23 for two people. Late-night revelers should keep in mind that rates double after midnight until 7am.

THE CHAPPAQUIDDICK FERRY The **On-Time ferry** (𝄐 508/627-9427; www.chappyferry.net) runs the 5-minute trip from Memorial Wharf, on Dock Street in Edgartown, to Chappaquiddick Island (a distance of about 500 ft.) from June to mid-October daily, every 5 minutes from 6:45am to midnight. Passengers, bikes, mopeds, dogs, and cars (three at a time) are all welcome. A round-trip is $4 per person, $12 for one car/one driver, $6 for one bike/one person.

[FastFACTS] MARTHA'S VINEYARD

ATMs ATMs can be found in multiple places on and near Main Street in all three down island towns: Vineyard Haven, Oak Bluffs, and Edgartown.

Business Hours In summer most retail stores are open from 9am to 6pm. Some stay open until 8pm in July and August.

Emergencies In case of an **emergency**, call 𝄐 **911** and/or head for the **Martha's Vineyard Hospital,** 1 Hospital Rd., Oak Bluffs (𝄐 **508/693-0410**), which has a 24-hour emergency room.

Safety Martha's Vineyard is a very safe place, but as when traveling anywhere, keep an eye on your personal belongings.

Where to Stay
EDGARTOWN
Expensive
Charlotte Inn ★★ The hotel version of a Ralph Lauren advertisement, this stately inn has a hushed quality about it. The rooms are full of intriguing antiques and knick-knacks, elaborate boudoir sets and statuary. The rooms are all completely distinct. Take room 14: You enter through mahogany doors to an elegant accommodation with a fireplace and a baby grand. It's time travel, Vineyard-style.

27 S. Summer St. (in the center of town), Edgartown, MA 02539. 𝄐 **508/627-4151.** www.relais chateaux.com/charlotte. 19 units. Summer $425–$750 double; $895–$1,000 suite. No children 13 and under. **Amenities:** Restaurant.

Harbor View Hotel & Resort ★★ Still a grand old hotel, the Harborview occupies a commanding spot. Relaxing in a rocking chair on the huge verandah overlooking the harbor is something guests here have been doing for more than 100 years. The 114 rooms here are in three areas: the main building, the Governor Mayhew building, and in cottages on the grounds. Rooms have in common a high-toned elegance, on the fancy side of beachy. The two restaurants, Water Street and Henry's, serve, between them, three meals a day.

131 N. Water St. (about ½ mile northwest of Main St.), Edgartown. 𝄐 **800/225-6005** or 508/627-7000. www.harbor-view.com. 114 units. Summer $420–$650 double; $1,200 1-bedroom suite; $1,500 2-bedroom suite; $1,800–$2,100 3-bedroom suite. **Amenities:** 2 restaurants; babysitting; concierge; fitness center; heated outdoor pool; room service; spa; Wi-Fi (free).

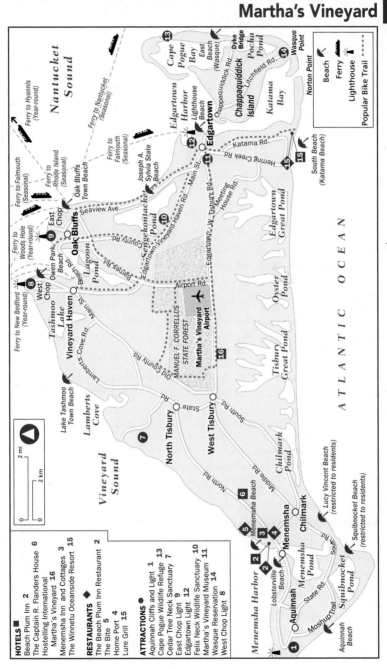

HOTELS ■
Beach Plum Inn **2**
The Captain R. Flanders House **6**
Hostelling International
Martha's Vineyard **16**
Menemsha Inn and Cottages **3**
The Winnetu Oceanside Resort **15**

RESTAURANTS ◆
The Beach Plum Inn Restaurant **2**
The Bite **5**
Home Port **4**
Lure Grill **15**

ATTRACTIONS ●
Aquinnah Cliffs and Light **1**
Cape Pogue Wildlife Refuge **13**
Cedar Tree Neck Sanctuary **7**
East Chop Light **9**
Edgartown Light **12**
Felix Neck Wildlife Sanctuary **10**
Martha's Vineyard Museum **14**
Wasque Reservation **14**
West Chop Light **8**

The Hob Knob ★★★   This very stylish B&B was inspired by the owner's grand-parents, bon vivants who gallivanted around the Ohio countryside, overflowing silver tumblers in hand. Now an eco-friendly boutique hotel, the building has served as a lodging house since at least 1947, when a windblown Senator John F. Kennedy is said to have stayed here during a sailing regatta. The interior is exceptionally stylish with a sense of humor—a cow theme crops up here and there.

128 Main St. (on Upper Main St., in the center of town), Edgartown. ✆**800/696-2723** or 508/627-9510. www.hobknob.com. 17 units, 3-bedroom and 4-bedroom cottage. Summer $485–$720 double. Rates include full breakfast and afternoon tea. No children 6 and under. **Amenities:** Rental bikes ($20 per day); exercise room; room service; spa; Wi-Fi (free).

The Victorian Inn ★★   This handsome old whaling captain's house is a block from Edgartown Harbor. This is a very well-run property, spotlessly clean and well maintained. Rooms are decorated in an old-fashioned style, with handsome antique reproductions, and some with romantic canopied beds. The breakfast is so plentiful that you might be able to skip lunch.

24 S. Water St. (in the center of town), Edgartown. ✆**508/627-4784.** www.thevic.com. 14 units, 2 with tub/shower combination, 12 with shower only. Summer $260–$425 double. Rates include full breakfast and afternoon tea. Closed Nov–Mar. **Amenities:** Wi-Fi (free).

Vineyard Square Hotel ★★   A large boutique hotel, centrally located in Edgartown, the Vineyard Square is in a complex that includes a salon and day spa, fitness center, art gallery and boutique. The rooms have all been redone in recent years in what you might call "beach modern." The more expensive ones have views of Edgartown Harbor. There's quite a variety in size, with the smallest called "cozy" rooms. Continental breakfast is a large buffet spread for guests in season. The inn's roof deck, with wonderful harbor views, is outstanding.

38 N. Water St., Edgartown. ✆**800/627–4701** or 508/627–4711. www.vineyardsquarehotel.com. 28 units. Summer $360–$590 double; $590–$1,095 suite or efficiency. Rates include continental breakfast. Closed Dec–Mar. Pets allowed in designated rooms. **Amenities:** Restaurant; fitness room; spa; Wi-Fi (free).

Winnetu Oceanside Resort ★★★   This resort, set near one of the Vineyard's best full-surf beaches, has more amenities than any other island resort—and prices to match. The rooms are all suites with one to four bedrooms. Winnetu is very much set up with families in mind. There is a children's day program, a parent/toddler program, tennis club, heated swimming pools, a fitness facility, free fitness classes and yoga on the lawn, and, perhaps most important, shuttle transportation by land or water taxi to Edgartown's Main Street. A nearby sister compound has home rentals and vacation condos.

31 Dunes Rd. (at South Beach), Edgartown. ✆**866/335-1133** or ✆508/310-1733. www.winnetu.com. 54 units. Summer $602–$720 1-bedroom suite; $1,211–$1,695 2- to 4-bedroom suite; $1,485–$1,975 2-bedroom cottages. Closed Nov–Mar. **Amenities:** Restaurant; children's program (early June to early Sept); free in-season hourly shuttle to Edgartown; concierge; fitness room; general store; outdoor heated pool; putting green; tennis courts w/pro; Wi-Fi (free).

Moderate

Edgartown Inn ★   Built as the 1798 residence of the whaling captain Thomas Worth, this is perhaps the island's oldest continuously operating lodging house. Rooms have been upgraded in recent years so that now all have private baths. The inn has long been known for its country breakfasts, which are open to the public.

56 N. Water St., Edgartown. ✆**508/627-4794.** www.edgartowninn.com. 14 units. Summer $175–$295 double. Closed Nov–Mar. No children 6 and under.

The Jonathan Munroe House ★   A room in this elegant Victorian is a little less expensive than those in other B&Bs in Edgartown; it has a good location, across the street from the Whaling Church on Main Street but not in the thick of it. The rooms decorated with the likes of lacy canopy beds and floral upholstery, are well cared for, so are guests, particularly with the elaborate hot breakfasts that are served on the screened-in porch.

100 Main St., Edgartown. ✆ **877/468-6763** or 508/939-6004. www.jonathanmunroe.com. 7 units, 1 cottage. Summer $250–$315 double; $375 cottage. Rates include continental breakfast and wine-and-cheese hour. No children 11 and under. **Amenities:** Wi-Fi (free).

OAK BLUFFS
Expensive
Isabelle's Beach House ★   At what's the best in a line-up of B&Bs across from the ocean in Oak Bluffs, you could while away the afternoon in a rocker on the front porch. As is typical with a converted Victorian house, some of the rooms are a tad small. There are plenty of old-fashioned touches, like wicker beds and pedestal sinks in the bedrooms. Since the inn is oceanfront, when a storm blows in, the windows of the old place have quite a rattle.

83 Seaview Ave. (on the sound), Oak Bluffs. ✆ **800/674-3129** or 508/693-3955. www.isabelles beachhouse.com. 11 units. Summer $315–$395 double; $465 suite. Rates include continental breakfast. Closed late Oct to early May. **Amenities:** Wi-Fi (free).

The Oak Bluffs Inn ★   After seeing all the fancifully decorated gingerbread cottages in Oak Bluffs, you may want to stay in one yourself. Here it is, a big pink confection with elaborate trim and turrets. This is a terrific location for an easy walk to restaurants, shops, clubs, and the harbor. Rooms are simply and tastefully decorated in soothing muted colors.

64 Circuit Ave. (at the corner of Pequot Ave.), Oak Bluffs. ✆ **800/955-6235** or 508/693-7171. www. oakbluffsinn.com. 9 units. Summer $225–$380 double; $600 2-bedroom suite. Rates include continental breakfast. Closed Nov–Apr. **Amenities:** Wi-Fi (free).

Moderate
The Dockside Inn ★   The Dockside is a family-friendly hotel located just steps from Oak Bluffs Harbor. There are several clubs nearby, which may or not be a good thing—streets are definitely hopping around here until 1am. There are 2-person rooms and 4-person and 5-person suites. The rooms are comfortable, though similar in style to motel rooms.

9 Circuit Ave. Ext. (P.O. Box 1206), Oak Bluffs. ✆ **800/245-5979** or 508/693-2966. www.vineyard inns.com. 21 units. Summer $240–$260 double; $350 suite. Rates include continental breakfast. Closed late Oct to early Apr. Pets allowed. **Amenities:** 6-seat hot tub; Wi-Fi (free).

Wesley Hotel ★   This Victorian hotel, in continuous operation since 1879, used to be the go-to place for a moderately priced room, but prices have risen higher than some other nearby inns. It is a nice facility, a large hotel, overlooking Oak Bluffs Harbor. Rooms are rather modest, with motel-style decor.

70 Lake Ave. (on the harbor), Oak Bluffs. ✆ **800/638-9027** or 508/693-6611. www.wesleyhotel. com. 95 units, all with shower only. Summer $265–$315 double; $355–$375 suite. Closed late Oct to Apr. **Amenities:** Wi-Fi (free).

VINEYARD HAVEN (TISBURY)
Expensive
Mansion House on Martha's Vineyard ★   A big hotel right on Vineyard Haven's Main Street and steps from the ferry, this is a nice location for people who like

to be in the thick of it. This is one of the few Vineyard lodging choices with a pool and it's a beauty, a 75-foot pool in the basement. Some rooms have a view of the harbor from private balconies, but all are decorated in a modern minimalist style: fresh and clean. Beds are particularly comfortable.

9 Main St., Vineyard Haven. ℂ **800/332-4112** or 508/693-2200. www.mvmansionhouse.com. 32 units. $309–$409 double; $349–$619 suite. Rates include full buffet breakfast. **Amenities:** Restaurant; 75-foot pool, health club; room service; Wi-Fi (free). Some pet-friendly rooms.

CHILMARK (INCLUDING MENEMSHA) & WEST TISBURY
Expensive
Beach Plum Inn ★★ Under the same ownership as the Menemsha Inn next door, this is a upscale hotel with one of the island's top restaurants, the **Beach Plum Restaurant,** on site. The main inn building and cottages are set in a 7-acre garden property with colorful flowers throughout. The rooms, some in cottages and some in the main house, vary widely in size, but all are decorated in a pleasing French country style. Many of the rooms in the main house have balconies, screened-in porches, or patios, the better to enjoy harbor breezes.

50 Beach Plum Lane (off North Rd., ½ mile northeast of the harbor), Menemsha. ℂ **508/645-9454.** www.beachpluminn.com. 11 units. Summer $295–$675 double or cottage. Rates include full breakfast in season, continental off-season. Closed Jan–Apr. **Amenities:** Restaurant; babysitting by arrangement; croquet court; tennis court; private beach passes.

Menemsha Inn & Cottages ★★★ There are likely guests who stay at the Menemsha Inn just to have access to passes to the Vineyard's most beautiful private beaches, Lucy Vincent and Squibnocket. But there is so much more to love about this place. It's a brisk quarter-mile walk from this 25-acre estate to the center of the 300-year-old fishing village of Menemsha. But mostly a stay here is about getting away from it all. The Carriage House and the Tea House have 15 luxury rooms; the large stone fireplace in the Carriage House is a gathering spots for guests to plan their day. The mainstay suite is by itself, above the reception area in the inn's main building. In addition, there are 12 Sea View Cottages of 1- and 2-bedroom with kitchens, wood-burning fireplaces and great views of Menemsha Harbor.

12 Menemsha Rd. (about ½ mile northeast of the harbor), Menemsha. ℂ **508/645-2521.** www.menemshainn.com. 15 units, 12 cottages. Summer $315 double; $450–$735 suite; $1,995–$3,300 1-bedroom cottage, $3,995 per week 2-bedroom cottage. Rates include continental breakfast for rooms and suites. Closed Dec to mid-Apr. **Amenities:** Fitness room (step machine, treadmill, exercise bike, and free weights); tennis court; private beach passes. Dogs allowed in certain rooms.

Moderate
The Captain R. Flanders House ★ This 1700s country farmhouse is on the west end of the island, on 60 rolling acres of farmland, with horses and sheep grazing and the aptly named Bliss Pond. The house, simply decorated with period antiques, has four rooms, with two that share a bathroom and two with private bathrooms. There are two small stand-alone cottages, each with a bedroom, sitting area and kitchenette.

440 North Rd. (about ½ mile northeast of Menemsha), Chilmark. ℂ **508/645-3123.** www.captainflandersinn.com. 5 units, 2 with shared bathroom; 2 cottages. Summer $190 double with shared bathroom; $225 double with private bathroom; $300 cottage. Rates include continental breakfast. Closed Nov to early May. **Amenities:** Private beach pass; shuttle bus to beach, bikes to borrow; Wi-Fi (free).

Inexpensive

Hostelling International–Martha's Vineyard Set in a large forest in the geographic center of the island, this hostel isn't the conveniently located. Bikes are an option for getting around, but a shuttle bus also stops here. The facility is run with efficiency, and staff members are known for their friendliness, which, for a traveler, may be the most important quality of all. The rooms are set up with bunk beds, 4 to 10 beds per room.

525 Edgartown–West Tisbury Rd. (about 1 mile east of the town center), West Tisbury. http://capecod.hiusa.org. © **888/901-2087** or 508/693-2665. 67 beds, 1 family room. $29 for members; $39 for nonmembers; $150–$200 private room. Closed mid-Oct to mid-May.

Where to Eat

Note that outside Oak Bluffs, Edgartown, and Vineyard Haven (also known as Tisbury), all of Martha's Vineyard is "dry," but you can bring your own wine or other alcoholic beverage; some restaurants charge a small fee for uncorking. **Great Harbour Gourmet & Spirits,** 40 Main St., Edgartown (© **508/627-4390**), has a very good wine selection. There's also **Jim's Package Store,** at 27 Lake Ave., in Oak Bluffs (© **508/693-0236;** http://jimspackagestore.com).

EDGARTOWN
Expensive

Atria/Brick Cellar Bar ★★★ NEW AMERICAN Many of the Vineyard's fanciest restaurants, including Atria, also have a more casual dining area (and less expensive menu). The Brick Cellar Bar here, with live music, bumper pool, and fish tanks, has perhaps the Vineyard's best burger menu, from the PETA (vegetarian, with a marinated portobello) to the Atria classic, with cheddar, sautéed onions, mushrooms, apple-smoked bacon and béarnaise sauce. The pleasures of the bar cannot be overstated, but upstairs, the main dining room offers the more lauded experience. Traditional surf-and-turf is turned on its head with Georges Bank scallops and red wine-braised short ribs. A 2-pound lobster is wok-fired and served with whipped potatoes. It's all delicious.

137 Main St. (a short walk from the center of town). © **508/627-5850.** www.atriamv.com. Atria main courses $30–$48, Brick Cellar Bar $14–$22. June–Aug daily 5:30–10pm; call for off-season hours. Closed Dec to mid-Mar.

Chesca's ★ ITALIAN What distinguishes this classic Italian restaurant may be the live music, local bands like Johnny Hoy and the Bluefish, who play in the courtyard until sunset Thursday nights during the summer. There is a boisterous bar scene where you can catch a game on TV while dining. The casual and lively restaurant also includes an enclosed porch for a quieter dining experience. This is the place to bring a large group and enjoy a big bowl of pasta—perhaps lobster ravioli and seared scallops or pappardelle Bolognese?—for a fun night out.

At the Colonial Inn, 38 N. Water St. © **508/627-1234.** www.chescasmv.com. Main courses $28–$38. Mid-June to mid-Oct daily 5:30–9:30pm; call for off-season hours. Closed Nov to mid-Apr.

Restaurant Détente ★★ NEW AMERICAN Both this hidden gem and its menu are small but expertly executed and innovative. People book days in advance for dishes like with local monkfish with Spanish octopus, mint, grapefruit, and hazelnut ravioli. As a main course, choose between Vineyard fluke with buttermilk risotto or perhaps squid ink fettuccine with Menemsha lobster. It all gets pricey, but it's worth it for a special occasion.

15 Winter St. (in Nevin Sq., behind the Colonial Inn). ✆ **508/627-8810.** www.detentemv.com. Main courses $32–$38. 6-course tasting menu $70. June–Aug daily 5:30–10pm; call for off-season hours. Closed Jan to mid-Apr.

L'étoile ★★★ CONTEMPORARY FRENCH Long known for being the fanciest restaurant in a town of fancy restaurants, l'étoile now has a bar menu if you want the experience of eating the exquisite cuisine of Chef Michael Brisson without the intimidating prices. Locally caught and sourced fish, meat and vegetables are the mainstay here. What it all has in common is care in combinations, flavors, colors and presentation.

22 N. Water St. (off Main St.). ✆ **508/627-5187.** www.letoile.net. Main courses $28–$42; chef's tasting menu $99. Mid-June to mid-Sept 6–10pm; call for off-season hours. Closed Dec–Apr.

Water Street/Henry's Pub ★★ NEW AMERICAN Whether you prefer the fancy atmosphere of Water Street, a special occasion summer-only restaurant with big windows offering views out to Edgartown Lighthouse and Edgartown Harbor or the clubby, gastropub atmosphere of Henry's Pub, you are assured of good food. Both restaurants have a selection of small dishes ($9–$18) suitable for sharing in addition to the traditional menu ($17–$41). Bistro fare at Henry's includes local chicken with a sweet-potato puree and pig cheek Bolognese with fresh rigatoni. At Water Street, you might find unabashedly fancy choices on the menu, like Peking duck or pork shank with maple-roasted carrots. Desserts are not to be missed here, in particular the pear bombe, which is a pear mousse with a Chinese five-spice cake.

At the Harbor View Hotel, 131 N. Water St. ✆ **508/627-3761.** www.harbor-view.com/dining. Water Street main courses $23–$42; small plates $8–$19. June–Aug Mon–Sat 7-10:30am (at Water St. only), 11am–2pm (at Henry's only), and 6–10pm, Sun 11am–2pm and 6–9pm; call for off-season hours. Water Street closed mid-Sept to late May.

Moderate

Among the Flowers Cafe ★★ AMERICAN A charming little cafe, Among the Flowers is where to go for a moderately priced lunch or dinner that feels like visiting a friend. Outdoor seating on the patio is particularly pleasant. For breakfast, best bets are apple cinnamon French toast and omelets loaded with veggies. Lunch, though, is really the standout here, with lobster rolls, turkey wraps, and even scallop kebobs.

17 Mayhew Lane. ✆ **508/627-3233.** www.mvol.com/menu/amongtheflowers. Main courses $10–$18. Late June to early Sept daily 8am–9:30pm; late Apr to June and Sept to mid-Oct daily 8am–4pm. Closed late Oct to mid-Apr.

The Port Hunter ★ AMERICAN This is a casual flatbread pizza and burgers kind of place that is also the best live music venue in Edgartown. The menu always has creative specials like tempura shrimp with a ginger dipping sauce; catch of the day like grilled scup with mixed greens and vegetarian choices including pastas. There is also a raw bar with local shellfish. Fish tacos at the bar while listening to the Brothers Rye, an outlaw jug band out of Woods Hole, is a favorite Vineyard experience.

55 Main St. (in the center of town), Edgartown. ✆ **508/627-7747.** Main courses $10–$30. Mid-May to Nov daily 5:30–10pm; call for off-season hours.

The Seafood Shanty ★ SEAFOOD What distinguishes this seafood shack from others along the waterfront is the two levels of indoor and outdoor dining. The roof deck overlooking Edgartown Harbor is really the ultimate place to enjoy a meal in this quaint seaside town. The menu includes sushi and sashimi, with special rolls and platters served all day and evening. In addition, the owners strive to serve sustainable and locally caught seafood and shellfish, prepared in a healthful manner.

31 Dock St. ☏ **508/627-8622.** www.theseafoodshanty.com. Lunch $9–$17; dinner $14–$33. June–Aug daily 11am–10pm; call for off-season hours. Closed Nov to mid-May.

Inexpensive

Espresso Love ★★ AMERICAN   The place is a little difficult to find, tucked back behind a parking lot off Main Street in Edgartown. But once you find it, you'll be glad you did. The MV Blue Beast Sandwich (roast beef, caramelized onion, blue cheese, and mayo) may be reason enough to visit this deli/gourmet restaurant. It's a go-to place for breakfast and lunch, with burgers, salads and soups the mainstays. In season, they also serve dinner.

17 Church St. (off Main St., behind the courthouse). ☏ **508/627-9211.** www.espressolove.com. Main courses $12–$18. July–Aug daily 6:30am–9pm; off-season Mon-Sat 6:30am–6pm, Sun 6:30am–4pm.

MacPhail's Corner Cafe DINER   Six oranges go into each glass of fresh-squeezed juice and muffins are baked daily at this top-notch diner steps from the harbor. Breakfast is all day and the bacon, egg and cheese sandwich is a winner. For lunch, there is clam chowder, lobster rolls and huge cookies.

18 Dock St. (near the harbor), Edgartown. ☏ **508/939-3090.** All items under $15. July–Aug daily 8am–6pm.

The Newes from America ★★ PUB GRUB   If you're looking for a pub with atmosphere, this one has it. Set in the basement of a 1742 building, the Newes has beams, brick walls and a hearth. The pub food includes bangers and mash; curry fries; and of course fish and chips. The beer menu's extensive, too.

At The Kelley House, 23 Kelley St., Edgartown ☏ **508/627-4397.** www.kelley-house.com/dining_news_from_america.asp. Main courses $7–$10. Daily 11:30am–11pm.

OAK BLUFFS

Expensive

Martha's Vineyard Chowder Company ★★ NEW AMERICAN   Located across from the Flying Horses carousel, this restaurant has sort of a dark, clublike atmosphere when you enter (and the Dreamland nightclub is upstairs). As you might hope, the signature soup is indeed special—made from scratch with a thin cream base. Other highlights on the menu are fresh seared scallops with a corn and herb risotto and the prosciutto-wrapped fresh cod with potato gnocchi.

9 Oak Bluffs Ave. ☏ **508/696-3000.** www.mvchowder.com Main courses $19–$39. May–Nov daily 11:30am–10pm; call for off-season hours.

The Red Cat Kitchen at Ken 'N' Beck ★★★ NEW AMERICAN   Chef Ben DeForest has created a winner here, in this quirky little hole-in-the-wall on a side street in Oak Bluffs. DeForest's signature dish is Island Fresca, a soup of corn broth, tomatoes, corn, butter and topped with parmesan and basil oil. Fresh from the Vineyard, it tastes like a summer day. The rest changes with the season. You won't be disappointed.

14 Kennebec Ave., Oak Bluffs ☏ **508/696-6040.** www.redcatkitchen.com Main courses $19–$39. May–Nov daily 6–10pm; call for off-season hours.

Sweet Life Cafe ★★ FRENCH/AMERICAN   Oak Bluffs' top high-end choice has an atmosphere fit for a president (the Obamas made it one of their "date night" spots). The large outdoor patio, with tables lit by candles and under Japanese umbrellas, is lovely on a summer evening. Inside is casual elegance. If it's on the menu when you visit, try the striped-bass ceviche in season as an appetizer. Among the main courses, king salmon with broccoli-rabe risotto, sun-dried tomatoes and white anchovies is a pleasing—and filling—combination. Grass-fed sirloin comes with greens from the Vineyard's Morning Glory Farm and, at the other end of the dining spectrum, there's a a house-made fettuccine with roasted broccoli pesto on ginger carrot puree.

63 Circuit Ave., Oak Bluffs. © **508/696-0200.** www.sweetlifemv.com. Main courses $32–$40. Mid-May to Aug daily 5:30–9pm. Closed late Sept to mid-May.

Inexpensive

Coop de Ville ★ SEAFOOD   The beauty of this place is the outdoor raw bar where you can sit facing Oak Bluffs harbor and watching the boats come and go. There is no indoor seating, but there is an awning covers the seating. Fried fish, hamburgers, chicken wings, and lobster dinners are the staples here, washed down with a cold brew (10 on draft, 12 in bottles).

Dockside Market Place. © **508/693-3420.** www.coopdevillemv.com. Main courses $7–$20. June–Aug daily 11am–10pm; call for off-season hours. Closed late Sept–Apr.

Linda Jean's ★ DINER   A summer staple in Oak Bluffs since 1976, this diner with a long counter and cozy booths and tables is a particularly good choice for breakfast, although by mid-morning in season, the line waiting for a table goes out the door.

25 Circuit Ave., Oak Bluffs © **508/693-4093.** Main courses $6-24. June–Aug daily 8am–7pm; call for off-season hours.

Sharky's Cantina ★ MEXICAN   With many menu items under $10, this high-octane Mexican restaurant is a great place for budget travelers. On the menu are the usual burritos and chimichangas, but also an entire wings menu with fun flavors like tango mango teriyaki. Beverages are a specialty here, with carefully made margaritas and frozen drinks. Note that Sharky's gets fairly loud on weekend evenings in summer.

31 Circuit Ave. © **508/693-7501.** www.sharkyscantina.com. Main courses $11–$25. June–Aug daily 11am–12:30am; call for off-season hours.

Slice of Life ★ DELI   This cafe serves upscale deli food at breakfast, lunch and dinner at reasonable prices. A lunch favorite is the meatloaf sandwich on a ciabatta roll. At dinner, you could have pan-seared salmon with sweet potato hash or even fish and chips.

50 Circuit Ave. © **508/693-3838.** www.sliceoflifemv.com. Main courses $10–$23. June–Aug daily 7am–8pm; call for off-season hours.

Sweets

Mad Martha's ★   Just over a dozen homemade flavors leave you wishing there were even more at this classic ice cream parlor in Oak Bluffs. The scoops are huge and one is plenty, which is good because it is also $5. There is also a branch in Edgartown and one in Vineyard Haven.

117 Circuit Ave. (in the center of town). © **508/693-9151.** Daily 11am–midnight. Closed Oct–Apr.

Martha's Vineyard Gourmet Cafe & Bakery ★   You can't imagine the heavenly smell and then taste of a chocolate donut pulled fresh out of the oven at midnight on Martha's Vineyard. That is when people line up at Back Door Donuts (the alleyway in the back of this deli) for extraordinary baked goods—donuts and apple fritters—fresh out of the oven.

5 Post Office Sq. (in the center of town). © **508/693-3688.** Mid-Apr to Oct daily 6am–10pm. Back Door Donuts 7:30pm–1am. Call for off-season hours. Closed mid-Oct to mid-Apr.

Murdick's Fudge The top fudge on the island is at this little storefront; watching it being made is a fun treat for the kids. Besides the flagship, there are also locations in Edgartown and Vineyard Haven.

7 Circuit Ave., Oak Bluffs. © **508/627-8047.** www.murdicks.com/fudge. Summer daily 10am–11pm; call for off-season hours.

VINEYARD HAVEN (TISBURY)
Expensive

Le Grenier ★★ FRENCH It's the wonderful traditional French cuisine that brings people back year and year to one of the longest-running restaurants on the island. Chef-owner Jean Dupon from the Lyon region of France knows exactly how to satisfy with local ingredients. So you might start with mussels steamed in Pernod, move on to the flambéed lobster Normande (with apples and Calvados), and end with profiteroles au chocolate.

96 Main St. (in the center of town). © **508/693-4906.** www.legrenierrestaurant.com. Main courses $28–$39. Daily 5:30–9:30pm.

Copper Wok ★ PAN ASIAN Pan-Asian is how the cuisine is described at this sleek restaurant, which opened in 2014 in the Mansion House hotel, steps from the ferry in Vineyard Haven. Besides Chinese food, there are dishes from India and Thailand, as well as a full 20-seat sushi bar. The Chinese items on the menu are a bargain for the Vineyard; the sushi is on the pricey side, with rolls starting at $7 and going up to $23.

9 Main St. (at the Mansion House), Vineyard Haven © **508/693-3416.** www.copperwokmv. Main courses $12–$23. June-Sept daily 11:30am–9:30pm; call for off-season hours.

Moderate

Black Dog Tavern ★ NEW AMERICAN Back in 1969, Captain Robert Douglas, a local sailor, spent a late cold night in Vineyard Haven and wanted a good meal. There were no restaurants open, and the only food he could find was a packaged stale donut from a convenience store. From that experience, he got the idea of building a good year-round tavern on the harbor in Vineyard Haven, and the rest is (marketing) history. But the tavern remains, open all winter long for breakfast, lunch and dinner. You can still get a steaming cup of quahog chowder on a winter day here, as well as fish and chips and chicken potpie. Old-time favorites are clams casino, grilled swordfish and, for meat-lovers: bacon-wrapped meatloaf. Friday is lobster night: A complete lobster dinner will cost you $20. On sunny days, try to get a seat on the outdoor patio next to the harbor.

Beach St. Ext. (on the harbor). © **508/693-9223.** www.theblackdog.com. Main courses $19–$38. June to early Sept daily 7am–9pm. Call for off-season hours.

Saltwater ★★ NEW AMERICAN Chef Joe DaSilva, one of the island's best, has made this a destination. The dining room uses its location to full advantage with a wall of windows overlooking Lagoon Pond and a high-vaulted ceiling. On the starter menu, lump crab cakes with caper aioli are a longtime favorite. As for main courses, pan-seared scallops, pan-roasted salmon, herb roasted chicken are all standouts.

79 Beach Rd. (at Tisbury Marketplace; 10-min. walk from Main St.). ©**508/338-4666.** www.saltwater restaurant.com. Main courses $25–$35. Late June to mid-Oct Mon–Sat 11:30am–2pm, daily 5:30–9:30pm; call for off-season hours.

Inexpensive

Art Cliff Diner ★★ DINER   Every town should have a really good diner with a sense of fun. At Art Cliff, even the menu is playful. Green eggs and ham? That's an omelet with Swiss cheese, spinach and ham. There are frittatas, crepes and wonderful Drunken Sailor Pancakes (pecan pancakes with real rum sauce). Go early or late or you'll never make it in the door. If the wait's too long, there's always the food truck parked out front, with burgers, hotdogs and pulled-pork sandwiches, and Parmesan fries.

39 Beach Rd. (a short walk from Main St.). © **508/693-1224.** Reservations not accepted. Main courses all under $15. No credit cards. July–Aug Thurs–Tues 7am–2pm; call for off-season hours. Closed Nov to mid-Apr.

Takeout & Picnic Fare

Black Dog Bakery ★   The first place you pass as you get off the ferry in Vineyard Haven, this is where you get your coffee and snack for the ferry ride or something to tide you over for your next meal. Muffins are a specialty, as are dog biscuits.

11 Water St. (near the harbor). © **508/693-4786.** www.theblackdog.com. June–Sept daily 5:30am–8pm; off-season daily 5:30am–5pm (call ahead for details).

CHILMARK (INCLUDING MENEMSHA) & WEST TISBURY
Expensive

The Beach Plum Inn Restaurant ★★★ NEW AMERICAN   This secluded restaurant is one of the best on the island. A big long table is the focus point, though there are also individual tables. Chris Fischer, a 12th-generation islander who grew up on nearby Beetlebung Farm, runs the kitchen with a focus on local, be it a salad of North Tabor Farm greens or Menemsha mussels. Fischer believes food should be simple and authentic, from the island that he loves. In a restaurant with views of the harbor, you can't go wrong with fish, either.

At the Beach Plum Inn, 50 Beach Plum Lane (off North Rd.), Menemsha. ©**508/645-9454.** www. beachpluminn.com/restaurant.html. Main courses $32–$44. Mid-June to early Sept daily 5:30–9:30pm; call for off-season hours. Closed Dec to mid-May.

Home Port Restaurant ★★ SEAFOOD   At some point after 1930, when the Home Port opened on the slope overlooking Menemsha Harbor, it became not just a casual clam shack but an institution, a place that defined summer for Vineyard visitors. It's still a place for lobster dinners and sunsets, but now it's also about sustainable fisheries and using fish caught by local fishermen. Best bets are the fish taco or the varied fried fish platters. The three-course option, which for $9 extra gets you an appetizer and dessert with a main course, is a good deal. The sunset's thrown in for free.

512 North Rd., Menemsha. ©**508/645-2679.** www.homeportmv.com. Complete dinners $14–$47. July–Aug daily 5–9pm; call for off-season hours. To-go window 11:30–9pm. Closed Labor Day to mid-May.

State Road Restaurant ★★ NEW AMERICAN   The restaurant, located way off the tourist track in North Tisbury, bills itself as a "contemporary American tavern," and though it serves three meals a day and is open year-round, it is certainly more upscale than the usual tavern. The restaurant's stone fireplace, rough-hewn beamed ceiling, shingle-sided porch, and paintings by the rural master Alan Whiting make it resemble a farmhouse. The menu focuses on Island products, from the Vineyard greens salad to the Briar Patch farm rabbit with Parmesan polenta. The drinks list features ciders, craft beers and carefully selected wines by the glass and bottle.

688 State Rd. (5½ miles from the center of Vineyard Haven), West Tisbury. (©508/693-8582. Main courses $20–$48. July–Aug daily 8am–10pm; call for off-season hours.

Moderate

The Bite ★★ SEAFOOD   If you happen to be in Menemsha around sunset, you can't do much better for dinner than stopping in this unassuming clam shack by the harbor. This is fried seafood to go, simple and basic. The warm lobster rolls are superlative, as is the chowder.

29 Basin Rd. (off North Rd., about ¼ mile northeast of the harbor), Menemsha. (©508/645-9239. Main courses $18–$30. No credit cards. July–Aug daily 11am–8pm; call for off-season hours. Closed late Sept to mid-May.

Takeout & Picnic Fare

Alley's General Store   In business since 1858, this example of that endangered species the true New England general store, nearly foundered in the 1980s. Luckily, the Martha's Vineyard Preservation Trust interceded to give it a new lease on life, along with a much-needed structural overhaul. The stock is still the same, though: basically, everything you could possibly need, from scrub brushes to fresh-made salsa. The no-longer-sagging front porch still supports a popular bank of benches, along with a blizzard of bulletin-board notices. For local activities and events, check here first.

State Rd. (in the center of town), West Tisbury. (©508/693-0088. Summer Mon–Sat 7am–7pm, Sun 7am–6pm; winter Mon–Sat 7am–6pm, Sun 8am–5pm.

West Tisbury Farmers' Market   This seasonal outdoor market, open Wednesday from 2:30 to 5:30pm and Saturday from 9am to noon, is among the biggest and best in New England, and certainly the most rarefied, with local celebrities loading up on prize produce and snacking on pesto bread and other international goodies. The fun starts in June and runs for 18 Saturdays and 10 Wednesdays.

Old Agricultural Hall, West Tisbury. (©508/693-9561. www.westtisburyfarmersmarket.com.

Exploring: Beaches & Recreational Pursuits

BEACHES   Most down-island beaches in Vineyard Haven, Oak Bluffs, and Edgartown are open to the public and just a walk or a short bike ride from town. In season shuttle buses make stops at **State Beach,** between Oak Bluffs and Edgartown. Most of the Vineyard's magnificent up-island shoreline is privately owned or restricted to residents and thus off limits to transient visitors. Renters in up-island communities, however, can obtain a beach sticker (around $35–$50 for a season sticker) for those private beaches by applying with a lease at the relevant **town hall:** West Tisbury, © **508/696-0147;** Chilmark, © **508/645-2100;** or Aquinnah, © **508/645-2300.** Also, many up-island inns offer the perk of temporary passes to residents-only beaches such as Lucy Vincent Beach. In addition to the public beaches listed below, you might also track down a few hidden coves by requesting a map of conservation properties from the **Martha's Vineyard Land Bank** (© **508/627-7141;** www.mvlandbank.com). Below is a list of visitor-friendly beaches.

○ **Aquinnah Beach ★★★** (Moshup Beach), off Moshup Trail: Parking costs $15 a day (in season) at this peaceful half-mile beach just east (Atlantic side) of the colorful cliffs. Go early, as the lot is small and a bit of a hike from the beach. I suggest that all but one person get off at the wooden boardwalk along the road with towels, toys, lunches, and so on, while the remaining person heads back up to park. In season you can also take the shuttle buses from down-island to the parking lot at the Aquinnah (formerly Gay Head) cliffs and walk to the beach. Although it is against the law, nudists tend to gravitate here. Remember that climbing the cliffs or stealing clay for a souvenir here is against the law, for environmental reasons: The cliffs are suffering from rapid erosion. Restrooms are near the parking lot.

○ **East Beach ★★**, Wasque (pronounced *Way*-squee) Reservation, Chappaquiddick: Relatively few people bother biking or hiking (or four-wheel-driving) this far, so this beach remains one of the Vineyard's best-kept secrets (and an ideal spot for bird-watching). You should be able to find all the privacy you crave. If you're staying in Edgartown, the Chappy ferry is probably minutes by bike from your inn. Biking on Chappaquiddick is one of the great Vineyard experiences, but the roads can be sandy and are best suited for a mountain bike. You may have to dismount during the 5-mile ride to Wasque. Because of its exposure on the east shore of the island, the surf here is rough. Pack a picnic and make this an afternoon adventure. Sorry, no facilities. The area is owned by the Trustees of Reservations. It costs $180 for a season pass for nonmembers to drive a four-wheel-drive vehicle out to the beach. Most people park their car near the Dyke Bridge and walk the couple hundred yards out to the beach. Admission is $3 per person.

○ **Joseph A. Sylvia State Beach ★★★**, midway between Oak Bluffs and Edgartown: Stretching a mile and flanked by a paved bike path, this placid beach has views of Cape Cod and Nantucket Sound and is prized for its gentle and (relatively) warm waves, which make it perfect for swimming. The wooden drawbridge is a local landmark, and visitors and islanders alike have been jumping off it for years. Be aware that State Beach is one of the Vineyard's most popular; come midsummer, it's packed. The shuttle bus stops here, and roadside parking is also available—but it fills up fast, so stake your claim early. Located on the eastern shore of the island, this is a Nantucket Sound beach, so waters are shallow and rarely rough. There are no restrooms, and only the Edgartown end of the beach, known as Bend-in-the-Road Beach, has lifeguards.

○ **Lake Tashmoo Town Beach ★**, off Herring Creek Road, Vineyard Haven: The only spot on the island where lake meets ocean, this tiny strip of sand is good for swimming and surf-casting but is somewhat marred by limited parking and often brackish waters. Nonetheless this is a popular spot, as beachgoers enjoy a choice between the Vineyard Sound beach with mild surf or the placid lake beach. Bikers will have no problem reaching this beach from Vineyard Haven; otherwise you have to use a car to get to this beach.

○ **Lobsterville Beach ★★**, at the end of Lobsterville Road, in Aquinnah (formerly Gay Head; restricted): This 2-mile beauty on Menemsha Pond boasts calm, shallow waters, which are ideal for children. It's also a prime spot for birding—just past the dunes are nesting areas for terns and gulls. Surf-casters tend to gravitate here, too. The only drawback is that parking is for residents only. This is a great beach for bikers to hit on their way back from Aquinnah and before taking the bike ferry over to Menemsha.

o **Menemsha Beach** ★★, next to Dutchers Dock, in Menemsha Harbor: Despite its rough surface, this small but well-trafficked strand, with lifeguards and restrooms, is popular with families. In season it's virtually wall-to-wall colorful umbrellas and beach toys. The nearby food vendors in Menemsha are a plus here. *Tip:* This beach is the ideal place to watch a sunset. Get a lobster dinner to go at the famous **Home Port restaurant,** right next to the beach, grab a blanket and a bottle of wine, and picnic here for a spectacular evening. If you are staying at an up-island inn, Menemsha is a fun bike ride downhill. Energetic bikers can make it from down-island towns; plan to make it part of an entire day of scenic biking. Otherwise you'll need a car to get here.

o **Oak Bluffs Town Beach,** Seaview Avenue: This sandy strip extends from both sides of the ferry wharf, which makes it a convenient place to linger while you wait for the next boat. This is an in-town beach, within walking distance for visitors staying in Oak Bluffs. The surf is consistently calm and the sand smooth, so it's also ideal for families with small children. Public restrooms are available at the ferry dock, but there are no lifeguards.

o **Owen Park Beach,** off Main Street, in Vineyard Haven: A tiny strip of harborside beach adjoining a town green with swings and a bandstand will suffice for young children, who, by the way, get lifeguard supervision. There are no restrooms, but this is an in-town beach, and a quick walk from most Vineyard Haven inns.

o **South Beach** ★★★ (Katama Beach), about 4 miles south of Edgartown, on Katama Road: If you have time for only one trip to the beach and you can't get up-island, go with this popular, 3-mile barrier strand that boasts heavy wave action (check with lifeguards for swimming conditions), sweeping dunes, and, most important, relatively ample parking space. It's also accessible by bike path or shuttle. Lifeguards patrol some sections of the beach, and there are sparsely scattered toilet facilities. The rough surf here is popular with surfers. *Tip:* Families tend to head to the left, college kids to the right.

o **Wasque Beach** ★★, Wasque Reservation, Chappaquiddick: Surprisingly easy to get to (via the On-Time ferry and a bike or car), this half-mile-long beach has all the amenities—lifeguards, parking, restrooms—without the crowds. Wasque Beach is a Trustees of Reservations property, and if you are not a member of this land-preservation organization, you must pay at the gatehouse (www.thetrustees.org). To park your car here and go to the beach, it is $3 per car plus $3 per person. To drive your car on to the beach, it's $30 for a day pass, plus $3 per person. For a season pass to drive on to the other beaches on Chappaquiddick, it's $100 for Norton Point and $180 for Cape Pogue.

BICYCLING   What's unique about biking on Martha's Vineyard is that you'll find not only the smooth, well-maintained paths indigenous to the Cape, but also long stretches of road with virtually no traffic that, while rough in spots, pass through breathtaking country landscapes with sweeping ocean views. It is only a few miles but a very scenic ride between Vineyard Haven and Oak Bluffs. A few more miles gets you to Edgartown along a nice flat bike path.

The adventurous **mountain biker** will want to head to the 8 miles of trails in the **Manuel F. Correllus State Forest** (© **508/693-2540;** www.mass.gov/dcr/parks/southeast/corr.htm), a vast spread of scrub oak and pine smack-dab in the middle of the island that also boasts paved paths and hiking and horseback-riding trails. For those seeking an escape from the multitudes, the trails are so extensive that even during peak summer season, it is possible to not see another soul for hours. On most of the conservation land on the Vineyard, however, mountain biking is prohibited, for environmental reasons.

Bike rental operations are ubiquitous near the ferry landings in Vineyard Haven and Oak Bluffs, and there are also a few outfits in Edgartown. For information on bike rental shops, see "Getting Around," earlier in this chapter.

The chamber of commerce has a great bike map available at its office on Beach Road, in Vineyard Haven (see "Visitor Information," earlier in this chapter).

BIRD-WATCHING   **Felix Neck Wildlife Sanctuary,** Edgartown–Vineyard Haven Road, Edgartown (© 508/627-4850; www.massaudubon.org), is an easy 2-mile bike ride from Edgartown. A Massachusetts Audubon Property, it has a complete visitor center staffed by naturalists who lead bird-watching walks, among other activities. You'll see osprey nests on your right on the way to the center. Pick up a trail map at the center before heading out. Several of the trails pass Sengekontacket Pond, and the orange trail leads to Waterfowl Pond, which has an observation deck with bird-sighting information. Although it's managed by the conservation group Sheriff's Meadow Foundation, the 300-acre **Cedar Tree Neck Sanctuary** ★★★, in Tisbury, was acquired with the assistance of Massachusetts Audubon Society. There are several trails, but you'll eventually arrive out on a picturesque bluff overlooking Vineyard Sound and the Elizabeth Islands. Check out the map posted at the parking lot for an overview of the property. The range of terrain here—ponds, fields, woods, and bog—provides diverse opportunities for sightings. The Sanctuary is on State Road. Follow State to Indian Hill Road, then to Obed Daggett Road, and follow signs (www.sheriffs meadow.org). **Wasque Reservation** ★★★, on Chappaquiddick (see "Nature Trails," below), a sanctuary owned by the Trustees of Reservations and located on the eastern-most reaches of the island, can be accessed by bike or four-wheel-drive vehicle (see "Getting Around," earlier in this chapter). The hundreds of untouched acres here draw flocks of nesting shorebirds, including egrets, herons, terns, and Piping Plovers.

FISHING   For shellfishing you'll need to get information and a permit from the appropriate town hall (for the telephone numbers, see "Beaches," above). Popular spots for surf-casting (requires a $10 license available at town halls) include **Wasque Point** (Wasque Reservation), on Chappaquiddick (see "Nature Trails," below). Deep-sea excursions can be arranged aboard **North Shore Charters** (© 508/645-2993; www.bassnblue.com), out of Menemsha, locus of the island's commercial fishing fleet (you may recognize this weathered port from the movie "Jaws"). Charter costs are about $650 for a half-day.

Cooper Gilkes III, proprietor of **Coop's Bait & Tackle,** at 147 W. Tisbury Rd., in Edgartown (© 508/627-3909; www.coopsbaitandtackle.com), which offers rentals as well as supplies, is another authority. He's available as an instructor or charter guide and is even amenable to sharing hard-won pointers on local hot spots.

GOLF   The 9-hole **Mink Meadows Golf Course,** at 320 Golf Club Rd., off Franklin Street, in Vineyard Haven (© 508/693-0600; www.minkmeadowsgc.com), despite occupying a top-dollar chunk of real estate, is open to the general public. There is also the semiprivate, championship-level 18-hole **Farm Neck Golf Club,** off Farm Neck Way, in Oak Bluffs (© 508/693-3057). The Cafe at Farm Neck serves a wonderful lunch overlooking the manicured greens. In season greens fees at Mink Meadows are $55 for 9 holes and $80 for 18 holes; at Farm Neck, it's $150 (including cart) for 18 holes.

NATURE TRAILS   About a fifth of the Vineyard has been set aside for conservation, and much of it is accessible to energetic bikers and hikers. The **West Chop Woods,** off Franklin Street in Vineyard Haven, comprise 85 acres with marked walking trails. Midway between Vineyard Haven and Edgartown, the **Felix Neck Wildlife Sanctuary** (see "Bird-Watching," above) includes a 6-mile network of trails over varying terrain, from woodland to beach. Accessible by ferry from Edgartown, quiet Chappaquiddick is home to two sizable preserves. The **Cape Poge Wildlife Refuge ★★★** and **Wasque Reservation ★★★** (www.thetrustees.org), covering much of the island's eastern barrier beach, have 709 acres that draw flocks of nesting or resting shorebirds. Also on the island, 3 miles east on Dyke Road, is another Trustees of Reservations property, the distinctly poetic and alluring **Mytoi,** a 14-acre Japanese garden that is an oasis of textures and flora and fauna.

The 633-acre **Long Point Wildlife Refuge ★★★**, off Waldron's Bottom Road, in West Tisbury (gatehouse (✆ **508/693-7392;** www.thetrustees.org), offers heath and dunes, freshwater ponds, a popular family-oriented beach, and interpretive nature walks for children. In season the Trustees of Reservations charges a $10 parking fee, plus $3 per person ages 16 and older. The 4,000-acre **Manuel F. Correllus State Forest** (www.mass.gov/dcr/parks/southeast/corr.htm) occupies a sizable, if not especially scenic, chunk mid-island; it's riddled with mountain-bike paths and riding trails. This sanctuary was created in 1908 to try to save the endangered heath hen, a species now extinct. In season there are free interpretive and birding walks.

Up-island, along the sound, the **Menemsha Hills Reservation,** off North Road, in Chilmark (✆ **508/693-7662**), encompasses 210 acres of rocks and bluffs, with steep paths, lovely views, and even a public beach. The **Cedar Tree Neck Sanctuary,** off Indian Hill Road, southwest of Vineyard Haven (✆ **508/693-5207**), offers some 300 forested acres that end in a stony beach (alas, swimming and sunbathing are prohibited). It's still a refreshing retreat.

Some remarkable botanical surprises can be found at the 20-acre **Polly Hill Arboretum,** 809 State Rd., West Tisbury (✆ **508/693-9426;** www.pollyhillarboretum.org). Horticulturist Polly Hill developed this property over the past 40 years and allows the public to wander the grounds daily from sunrise until sunset. There are guided tours at 2pm. The visitors center and plant sale are open 9:30am to 4:30pm. This is a magical place, particularly mid-June to July when the Dogwood Allee is in bloom. Wanderers will pass old stone walls on the way to the Tunnel of Love, an arbor of bleached hornbeam. There are also witch hazels, camellias, magnolias, and rhododendrons. To get there from Vineyard Haven, go south on State Road, bearing left at the junction of North Road. The arboretum entrance is about a half-mile down on the right. There is a requested donation of $5 for adults.

WATERSPORTS   **Wind's Up,** 199 Beach Rd., Vineyard Haven (✆ **508/693-4252;** www.windsupmv.com), rents out canoes, kayaks, and various sailing craft, including sailboards, and offers instruction on-site, on a placid pond; it also rents surfboards and boogie boards. Canoes and kayaks rent for $16 per hour, $35 for a half-day, and $55 for a full day.

Museums & Historic Landmarks

Cottage Museum ★   As you walk around the 34-acre Camp Meeting Grounds in Oak Bluffs and admire the more than 300 tiny colorful cottages in the compound, you may find yourself wanting to take a look inside. This museum is your ticket. Decorated with period furnishings, it offers a glimpse into what the Campground was like when it was first started as a Methodist Revival colony in the 1800s. Back then, instead of cottages, there were tents where families would stay during the course of the multi-week religious meetings. Some families began to decorate their tents and expand them and eventually the tents became homes.

There would be three prayer services daily in the nearby 1878 Trinity Methodist Church; or the 1879 open-sided **Trinity Park Tabernacle ★★**, which today is used for Sunday morning services, but also concerts and sing-alongs. The tabernacle is the largest wrought-iron structure in the country.

1 Trinity Park (within the Camp Meeting Grounds), Oak Bluffs. ℂ **508/693-7784.** www.mvcma.org/museum.htm. Admission $2 (donation). Mid-June to Sept Mon–Sat 10am–4pm. Closed Oct to mid-June.

Flying Horses Carousel ★★ The oldest operating platform carousel in the country, the Flying Horses has been designated as a National Historic Landmark. But for generations of islanders, the carousel is just simply a lot of fun. Kids and their parents reach to grab the rings, hoping for a brass one, which gives the bearer a free ride. The horses are majestic steeds, intricately carved, with real horsehair and glass eyes. Charles Dare, a renowned maker of carousel, constructed this one in 1876 for Coney Island.

33 Circuit Ave. (at Lake Ave.), Oak Bluffs. ℂ **508/693-9481.** www.mvpreservation.org/carousel.html. Admission $2.50 per ride. Late May to early Sept daily 10am–10pm; call for off-season hours. Closed mid-Oct to mid-Apr.

Martha's Vineyard Museum ★★ A fascinating place, the Martha's Vineyard Museum tells the story of this multi-faceted island while preserving significant parts of its history. There are multiple buildings on the campus, including outdoor displays. The **Pease House Galleries** is the main museum building and your first stop. Artifacts of the Vineyard's history from pre-Colonial times to the present day is all here. Here you might find an exhibit on an oral history project with portrait photos of old time Vineyarders and quotes from them about how life used to be. Or you might see a photographic display of the Vineyard during the volatile 1960s. The 1740 **Cooke House** is a colonial house museum, not that distinct from others of its type. But it is fun to look at the **Fesnel lens** of the Gay Head Lighthouse, which sits on the lawn of the museum. The light's 1,000 prisms aided mariners from 1854 to 1951. Kids might like to look in the **Carriage Shed** where there is a whaleboat, pieces of a railroad train and more. History buffs will want to visit the **Gale Huntington Library,** the island's archive of source material from the 17th to the 21st century. Here you can look at a whaler's log complete with doodles in the margins of whales killed during the journey.

59 School St. (corner of Cooke St., 2 blocks southwest of Main St.), Edgartown. ℂ **508/627-4441.** www.mvmuseum.org. Admission $7 adults, $6 seniors, $4 children 6–15. Mid-May to mid-Oct Mon–Sat 10am–5pm, Sun noon-5pm; mid-Oct to mid-May Mon–Sat 10am–4pm.

Shopping

ARTS & CRAFTS A little art gallery cluster called "The Arts District" in Oak Bluffs, just beyond the "gingerbread" cottage colony, is worth a visit. A short walk away, on Dukes County Avenue, there are interesting shops, including **Alison Shaw Gallery** (ℂ **508/696-7429;** www.alisonshaw.com), featuring the exquisite photographs of this artist; and **Dragonfly Gallery** (ℂ **508/693-8877;** www.mvdragonfly.com), showing a range of mediums.

Chilmark Pottery, 145 Fieldview Lane, off State Road (about 4 miles southwest of Vineyard Haven), West Tisbury (𝄐 508/693-6476), features tableware fashioned to suit its setting. Geoffrey Borr takes his palette from the sea and sky and produces serviceable stoneware with clean lines and a long life span.

The Field Gallery, 1050 State Rd. (in the center of town), West Tisbury (𝄐 508/693-5595; www.fieldgallery.com), set in a rural pasture, is where Tom Maley's playful figures have enchanted locals and passersby for decades. You'll also find paintings by Albert Alcalay and drawings and cartoons by Jules Feiffer. The Sunday evening openings are high points of the summer social season. Closed mid-October to mid-May.

Don't miss the **Granary Gallery at the Red Barn,** 636 Old County Rd. (off Edgartown–West Tisbury Rd., about one-quarter mile north of the intersection), West Tisbury (𝄐 800/472-6279; www.granarygallery.com), which displays astounding prints by the late longtime summerer Alfred Eisenstaedt, dazzling color photos by local luminary Alison Shaw, and a changing roster of fine artists—some just emerging, some long since "discovered." A fine selection of country and provincial antiques is also sold here. Open April to December, and by appointment only January through March.

Another unique local artisans' venue is **Martha's Vineyard Glass Works,** 683 State Rd., West Tisbury (𝄐 508/693-6026; www.mvglassworks.com). World-renowned master glass blowers sometimes lend a hand at this handsome rural studio/shop just for the fun of it.

BOOKS **Bunch of Grapes Bookstore,** 44 Main St., Vineyard Haven (𝄐 508/693-2291; www.bunchofgrapes.com), has risen from the ashes after a fire destroyed the second floor a couple years ago. **Edgartown Books,** 44 Main St., Edgartown (𝄐 508/627-8463; www.edgartownbooks.net), has a lively presentation of timely titles highlighting local endeavors; inquire about readings and signings. Closed January to March.

FASHION **The Great Put On,** 1 Dock St. (in the center of town), Edgartown (𝄐 508/627-5495), dates back to 1969 but always keeps up with the latest styles, including lines by Vivienne Tam, Moschino, and BCBG. **Saffron,** at 65 Main St., Edgartown (𝄐 508/627-7088), offers a hip selection of island ware. **Katydid** is another high-fashion option, at 38 Main St., in Edgartown (𝄐 508/627-1232).

GIFTS/HOME DECOR My favorite place for gifts in Oak Bluffs is **Craftworks,** 149 Circuit Ave. (𝄐 508/693-7463), which is filled to the rafters with whimsical, colorful contemporary American crafts, some by local artisans.

Carly Simon owns a shop called **Midnight Farm,** 44 Main St., Vineyard Haven (𝄐 508/693-1997; www.midnightfarm.net), named after her popular children's book. This home store offers a world of high-end, carefully selected, and imaginative gift items starting with soaps and candles and including children's clothes and toys, rugs, furniture, books, clothes, and glassware.

JEWELRY Stop by **C. B. Stark Jewelers,** 53A Main St., Vineyard Haven (𝄐 508/693-2284; www.cbstark.com), where proprietor Cheryl Stark started fashioning island-motif charms back in 1966.

SEAFOOD Feel like whipping up your own lobster feast? For the freshest and biggest crustaceans on the island, head to the **Net Result,** 79 Beach Rd., Vineyard Haven (𝄐 508/693-6071; www.mvseafood.com). Run by the Larsen family, here you'll also find everything shrimp, scallops, swordfish, bluefish, and tuna, as well as prepared foods, including sushi. If you're up-island, stop by **Larsen's Fish Market,** right on the docks at Menemsha Harbor.

Martha's Vineyard After Dark

PUBS, BARS, DANCE CLUBS & LIVE MUSIC

Dreamland MV ★★   Built in 1900, this historic ballroom was restored from top to bottom in 2012 and turned into a nightclub upstairs and the Chowder House downstairs. This is the place to see bands from off-island, reggae and rock and everything in between. Closed January to mid-May. 9 Oak Bluffs Ave. (in the center of town), Oak Bluffs. ② **508/560-1932.** Cover varies.

The Lampost/The Dive Bar ★   Young and loud are the watchwords at this pair of clubs; the larger features live bands or DJs and a dance floor, the smaller (down in the basement), acoustic acts. This is where the young folk go, and the performers could be playing blues, reggae, R&B, or '80s music. Call for a schedule. Closed November to March. 111 Circuit Ave. (in the center of town), Oak Bluffs. ② **508/696-9352.** Cover $1–$5.

Flatbread Company ★★   The dance club at the airport features top musicians, comedy, theme nights, and teen nights. Doors open on show nights at 7pm. Food is served until 11pm. Open April to mid-January. 17 Airport Rd. (at Martha's Vineyard Airport), Edgartown. ② **508/693-1137.** www.flatbreadcompany.com. Tickets $10–$30. Take Edgartown–West Tisbury Rd. to the airport. Closed Nov–Apr. Cover $18–$25.

Offshore Ale Company   In 1602, the first barley in the New World was grown on Martha's Vineyard. The Vineyard's only brewpub features eight locally made beers on tap ($2.75–$5). It's an attractively rustic place, with high ceilings, oak booths lining the walls, and peanut shells strewn on the floor. Local acoustic performers entertain 6 nights a week in season. Open June to September daily, noon to midnight; call for off-season hours. 30 Kennebec Ave., Oak Bluffs. ② **508/693-2626.** www.offshoreale.com. Cover $2–$3.

The Ritz Café ★   Locals and visitors alike flock to this down-and-dirty hole-in-the-wall that features live music every night in season (don't miss Ballyhoo, original roots music including washboard) and on weekends year-round. The crowd—a boozing, brawling lot—enjoy the pool tables in the back. Call for a schedule. 4 Circuit Ave., Oak Bluffs. ② **508/693-1454.** www.theritzcafe.com. Cover $3.

The Sand Bar & Grille   This cool-cat bar is the place to hang out in Oak Bluffs near the harbor to listen to the latest local bands. 6 Circuit Ave. (in the center of town), Oak Bluffs. ② **508/693-7111.**

LOW-KEY EVENINGS

Old Whaling Church ★★   This magnificent 1843 Greek Revival church functions primarily as a 500-seat performing-arts center offering lectures and symposiums, films, plays, and concerts. It's also the Edgartown United Methodist Church, with a 9am service on Sundays. 89 Main St. (in the center of town), Edgartown. ② **508/627-4440.** www.mvpreservation.org/whale.html. Ticket prices vary.

THEATER & DANCE

Vineyard Playhouse   In an intimate (112-seat) black-box theater, carved out of an 1833 church-turned-Masonic lodge, Equity professionals put on a rich season of favorites and challenging new work, followed, on summer weekends, by musical or comedic cabaret in the gallery/lounge. Children's theater selections are performed on Saturdays at 10am. Townspeople often get involved in the outdoor Shakespeare production, a 3-week run starting in mid-July, at the Tashmoo Overlook Amphitheatre, about 1 mile west of town. Tickets for the 5pm performances Tuesday to Sunday run only $10 to $15. MasterCard and Visa are accepted. Open June to September Tuesday to Saturday at 8pm, Sunday at 7pm; call for off-season hours. 24 Church St. (in the center of town), Vineyard Haven. ⓒ **508/696-6300.** www.vineyardplayhouse.org. Tickets $15–$30.

NANTUCKET

Herman Melville wrote in "Moby-Dick," "Nantucket! Take out your map and look at it. See what a real corner of the world it occupies; how it stands there, away off shore . . ." More than 100 years later, this tiny island 30 miles off the coast of Cape Cod still defines itself, in part, by its isolation. At only 3½ by 14 miles in size, Nantucket is smaller and more insular than Martha's Vineyard. But charm-wise, Nantucket stands alone—all the creature comforts of the 21st century wrapped in an elegant 19th-century package.

Essentials

VISITOR INFORMATION

For information, contact the **Nantucket Island Chamber of Commerce,** at 48 Main St., Nantucket, MA 02554 (ⓒ **508/228-1700;** www.nantucketchamber.org).

When you arrive, you should also stop by the **Nantucket Visitor Services and Information Bureau** at 25 Federal St. (ⓒ **508/228-0925**), which is open 9am to 5pm daily from June to September, but closed on Sundays from October to May. Visitor Services is where to call if you are having trouble finding an available room. They have the most up-to-date accommodations availability listings. They can also help with 1-night stays and special events listings.

Nantucket Accommodations, P.O. Box 217, Nantucket, MA 02554 (ⓒ **866/743-3440** or 508/228-9559; www.nantucketaccommodation.com), a fee-based private service, can arrange advance reservations for 95 percent of the island's lodgings. Last-minute travelers can use the **Nantucket Visitors Service and Information Bureau** (ⓒ **508/228-0925**), a daily referral service, rather than a booking service. It always has the most updated list of available accommodations.

GETTING THERE

BY FERRY The two companies that offer ferry service from Hyannis to Nantucket are the **Steamship Authority** and **Hy-Line Cruises.** Their terminals are on opposite sides of Hyannis Harbor. Tickets on the Steamship Authority are less expensive than tickets on the Hy-Line, by about $10. Parking in the Steamship Authority lots is also a couple dollars less expensive.

From the South Street Dock in Hyannis, the **Steamship Authority** (ⓒ **508/477-8600,** or 508/228-3274 on Nantucket; www.steamshipauthority.com) operates year-round ferry service (including cars, passengers, and bicycles) to Steamboat Wharf in Nantucket using both **high-speed** ferries—which get you there in 1 hour—and **conventional** ferries, which take 2 hours and 15 minutes and cost about half the price.

Only the conventional ferries have space for cars, but there is no need to bring a car to the island because of its small size and superior public transportation and taxicab system.

Steamship Authority high-speed ferry: The Steamship Authority's **fast ferry to Nantucket, MV** *Iyanough* (ⓒ **508/495-3278**), is for passengers only (no cars). It takes 1 hour and runs four to five times a day. Tickets in season cost $36.50 one-way ($69 round-trip) for adults, $18.75 one-way ($35 round-trip) for children 5 to 12, and it is free for children 4 and under. Bikes cost $14 round-trip. Passenger reservations are highly recommended.

Parking costs $5 to $20 per day. There are four lots. The first to fill up is at the terminal on South Street. The second to fill up is just a block from the ferry terminal on Lewis Bay Road across from the entrance to Cape Cod Hospital. You walk out the back exit of the parking lot onto School Street and you are across the street from the terminal on South Street. The third lot that is used is on Yarmouth Road, about 6 blocks from the terminal. A free shuttle bus runs continually to transport passengers to the terminal. The fourth lot is Brooks Road, which is several miles away on the north side of Route 28 in Hyannis, next to the airport property. A free shuttle bus connects the parking lot to the ferry terminal.

Steamship Authority conventional ferry: A one-way ticket on the Steamship Authority traveling on the conventional ferry is $17.50 ($35 round-trip) for adults, $9 ($18 round-trip) for children 5 to 12, and $14 extra round-trip for bikes. Remember that Steamship Authority parking costs $15 per day in season ($12 off-season). You can't make advance passenger reservations for the traditional ferry, and there is no need to; there is plenty of space. Also, no need for parking reservations for the Steamship Authority.

Bringing a car to Nantucket: A round-trip fare, if you are bringing a car, costs a whopping $400 to $450 (depending on the length of the car) from April through October; during the off season, from November through March, it's $280 to $320. (Do you get the impression they don't want you to bring a car?)

If you must bring a car to the island, you need to reserve *months in advance* to secure a spot on the conventional ferry, as only five boats make the trip daily in season (three boats daily off-season). Before you call, have alternative departure dates. When bringing a car to the island, remember to arrive at least 1 hour before departure to avoid your space being released to standbys. If you arrive without a reservation and plan to wait in the standby line, there is no guarantee you will get to the island that day. There is a $10 processing fee for canceling reservations 14 days in advance of the trip; no refunds are issued if the cancellation is made less than 14 days before the trip.

No advance reservations are required for passengers traveling without cars on the conventional (slow) ferry.

Note: The Steamship Authority charges different rates for different length cars. You will need to specify the make and model of your car when you place your reservation.

Car rates do not include drivers or passengers; you must get tickets for each person going to the island.

The other organization that runs ferries from Hyannis to Nantucket is **Hy-Line Cruises,** Ocean Street Dock; for high-speed ferry reservations, call *©* **800/492-8082** or 508/228-3949; www.hy-linecruises.com). The ferries go from the dock on Ocean Street in Hyannis to Straight Wharf on Nantucket.

Hy-Line Cruises fast ferry: Hy-Line offers year-round service with its high-speed passenger catamaran, the *Grey Lady,* which makes five to six hourly trips per day. The cost of a one-way fare is $41 for adults ($77 round-trip), $29 for children 5 to 12 ($51 round-trip), and $7 extra for bicycles ($14 round-trip).

It's best to reserve in advance for your ferry ticket and for a parking space. Parking costs $17 per day in summer (only $5 in winter and $10 in spring and fall). Pets are allowed on the *Grey Lady.*

Hint: It pays to buy a round-trip ticket on the Hy-Line or the Steamship Authority fast ferry. It's cheaper than buying two one-way tickets.

Hy-Line Cruises conventional ferry: From early May through October, Hy-Line's standard 1-hour-and-50-minute ferry service on the Great Point is also offered. Round-trip tickets are $45 for adults ($22.50 one-way), free for children 5 to 12, and $14 extra

for bikes. On busy holiday weekends, you may want to order tickets in advance; otherwise, be sure to buy your tickets at least a half-hour before your boat leaves the dock.

The standard ferry Great Point also has a **first-class section** with a private lounge, bathrooms, a bar, and a snack bar; a continental breakfast or afternoon cheese and crackers is also served onboard. No pets are allowed on the *Great Point* ferry in the first-class section. Tickets in the first-class section are $60 round-trip ($30 one-way), for all ages.

Hy-Line's **Around the Sound** cruise is a 1-day round-trip excursion from Hyannis, with stops in Nantucket and Martha's Vineyard, that runs from mid-June to mid-September. The price is $79 for adults, $44 for children 5 to 12, and $21 extra for bikes.

Hy-Line runs one passenger-only high-speed ferry **from Oak Bluffs,** on Martha's Vineyard, to Nantucket, from mid-June to mid-September (there is no car-ferry service btw. the islands). The trip time from Oak Bluffs is 1 hour and 10 minutes. The one-way fare is $36 for adults, $24 for children 5 to 12, and $7 extra for bikes.

From Harwich Port: You can avoid the summer crowds in Hyannis and board one of **Freedom Cruise Line's** (702 Rte. 28, in Harwich Port, across from Brax Landing; ☎ **508/432-8999;** www.nantucketislandferry.com) passenger-only ferries to Nantucket. From mid-May to early October, boats leave from Saquatucket Harbor in Harwich

Port. They make two or three trips a day in season and one trip per day in the shoulder season. The trip takes 1 hour and 15 minutes. A round-trip ticket is $74 for adults, $51 for children 2 to 11, $6 for children 1 and under, and $14 extra for bikes. Parking is free for day-trippers; it's $17 overnight. Advance reservations are highly recommended.

A hint: All the ferries are equipped with Wi-Fi.

BY AIR   You can also fly into **Nantucket Memorial Airport** (© **508/325-5300**), which is about 3 miles south of Nantucket Road, on Old South Road. The flight to Nantucket takes about 30 to 40 minutes from Boston, 20 minutes from Hyannis, and a little more than an hour from New York City airports. Keep in mind, there is frequent shuttle bus service from Nantucket Airport terminal to town for $2.

Airlines providing service to Nantucket include: **Cape Air/Nantucket Airlines** (© **866/227-3247** or 508/771-6944; www.flycapeair.com), year-round from Hyannis (about $126 round-trip, $57–$69 one-way), Boston (about $350 round-trip, $175 one-way), Martha's Vineyard ($49 each way), and New Bedford ($99 each way); **Island Airlines** (© **800/248-7779** or 508/771-7774; www.islandair.net), year-round from Hyannis ($138 round-trip); and **US Airways Express** (© **800/428-4322;** www.usairways.com), year-round from Boston ($383 round-trip) and LaGuardia Airport in New York City ($655 round-trip). **Delta Airlines, United Airlines,** and **JetBlue Airways** run flights from JFK Airport in New York City to Nantucket. Delta and United charges charge about $500 round-trip for a 1-hour-and-20-minute flight. Jet Blue charges $318 to $374 round-trip for a 1-hour-and-10-minute flight.

Island Airlines and Nantucket Airlines both offer year-round charter service to the island. Another recommended charter company is **Ocean Wings** (© **800/253-5039;** www.flyoceanwings.com).

GETTING AROUND

Nantucket is easily navigated on bike, moped, or foot, and also by shuttle bus or taxi. If you're staying outside of Nantucket Town, however, or if you simply prefer to explore by car, you might want to bring your own car or rent one when you arrive. Adventure-minded travelers may even want to rent a jeep or other four-wheel-drive vehicle, which you can take out on the sand—a unique island experience—on certain sections of the coast (a permit is required—see "By Car & Jeep," below). Keep in mind that if you do opt to travel by car, in-town traffic can reach gridlock in the peak season, and parking can be a nightmare.

BY BIKE & MOPED   When I head to Nantucket for a few days, biking is my preferred mode of transportation. The island itself is relatively flat, and paved bike paths abound—they'll get you from Nantucket Town to Siasconset, Surfside, and Madaket. There are also many unpaved back roads to explore, which make mountain bikes a wise choice when pedaling around Nantucket.

A word of warning to bikers: One-way street signs and all other traffic rules apply to you, too! This law is enforced in Nantucket Town, and don't be surprised if a tanned but stern island policeman requests that you get off your bike and walk. Helmets are required for children 15 and under. Bikers should also remember not to ride on the sidewalks in town, which are busy with pedestrians strolling and exiting shops.

Mopeds and scooters are also prevalent, but watch out for sand on the roads. Be aware that local rules and regulations are strictly enforced. Mopeds are not allowed on sidewalks or bike paths. You'll need a driver's license to rent a moped, and state law requires that you wear a helmet. The following shops rent bikes and scooters (all are within walking distance of the ferries): **Cook's Cycle Shop, Inc.,** 6 S. Beach St.

(☎ **508/228-0800**), which rents bikes and mopeds; **Nantucket Bike Shop,** at Steamboat and Straight wharves (☎ **508/228-1999;** www.nantucketbikeshop.com), which rents bikes and scooters; and **Young's Bicycle Shop,** 6 Broad St., at Steamboat Wharf (☎ **508/228-1151;** www.youngsbicycleshop.com), which rents bikes and also does repairs. Bike rentals average $20 to $30 for a full day. Most places renting scooters or mopeds require a valid driver's license and the operator to be 18 or older. Rentals cost about $70 for a one-seater or $90 for a two-seater for 24 hours.

BY SHUTTLE BUS   Inexpensive shuttle buses, with bike racks and accessibility for those with disabilities, make frequent loops through Nantucket Town and beaches, and to outlying spots. For routes and stops, contact the **Nantucket Regional Transit Authority** (☎ **508/228-7025;** www.nrtawave.com), or pick up a map and schedule at the visitor center on Federal Street or the chamber of commerce office on Main Street (see "Visitor Information," above). The shuttle permits you to bring your clean, dry dog along, too. There's room for two bikes on a first-come, first-served basis. The cost is $1 to $2, and exact change is required. A 3-day pass can be purchased at the visitor center for $10.

Shuttle routes and fares are pretty simple. Downtown shuttle stops are located on the corner of Salem and Washington streets (for South, Miacomet, and Airport loops); on Broad Street, in front of the Foulger Museum (for Madaket Loop and Beach Express); and on Washington Street, at the corner of Main Street (for 'Sconset loops). Most shuttles run approximately every 30 minutes for most of the season; from July until Labor Day, the Mid-Island Loop runs every 15 minutes, and the Miacomet Loop every 20 minutes.

BY CAR & JEEP   I recommend a car if you'll be here for more than a week or if you're staying outside Nantucket Town. However, there are no in-town parking lots; parking, although free, is limited to Nantucket's handful of narrow streets, which can be a problem in the busy summer months. Also, gas is much more expensive on Nantucket than it is on the mainland.

Four-wheel-drive vehicles are your best bet, as many beaches and nature areas are off sandy paths; be sure to reserve at least a month in advance, if you're coming in summer. If you plan on doing any four-wheeling in the sand, you need to get an **Over-Sand Permit** ($140) from the **Nantucket Police Department** (☎ **508/228-1212**). To drive in the **Coskata-Coatue** nature area, you need a separate permit from the **Trustees of Reservations,** at the gatehouse (☎ **508/228-0006**), which costs about $140 for a season pass, or a $35 gate fee for a day-rental four-wheel-drive that comes with the Over-Sand Permit. Dogs are not allowed, even in a car.

The following on-island rental agencies offer cars, Jeeps, and other four-wheel-drive vehicles: **Hertz,** at the airport (☎ **800/654-3131** or 508/228-9421; www.hertz.com); **Nantucket Windmill Auto Rental,** at the airport (☎ **800/228-1227** or 508/228-1227; www.nantucketautorental.com); and **Young's 4×4 & Car Rental,** 6 Broad St., at Steamboat Wharf (☎ **508/228-1151;** www.youngsbicycleshop.com). A standard car costs about $129 to $139 per day in season; a four-wheel-drive rental is about $199 to $229 per day (including an Over-Sand Permit).

BY TAXI   You'll find taxis (many are vans that can accommodate large groups or those traveling with bikes) waiting at the airport and at all ferry ports. During the busy summer months, I recommend reserving a taxi in advance to avoid a long wait upon arrival. Rates are flat fees, based on one person riding before 1am, with surcharges for additional passengers, bikes, and dogs. The most centrally located taxi stand is at the bottom of Main Street, in front of the Club Car restaurant. A taxi from the airport to Nantucket Town will cost about $15, plus $1 for each additional person. Reliable cab companies on the island include **All Point Taxi & Tours** (© 508/228-5799); **Canty's Cab** (© 508/228-2888); **Chief's Cab** (© 508/284-8497), which is run by the island's former fire chief; **Lisa's Taxi** (© 508/228-2223); and **Val's Cab Service** (© 508/228-9410).

[FastFACTS] NANTUCKET

ATMs/Banks **Automated teller machines (ATMs)** can be difficult to locate on Nantucket. **Nantucket Bank** (© 508/228-0580), has five locations: 2 Orange St., 104 Pleasant St., 1 Amelia Dr., the Hub on Main Street, and the airport lobby, all open 24 hours. **Pacific National Bank** has four locations: the A&P Supermarket (next to the wharves), the Stop & Shop (open 24 hr. seasonally), the Steamship Wharf Terminal, and the Pacific National Bank lobby (open during bank hours only).

Emergencies In case of a **medical emergency,** the **Nantucket Cottage Hospital,** 57 Prospect St. (© 508/825-8100; www.nantuckethospital.org), is open 24 hours.

Safety Nantucket is a very safe destination. But, as in any circumstance, when traveling, keep an eye on your belongings.

Where to Stay
VERY EXPENSIVE

Beachside at Nantucket ★   Simple and clean and a little nondescript, the Beachside is the equivalent of a Hampton's Inn on the island. But then again, you will not be spending much time in your room anyway, right? It's a 10-minute walk to Steamboat Wharf and the heart of downtown in one direction and about the same distance to Jetties Beach the other way. The rooms are more spacious than what you might find in a historic house B&B; the "poolside' rooms are more private.

30 N. Beach St. (about ¾ mile west of the town center). ©**800/322-4433** or 508/228-2241. www. thebeachside.com. 90 units. Summer $315–$415 double; $425–$750 suite. Rates include continental breakfast. Closed late Oct to late Apr. **Amenities:** Heated outdoor pool; Wi-Fi (free). Dogs allowed.

Cliffside ★★★   If you can swing the hefty nightly room rate and the 4-night minimum stay, this beachfront property is the ultimate place to stay on Nantucket. The name "beach club" is apt, because when you walk into the unpretentious lobby, you feel like you are entering an old-money private club, one where the fresh-faced staff acts genuinely glad to see you. The on-site restaurant, Galley Beach, is one of the island's best, and all the amenities, from the health club to the in-room extras are top-notch. But the biggest selling point is the beach. Get one of the Beach Club rooms, with private decks right on the sand. They cost a little more but are worth it. Better yet, reserve slightly off-season, in May or October, to get a much better rate for the same room. Then just cross your fingers on the weather.

46 Jefferson Ave. (about 1 mile from town center). © **800/932-9645** or 508/228-0618. www. cliffsidebeach.com. 25 units, 1 cottage. Summer $585–$995 double; $695–2,675 suite; $1,115 3-bedroom apt; $1,025-1,320 cottage. There is a 5.3 percent service charge in addition to taxes. Rates include continental breakfast. Closed mid-Oct to mid-May. **Amenities:** Restaurant; babysitting; concierge; exercise facility; pool; steam saunas; indoor hydrotherapy spa; Wi-Fi (free).

The Cottages/Woof Cottages at the Boat Basin ★★★   On a wharf alongside Nantucket Harbor, the Wharf Cottages comprise 24 units with 1-, 2-, and 3-bedroom

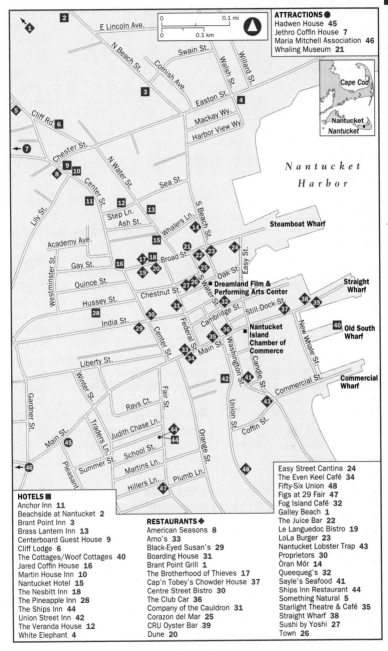

E Lincoln Ave.

N Beach St.

Cornish Ave.

Swain St.

Walsh St.

Willard St.

Easton St.

Mackay Wy.

Harbor View Wy.

Cliff Rd.

Chester St.

N Water St.

Sea St.

S Beach St.

Nantucket Harbor

Steamboat Wharf

Lily St.

Center St.

Step Ln.

Ash St.

Whalers Ln.

Academy Ave.

Westminster St.

Gay St.

Broad St.

Quince St.

Chestnut St.

Oak St.

Easy St.

Dreamland Film & Performing Arts Center

Straight Wharf

Hussey St.

Slater St.

Cambridge St.

Still Dock St.

New Whale St.

India St.

Center St.

Federal St.

Main St.

Nantucket Island Chamber of Commerce

Old South Wharf

Liberty St.

Winter St.

Washington St.

Candle St.

Commercial St.

Commercial Wharf

Gardner St.

Main St.

Traders Ln.

Rays Ct.

Fair St.

Judith Chase Ln.

Orange St.

Union St.

Coffin St.

School St.

Summer St.

Martins Ln.

Pleasant St.

Hillers Ln.

Plumb Ln.

ATTRACTIONS ●
Hadwen House **45**
Jethro Coffin House **7**
Maria Mitchell Association **46**
Whaling Museum **21**

Cape Cod

Nantucket

Nantucket

HOTELS ■
Anchor Inn **11**
Beachside at Nantucket **2**
Brant Point Inn **3**
Brass Lantern Inn **13**
Centerboard Guest House **9**
Cliff Lodge **6**
The Cottages/Woof Cottages **40**
Jared Coffin House **16**
Martin House Inn **10**
Nantucket Hotel **15**
The Nesbitt Inn **18**
The Pineapple Inn **28**
The Ships Inn **44**
Union Street Inn **42**
The Veranda House **12**
White Elephant **4**

RESTAURANTS ◆
American Seasons **8**
Arno's **33**
Black-Eyed Susan's **29**
Boarding House **31**
Brant Point Grill **1**
The Brotherhood of Thieves **17**
Cap'n Tobey's Chowder House **37**
Centre Street Bistro **30**
The Club Car **36**
Company of the Cauldron **31**
Corazon del Mar **25**
CRU Oyster Bar **39**
Dune **20**

Easy Street Cantina **24**
The Even Keel Café **34**
Fifty-Six Union **48**
Figs at 29 Fair **47**
Fog Island Café **32**
Galley Beach **1**
The Juice Bar **22**
Le Languedoc Bistro **19**
LoLa Burger **23**
Nantucket Lobster Trap **43**
Proprietors **30**
Òran Mór **14**
Queequeg's **32**
Sayle's Seafood **41**
Ships Inn Restaurant **44**
Something Natural **5**
Starlight Theatre & Café **35**
Straight Wharf **38**
Sushi by Yoshi **27**
Town **26**

options. Your neighbors are the private yachts that line the harbor. These are sweet units, with kitchen and comfortable seating areas, beautifully maintained and decorated in a nautical modern style. The complimentary bicycles are first-come, first-serve.

24 Old South Wharf (in the center of town). ℭ **866/838-9253** or 508/325-1499. www.thecottages nantucket.com. 33 units. Summer $445–$750 studio and 1-bedroom; $750–$1,145 2-bedroom; $1,090–$1,240 3-bedroom. AE, MC, V. Closed mid-Oct to May. Pet-friendly. **Amenities:** Wi-Fi (free).

Nantucket Hotel & Resort ★★

Thoroughly modern and renovated, but with generous nods to the island's rich history, this grand lady of island hospitality caters to those who prefer a full-service experience. It is especially geared to families with children. The hotel can handle groups of anywhere from 2 to 17 people in its tastefully designed and comfortable rooms. There is a complimentary children's program during the day and 3 nights a week with a fee. You can hop aboard either the antique fire truck or antique bus to be shuttled to Surfside or Jetties Beach.

77 Easton St. (a few blocks from the center of town). ℭ **508/228-4747.** www.thenantuckethotel. com. 12 units, Summer $450–$1,095 double; $990–$1,350 2-bedroom. **Amenities:** Restaurant, 2 outdoor heated pools (1 adults only), fitness facility and spa, fitness classes, kids' program, shuttle; Wi-Fi (free).

The Pineapple Inn ★★

This B&B is one of the Summer House group of small inns and B&Bs, so if one is booked up, they can refer you to the other. A stay here also means that you can take advantage of the pool, private beach, and other amenities at the Summer House Inn and Cottages in 'Sconset. As for the Pineapple, it is a lovely property with rooms that are, for the most part spacious, and it has a good location, steps from downtown shops and restaurants.

10 Hussey St. (in the center of town). ℭ **508/228-9992.** www.thesummerhouse.com/pineapple. 12 units, 8 with tub/shower combination, 4 with shower only. Summer $230–$375 double. Rates include continental breakfast. Closed early Dec to mid-Apr. No children 8 or under. **Amenities:** Wi-Fi (free).

Union Street Inn ★★

The Union Street Inn is a B&B that acts like a hotel, with refinements that bring it several notches above the usual "mom and pop" operation. The entire inn has been recently renovated in a combination of bright and rich colors, with luxurious wallpapers and wood paneling. This is the only Nantucket B&B to serve a full breakfast (it's a zoning thing), and there are fresh cookies in the afternoon.

7 Union St. (in the center of town), Nantucket. ℭ **888/517-0707** or 508/228-9222. www.unioninn. com. 12 units, 1 with tub/shower combination, 11 with shower only. Summer $299–$499 double; $579 suite. Rates include full breakfast. Closed Nov–Mar. **Amenities:** Wi-Fi (free).

The Veranda House ★★

Calling itself a retro-chic boutique hotel, the Veranda House, originally built in 1684, is one of the island's most stylish B&Bs. Inside, it looks like nothing else on island: There's rattan mixed with club chairs mixed with zebra striped benches in the common areas. The rooms have colorful artwork and accents. The smallest ones are well priced for budget travelers, particularly off-season.

3 Step Lane (a few blocks from town center). ℭ **877/228-0695** or 508/228-0695. www.theveranda house.com. 18 units. Summer $319–$629 double; $649 suite. Rates include continental breakfast. Closed mid-Oct to late May. **Amenities:** Wi-Fi (free).

The Wauwinet ★★

If refuge is what you want, refuge is what you'll get at this luxury property at the head of the harbor, a 20-minute car ride from town. It's also at the edge of some 1,400 acres of Nantucket's most cherished, protected land. The property has 32 guestrooms and 6 cottages that are richly appointed with equestrian oil paintings and fine linens and have views of the bay or the garden (planted with opulent hydrangeas). The manicured lawn leads to a private beach on the harbor side, and there's a path to a private beach on the Atlantic side. Complimentary Sunfish sailboats and bicycles are available during the day, and a shuttle runs back and forth to town hourly. Other perks include a bay cruise, excursions to Great Point Lighthouse, lawn games and tennis (two courts). The restaurant, Topper's, is excellent.

120 Wauwinet Rd. (about 8 miles east of Nantucket center), Nantucket.© **800/426-8718** or 508/228-0145. www.wauwinet.com. 25 units, 10 cottages. Summer $680–$1,250 double; $1,020–$1,450 1- and 2-bedroom cottages. Rates include full breakfast and afternoon wine and cheese. Closed mid-Oct to mid-May. Children 12 and older only. **Amenities:** Restaurant; mountain bikes on loan; concierge; croquet lawn; room service; spa; 2 clay tennis courts; rowboats, sailboats, sea kayaks; Wi-Fi (free).

White Elephant ★★★ The White Elephant has long been one of the islands top luxury accommodations. A 2-minute walk from Steamboat Wharf, many of the finely appointed rooms and suites have harbor views and private decks—others have garden views—several with their own fireplace. Garden-view cottages have 1, 2, or 3 bedrooms and a there is a 3-bedroom loft. The Brant Point Grill provides a decent breakfast but is best known as one of the island's best steak joints.

50 Easton St. (P.O. Box 1390), Nantucket.© **800/445-6574** or 508/228-2500. www.whiteelephant hotel.com. 52 units, 11 cottages (61 with tub/shower combination, 2 with shower only). Summer $800–$850 double; $1,100 1-bedroom cottage; $2,150 2-bedroom cottage; $2,430 3-bedroom cottage. Rates include full breakfast. Closed Nov–Mar except for 1 week during Christmas Stroll, in early December. **Amenities:** Restaurant (lobster and steakhouse, serving lunch and dinner daily, plus an afternoon raw bar); concierge; exercise room; room service; spa; Wi-Fi (free).

MODERATE

Brant Point Inn ★ Located about halfway between downtown and Jetties Beach, the Brant Point Inn and its almost-identical twin across the driveway, the Atlantic Mainstay, have fairly spacious rooms with queen or twin beds decorated in a homey country style, with wooden post-and-beam construction throughout. A common living room is for reading and relaxation.

6 N. Beach St. (a few blocks west of town).© **508/228-5442.** www.brantpointinn.com. 8 units. Summer $245 double; $225–$345 suite. Rates include continental breakfast. Closed Nov–Apr.

Brass Lantern Inn ★★ This is a very good moderately priced option by virtue of its location—far enough from the thick of things to be very quiet but close enough for a quick walk—and its amenities, which are a step up from some similar B&Bs.

11 N. Water St. (in the center of town).© **800/377-6609** or 508/228-4064. www.brasslanternnantucket. com. 16 units, 8 with tub/shower combination, 8 with shower only. Summer $315–$395 double; $550–$650 2-bedroom suite. Rates include continental breakfast. Dogs allowed. **Amenities:** Wi-Fi (free).

Centerboard Guest House ★★ Located in the center of town, this whaling captain's home has always been one of the better area B&Bs. It is the only one in the Victorian style, lending it a certain elegance that comes with the 12-foot ceilings and spacious rooms. The rooms are luxurious, and the bedding is particularly plush here.

8 Chester St. © **877/228-2811** or 508/228-9696. www.centerboardguesthouse.com. 7 units. Summer $399–$450 double; $575 suite. Rates include continental breakfast. Closed Nov–Apr.

Cliff Lodge ★ This 1771 captain's home is along the initial ascent of Nantucket's Cliff Road, where some of the island's oldest and most sought after homes are located. A climb to the widow's walk gives a panorama of downtown Nantucket and the harbor.

The bright and cheery rooms range from a tiny single tucked into an alcove to a spacious room on the first floor with a king-sized bed. The apartment is a good fit for a small family. Wine and cheese is served in the afternoon.

9 Cliff Rd. (a few blocks from the center of town). ℭ**508/228-9480.** www.clifflodgenantucket.com. 12 units. Summer $155 single; $195–$320 double; $485 apt. Rates include continental breakfast. No children 10 and under.

Jared Coffin House ★ This inn, with its majestic brick facade, has a terrific location, just steps from all restaurants and stores in the downtown center. The rooms have been freshened up, but still retain a feeling of yesteryear, particularly in the old wallpaper and furnishings.

29 Broad St. (at Centre St.). ℭ**800/248-2405** or 508/228-2400. www.jaredcoffinhouse.com. 60 units, 52 with tub/shower combination, 8 with shower only. Summer $155 single; $325–$470 double. **Amenities:** Wi-Fi (free).

The Ships Inn ★ The abolitionist Lucretia Mott was born in this 1831 house, and today it is one of the island's best moderately priced inns. Rooms are fresh and cheerful, not overly frilly. None are alike, and unfortunately some are small or awkwardly configured. A very good restaurant is in the basement.

13 Fair St. (a few blocks from town center). ℭ **888/872-4052** or 508/228-0040. www.shipsinn nantucket.com. 12 units, 2 with shared bathroom. Summer $155 single with shared bathroom; $295 double. Rates include continental breakfast. Closed late Oct to mid-May. **Amenities:** Restaurant; Wi-Fi (free).

INEXPENSIVE

Anchor Inn ★ In 1806 Captain Archaelus Hammond, considered the first man from Nantucket to kill a sperm whale in the Pacific Ocean, built the building that now houses the Anchor Inn, and it still has the old floorboards and antique paneling from days gone by. The rooms, each named after a whaling ship, are simple, and some are smallish, but for authentic Nantucket feel and hospitality, this inn can't be beat.

66 Centre St. (in the center of town). ℭ**508/228-0072.** www.anchor-inn.net. 11 units, 2 with tub/ shower combination, 9 with shower only. Summer $289 double. Rates include continental breakfast. Closed Jan–Feb. **Amenities:** Wi-Fi (free).

Robert B. Johnson Memorial Hostel The price is under $40 a night and the location is priceless. Yards away from a private walk to the popular Surfside Beach, this hostel was once a life-saving station where men headed out in treacherous conditions to rescue sailors from shipwrecks along the island's south shore. Now it is a lifesaver of another sort, saving cash-strapped visitors from being priced off the island.

31 Western Ave. (on Surfside Beach, about 3 miles south of Nantucket Town). http://capecod. hiusa.org. ℭ **888/901-2084** or 508/228-0433. 49 beds. $32–$35 for members; $35–$38 for nonmembers; $178 private room. Closed mid-Sept to mid-May.

Where to Eat

During the 2 Nantucket Restaurant Weeks (early June and late Sept), you can get three-course menus for the same price as an entree costs on a typical night. Think of it as two or three meals for the price of one.

VERY EXPENSIVE

American Seasons ★★ AMERICAN A leader among Nantucket's restaurants for 25 years, American Seasons emphasizes regional cuisines. Faroe Island salmon with smoked potato and a red onion crème fraîche shares space on the menu with buttermilk chicken with yellow-eye peas and pimento fried biscuits, smoked chicken hocks, and giblet gravy. The candlelit dining room is decorated with old-fashioned Americana and pleasing agrarian-themed murals. Seating in the summer is outside on a trellis-covered patio.

80 Centre St. (2 blocks from the center of town). © **508/228-7111.** www.americanseasons.com. Main courses $26–$38. Apr to mid-Dec daily 5:30–9:30pm. Closed mid-Dec to Mar.

Black-Eyed Susan's ★★ ASIAN/AMERICAN   Foodie friends have said they would like to have every meal at this funky diner. Some seating is right at the counter: The food is cooked right behind it, for all to see—and even better, to smell. Breakfasts of huevos ranchos or Pennsylvania Dutch buttermilk pancakes with Jarlsberg cheese will leave you so full that you might want to skip lunch and can arrive early for dinner. At that hour, you might have your choice of tandoori salmon with mango coulis; beef tenderloin in red wine sauce with rigatoni; or paprika-dusted diver scallops with a lemon-Madeira demi-glace and kale risotto. Note that the diner's cash only; there's an ATM not far away on Centre Street. It's also BYOB: A liquor store is a few blocks away, on Main Street. Finally, they don't take reservations, so that the line out the door. A typical wait in season is an hour.

10 India St. (in the center of town). © **508/325-0308.** www.black-eyedsusans.com. Main courses $24–$29. Apr–Oct daily 7am–1pm; Mon–Sat 6–10pm. Closed Nov–Mar.

The Chanticleer ★★★ FRENCH   This famous restaurant in a rose-covered cottage has become even better in recent years. The chef-owner Jeff Worster has reinvented the strictly French menu to reflect modern ways of dining. That means, just taking a sampling from the appetizers menu, that the seared tuna au poivre is served with Green Goddess dressing, and roasted butternut squash comes with an apple bisque with ginger crème fraîche, Thai curry, and a lobster egg roll. Still, this remains one of the island's most formal dining experiences—a place for special occasions.

9 New St., Siasconset (on the south side of the island). © **508/257-4499.** www.thechanticleer.net. Jackets preferred for men. Main courses $24–$46. June–Aug Tues–Sun 11:30am–2pm and 6–9:30pm; call for off-season hours. Closed mid-Oct to late May.

The Club Car ★ CONTINENTAL   No list of restaurants on Nantucket would be complete without the Club Car, a classic since it was founded in 1977. The restaurant has stuck to the same formula for decades, classic French cuisine served in a traditionally fancy dining room. Diners return year after year for the beef Wellington night, the famous crab cakes, and shrimp scampi. After dinner, diners can wander into the club car section—an actual train car from when a train used to run from downtown Nantucket out to 'Sconset. This piano bar is loads of fun in the summer.

1 Main St. © **508/228-1101.** www.theclubcar.com. Main courses $34–$45. July–Aug daily 11am–4pm and 6–9:30pm; call for off-season hours. Closed late Oct to Apr.

Company of the Cauldron ★★★ NEW AMERICAN   A longtime contender for the honor of most romantic restaurant on Nantucket, this place maintains its special qualities year after year. You enter its little red building from the tree-shaded sidewalk while candles flicker and a harpist performs classical music. There's just one three-course, fixed-price menu every night, so that everyone is served the same dishes and it feels a bit like a private dinner party. You check the menus in advance to be sure they are serving something you want. For example, it might be grilled shrimp; beef

Wellington and, for dessert, vanilla panna cotta. Monday's single seating always includes lobster four ways (bisque, salad, steamed, and grilled).

5 India St. (btw. Federal and Centre sts.). ℭ**508/228-4016.** www.companyofthecauldron.com. Fixed-price dinner $70–$89. Early July to early Sept Tues–Sun seatings 6:45 and 8:45pm, Mon seating 7pm only; call for off-season hours. Closed mid-Oct to mid-Apr, except Thanksgiving weekend and the first 2 weeks of Dec.

Corazon del Mar ★★ LATIN   A favorite of locals and visitors alike, this is authentic Latin restaurant with a spirit of fun infused in every dish. It is a little less expensive than some of the other spots in town, and with its brightly colored walls, has significantly more pizzazz. Downstairs has just a half-dozen tables and a bar; the upstairs has a few more tables and a tequila bar. Lunch here has a great menu (bacon-wrapped hotdogs; spicy beef jerk burrito; build your own Mexican street sandwich) and is very reasonably priced ($11–$14). Dinner includes the raw bar and ceviche menu with the likes of mini yellowfin tuna tacos; and lobster and shrimp tostada.

21 S. Water St. ℭ**508/228-0815.** www.corazonnantucket.com. Main courses $23–$32. July–Aug daily 11:30am–2:30pm, 5:30–9:30pm; call for off-season hours. Closed Nov to early May.

Cru Oyster Bar ★ SEAFOOD   Formerly the Ropewalk, this upscale raw bar with an enviable location has long been the place where the yachting crowd goes to toast the day. And why not? They can hop off their boats and be at the bar in a few steps. There are a dozen kinds of oysters on the menu, a revolving selection from around the region. The bistro-style menu has classics like steak frites and seared sea scallops with lobster broth. Keep in mind, the million-dollar view and up-close look at the rich and famous is reflected in your check. Wine is $17 a glass and appetizers hover around $20 apiece.

1 Straight Wharf. ℭ**508/228-9278.** www.theropewalk.com. Main courses $23–$33. Late May to Aug daily 11am–10pm. Call for off-season hour. Closed mid-Oct to Apr.

Dune ★★ NEW AMERICAN   Sleek and modern, Dune may seem at first a little out of place on Nantucket, but the chef-owner, Michael Getter, a longtime resident, knows what he's doing. Lovely colorful choices here change with the seasons, but you will certainly see items on the menu you have never seen anywhere else. A spring offering might be a pea bisque with smoked mushrooms and ham with lavender yogurt. A grilled steak comes with bok choy and green garlic potato puree.

20 Broad St. ℭ**508/228-5550.** www.dunenantucket.com. Main courses $28–$38. July–Sept daily noon–3pm and 6–10pm; call for off-season hours.

Galley Beach ★★★ NEW AMERICAN   This is really more of an experience than a restaurant. An intake of breath is the typical response as you walk into the dining room set right on a beautiful wide beach with views across the sand to the ocean. Salt breezes accompany your meal. You might expect a place this fabulous to have so-so food because people will come no matter what. But not so here. The menu is wonderfully summery. On the starter list, you might have cured salmon tartare with crème fraîche and caviar, or crab tortellini with fennel cream and ginger vinaigrette. As a main course, there is the luxurious warm lobster tail r the pork belly with roast parsnips and picked pear. This restaurant boldly prices most of its entrees in the $40-range; that delicious lobster tail is $59.

At Cliffside Beach Club, 54 Jefferson Ave. ℭ**508/228-9641.** www.galleybeach.net. Main courses $32–$59. Summer Mon–Fri 11:30am–2:30pm and 5:30–10pm, Sat–Sun 10am–2:30pm and 5:30–10pm; call for off-season hours. Closed late Sept to late May.

Le Languedoc Bistro ★★ NEW AMERICAN/FRENCH Run since 1978 with the same owners, this bistro has remains a place where locals feel comfortable coming in for a warm lunch, a cheeseburger with garlic fries perhaps or a bowl of lobster bisque on a crisp fall day. The beauty of the dinner menu is that you can order half-portions for a more affordable meal that still lets you appreciate the riches of this food. Among the appetizers are the roasted fresh quail and veal sweetbreads saltimbocca. Main courses include the foie-gras-infused chicken or pan-roasted lobster with creamy polenta.

24 Broad St. ☎ **508/228-2552.** www.lelanguedoc.com. Main courses $28–$39 (half-portions $15–$16). June–Sept Tues–Sun 11:30am–2pm and 5:30–9:30pm; call for off-season hours. Closed mid-Dec to mid-May.

Nantucket Lobster Trap ★ SEAFOOD This is Nantucket's version of your typical clam shack, though keep in mind, it is far more expensive than the Cape Cod version. Seating is at picnic tables, and there's an extensive raw bar and an outdoor patio area. The standard fried fish dinners are on the menu as well as lobster dinners. There are also some pasta entrees that take advantage of the seafood, such as linguini with clam sauce and lobster scampi.

23 Washington St. ☎ **508/228-4200.** www.nantucketlobstertrap.com. Main courses $24–$30. June–Sept daily 5–10pm; call for off-season hours. Closed late Oct to early May.

Òran Mór Bistro ★★★ INTERNATIONAL Climbing the copper steps in this historic building to enter Òran Mór, you can tell you are in for a special evening. The vibe is surprisingly down to earth. No white tablecloths or crystal here, and the small handsome bar and attentive service put you at ease. The first course might be marinated grilled baby octopus, or perhaps a Nantucket lobster po'boy atop grilled focaccia. As for the main course, you might find beer-braised pork short ribs with a parsnip puree or a miso-marinated cod with sweet-potato lasagna. Desserts are a sublime specialty: Save room for vanilla cream-filled brioche doughnuts with brown butter and roasted pear puree.

2 S. Beach St. (in the center of town). ☎ **508/228-8655.** www.oranmorbistro.com. Main courses $26–$32. June to mid-Oct daily 6–9:30pm; mid-Oct to mid-Dec and mid-Apr to May Thurs–Tues 6–9pm. Closed mid-Dec to mid-Apr.

The Proprietors Bar & Table ★★ NEW AMERICAN Although much of the food here has global inspirations, the focus is on sourcing ingredients from small Nantucket and New England farms. The menu has mostly small plates of light bites, and hungry people will need three or four to satisfy them, so you might want to just come for a drink and an appetizer if you're on a budget. You might choose the duck fat potatoes with figs and smoked blue cheese or the eggplant puree with orange blossom honey. The flavors are a revelation. The dining room is very beautiful, a sort of hip ode to the island's history. It's fun to sit at the bar and soak in the atmosphere.

9 India St. ☎ **508/228-7477.** www.proprietorsnantucket.com. Main courses $35–$41. Half portions $12–$18. July and August 11:30am–2pm, 5:30–10pm; call for off-season hours. Closed Dec to mid-May.

Straight Wharf ★★★ NEW AMERICAN Perhaps the most lauded chefs on an island of lavishly praised chefs, Amanda Lydon and Gabriel Frasca run the elegant Straight Wharf beside Nantucket Harbor as a sort of chef's restaurant, a place where foodies flock for the best of the best in creative cuisine. The menus change nightly, adjusting to what's fresh at the market. In contrast to come of the other Nantucket restaurants, this food is neither heavy nor overly rich. You might begin with a butter pear and celery salad and continue with the seared Nantucket fluke with island vegetables and garden herbs, adding on pan-roasted broccoli rabe and heirloom grits. Finish the meal off with a chilled melon soup with a cantaloupe sorbet. See what I mean? Ethereal.

6 Harbor Sq. (on Straight Wharf). ℂ 508/228-4499. www.straightwharfrestaurant.com. Main courses $26–$39. July–Aug Tues–Fri 11:30am–2pm and 5:30–9:45pm, Sat–Sun 11am–2pm and 5:30–10pm; call for off-season hours. Closed late Sept to mid-May.

Town ★★ INTERNATIONAL   The peaceful aesthetic when you enter Town is not an illusion. This restaurant featuring global cuisine is all about balancing the yin and the yang. The decor inside and on the outdoor patio is features muted colors and soft textures, black and ivory, wicker and rattan, cozy booths and cushioned couches. Besides sushi, you might find red Thai curried chicken and orecchiette with grilled eggplant At the outdoor Tree Bar, which is under a shady tree, you can order appetizers from the menu like salt cod fritters with tomato confit, and sweet corn bisque.

4 E. Chestnut St. ℂ 508/325-TOWN [8696]. www.townnantucket.com. Main courses $24–$32. July–Aug Mon–Fri 5:30–9pm, Sat and Sun 11am–2:30pm and 5:30–9pm.

MODERATE

Centre Street Bistro ★★★ NEW AMERICAN   At this little cafe, two of the island's top chefs, Ruth and Tim Pitts, creating wonderfully creative meals in an intimate atmosphere. It's a very unpretentious place to have what is sure to be a memorable meal—the menu changes nightly. Main courses on a given night might include tofu pad Thai, sesame-crusted shrimp with red curry rice, and pan-seared duck breast with fruit chutney and homemade ricotta gnocchi. The restaurant is BYOB; the nearest liquor store is a few blocks away on Main Street.

29 Centre St. ℂ 508/228-8470. www.nantucketbistro.com. Main courses $19–$25. June–Sept Mon and Wed–Fri 11:30am–2pm and 5:30–9:30pm; Sat–Sun 8am–1pm and 6–9pm; call for off-season hours.

Sayle's Seafood ★★   A great bargain option is to pick up fried seafood platters or fish sandwiches at Sayle's, which is a short walk from the harbor, and eat it by the water. This is water-view dining on the cheap, and the fish here is among the best you can get on the island.

99 Washington St. Ext. ℂ 508/228-4599. www.saylesseafood.com. $7–$25. No credit cards. May–Nov daily 8am–9pm.

Sushi by Yoshi ★★   On an island 30 miles out to sea, it makes sense that you would be able to find terrific sushi. Here is your supplier. The small storefront lends itself to takeout, and what could be better than a sushi feast while sitting by the harbor watching the sunset? Be ready for a long wait here on summer nights.

2 E. Chestnut St. ℂ 508/228-1801. www.sushibyyoshi.com. Rolls from $9 and up. May to mid-Oct Sun–Thurs 11:30am–8:30pm, Fri–Sat 11:30am–9pm; mid-Oct to Apr Thurs–Sat 11:30am–9pm, Sun–Wed 5–9pm.

INEXPENSIVE

Arno's ★ INTERNATIONAL   A low-cost option for family dining, this restaurant near the top of Main Street has a pleasing brick interior and a very extensive menu. Serving three meals a day in season, it is a go-to place for a quick bite at any time of day. Sandwiches, salads and soups are the mainstays here.

41 Main St. ℂ **508/228-7001.** www.arnos.net. Main courses $9–$17. June–Oct daily 8am–10pm. Call for off-season hours. Closed Jan–late April.

The Brotherhood of Thieves ★ PUB The unusual name of this 1840s bar comes from an 1844 anti-slavery pamphlet written on Nantucket. It's best for classic pub fare like burgers or even a fish burrito, washed down with craft beer (they have a couple dozen unusual ones available on tap and in bottles.)

23 Broad St. ℂ **508/228-2551.** www.brotherhoodofthieves.com. Main courses $12–$26. Mar–Jan Mon–Sat 11:30am–midnight; Sun noon–10pm. Closed Feb.

Starlight Theatre and Cafe ★★ AMERICAN A budget night out on Nantucket can actually include dinner and a movie. Run by a local family, the theater shows first-run features year-round. There are special deals for dinner and a movie, and the fare here is unexpectedly different. From duck tacos to a Cajun spiced pork sandwich, this is definitely a step up from your usual burger joint, though they do have those too.

1 N. Union St. ℂ **508/228-4479.** www.starlightnantucket.com. All items under $15. July–Aug Mon–Sat 11:30am–9pm, Sun 9am–9pm; call for off-season hours.

TAKEOUT & PICNIC FARE

Broad Street, just steps from Steamboat Wharf, is the place to go for cheap takeout eats any time. Good choices are **Island Coffee,** 4 Broad St. (ℂ **508/228-2224**), where you can treat yourself to rich coffee and chocolate croissants with Nutella; **Walter's Deli,** 10 Broad St. (ℂ **508/228-0010**), for sandwiches; and **Stubby's,** 8 Broad St. (ℂ **508/228-0028**), for burgers. Walter's and Stubby's are open until 2am.

Bartlett's Farm ★★ In the 1800s, Nantucket had 100 family farms, and one was run by the Bartlett family on a large parcel near Hummock Pond. Today, it's is Nantucket's oldest and largest (125 acres) farm; the seventh generation is running the operation. A Bartlett's truck with its wonderful fresh produce is parked in town in the summer. It's well worth the trip to head out to the farm, where you can stock up on goodies, including prepared foods.

33 Bartlett Farm Rd. ℂ **508/228-9403.** www.bartlettsfarm.com. Apr–Dec daily 7:30am–8pm. Take Main St. to Civil War monument; take left on Milk St. to Hummock Pond Rd., and follow to Bartletts Farm Rd.

Cisco Brewery ★★ It used to be that the typical Nantucket visitor would not get to Cisco Brewery because it is too far to drive from the downtown area. But now a free shuttle bus, leaving from the Nantucket Visitor Services Center at 12:30pm) will take you there. The fun part is that they have live music on the property many afternoons. They invite different island restaurants to provide food service: Buy a drink at the brewery and enjoy a concert of local music.

5 Bartlett Farm Rd. ℂ **508/325-5929.** www.nantucketvineyard.com. Apr–Dec Mon–Sat 10am–7pm; Sun noon–6pm.

Easy Street Cantina ★ Among the many fast food places along Broad Street, this is your best bet for a good meal to go, mainly by virtue of the size of the menu and the choices you have. But this isn't typical fast-food fare. The fish tacos are nicely spiced and come with homemade slaw, and the breakfast sandwiches are sublime.

2 Broad St. ℂ **508/228-5418.** All under $15. July–Aug daily 7:30am–10pm. Call for off-season hours.

Something Natural ★★ This is the place to stop on your bike while heading out for a day at Jetties Beach. Big overstuffed sandwiches (they sell halfs too) and homemade cookies are the specialties.

50 Cliff Rd. ☏ **508/228-0504.** www.somethingnatural.com. Apr to mid-Oct daily 8am–6:30pm. Closed mid-Oct to Mar.

SWEETS

The Juice Bar ★★ This is *the* ice cream shop on the island, and the place where people gather when the bars let out to have one last treat before bedtime. With home-made ice cream and frozen yogurt, it is crowded most of the day.

12 Broad St. ☏**508/228-5799.** June–Aug Sun–Thurs 10am–9pm, Fri–Sat 10am–11:30pm; mid-Apr to May and Sept to mid-Oct daily 11am–9pm. Closed mid-Oct to mid-Apr.

Exploring: Beaches & Recreational Pursuits

BEACHES In distinct contrast to Martha's Vineyard, virtually all of Nantucket's 110-mile coastline is free and open to the public. Though the pressure to keep people out is sometimes intense (especially when four-wheel-drivers insist on their right to go anywhere, anytime), islanders are proud that they've managed to keep the shoreline in the public domain.

Each of the following areas tends to attract a different crowd.

o **Children's Beach ★**: This small beach is a protected cove just west of busy Steamship Wharf. It has a park, a playground, restrooms, lifeguards, a snack bar (the beloved Downy Flake, famous for its homemade doughnuts), and even a bandstand for free weekend concerts.

o **Cisco Beach ★★**: About 4 miles from town, in the southwestern quadrant of the island (from Main St., turn onto Milk St., which becomes Hummock Pond Rd.), Cisco enjoys vigorous waves—great for the surfers who flock here, not so great for the waterfront homeowners. Restrooms are available, and lifeguards are on duty.

o **Coatue ★**: This fishhook-shaped barrier beach, on the northeastern side of the island, at Wauwinet, is Nantucket's outback, accessible only by four-wheel-drive vehicles, watercraft, or the very strong-legged. Swimming is strongly discouraged because of fierce tides.

o **Dionis Beach ★★★**: About 3 miles out of town (take the Madaket bike path to Eel Point Rd.) is Dionis, which enjoys the gentle sound surf and steep, picturesque bluffs. It's a great spot for swimming, picnicking, and shelling, and you'll find fewer children than at Jetties or Children's beaches. Stick to the established paths to prevent further erosion. Lifeguards patrol here, and restrooms are available.

o **Jetties Beach ★★★**: Located about a half-mile west of Children's Beach, on North Beach Street, Jetties is about a 20-minute walk, or an even shorter bike ride, shuttle bus ride, or drive, from town (there's a large parking lot, but it fills up early on summer weekends). It's another family favorite for its mild waves, lifeguards, bathhouse, and restrooms. Facilities include the town tennis courts, volleyball nets, a skate park, and a playground; watersports equipment and chairs are also available to rent. There is also The Jetties, an upscale concession stand, complete with bar, serving lunch and dinner. The Fourth of July fireworks are held here. Every August, Jetties hosts an intense sand-castle competition.

o **Madaket Beach ★★★**: Accessible by Madaket Road, the 6-mile bike path that runs parallel to it, and by shuttle bus, this westerly beach is narrow and subject to pounding surf and sometimes serious crosscurrents. Unless it's a fairly tame day, you might content yourself with wading. It's the best spot on the island for admiring the sunset. Facilities include restrooms, lifeguards, and mobile food service.

o **Siasconset ('Sconset) Beach ★★**: The eastern coast of 'Sconset is as pretty as the town itself and rarely, if ever, crowded, perhaps because of the water's strong sideways tow. You can reach it by car, by shuttle bus, or by a less scenic and somewhat hilly (at least for Nantucket) 7-mile bike path. Lifeguards are usually on duty, but the closest facilities (restrooms, grocery store, and cafe) are back in the center of the village.

o **Surfside Beach ★★★**: Three miles south of town via a popular bike/skate path, broad Surfside—equipped with lifeguards, restrooms, and a surprisingly accomplished little snack bar—is appropriately named and commensurately popular. It draws thousands of visitors a day in high season, from college students to families, but the free parking lot can fit only about 60 cars. You do the math—or better yet, ride your bike or take the shuttle bus.

BICYCLING   Several lovely, paved bike paths radiate from the center of town to outlying beaches. The **bike paths** run about 6¼ miles west to Madaket, 3½ miles south to Surfside, and 8¼ miles east to Siasconset. To avoid backtracking from Siasconset, continue north through the charming village and return on the Polpis Road bike path. Strong riders could do a whole circuit of the island in a day. Picnic benches and water fountains stand at strategic points along all the paths.

For a free map of the island's bike paths (it also lists Nantucket's bicycle rules), stop by **Young's Bicycle Shop,** at Steamboat Wharf (ⓒ **508/228-1151;** www.youngsbicycle shop.com). It's definitely the best place for bike rentals, from basic three-speeds to high-tech suspension models. In operation since 1931—check out the vintage vehicles on display—they also deliver to your door. See "Getting Around," above, for more bike rental shops.

FISHING   For shellfishing you'll need a permit from the **marine coastal resources office** at 34 Washington St. (ⓒ **508/228-7261**), which costs $25 for nonresidents for the season. You'll see surf-casters all over the island ($10 permit required). Deep-sea charters heading out of Straight Wharf include Capt. Bob DeCosta's *The Albacore* (ⓒ **508/228-5074;** www.albacorecharters.com), Capt. Josh Eldridge's *Monomoy* (ⓒ **508/228-6867;** www.monomoychartersnantucket.com), and Capt. David Martin's *Absolute* (ⓒ **508/325-4000;** www.absolutesportfishing.com). On the *Absolute,* a 5-hour bass-fishing trip for up to six people costs $1,100; for 2½ hours, it is $550.

GOLF   Two pretty courses are open to the public: the 18-hole **Miacomet Golf Course,** 12 W. Miacomet Rd. (ⓒ **508/325-0333;** www.miacometgolf.com), and the 9-hole **Siasconset Golf Club,** off Milestone Road (ⓒ **508/257-6596**). You'll pay $125 for 18 holes at Miacomet. At Siasconset, playing 9 holes costs $35.

NATURE TRAILS   About one-third of Nantucket's 42 square miles are protected from development. Contact the **Nantucket Conservation Foundation,** at 118 Cliff Rd. (ⓒ **508/228-2884;** www.nantucketconservation.com), for a map of its holdings ($4), which include the 205-acre **Windswept Cranberry Bog** (off Polpis Rd.), where bogs are interspersed amid hardwood forests; and a portion of the 1,100-acre **Coskata-Coatue Wildlife Refuge,** comprising the barrier beaches beyond Wauwinet (see "Organized Tours," below). **The Maria Mitchell Association** (see "Museums & Historic Landmarks," below) sponsors guided birding and wildflower walks in season.

WATERSPORTS   **Jetties Sailing Center** manages the concession at **Jetties Beach** (ⓒ **508/228-5358**), which offers lessons and rents out kayaks, sailboards, sailboats, and more. Rental rates for single kayaks are $20 to $25 per hour; sailboards $20 to $25 per hour; and Sunfish $35 per hour. **Sea Nantucket,** on tiny Francis Street Beach, off Washington Street (✆ 508/228-7499), also rents stand-up paddleboards and kayaks; it's a quick sprint across the harbor to beautiful Coatue. Single kayaks rent for $40, and tandems for $70, for 4½ hours. **Nantucket Island Community Sailing** (✆ **508/228-6600;** www.nantucketcommunitysailing.org) gives relatively low-cost private and group lessons from the Jetties pier for adults (16 and up) and children; a seasonal adult membership covering open-sail privileges costs $250 for 4 weeks. One 2-hour private lesson costs $125.

Gear for scuba diving, fishing, and snorkeling is readily available at the souvenir shop **Sunken Ship,** on South Water and Broad streets, near Steamboat Wharf (✆ **508/228-9226;** www.sunkenship.com). Snorkeling gear costs $20 per day, and scuba-diving gear costs $50 per day. A 2-week scuba-diving course is $550.

Museums & Historic Landmarks

Hadwen House ★★   In the mid–19th century when Nantucket was a wealthy boomtown because of the success of sea captains in the whaling industry, there sprang up luxe houses like this Greek Revival beauty on Upper Main Street. Docents give a good feeling for the time period as they give tours around this 1845 mansion, a twin to the house next door. Whaling merchant William Hadwen hired a builder who specialized in intricate carving the construct the house's five-bayed facade, colossal pilasters and pedimented ionic portico. The house is a symbol of the wealth and prosperity of the island at that time. Inside is period furniture and outside are gardens maintained in period style.

96 Main St. (at Pleasant St., a few blocks southwest of the town center). ✆ **508/228-1894.** www.nha.org. Admission for historic sites only (not Whaling Museum) $6 adults, $3 children; also included in Nantucket Historical Association's History Ticket ($120 adults, $5 children). June–Sept Mon–Sat 10am–5pm, Sun noon–5pm; call for off-season hours. Closed Dec–Mar.

Jethro Coffin House ("The Oldest House") ★★   If you're only going to see one historical site, it should be the Whaling Museum, but if you have time for two sites, this should be your second choice. On an island of historic buildings, this is officially the oldest, built in 1686 as a wedding gift for Jethro Coffin, a blacksmith, and his wife Mary Gardner, it is the sole surviving structure from the island's original 17th-century English settlement. The interior gives an example of the spare existence of the early settlers. A kitchen garden and an apple orchard also help put the house into historic perspective.

16 Sunset Hill Lane (off W. Chester Rd., about ½ mile northwest of the town center). ✆ **508/228-1894.** www.nha.org. Admission for historic sites only (not the Whaling Museum) $6 adults, $3 children; also included in Nantucket Historical Association's History Ticket ($20 adults, $5 children). Late May to mid-Oct daily noon–5pm. Closed mid-Oct to late May.

Maria Mitchell Association ★   Maria Mitchell (1818–89), considered America's first professional astronomer, grew up on Nantucket, looking at the stars. She used to scan the sky from the roof of the Pacific National Bank, where her father was a cashier. While in her 20s, she was scanning the skies one day with a telescope when she found an object not in her charts. She had discovered a comet. She later became a professor of astronomy at Vassar and traveled the world giving talks on her discovery. The Maria Mitchell Association on Nantucket has developed a campus of five buildings, including two observatories, developed to scientific inquiry and education. Perhaps most of interest for any member of the family is the **Loines Observatory** at

59 Milk St. Ext. (© **508/228-9273**). It is open for viewing the stars July and August on Monday, Wednesday and Friday from 9 to 10:30pm; September to June, it's open 2 nights per month near to the first quarter of the moon. The **Hinchman House Natural Science Museum** (© **508/228-0898**) at 7 Milk St. (at Vestal St.) houses a visitor center with science exhibits. Programming for adults and children include bird-watching, nature walks and discovery classes. A small **aquarium** is at 28 Washington St. and is open Monday to Saturday 9am to 4pm.

4 Vestal St. (at Milk St., about ½ mile southwest of the town center). © **508/228-9198.** www.mmo. org. Admission to each site $6 adults, $5 children; museum pass (for birthplace, aquarium, science museum, and Vestal St. Observatory) $10 adults, $8 children ages 6–12. Early June to late Aug Tues–Sat 10am–4pm; call for off-season hours.

Nantucket Shipwreck and Lifesaving Museum ★

The Lifesaving Museum preserves the memory of those islanders who risked their lives to save shipwrecked mariners. The building is a replica of Nantucket's Life-saving station. Inside is an interesting display of objects on the topic including historic photos and actual surf-boats from the Massachusetts Humane Society, the predecessor of the Coast Guard. The collection includes film footage of the sinking of the *Andrea Doria*, which took place off the coast of Nantucket in 1956. Kids will like the exhibit on Coast Guard sea dogs. The museum is about 3 miles from town and is a nice stop by bike for those riding the path to Surfside Beach.

158 Polpis Rd. (3½ miles east of town; on the bike path and with a shuttle bus stop). © **508/228-1885.** www.nantucketshipwreck.org. Admission $6 adults, $4 children 6–18; free ages 5 and under. Late May to mid-Oct daily 10am–5pm.

Whaling Museum ★★★

One of the region's top museums, this is a must see on Nantucket. The museum building is a former candle factory that was built by the Mitchell family immediately following Nantucket's Great Fire of 1846. It was oper-ated as a candleworks until the end of whaling in 1860. Included in the museum is an 1847 candle factory and a 46-foot sperm whale skeleton. Besides a comprehensive history of the island of Nantucket and also of whaling, the museum has fine collections of the island arts of Nantucket baskets, scrimshaw and sailor's valentines.

13 Broad St. (in the center of town). © **508/228-1894.** www.nha.org. All Access Pass $20 adults, $18 students and seniors, $5 children 6–17 (includes Whaling Museum and historic sites). Late May to Nov daily 10am–5pm. Closed Dec to late May.

Shopping

ANTIQUES   **Rafael Osona Auctions** is the island's top antiques vendor, where the high prices reflect the high value of the items on view. Specialties include highly sought-after examples of Nantucket crafts like lightship baskets, scrimshaw, and sailors' valentines. It is located at the American Legion Hall at 21 Washington St. (© **508/228-3942;** www.nantucketauctions.com). Auctions take place May to December; see web-site for dates and viewing times.

ART & CRAFTS   The **Artists' Association of Nantucket** has the widest selection of work by locals, and the gallery at 19 Washington St. (© **508/228-0294;** www.nantucket arts.org) is impressive. In February and March, it's open by appointment only.

Exquisite art-glass pieces, as well as ceramics, jewelry, and basketry, can be found at **Dane Gallery,** 28 Centre St. (© **508/228-7779;** www.danegallery.com), where own-ers Robert and Jayne Dane show top-quality work. You'll be amazed at the colors and shapes of the glassware.

BARGAINS **Nantucket Cottage Hospital Thrift Shop,** 17 India St. (© 508/228-1125; www.nantuckethospital.org), is where you go to find a Dior gown—or just an elegant summer dress—at bargain-basement prices.

BOOKS **Mitchell's Book Corner,** 54 Main St. (© 508/228-1080; www.mitchells bookcorner.com), features an astute sampling of general-interest books and an entire room dedicated to regional and maritime titles. **Nantucket Bookworks,** 25 Broad St. (© 508/228-4000; www.nantucketbookworks.com), is a charming bookstore, strong on customer service and with a central location.

CHOCOLATE **Ambrosia Chocolate & Spices,** 29 Centre St. (© 508/292-3289), is an exquisite little organic chocolate and spice shop. Its specialty of the house is the otherworldly hazelnut "noisette," a delicate treat for coco connoisseurs. **Aunt Leah's Fudge,** located in the courtyard on Straight Wharf, a few steps from the Hy-Line ferry (© 800/824-6330; www.auntleahs.com), is where you find cranberry port-wine truffles and other undreamt-of delicacies, only with basic bonbons. **Petticoat Row Bakery,** located at 35 Centre St. (© 508/228-3700; www.petticoatrowbakery.com), has beautiful cupcakes, cookies, and muffins ready for purchase, but also excels in special orders.

Sweet Inspirations, 26 Centre St. (© 508/228-5814; www.nantucketchocolate. com), has been satisfying sweet tooths on Nantucket since 1981. This is artisan chocolate, carefully crafted on-site. Even better, the beautiful Nantucket-themed packaging makes this a great place to come for gifts. The Rainbow Fleet tin containing chocolate scallop shells, clipper-ship medallions, and Nantucket mints, among other chocolates, is a delight.

FASHION **Blue Beetle,** 12 Main St. (© 508/228-3227; www.bluebeetlenantucket. com), is the place to find summer cocktail dresses, cashmere throws, and the bling to pull it all together.

Eco-fashionista **Cheryl Fudge,** 24 Easy St. (© 508/228-9155; www.cherylfudge. com), sells what she calls up-cycled clothing, turning scarves into halter tops, for instance. Her funky dresses and vintage jewelry and ACK Green line of organic clothing have a passionate following. **Current Vintage,** 4 Easy St. (© 508/228-5073; www. currentvintage.com), is one of the most original shops to open in recent years, with gorgeous vintage gowns and accessories, such as antique bags and jewelry, as well as special wines from small wineries.

Haul Over, 7 Salem St. (© 508/228-9010), is where you go for basic, wear-it-all-summer-long sportswear, perfect for a day on the sailboat or an evening singing oldies at the piano bar at the Club Car.

Hepburn, 3 Salem St. (© 508/228-1458), sells ultrafashionable women's clothing and accessories, a cut above the usual fare.

Martha's Vineyard may have spawned "Black Dog" fever, but this island boasts the inimitable "Nantucket reds"—cotton clothing that starts out tomato red and washes out to salmon pink. The fashion originated at **Murray's Toggery Shop,** 62 Main St. (© 800/368-2134 or 508/228-0437; www.nantucketreds.com). Legend has it that the original duds were colored with an inferior dye that washed out almost immediately. However, customers so liked the thick cottons and instant aged look that the proprietor was forced to search high and low for more of the same fabric. Roland Hussey Macy, founder of Macy's, got his start here in the 1830s. Today's management also keeps up with current trends.

You'll find **Lilly Pulitzer's In The Pink,** which has sensational minidresses, at 5 S. Water St. (© 508/228-0569).

Zero Main, at 34 Centre St. (℡ **508/228-4401**), has a limited but fine selection of elegant yet casual women's clothes, shoes, and accessories.

GIFTS/HOME DECOR   Nantucket Looms, at 51 Main St. (℡ **508/228-1908;** www.nantucketlooms.com), is the place to ogle exquisite brushed-mohair chaise throws and other handmade woven items. The weaving studio is upstairs, where they also make blankets and sweaters of cotton and cashmere.

Erica Wilson Needle Works, 25 Main St. (℡ **508/228-9881;** www.ericawilson. com), features the designs of its namesake, an islander since 1958 and author of more than two dozen books on needlepoint. The shop offers hands-on guidance for hundreds of grateful adepts, as well as kits and handiwork of other noteworthy designers.

JEWELRY   Diana Kim England Goldsmiths, 56 Main St. (℡ **800/343-1468** or 508/228-3766; www.dianakimengland.com), is a team of five goldsmiths that have almost 70 years of combined experience in making jewelry. You'll find gold baskets and pearls, as well as unique custom pieces.

NEWSSTAND   The Hub, 31 Main St. (℡ **508/325-0200**), offers a selection of newspapers, magazines, and books, as well as greeting cards by local artists.

TOYS   The Toy Boat, 41 Straight Wharf (℡ **508/228-4552;** www.thetoyboat.com), is keen on creative toys that are also educational. In addition to the top commercial lines, owner Loren Brock stocks lots of locally crafted, hand-carved playthings, such as "rainbow fleet" sailboats, part of the Harbor Series that includes docks, lighthouses, boats, and everything your child needs to create his or her own Nantucket Harbor. There are also stackable lighthouse puzzles replicating Nantucket's beams.

Nantucket After Dark

Nantucket usually has an attractive crowd of bar-hoppers making the scene around town. You'll find good singles scenes at the **Boarding House** and **The Club Car,** which are reviewed earlier as restaurants, or **Slip 14 on South Wharf** at 14 Old South Wharf (℡ **508/228-2033;** www.slip14.com). Live music comes in many guises on Nantucket, and there are a number of good itinerant performers who play at different venues. Meanwhile, it may be Reggae Night at **The Chicken Box,** 16 Daves St. (℡ **508/228-9717;** www.thechickenbox.com), when the median age of this rocking venue rises by a decade or two. For a fun, down-low bar outside of town, try the **Muse,** 44 Surfside Rd. (℡ **508/228-1471**). Cover about $5.

Theatre buffs will want to spend an evening at the **Theatre Workshop of Nantucket,** 2 Centre St. (at the Methodist Church; ℡ **508/228-4305;** www.theatreworkshop.com). This shoebox-size theater assays thought-provoking plays as readily as summery farces. The season runs 8 months, well into the fall. Tickets are $25. You can catch the children's productions ($12) from mid-July to mid-August.

PLANNING
YOUR TRIP
TO BOSTON

A visit to Boston requires as much or as little forethought as you want, taking into account one important general rule: The later you plan, the more you'll pay.

GETTING TO BOSTON

By Plane

The main gateway to New England is **Logan International Airport** (**BOS; ℂ 800/23-LOGAN** [235-6426]; www.flylogan.com), which is across the harbor from downtown, at the East Boston end of the Sumner, Callahan, and Ted Williams tunnels.

The airport has four terminals—A, B, C, and E (there's no D). Each has ATMs, free Wi-Fi, rocking chairs, and an information booth (near baggage claim). Terminals A, B, and E have bank branches that handle currency exchange. Terminals A and C have children's play spaces (they're after security).

Boston is an increasingly popular direct destination for international travelers, but many itineraries go through another American or European city. International routes and schedules change constantly; double-check details (especially if you're traveling in the winter) well in advance.

ALTERNATE AIRPORTS Travelers with more time than money may find cheaper fares to Providence, Rhode Island (PVD), or Manchester, New Hampshire (MHT), than to Boston. Allow at least 2 hours to reach Boston, and factor the price of travel to and from your final destination into your budget. Check each airport's website for up-to-date information about ground transportation options.

T. F. Green Airport (ℂ **888/268-7222;** www.pvdairport.com) is in the Providence suburb of Warwick, about 60 miles south of Boston. It's a manageable alternative to Logan if you're continuing to Cape Cod or the islands. **Manchester–Boston Regional Airport** (ℂ **603/624-6539;** www.flymanchester.com) is in southern New Hampshire, about 51 miles north of Boston.

GETTING INTO TOWN FROM THE AIRPORT

The Massachusetts Port Authority, or **MassPort,** operates Logan Airport and coordinates ground transportation. If the information-packed website (www.flylogan.com) doesn't have the information you need, call the toll-free line (ℂ **800/235-6426**), which is staffed daily from 7am to 11:55pm.

The trip into central Boston takes 10 to 45 minutes, depending on traffic, your destination, and the time of day. If you must travel during rush hours, allow plenty of time or plan to take public transit (and pack accordingly).

Unless you need a **rental car** right away, wait to start the rental until you're going on a day trip or other excursion. You'll avoid airport fees, tunnel tolls, hotel parking charges, and, most important, Boston traffic.

You can reach central Boston from the airport by bus, subway, cab, boat, or van. See "Getting Around" in chapter 4 for information about paying your fare on the Boston area's **public transit system, the MBTA, known as "the T"** (© 617/222-3200; www.mbta.com).

BY BUS   To reach downtown Boston and make connections to many other destinations, take the MBTA Silver Line SL1 **bus.** It stops at each airport terminal and runs to South Station by way of the Seaport District. The trip takes about 20 minutes. Silver Line trips leaving the airport are free. The **fare** from South Station to the airport is $2.10 (with a pass or CharlieCard) or $2.60 (with a CharlieTicket or cash). At South Station, you can board the Red Line subway, the commuter rail to the southern suburbs, or the seasonal CapeFLYER train to Hyannis.

If your destination is in or near the Back Bay, take the **Back Bay Logan Express,** which runs to and from the Hynes Convention Center and Copley Square. Under a 2-year MassPort pilot program instituted in April 2014, buses leave the airport every 20 minutes daily from 6am to 10pm; airport-bound service runs from 5am to 9pm. The one-way fare is $5, payable by credit or debit card; MBTA pass holders ride free.

BY SUBWAY   The MBTA **subway** takes about 10 minutes to reach downtown from the airport, but first you have to get from the terminal to the subway station (which is actually aboveground). Free **shuttle buses** run from each terminal to Airport station from 4am to 1am every day, year-round. Airport is a stop on the Blue Line, which has stops downtown at Aquarium, State (where you can transfer to the Orange Line), and Bowdoin. *Note:* Government Center, where travelers normally transfer between the Blue and Green Lines of the T, is closed for construction through 2016.

The **fare** is $2.10 (with a pass or CharlieCard) or $2.60 (with a CharlieTicket or cash). You'll find fare kiosks at the station—where T employees can walk you through the process of loading value onto a CharlieCard or putting a pass onto a CharlieTicket—and in each terminal, near the exits closest to the public transit pick-up area.

BY TAXI   Just getting into a **cab** at the airport costs a whopping $10.10 (that's $7.50 in fees plus the initial $2.60 fare). The total fare to downtown or the Back Bay usually runs $20 to $45, and it may be more in bad traffic. Depending on traffic, the driver might use the Ted Williams Tunnel for destinations outside downtown, such as the Back Bay. On a map, this doesn't look like the fastest route, but often it is.

BY BOAT   The trip to the downtown waterfront in a weather-protected **boat** takes about 10 minutes—after you reach the dock. Service is available from early morning through early evening, with reduced schedules on weekends. The free no. 66 shuttle bus connects all four airport terminals to the dock. On trips leaving the airport, ask the shuttle driver to radio ahead for water-taxi pickup; on the way back, call ahead for service.

Two on-call water-taxi services serve the downtown waterfront and other points around Boston Harbor: **Rowes Wharf Water Transport** (© 617/406-8584; www.roweswharfwatertransport.com) and **Boston Harbor Cruises** (© 617/422-0392; www.bostonharborcruises.com/water-taxi). One-way fares start at $10.

Seven times each weekday, a scheduled ferry ($13) operated by **Boston Harbor Cruises** (☎ 888/733-9425 or 617/227-4321; www.bostonharborcruises.com) connects Logan to Long Wharf, behind the Marriott Long Wharf hotel.

BY SHUTTLE & LIMO   Some hotels have their own **shuttles** or **limousines;** check when you reserve your room. The airport website (www.flylogan.com) lists private companies that operate **shuttle-van service** to local hotels. They include **SuperShuttle** (☎ 800/BLUE-VAN [258-3826]; www.supershuttle.com). One-way prices start at $16 per person and are subject to fuel surcharges as gas prices fluctuate. Reservations are recommended.

To arrange private limo service, call ahead for a reservation, especially at busy times. Your hotel can recommend a company, or try **Boston Coach** (☎ 800/672-7676; www.bostoncoach.com), **Carey Limousine** (☎ 800/336-4646; www.carey.com), or **Commonwealth Worldwide** (☎ 800/558-5466 or 617/787-5575; www.commonwealth limo.com). **PlanetTran** (☎ 888/756-8876; www.planettran.com) uses only hybrid vehicles.

By Car

Renting a car for a long trip will almost certainly be more expensive and less conve-nient than any other means of reaching Boston. It's not that driving *to* Boston is diffi-cult. But parking is scarce and expensive, gasoline is pricey, traffic is terrible, and the drivers are famously reckless. If you're thinking of driving to Boston only because you want to use the car to get around town, think again.

It's impossible to say this often enough: When you reach your hotel, **leave your car in the garage** and walk or use public transportation. Save the car for day trips.

If you must drive, or if you decide to rent a car for day tripping, try to book a hotel or a special package that includes parking. If you pay for parking, expect it to cost at least $30 a day downtown, and build that into your budget along with gas, tolls, and parking.

Three major highways converge in Boston. **I-93/Route 3,** the Southeast Expressway, connects Boston with the south, including Cape Cod. **I-93/U.S. 1** extends north to Canada. **I-90,** also known as the Massachusetts Turnpike ("Mass. Pike" to the locals), is an east-west road that originates at Logan Airport, links up with the New York State Thruway, and extends to Seattle. It's the only toll road in Massachusetts. To avoid driving downtown, exit the Mass. Pike at Cambridge/Allston or at the Prudential Center in the Back Bay.

The main north-south East Coast highway, **I-95** (Massachusetts Rte. 128), passes through the area as a beltway about 11 miles from downtown that intersects the Mass. Pike and I-93 (twice). It connects Boston to highways in Rhode Island, Connecticut, and New York to the south, and New Hampshire and Maine to the north.

Note: **E-ZPass** transponders work in designated lanes on all roads that use the system, including the Mass. Pike. If you have a prepaid device from another system, check before you leave home to see whether it works with E-ZPass.

The approaches to Cambridge are **Storrow Drive** and **Memorial Drive,** which run along either side of the Charles River. Storrow Drive has a Harvard Square exit that leads across the Anderson Bridge to John F. Kennedy Street and into the square. Memorial Drive intersects with Kennedy Street; turn away from the bridge to reach the square.

Boston is about 53 miles from the **Sagamore Bridge** and 57 miles from the **Bourne Bridge;** the trip to or from Cape Cod takes at least an hour and can be much longer in the summer, especially on weekends. **New York City** is 218 miles from Boston; driving time is about 4½ hours. The 992-mile drive from **Chicago** to Boston takes around 21 hours; from **Washington, D.C.,** plan on 8 to 9 hours to cover the 468 miles.

In an emergency, you can call the **State Police** on a cellphone by dialing ℂ **911.** The American Automobile Association, or **AAA** (ℂ **800/AAA-HELP** [800/222-4357]; www.aaa.com) provides members with maps, itineraries, and other travel information, and arranges free towing if you break down. The Massachusetts Turnpike is a privately operated road that arranges its own towing. If you break down there, ask the AAA operator for advice.

By Train

Boston has three rail centers: **South Station,** 700 Atlantic Ave. (at Summer St.), near the Waterfront and the Financial District (www.south-station.net); **Back Bay Station,** 145 Dartmouth St. (btw. Huntington and Columbus aves.), across from the Copley Place mall; and **North Station,** on Causeway Street under the TD Garden arena. **Amtrak** (ℂ **800/872-7245** or 617/482-3660; www.amtrak.com) serves all three, and each is also a stop on the MBTA **subway.** From South Station, you can take the Red Line subway to Cambridge or to Park Street, the system's hub, where you can transfer to the Green and Orange lines. The Orange Line subway links Back Bay Station and Downtown Crossing, where there's a walkway to Park Street station. North Station is a Green and Orange Line stop.

Amtrak runs to South Station from New York and points south and in between, with stops at Route 128 and Back Bay. The MBTA **commuter rail from South Station** serves destinations including Plymouth and Providence, Rhode Island, as well as the seasonal **CapeFLYER** train to Hyannis.

Amtrak's **Downeaster** service (www.amtrakdowneaster.com) connects North Station to Brunswick, Maine, with multiple stops en route, including Portland. The **commuter rail from North Station** runs to numerous suburbs, including Porter Square in Cambridge.

Especially on long trips, Amtrak may not be cheaper than flying. Like the airlines, it adjusts fares depending on demand, so plan as far ahead as possible to get the lowest fares. Discounts are never available Friday or Sunday afternoon. Always remember to ask for the discounted rate.

Standard service from **New York** takes at least 4½ hours. High-speed Acela Express service is scheduled to take just over 3 hours. From **Washington, D.C.,** count on a grueling 7½ to 8½ hours for the slowest service, 6 hours for the Acela.

By Bus

The bus is a popular way to reach Cape Cod from Boston and is the only way out of many small New England towns. If you're coming from almost anywhere else, consider long-distance bus travel a last resort. An exception is the **New York** route, which is so desirable that numerous operators, including Greyhound and Peter Pan, offer service. It's frequent and relatively fast (4–4½ hr.), and the price is about half the regular train fare.

The Boston bus terminal, formally the **South Station Transportation Center,** is on Atlantic Avenue next to the train station. The major interstate lines are **Greyhound**

(📞 **800/231-2222** or 617/526-1816; www.greyhound.com) and **Peter Pan** (📞 **800/343-9999;** www.peterpanbus.com). **Plymouth & Brockton** (📞 **508/746-0378;** www.p-b.com) serves Cape Cod.

For bargain-hunters, the trip from South Station to midtown Manhattan can cost as little as $1—if you book at exactly the right moment—on **BoltBus** (📞 **877/265-8287;** www.boltbus.com) or **MegaBus** (📞 **877/462-6342;** www.megabus.com). Fares top out around $30, subject to fuel-price adjustments, and include on-board Wi-Fi access. *Note:* The discount operators known as "Chinatown buses" have experienced so many serious safety issues that the federal government actually shut down one of the largest companies; proceed with caution.

The business-oriented **LimoLiner** (📞 **888/546-5469;** www.limoliner.com) connects the Back Bay Hilton, 40 Dalton St., to the Hilton New York, 1335 Ave. of the Americas (with an on-request stop in Framingham, Massachusetts). The luxury coach seats 28 and has Internet access, work tables, leather seats, and an on-board attendant. The one-way fare is $89.

Go Buses (📞 **855/888-7160;** www.gobuses.com) steer clear of Boston traffic. From New York, they serve Riverside station in Newton, which is also a Green Line stop, and Alewife station in Cambridge, the northern terminus of the Red Line. One-way fares start at $15.

By Cruise Ship

Cruise ships arrive at the **Black Falcon Cruise Terminal,** 1 Black Falcon Ave., South Boston (📞 **800/294-2791;** www.massport.com/port-of-boston). Cabs are easy to find—the drivers know the cruise schedule—and a trolley shuttle operates when ships are in port. The terminal is across the street from the Design Center Place stop on the Silver Line SL2 bus route, which serves the nearest subway stop, South Station; if you prefer to walk, it's about a mile away. Before heading out, make sure you have the number of a cab company programmed into your phone, and leave plenty of time for the trip back to the dock.

[FastFACTS] BOSTON, CAPE COD & THE ISLANDS

ATMs/Banks Automated teller machines (ATMs), also known as cash machines, are widely available throughout eastern Massachusetts. You'll find them in and near all banks, most convenience stores and gas stations, and many grocery stores, subway stations, and cash-only businesses. Banks are open weekdays from 9am to 4pm or later and sometimes on Saturday morning; most offer 24-hour access to ATMs.

Cirrus (📞 **800/4CIRRUS** [800/424-7787]; www.mastercard.com), **PLUS** (📞 **800/THE-PLUS** [843-7587]; www.visa.com), and **NYCE** (www.nyce.net) are the major networks in the eastern United States. Look at the back of your card to see which network you're on, then call, check online, or download a smartphone app to find ATM locations.

Be sure you know your **personal identification number (PIN)** and your daily **withdrawal limit** before you depart. If you have a five- or six-digit PIN, ask your bank whether it will work; you may need to change it to a four-digit number. Also keep in mind that most banks impose a fee every time you use your card at a different bank's ATM, and the bank from which you withdraw cash may charge its own fee. At Massachusetts ATMs, a message should appear—onscreen or on a sticker near the keypad—specifying the amount of the charge.

Customs National customs agencies regulate what visitors to the United Stated may bring with them and what they may take home. For details, consult your nearest U.S. embassy or consulate, or check with **U.S. Customs & Border Protection** (☎ **877/CBP-5511** [227-5522] or 202/325-8000; www.cbp.gov).

Dentists The front-desk staff at your hotel or other lodging can often recommend a dentist. The **Massachusetts Dental Society** website (www.massdental.org) lets you search for a member by location.

Drinking Laws The legal age for purchase and consumption of alcoholic beverages is 21. Proof of age is required and often requested at bars, nightclubs, sports arenas, and restaurants, particularly near college campuses (in the Boston area, that's everywhere), so it's always a good idea to bring ID when you go out. Liquor stores and some supermarkets and convenience stores sell alcohol Monday though Saturday during regular business hours; in communities where selling alcohol on Sunday is allowed, sales still don't begin until noon. Happy hours with discounted drinks are illegal, but discounted food is permitted. Most restaurants have full liquor licenses, but some serve only beer, wine, and cordials. Last call typically is 30 minutes before closing time, which varies by community (in Boston, 1am in bars, 2am in clubs).

Do not carry open containers of alcohol in your car or any public area that isn't zoned for alcohol consumption. The police can fine you on the spot. Don't even think about driving while intoxicated.

Electricity Like Canada, the United States uses 110–120 volts AC (60 cycles), compared to 220–240 volts AC (50 cycles) in most of Europe, Australia, and New Zealand. Downward converters that change 220–240 volts to 110–120 volts are difficult to find in the United States, so bring one with you.

Embassies & Consulates All embassies are in the nation's capital, Washington, D.C. Some consulates are in major U.S. cities, and most nations have a mission to the United Nations in New York City. If your country isn't listed below, call directory assistance in Washington, D.C. (☎ **202/555-1212**), or check **www.embassy.org/embassies**.

The embassy of **Australia** is at 1601 Massachusetts Ave. NW, Washington, DC 20036 (☎ **202/797-3000;** www.usa.embassy.gov.au).

The embassy of **Canada** is at 501 Pennsylvania Ave. NW, Washington, DC 20001 (☎ **202/682-1740;** www.canadainternational.gc.ca/washington). The local Canadian consulate is at 3 Copley Place, Ste. 400, Boston, MA 02116 (☎ **617/247-5100;** www.boston.gc.ca).

The embassy of **Ireland** is at 2234 Massachusetts Ave. NW, Washington, DC 20008 (☎ **202/462-3939;** www.embassyofireland.org). The local Irish consulate is at 535 Boylston St., 5th floor, Boston, MA 02116 (☎ **617/267-9330;** www.consulategeneral ofirelandboston.org).

The embassy of **New Zealand** is at 37 Observatory Circle NW, Washington, DC 20008 (☎ **202/328-4800;** www.nzembassy.com/usa). Contact the **honorary consul** to the New England area at P.O. Box 1318, 57 N. Main St., Concord, NH 03302 (☎ **603/225-8228**).

The embassy of the **United Kingdom** is at 3100 Massachusetts Ave. NW, Washington, DC 20008 (☎ **202/588-6500;** http://ukinusa.fco.gov.uk). The Boston-area **British consulate** is at 1 Broadway, Cambridge, MA 02142 (☎ **617/245-4500**).

Emergencies Call ☎ **911** for fire, ambulance, or the police. This is a free call from pay phones. Dialing 911 on a cellphone connects you to a state police dispatcher, who transfers the call to the local authorities.

Health The greatest threat to your health is the same as in the rest of North America: overexposure to the summer sun. Be sure to pack sunblock, sunglasses, and a hat, and don't forget to stay hydrated.

Insurance   Whether you should invest in travel insurance depends on numerous factors, including how far you're traveling, how much you're spending, how set your schedule is, and your physical condition. For domestic travelers, most reliable healthcare plans provide coverage if you get sick away from home. If you require additional medical insurance, try **Travel Assistance International** (✆ **800/821-2828** or 317/818-2098; www.travelassistance international.com), **Travel Guard International** (✆ **800/826-4919;** www. travelguard.com), or **Allianz Global Assistance** (✆ **866/884-3556;** www. allianztravelinsurance.com). International travelers should note that unlike many other countries, the United States does not usually offer free or low-cost medical care to visitors (or citizens).

Internet Access   Most public libraries and many businesses in eastern Massachusetts offer Wi-Fi access, which is often but not always free. (High-end hotels tend to charge guests a daily fee for access, while room rates at many cheaper lodgings include Wi-Fi.) See "Fast Facts" in chapters 4, 5, and 6 for specifics.

Legal Aid   While driving, if you are pulled over for a minor infraction (such as speeding), never attempt to pay the fine directly to a police officer; this could be construed as attempted bribery, a much more

serious crime. Pay fines by mail, or directly into the hands of the clerk of the court. If accused of a more serious offense, say and do nothing before consulting a lawyer. In the U.S., the burden is on the state to prove a person's guilt beyond a reasonable doubt, and everyone has the right to remain silent, whether he or she is suspected of a crime or actually arrested. Once arrested, a person can make one telephone call to a party of his or her choice. The international visitor should call his or her embassy or consulate.

Mobile Phones   Most Americans call mobile phones "cellphones." The major North American service providers all cover eastern Massachusetts, though coverage can be spotty in thinly populated areas, especially near beaches. Don't count on reliable service in rural areas, especially if your phone is on the GSM network, which most of the world uses. Among major U.S. carriers, AT&T and T-Mobile are compatible with GSM, and Sprint and Verizon use CDMA.

If you're traveling from overseas and haven't used your phone internationally before, call your provider before you leave home to determine whether your phone will work where you're going, whether you'll be able to send and receive SMS (text messages), and how much everything will cost.

If you plan to call home frequently, the cheapest option in many cases is **Skype** (www.skype.com) or a similar service. Sign up before you leave home, and you can place calls from a computer or mobile device. Calls to other Skype users are free; add credit to your account to call non-members.

If you want a phone just for emergencies and don't have to know your number ahead of time, I suggest that you visit one of the area's numerous freestanding cellphone stores or **Radio Shack** (✆ **800/843-7422;** www.radioshack.com) and buy a prepaid phone to use during your visit. Phones sell for as little as $15, but calling time can cost as much as 35¢/minute. Make sure you're choosing a provider that allows you to activate international calling immediately (try making an international call while you're still in the store). Most important, be sure you understand all fees and per-minute charges and have enough money loaded onto the phone to cover the calls you're likely to make and receive.

In Boston, a reliable outlet for "unlocked" cellphones—which recognize any carrier's SIM card—is **Mega Mobile,** 278 Washington St., Downtown Crossing (✆ **617/573-0073;** www.megamobile boston.com). It also sells international SIM cards and does repairs. If you prefer to **rent** a phone, you can have it shipped to you before you leave from **InTouch USA** (✆ **800/872-7626**

WHAT THINGS COST IN BOSTON

	$
Taxi from airport to downtown or Back Bay	20.00–45.00
Water shuttle from airport to downtown	10.00
MBTA subway fare (w/ CharlieCard)	2.10
Double room at moderately priced hotel	169.00–299.00
Lunch for one at inexpensive restaurant	8.00–14.00
Three-course dinner for one, without wine, at moderately priced restaurant	20.00–30.00
Glass of beer	3.50–8.00
Cup of coffee	2.00 and up
Adult admission to the Museum of Fine Arts	25.00
Child (7–17) admission to the Museum of Fine Arts	Free

or 703/222-7161; www.intouchusa.us). Rates start at $29 a week, plus a shipping charge.

Money & Costs Frommer's lists exact prices in the local currency. The currency conversions quoted above were correct at press time. However, rates fluctuate, so before departing, consult a currency exchange website such as **www.oanda.com/convert/classic** or **www.xe.com/ucc** to check up-to-the-minute rates.

Like other large American cities, Boston can be an expensive destination. At the high end, it's nearly as costly as New York. The average hotel room rate in Boston and Cambridge in 2013 was $222—and that includes deep off-season discounts. The area does offer numerous ways to offset the price of lodging. Some attractions offer free or discounted admission at certain times, and the performing arts provide

options for every budget. Dining choices, from hole-in-the-wall noodle joints to acclaimed special-occasion restaurants, are equally diverse.

If you're visiting from overseas, exchange enough petty cash to cover airport incidentals, tipping, and transportation to your hotel before you leave home, or withdraw money upon arrival at an airport ATM (see "ATMs/Banks," above).

Beware of hidden **credit card fees** while traveling. Check with your credit or debit card issuer to see what fees, if any, it charges for overseas transactions. Fees can amount to 3 percent or more of the purchase price. Check with your bank before departing to avoid any surprise charges on your statement.

Stores and restaurants that accept credit cards generally accept **debit cards,** and some stores and most U.S. post offices

enable you to receive "cash back" on your debit card purchases as well. If you don't keep a large checking balance, be aware that most banks "freeze" a portion of your account when you initiate a purchase without a definite total, such as a car rental or tank of gas.

Credit cards and debit cards are much more often used and are usually more convenient, but **traveler's checks** are still accepted in the U.S. You shouldn't have trouble using traveler's checks at any tourist-friendly business. International visitors should make sure that they're denominated in U.S. dollars; foreign-currency checks are often difficult to exchange.

Pharmacies The area's major drugstore chains are **CVS** ((🕻 888/607-4287; www.cvs.com), **Rite Aid** ((🕻 800/748-3243; www.riteaid.com), and **Walgreens** ((🕻 877/925-4733; www.walgreens.com).

THE VALUE OF THE U.S. DOLLAR VS. OTHER POPULAR CURRENCIES

US$	C$	£	€	A$	NZ$
1.00	1.10	0.60	0.72	1.08	1.17

Senior Travel Mention that you're a senior citizen when you make your travel reservations. Many businesses offer discounts to seniors with identification (a driver's license, passport, or other document that shows your date of birth). The cut-off age is usually 65, sometimes 62. Restaurants and movie theaters usually offer discounts only at off-peak times, but many museums and other attractions offer reduced rates—usually the equivalent of the student price—at all times. If you'll be using public transportation in the Boston area, look into the Senior Charlie Card (© **800/543-8287** or 617/222-5976; TTY 617/222-5854; www.mbta.com).

Taxes The United States has no value-added tax (VAT) or other indirect tax at the national level. Every state, county, and city may levy its own local tax on all purchases, including hotel and restaurant checks and airline tickets. These taxes will *not* appear on price tags. The 6.25 percent

Massachusetts sales tax does not apply to groceries, prescription drugs, newspapers, or clothing that costs less than $175. The state tax on meals and takeout food is 6.25 percent, but some communities charge more; in Boston and Cambridge, the total tax is 7 percent. The state lodging tax is 5.7 percent, and individual municipalities can tack on as much as 6.5 percent. With the 2.75 percent convention center financing fee, the total is 14.45 percent in Boston and Cambridge.

Tipping Tip hotel **bellhops** at least $1 per bag ($5 or more if you have a lot of luggage) and tip the **housekeeping staff** $2 per day (more if you've left a big mess). Tip the **doorman** or **concierge** only if he or she has provided a specific service (for example, calling a cab for you or obtaining difficult-to-get theater tickets). Tip the **valet-parking attendant** $1 or $2 every time you get your car.

In restaurants, bars, and nightclubs, tip **service staff** and **bartenders** 15 percent to 20 percent of the check, tip **checkroom attendants** $1 or $2 per garment, and tip **valet-parking attendants** $1 per vehicle.

Tip **cabdrivers** 15 to 20 percent of the fare; tip **skycaps** at airports at least $1 per bag ($5 or more if you have a lot of luggage); and tip **hairdressers** and **barbers** 15 to 20 percent.

Toilets You won't find public toilets or "restrooms" on the streets in most U.S. cities; seek them out in visitor information centers, hotel lobbies, bars, restaurants, museums, department stores, malls and shopping centers, railway and bus stations, and service stations. Large hotels and fast-food restaurants are often the best bet for clean facilities. Restaurants and bars in heavily visited areas typically reserve their restrooms for patrons.

PLANNING YOUR TRIP TO CAPE COD & THE ISLANDS

The Cape is really many capes: tony in some places, tacky in others; in patches a nature lover's dream, a living historical treasure, or a hotbed of creativity. Planning a trip to Cape Cod is a little more complex than packing flip-flops and suntan lotion. But remember, this is a destination that is supposed to be about relaxation, lying on a sun-kissed beach, listening to the lapping surf, or walking along a wildflower-lined path to watch the sun set over the horizon. These simple pleasures are why people have been coming to Cape Cod, Nantucket, and Martha's Vineyard to vacation for more than a century. This chapter will tell you what you need to plan your trip to this part of the world and steer you there smoothly; international visitors will find essential information, helpful tips, and advice on the more common problems that surface while vacationing on Cape Cod and the islands.

Visiting Cape Cod means traveling over either the Bourne Bridge or the Sagamore Bridge. Most visitors arrive by car, but you can also take a bus or even travel by plane to one of several small airports in the region. You'll need a place to stay in one of the Cape's 15 towns or on one of the islands, and this book is loaded with options. You'll also need a way to get around. Public transportation leaves much to be desired in most Cape Cod towns, although several have good beach shuttles in season. Public transportation on both Martha's Vineyard and Nantucket, on the other hand, is excellent. There is also the option of bringing or renting a bike, a great way to travel from your rental house or hotel to the beach. There's lots more nitty-gritty information below, from information on passports and dates for festivals to weather predictions and tips on dining. To pinpoint where you want to go in the area and what you want to do, peruse the region-by-region chapters.

For additional help in planning your trip and for more on-the-ground resources in Cape Cod and the islands, see "Fast Facts: Cape Cod & the Islands," later in this chapter.

GETTING THERE

By Plane

Most major carriers offer service to **Boston's Logan Airport,** and from there it's a quick half-hour commuter flight on Cape Air to **Hyannis** or **Provincetown** (about $220 round-trip), or the islands (to **Martha's Vineyard** or **Nantucket,** about $350 round-trip).

Jet Blue flies between Hyannis on Cape Cod and JFK Airport in New York City. The seasonal service will run from late June to early September. One flight a day will leave JFK at 11:59am and arrive in Hyannis at 1:05pm. A flight will depart Hyannis at 1:45pm and arrive at JFK at 2:53pm. The 1 hour and 8 minute trip costs about $98 round-trip. Other carriers to the Cape and islands are **Cape Air/Nantucket Airlines** (© 866/227-3247 or 508/771-6944; www.flycapeair.com) and **Island Airlines** (© 508/228-7575; www.islandair.net). To find out which airlines travel to area airports, where you can get connecting flights to the Cape and islands, see p. 238.

Flying to Nantucket from Hyannis takes about 20 minutes, depending on the weather; costs about $138 round-trip; and is a great way to avoid the hectic ferry scene. Island Airlines and Cape Air make the most frequent trips from Hyannis to Nantucket. These two air carriers alone operate more than 50 flights per day, and both offer charter flights.

The commuter flights have their own little fare wars, so it's worth comparing costs. And though flights may lessen in frequency during the off season, fares sometimes descend as well.

GETTING INTO TOWN FROM THE AIRPORT

Visitors to the Cape and islands who are flying into Boston's Logan Airport or T.F. Green Airport in Providence, Rhode Island, can rent a car and drive to Cape Cod in about 1½ hours (from Boston) or an hour (from Providence). Driving maps are generally available at car rental locations.

The major route from Boston's Logan Airport is I-93 S. to Route 3, which ends at the Sagamore Bridge. The Sagamore Bridge is best used to access all the Cape towns and the island of Nantucket, but not Falmouth or the island of Martha's Vineyard. For those destinations, plus parts of Bourne, the best route from Logan Airport is I-93 to Route 24 to I-495, which turns into Route 25 near the Bourne Bridge.

From Providence, Rhode Island, take I-195 all the way to Route 25 and the Bourne Bridge.

By Bus

Greyhound (© 800/231-2222; www.greyhound.com) connects Boston with the rest of the country, and **Bonanza Bus Lines/Peter Pan** (© 800/343-9999 or 508/548-7588; www.peterpanbus.com) covers a good portion of southern New England. Logan Airport to Falmouth costs about $30 each way.

Bonanza links Boston's Logan Airport and South Station with Bourne, Falmouth, and Woods Hole; its buses from New York reach the same destinations, plus Hyannis. From New York to Hyannis or Woods Hole, the 6-hour ride costs about $74 each way.

Plymouth & Brockton (© 508/746-0378; www.p-b.com) offers service from Logan and South Station to Hyannis by way of Sagamore and Barnstable, and offers connections from there to the towns of Yarmouth, Dennis, Brewster, Orleans, Eastham, Wellfleet, Truro, and Provincetown.

A WORD ABOUT traffic

Cape Cod traffic is nothing if not predictable. You do not want to be driving over the Bourne or Sagamore bridges onto the Cape on a summer Friday between 4 and 8pm. Saturday between 10am and 3pm is an equally bad time to arrive. Most of all, you do not want to try to get off the Cape on a Sunday or a holiday Monday between 2 and 8pm, when traffic can back up nearly 20 miles from the Sagamore Bridge. If you find yourself in one of the infamous Cape Cod traffic jams, there are options. Here are my personal traffic-beating tips.

1. The Bourne Bridge is almost always a less crowded route than the Sagamore Bridge. You can connect to Route 6 from the Bourne Bridge via the canal road, or see number 3 below.
2. When heading off the Cape on Route 6, turn off at exit 5. Take Route 149 south to Route 28. At the Mashpee Rotary, take Route 151 to Route 28 in North Falmouth. Take Route 28 to the Bourne Bridge.
3. To get onto the Cape to points east of Yarmouth, follow step 2 above in reverse.
4. If you are traveling to Nantucket and plan to park your car in Hyannis, watch the signs on Route 6 to see which parking lot is open. If the Brooks Road lot is open, there is no need to drive all the way to the ferry terminal. Instead you will park your car at the lot, which is off Route 28, and take a free shuttle bus to the terminal. Knowing in advance which lot you will park in will save you a lot of time in the long run.
5. If you are heading to Martha's Vineyard from points south, such as New York or Connecticut, consider taking a passenger ferry from Rhode Island or New Bedford (see chapter 9). Otherwise be alert to the signs on Route 28 about parking lots. These signs are accurate. If they say the lot is full in Woods Hole, you will not be allowed to park there, so don't bother driving down to check it out. Follow the signs to the open parking lots, and a free shuttle bus will take you to the ferry.

From Logan to Hyannis takes about 2 hours on the P&B; to Provincetown it's about 3½ hours (including the transfer in Hyannis).

The fare from Logan to Provincetown on P&B is $63 round-trip, $35 one-way; it's $52 round-trip and $29 one-way from South Station in Boston. To Hyannis it's $45 round-trip from Logan, $25 one-way; $34 from South Street Station round-trip, and $17 one-way.

Note: If you plan to catch a ferry, don't count on the bus arriving on time (there's no telling what the traffic may do). Plan to take the second-to-last ferry of the day, so you have a backup—and even so, schedule your arrival with an hour to spare.

By Car

Visitors from the south (New York, for example) will approach the Cape Cod Canal via I-95 to I-195 to Route 25 and over the Bourne Bridge. Those coming from Boston can either come that way (reaching Rte. 25 via I-93 to Rte. 24 and I-495) or head directly south from Boston on I-93 to Route 3, heading over the Sagamore Bridge.

The bridges are only 3 miles apart, with connecting roads on both sides of the canal, so either bridge will do. The best option will depend on where you're going. If you're planning to head south to Falmouth or take a ferry to Martha's Vineyard, you'll want to take the Bourne Bridge and follow Route 28 about 10 miles to Falmouth. If you're heading farther east of the Sagamore Bridge to any of the other 14 towns on the Cape or to Nantucket, you'll want to travel over the Sagamore Bridge and take Route 6 or its scenic sidekick, the meandering Route 6A, which merges with Route 28 in Orleans. From Orleans the main road is Route 6 all the way to Provincetown.

Those traveling to Nantucket should take the Sagamore Bridge and drive down Route 6 until reaching exit 7. From there you can follow signs to one of the two ferry terminals (Steamship Authority or Hy-Line), both on Hyannis Inner Harbor.

The big challenge, actually, is getting over either bridge, especially on summer weekends, when upward of 100,000 cars all try to cross at once. Savvy residents avoid at all costs driving onto the Cape on Friday afternoon or joining the mass exodus on Sunday (or Mon, in the case of a holiday weekend), and you'd be wise to follow suit. Call **SmarTraveler** (© **617/374-1234,** or cellular *1) for up-to-the-minute news on congestion and alternate routes, as well as parking availability in the pay-per-night parking lots that serve the island ferries.

Traffic can throw a major monkey wrench into these projections, but on average, driving time from New York to Hyannis is 5 hours (with no traffic) to 7 hours; and to drive from Boston to Hyannis is 1½ to 2 hours. It'll take about a half hour to 45 minutes more to drive all the way to Provincetown.

Traffic can be a nightmare on peak weekends. Cars are enough of a bother on the Cape itself: If you're not planning to cover much ground, rent a bike instead (some B&Bs offer "loaners"). On the islands, cars are superfluous. Cars are expensive to ferry back and forth ($200 one-way to Nantucket in season, and that's if you manage to make a reservation months, even a year, in advance or are willing to sit in "standby" for many hours). They'll also prove a nuisance in the crowded port towns, where urban-style gridlock is not uncommon. Should you change your mind and decide to go motoring once you arrive, you can rent a car or jeep (for off-roading) on the islands for less than the cost of bringing your own vehicle over (see "Getting Around," below).

By Train

The Cape Flyer (© **508/775-8504;** www.capecodrta.org) train travels from Boston to Hyannis on weekends from late May through Labor Day. The trip takes about 2 hours and 15 minutes, about 45 minutes more than driving if you don't hit traffic (which you will in the summer). Service to the Cape is offered from South Station in Boston, Braintree, Middleborough/Lakeville, Wareham Village and Buzzards Bay. When you arrive in Hyannis, you'll have access to taxis, buses, planes and island ferries.

From South Station in Boston to Hyannis is $40 round-trip ($22 one-way). Bikes are free, as are kids 12 and under.

The train leaves from Boston on Fridays at 5:12pm and arrives in Hyannis at 7:50pm. On Saturday and Sunday, the train leaves Boston at 8am and arrives in Hyannis at 10:18am. On the return trip, the train leaves Hyannis at 6:30pm on Saturdays and Sundays and arrives in Boston at 8:45pm. On Fridays the train leaves Hyannis at 8:30pm and arrives in Boston at 10:45pm.

TRAVEL TIMES TO CAPE COD & THE ISLANDS

New York to Hyannis (by bus or car)	5–7 hours, depending on traffic
Boston to Hyannis	1½ hours, with no traffic
Sagamore Bridge to Orleans	45 minutes off season; up to 2 hours high season
Sagamore Bridge to Provincetown	1¼ hours, with little traffic
Hyannis to Sagamore Bridge	30 minutes; Sunday afternoons in season, 2 hours
Bourne Bridge to Woods Hole	35 minutes; Friday afternoons in season, 1¼ hours
Hyannis to Nantucket by plane	20 minutes
Hyannis to Nantucket by Steamship Authority or Hy-Line high-speed catamaran	1 hour
Hyannis to Nantucket by slow Steamship Authority or Hy-Line ferries	2¼ hours
Woods Hole to Martha's Vineyard aboard the Steamship Authority ferries	45 minutes
Falmouth to Edgartown, Martha's Vineyard, aboard the *Pied Piper*	1 hour
Falmouth to Oak Bluffs, Martha's Vineyard, aboard the *Island Queen*	35 minutes

GETTING AROUND

By Car

Once you've made it over one of the bridges guarding the Cape Cod Canal—or bypassed the bridges by flying or boating in—getting around is relatively easy. Traveling by car does offer the greatest degree of flexibility, although you'll probably wish no one else knew that. Traffic is frustrating enough, but parking is yet another problem. In densely packed towns, such as Provincetown, finding a free, legal space is like winning the lottery. Parking is also problematic at many beaches. Some are closed to all but residents, and visitors will almost always have to pay a day rate of about $10 to $20. Renters staying a week or longer can arrange for a discounted weeklong or month-long sticker through the local town hall (you'll probably need to show your lease as well as your car registration). You can usually squeeze into the Cape Cod National Seashore lots if you show up early (by 9am); here the fee is $15 a day, or $45 per season.

Further complicating the heavy car traffic on the Cape is the seemingly disproportionate number of bad drivers. A few key traffic rules: A right turn is allowed at a red light after stopping, unless otherwise posted. In a rotary (aka a traffic circle), cars within the circle have the right of way until they manage to get out. Four-way stops call for extreme caution or extreme courtesy, and sometimes both.

Rental cars are available at the Hyannis Airport and at branch offices of major chains in several towns. The usual maze of rental offers prevails. Almost every rental firm tries to pad its profits by selling loss-damage waiver (LDW) insurance at a cost of $8 to $15 extra per day. Before succumbing to the hard sell, check with your insurance carrier and credit card companies; chances are you're already covered. If not, the LDW may prove a wise investment. Exorbitant charges for gasoline are another ploy to look out for; be sure to top off the tank just before bringing the car in.

By Bus

To discourage congestion and provide a pleasant experience, a growing number of towns offer free or low-cost in-town shuttles in season. You'll find such services in Falmouth, Woods Hole, Mashpee, Hyannis, Dennis, Yarmouth, Harwich, Martha's Vineyard, and Nantucket. Each town's chamber of commerce can fill you in, or call the **Cape Cod Regional Transit Authority** (℃ **800/352-7155**; www.capecodtransit. org). For commercial bus service between towns, see "Getting There," earlier in this chapter.

By Bike

The bicycle is the ideal conveyance for the Cape and islands, for distances great and small. The Cape has some extremely scenic bike paths, including the glorious Cape Cod Rail Trail, which meanders through seven towns for more than 25 miles. Two wheels are the best way to explore Nantucket's flat terrain, and scenic bike routes run through all six towns on Martha's Vineyard. You'll find a rental shop in just about every town (see "Bicycling," in previous chapters)—or better yet, bring your own.

By Taxi

You'll find taxi stands at most airports and ferry terminals. The islands also offer jitney services with set rates, such as **Adam Cab,** on Martha's Vineyard (℃ **800/281-4462** or 508/627-4462), and **Chief's Cab,** on Nantucket (℃ **508/284-8497**). Several offer bike racks or can arrange for bike transportation with advance notice—call around until you find what you need. Some companies offer sightseeing tours. Among the larger taxi fleets on the Cape are **Falmouth Taxi** (℃ **508/548-3100**), **Hyannis Taxi Service** (℃ **508/775-0400**), and Provincetown's **Mercedes Cab** (℃ **508/487-3333**), which delivers elegance at no extra charge. Other cab companies are listed in the Yellow Pages, as are limousine liveries.

[FastFACTS] CAPE COD & THE ISLANDS

Fishing A license is now required for saltwater fishing. Previously, licenses were needed only for freshwater fishing and shellfishing. The new license costs $10. To get a license, go online to www.mass.gov/marinefisheries or call ℃ **866/703-1925**.

Health You'll find numerous large chain pharmacies on Cape Cod; there's a CVS and Brooks Drugstore in almost every town. In the Outer Cape towns of Wellfleet and Truro and in some of the towns up-island on Martha's Vineyard, you might be a half-hour drive from a pharmacy, so it's best to come prepared with everything you need.

Sun   Even in this northerly clime, **sunburn** is a real hazard. For most skin types, it's safest to start with a lotion with a high SPF and work your way down. Be sure to reapply often and according to the directions, and no matter how thoroughly you slather on lotion, try to stay in the shade during prime frying time—11am to 2pm. Kids should always wear sunscreen with a high SPF number, or a cover-up such as a T-shirt, if they're going to be playing outside for long periods of time. Sunglasses with UVP (ultraviolet protection) lenses will help shield your eyes.

Insects   The sea breezes keep most **mosquitoes** on the move, but not always, so pack some bug spray. Birds on the Cape have been diagnosed with **West Nile virus,** so it's a good idea to avoid mosquito bites if at all possible. Mosquitoes are the carrier of this disease, but the chances of catching West Nile are very low.

The most dangerous insects are pinhead-size **deer ticks,** which transmit **Lyme disease.** Widespread along the Massachusetts coast, they're especially active just when you're apt to be there: April through October. Nantucket has the highest concentration of Lyme disease in the country. A vaccine tested there is now on the market. Ask your doctor if you should consider the vaccine. If caught in its early stages—symptoms include a ring-shaped rash and flulike achiness—the disease is easily countered with antibiotics; if it's left untreated, however, the effects could eventually prove fatal.

Avoid walking in brush or high grass. If bushwacking is unavoidable, cover up in light-colored clothing (the better to spot any clinging ticks), consisting of a long-sleeve shirt and long pants tucked into high white socks. Camping stores such as EMS sell bush pants that are perfect for this purpose—they're actually comfortable in warm weather. For double protection, spray your clothes and hands (but not face) with a DEET-based insect repellent. Check your clothes before removing them, and then check your body; it helps to use a mirror or call upon a significant other. Showering after such an outing is a good safeguard. If, despite your best precautions, you find you've brought home a parasite, remove it with tweezers by pulling directly outward, if you can manage to do so without squeezing the body (that would serve only to inject more bacteria into your bloodstream). Dab the bite with alcohol to help disinfect it, and save the tick in a closed jar. If you're within a few minutes of a medical facility, have a doctor deal with the extraction; if you do it yourself, go for testing and treatment as soon as you can and take the tick with you. The **Lyme Disease Foundation** (✆ **860/870-0070;** 24-hour hotline: 800/886-LYME [5963]) distributes brochures to tourist areas and is also able to field questions. Other good sources of information are the **Centers for Disease Control** (✆ **888/232-3228** and the **Massachusetts Department of Public Health** (✆ **866/627-7968**).

Plants   Poison ivy—with its shiny, purplish, three-leafed clusters—is ubiquitous and potent on the Cape and islands. If you so much as brush past a frond, the plant's oil is likely to raise an itchy welt. Clothing that has been in contact with the plant can spread the harmless but irritating toxin to your skin; it's even transmitted by smoke. If you think you've been exposed, wash with soap immediately so the oil doesn't spread on your body. Calamine lotion—available at all drugstores—should help soothe the itching. You won't spread the rash by scratching, because it's the oil that does the spreading, but scratches could get infected, so resist the temptation.

Hospitals   The **Cape Cod Hospital,** at 27 Park St., Hyannis (✆ **508/771-1800**), offers 24-hour emergency medical service and consultation, as does the **Falmouth Hospital,** at 100 Ter Heun Dr. (℃ **508/548-5300**). On the islands, contact the **Martha's Vineyard Hospital,** on Linton Lane, in Oak Bluffs (℃ **508/** **693-0410**), or **Nantucket Cottage Hospital,** at 57 Prospect St. (℃ **508/ 825-8100**).

Money Every town on the Cape has multiple **ATMs** (automated teller machines), sometimes referred to as "cash machines," or "cashpoints." These are the easiest and best source of cash when you're away from home.

Index

See also Accommodations and Restaurant indexes, below.

General Index

A

Abiel Smith School (Boston), 72, 73
Abolitionists, 11
The Academy Playhouse (Orleans), 191
Accommodations. *See also specific towns and islands; and* Accommodations Index
  Boston, 42–52
  Cambridge, 52–54
Ace Ticket, 124
Acme Fine Art (Boston), 99
Adams, Samuel, grave of, 77
African-American History Month (Boston), 15
African Americans
  Boston, 11, 15, 20, 72, 73, 76–77
  Cambridge African American Heritage Trail, 95
  Zion Union Heritage Museum (Hyannis), 164–165
African Meeting House (Boston), 72, 73
Agricultural Society Livestock Show and Fair (Martha's Vineyard), 18
Air travel
  Boston, 256–257
  Cape Cod and the islands, 266
  Martha's Vineyard, 213–214
  Nantucket, 238
Alcott, Louisa May, 11
Algiers Café & Restaurant (Boston), 123
Alley's General Store (Martha's Vineyard), 227
Alpha Gallery (Boston), 99–100
Alternative Entertainment (Boston), 123–124
Ambassador Brattle/Yellow Cab (Cambridge), 38
Ambrosia Chocolate & Spices (Nantucket), 254
American Repertory Theater (Cambridge), 114
America's Hometown Shuttle trolley (Plymouth), 127
America's Hometown Thanksgiving (Plymouth), 19
An Evening with Champions (Allston), 19
Angel Foods (Provincetown), 205
Antiques and collectibles
  Boston and Cambridge, 99
  Brewster, 181
  Dennis, 175

Nantucket, 253
Orleans, 190
Sandwich, 139
Wellfleet, 195
Antiques Center of Cape Cod (Dennis), 175
Apps, 33
Aptucxet Strawberry Festival (Bourne), 17
Aptucxet Trading Post Museum (Sandwich), 140–141
Aquinnah Beach (Moshup Beach), 228
Ars Libri Ltd. (Boston), 101
Art House (Provincetown), 209
Arthur M. Sackler Museum (Cambridge), 88
The Artists' Association of Nantucket, 253
Arts Alive Festival (Falmouth), 17
Art's Dune Tours (Provincetown), 207
ArtsEmerson: The World on Stage (Boston), 111
Arts Stroll (Hyannis), 163
ArtStrand Gallery (Provincetown), 208
Ashumet Holly and Wildlife Sanctuary, 149
The Atlantic House (Provincetown), 208
Atlantic White Cedar Swamp Trail, 194
ATMs and banks, 260–261
August Moon Festival (Boston), 18
Aunt Leah's Fudge (Nantucket), 254

B

The Back Bay (Boston), 35, 49–52, 97
Ballymeade Country Club (Falmouth), 149
Band concerts, Chatham, 186
Barbara Krakow Gallery (Boston), 100
Barnes & Noble (Boston), 101
Barnes & Noble (Hyannis), 163
Barnes & Noble at Boston University, 101
Barnstable and environs, 153–166. *See also* Mid Cape
Barnstable County Fair (East Falmouth), 18
Bartlett's Farm (Nantucket), 249
Baseball, 125, 141
Basketball, Boston, 126
Bass Hole boardwalk, 168
Bass River Beach, 168
Battle of Bunker Hill (Boston), 10
Battle of Bunker Hill Museum (Boston), 84
Battle Road Committee (Boston), 16
Bay Lady II (Provincetown), 207
Bay State Cruise Company, 94

Beachcomber (Chatham), 185, 186
The Beachcomber (Wellfleet), 196
Beacon Hill (Boston), 26–27, 35
Beacon Hill Chocolates (Boston), 105
Beantown Trolley (Boston), 93
Beat Hôtel (Boston), 114
Bed and Breakfast Associates Bay, 44
Beech Forest Trail, 194
The Beehive (Boston), 114
Ben & Bill's Chocolate Emporium (Falmouth), 147–148
Ben & Jerry's (Boston and Cambridge), 66
Berklee Beantown Jazz Festival (Boston), 120
Berklee Performance Center (Boston), 113
Berk's Shoes (Boston), 104
Berta Walker Gallery (Provincetown), 208
Big Apple Circus (Boston), 16
Biking, 270
  Boston and Cambridge, 40, 96
  Dennis, 174
  Falmouth, 148–149
  Martha's Vineyard, 214, 229–230
  Nantucket, 238–239, 251
  Provincetown, 205–206
  Sandwich, 137
  Shining Sea Bikeway, 30–31
Bird Watcher's General Store (Orleans), 190
Bird-watching, Martha's Vineyard, 230
Black Heritage Trail (Boston), 72, 73
Black Ink (Boston), 106
Black Nativity (Boston), 20
The Black Rose (Boston), 116
Bleacher Bar (Boston), 116
Blue Beetle (Nantucket), 254
Blue Hills Bank Pavilion (Boston), 113
Blue Man Group (Boston), 114
Boating, 149, 190, 195, 207
Boat trips and cruises. *See also* Ferries; Water taxis
  Boston and Cambridge, 93–94, 257–258
  Boston Harbor Islands, 95
  Mid Cape, 162
  Plymouth, 128
  Provincetown, 207
  Sandwich, 141
Bobby From Boston, 104
Bob Slate Stationer (Cambridge), 101
Bodega (Boston), 103
Booksmith/Musicsmith (Orleans), 190
Boomerangs (Boston), 104–105
BosTix, 108

Accommodations

Restaurants